Blueprints

Constitutional and Administrative Law

Blueprints

Your plan for learning

Constitutional and Administrative Law

Chris Monaghan

University of Greenwich

PEARSON

Harlow, England • London • New York • Boston • San Francisco • Toronto • Sydney • Auckland • Singapore • Hong Kong
Tokyo • Seoul • Taipei • New Delhi • Cape Town • São Paulo • Mexico City • Madrid • Amsterdam • Munich • Paris • Milan

Pearson Education Limited
Edinburgh Gate
Harlow CM20 2JE
United Kingdom
Tel: +44 (0)1279 623623
Web: www.pearson.com/uk

First published 2015 (print and electronic)

ISBN: 978-1-447-90497-7 (print)
978-1-447-90498-4 (PDF)
978-1-292-01513-2 (eText)

British Library Cataloguing-in-Publication Data
A catalog record for the print edition is available from the Library of Congress

Library of Congress Cataloging-in-Publication Data
Monaghan, Christopher, author.
  Constitutional and administrative law / Chris Monaghan.
    pages cm. -- (Blueprints)
  Includes bibliographical references and index.
  ISBN 978-1-4479-0497-7
  1. Constitutional law--Great Britain.   2. Administrative law--Great Britain.   3. Parliamentary practice--Great Britain.   4. Judicial review--Great Britain.   I. Title.   II. Title: Your plan for learning constitutional and administrative law.
  KD3989.M66 2015
  342.41--dc23

2014027718

10 9 8 7 6 5 4 3 2 1
18 17 16 15

Print edition typeset in 10/12pt Helvetica Neue LT Pro by 35
Print edition printed in Malaysia (CTP-PPSB)

NOTE THAT ANY PAGE CROSS REFERENCES REFER TO THE PRINT EDITION

Brief contents

Contents

PART 1

Constitutional fundamentals 2

1 Introduction to the constitution of the United Kingdom 5

2 The sources of the United Kingdom's constitution 35

3 The separation of powers 59

13 Grounds for judicial review 387

Table of cases and statutes

TABLE OF CASES

Canada

European Court of Human Rights

TABLE OF STATUTES

TABLE OF STATUTORY INSTRUMENTS

Canada

Acknowledgements

Over the years I have been fortunate enough to have taught Constitutional and Administrative Law to students who have been genuinely interested in the concepts explored in this book and this has made teaching the subject highly rewarding. I hope that students on LLB, GDL and ILEX programmes will find this book to be useful as an introduction to the subject. Constitutional and Administrative Law is highly relevant to your study of law, and I have sought to give contemporary examples to illustrate how what you watch on the news, or read in newspapers, is linked to the topics that you will learn during your studies. This book has been written as an introduction to the subject and there is a considerable amount of interesting material available that will help you to build upon the concepts explored in this book. At the end of each chapter I have provided a list of further reading, which includes journal articles, books and links to online resources.

The idea of writing *Blueprints Constitutional and Administrative Law* was originally suggested by Zoe Botterill and encouraged by Christine Stratham, the *Blueprints* series editor, at Pearson. Throughout the writing process I have received considerable support from my editors Owen Knight and Stuart Hay. I would also like to thank my project editor Dhanya Ramesh and copy-editor Jim Caunter, who along with the rest of the editorial and production team at Pearson have seen the book through to production. I would like to thank Pearson for allowing me to update the text in light of the result of the Scottish referendum on independence in September 2014.

Writing *Blueprints Constitutional and Administrative Law* has proved to be a highly enjoyable process and I am grateful to all the invaluable comments that I have received from the anonymous academic and student reviewers who have reviewed each of the chapters.

Finally, I would like to thank my wife, Nicola, for all her support and encouragement throughout the writing process. Writing this book has dominated many a weekend and Nicola has been understanding and supportive during this time.

This book is dedicated to my parents, Michael and Marie.

I accept full responsibility for any errors or omissions in the text. The law is stated as it stood on 1st January 2014.

Chris Monaghan
Hertfordshire, May 2014

PUBLISHER'S ACKNOWLEDGEMENTS

We are grateful to the following for permission to reproduce copyright material:

Text

Extract on page 54 from Manuel *v.* Attorney-General [1983] 1 Ch 77; Extract on page 78 from Willis *v.* Baddeley [1892] 2 QB 324 at 326; Extracts on page 82, page 283 from British Broadcasting

Corporation *v.* Johns [1964] WLR 1071; Extracts on page 87, page 380 from R *v.* HM Treasury *ex p.* Smedley [1985] QB 657; Extracts on page 104, page 120, page 241 from R *v.* Secretary of State for the Home Department *ex p.* Simms [2000] 2 AC 115; Extract on page 122 from British Coal Corporation *v.* The King [1935] AC 500; Extract on page 122 from Madzimbamuto *v.* Lardner-Burke [1969] 1 AC 614; Extracts on page 124 from British Railway Board *v.* Pickin [1974] AC 765; Extract on page 129 from Vauxhall Estates Ltd *v.* Liverpool Corporation [1932] 1 KB 733; Extract on page 129 from Brown *v.* The Great Western Railway Company (1882) 9 QBD 744; Extract on page 129 from Ellen Street Estates Ltd *v.* Minister of Health [1934] 1 KB 590; Extract on page 134 from R *v.* Secretary of State for Transport *ex p.* Factortame Ltd (No.1) [1990] 2 AC 85; Extract on page 134 from R *v.* Secretary of State for Transport *ex p.* Factortame Ltd (No.2) [1991] 1 AC 603; Extracts on pages 126–7, page 118 from Duport Steels Ltd *v.* Sirs [1980] 1 WLR 142; Extract on page 202 from Attorney-General *v.* Jonathan Cape Ltd [1976] QB 752; Extract on page 212 from Parliamentary Resolutions on Ministerial Accountability, 2007, © Parliamentary Copyright 1997. Contains Parliamentary information licensed under the Open Parliament Licence *v.* 1.0; Extract on page 227 from *Just Law*, Vintage (Kennedy, H. 2005) p. 151; Extract on page 240 from Shaw *v.* DPP [1962] AC 220; Extract on page 242 from R *v.* Secretary of State for Social Service *ex p.* Council for the Welfare of Immigrants [1997] 1 WLR 275 at 293; Extract on page 244 from Just Law, Vintage (Kennedy, H. 2005) p. 127; Extracts on page 245, page 393 from R *v.* Secretary of State for the Environment *ex p.* Nottinghamshire County Council [1986] AC 240; Extracts on page 276, page 276, page 279 from Attorney-General *v.* De Keyser's Royal Hotel Ltd [1920] AC 508; Extract on page 278 from R *v.* Secretary of State for the Home Department *ex p.* Fire Brigades Union and Others [1995] 2 WLR 464; Extract on page 280 from Burmah Oil Co (Burma Trading) Ltd *v.* Lord Advocate [1965] AC 75; Extracts on page 281, pages 281–2 from R *v.* Secretary of State for the Home Department *ex p.* Northumbria Police Authority [1988] 2 WLR 590; Extracts on page 284, page 390, page 392, page 401, page 412 from Council of Civil Service Unions *v.* Minister of State for the Civil Service [1985] AC 374; Extracts on pages 277–8, page 278, page 279 from Laker Airways Ltd *v.* Department of Trade [1977] QB 546; Extract on page 309 from Keir Starmer under attack after Tory human rights broadside, *The Times*, 22/10/2009 (Hines, N. and Gibb, F.); Extract on page 326 from Douglas *v.* Hello! Ltd (No.1) [2001] QB 967; Extract on page 341 from Express Newspapers Ltd *v.* McShane [1979] 1 WLR 390; Extract on page 352 from R *v.* Howell (Errol) [1982] QB 416; Extract on page 321 from R *v.* Liverpool Corp *ex p.* Liverpool Taxi Fleet Operators Association [1972] 2 QB 299; Extract on page 369 from Liversidge *v.* Anderson [1942] AC 206; Extract on page 372 from R *v.* Panel on Takeovers and Mergers *ex p.* Datafin Plc [1987] QB 815; Extract on page 378 from O'Reilly *v.* Mackman [1983] 2 AC 237; Extract on page 381 from R *v.* Secretary of State for the Environment *ex p.* Rose Theatre Trust Co (No.2) [1990] 1 QB 504; Extract on page 382 from R *v.* Secretary of State for Foreign and Commonwealth Affairs *ex p.* World Development Movement Ltd [1995] 1 WLR 386; Extract on page 392 from Associated Provincial Picture Houses Ltd *v.* Wednesbury Corporation [1948] 1 KB 223; Extract on page 392 from Short *v.* Poole Corporation [1926] Ch 66; Extract on page 394 from R *v.* Secretary of State for the Home Department *ex p.* Bugdaycay [1987] AC 514; Extract on page 394 from R *v.* Ministry of Defence *ex p.* Smith [1996] QB 517; Extract on page 395 from R *v.* Secretary of State for the Home Department *ex p.* Brind [1991] 1 AC 696; Extract on page 396 from De Freitas *v.* Permanent Secretary of Ministry of Agriculture, Fisheries, Lands and Housing [1999] 1 AC 69; Extract on page 401 from Congreve *v.* Home Office [1976] QB 629; Extract on page 402 from Attorney-General *v.* Fulham Corporation [1921] 1 Ch 440; Extract on page 403 from Wheeler *v.* Leicester City Council [1985] AC 1054; Extract on page 405 from R *v.* Governor of Brixton Prison *ex p.* Enahoro [1963] 2 QB 455; Extract on page 408 from Schmidt *v.* Secretary of State for Home Affairs [1969] 2 Ch 149; Extract on page 409 from Attorney-General of Hong Kong *v.* Ng Yuen Shiu [1983] 2 AC 629; Extract on page 409 from R *v.* North and East Devon Heath Authority *ex p.*

Coughlan [2001] QB 213; Extract on page 410 from R *v.* Secretary of State for Education and Employment *ex p.* Begbie [2000] 1 WLR 1115; Extracts on page 413 from Ridge *v.* Baldwin [1964] AC 40 HL; Extract on page 414 from Lloyd *v.* McMahon [1987] AC 625; Extract on page 415 from R *v.* Secretary of State of the Home Department *ex p.* Doody [1994] 1 AC 531; Extract on page 416 from R *v.* Army Board of the Defence Council *ex p.* Anderson [1991] 3 WLR 42; Extract on page 416 from Enderby Town Football Club *v.* Football Association [1971] Ch 591; Extract on page 418 from R *v.* Sussex Justices *ex p.* McCarthy [1924] 1 KB 256; Extract on page 420 from R *v.* Bow Street Metropolitan Stipendiary Magistrate *ex p.* Pinochet Ugarte (No.1) [2000] 1 AC 61; Extract on page 420 from R *v.* Bow Street Metropolitan Stipendiary Magistrate *ex p.* Pinochet Ugarte (No.3) [2000] 1 AC 147; Extract on pages 410–11 from R (Bibi) *v.* Newham London Borough Council [2002] 1 WLR 237; Extract on pages 412–13 from Local Government Board *v.* Arlidge [1915] AC 120

In some instances we have been unable to trace the owners of copyright material, and we would appreciate any information that would enable us to do so.

How to use this guide

Blueprints was created for students searching for a smarter introductory guide to their legal studies

This guide will serve as a primer for deeper study of the law – enabling you to get the most out of your lectures and studies by giving you a way in to the subject which is more substantial than a revision guide, but more succinct than your course textbook. The series is designed to give you an overview of the law, so you can see the structure of the subject and understand how the topics you will study throughout your course fit together in the big picture. It will help you keep your bearings as you move through your course study.

Blueprints recognises that students want to succeed in their course modules

This requires more than a basic grasp of key legislation; you will need knowledge of the historical and social context of the law, recognition of the key debates, an ability to think critically and to draw connections among topics.

Blueprints addresses the various aspects of legal study, using assorted text features and visual tools

Each Blueprints guide begins with an **Introduction**, outlining the parameters of the subject and the challenges you might face in your studies. This includes a **map** of the subject highlighting the major areas of study.

Each **Part** of the guide also begins with an Introduction and a map of the main topics you need to grasp and how they fit together.

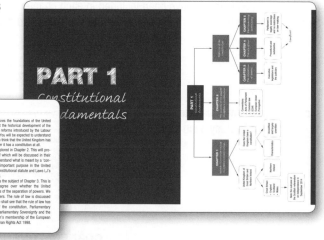

Each guide includes advice on the specific **study skills** you will need to do well in the subject.

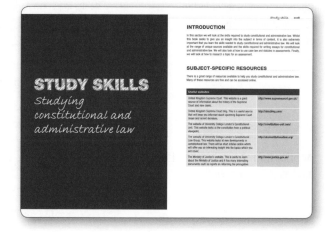

Each chapter starts with a **Blueprint** of the topic area to provide a visual overview of the fundamental buildings blocks of each topic, and the academic questions and the various outside influences that converge in the study of law.

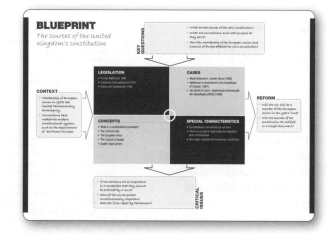

A number of text features have been included in each chapter to help you better understand the law and push you further in your appreciation of the subtleties and debates:

Setting the scene illustrates why it is important to study each topic.

Setting the scene

Many people use the word constitution without really knowing what it means. We will look at what the word constitution means and why every country, organisation or sports club will require a constitution to enable it to work effectively. We will look at the constitution of the United Kingdom. It is important to appreciate just how controversial an area this is. If you ask your lecturers whether the United Kingdom has a constitution, you might receive a number of very different responses. This is because many academics argue that the United Kingdom does not have a constitution. They argue that this so because it is not codified, i.e. written down in a single document such as the constitution of the United States of America. So does this mean that the United Kingdom's constitution is unwritten? Technically large parts of what we consider to be constitutional sources are written down, such as important statutes. However, other sources of the constitution are unwritten, such as constitutional conventions.

Cornerstone highlights the fundamental building blocks of the law.

CORNERSTONE

Coalition government

Where no one political party is able to form a government on its own it will need to form a **coalition** with another party. Coalition governments are common in countries such as Italy and Germany. However, in the United Kingdom they are very rare and the formation of the Conservative and Liberal Democrat coalition in 2010 was the first peace-time coalition government since the Second World War.

Application shows how the law applies in the real world.

APPLICATION

In light of the decision in *Entick* v. *Carrington*, imagine that the Home Secretary had received permission from the king to issue the warrant. Would this have made a difference? The answer would be no. However, had the Home Secretary received the authority to issue the warrant from an Act of Parliament then he could have lawfully issued the warrant and no trespass would have been committed.

Intersection shows you connections and relationships with other areas of the law.

INTERSECTION

The role of the monarch was gradually restricted by Parliament. For example, the ability to raise taxation was controlled by the need for parliamentary approval. However, as we shall see in Chapter 5, the idea of Parliamentary Sovereignty was not established until the start of the seventeenth century. This led to a conflict with the Stuart kings who believed that their prerogative power were absolute.

Reflection helps you think critically about the law, introducing you to the various complexities that give rise to debate and controversy.

Do you think that if MPs had a say over who became a member of the Supreme Court, the candidates' views on divorce, religion, politics and abortion might influence their decision? Kenneth Clarke MP, the previous Lord Chancellor, when appearing before the House of Lords Constitutional Reform Committee was critical of introducing confirmation hearings for the appointment of members of the Supreme Court:

'I think there's a danger that they would become political . . . The US experience is just shocking. Some US confirmation hearings are just consumed by the social attitudes of the judge and his sexual history . . . Anything that got near that would be deplorable. Sooner or later you would have some stray MP asking what a judge's views are on this or that. A certain partisanship could creep in.'

REFLECTION

Context fills in some of the historical and cultural background knowledge that will help you understand and appreciate the legal issues of today.

Lord Denning has recounted that after the decision in *Heatons Transport (St Helens) Ltd* v. *Transport and General Workers Union* [1972] 3 WLR 73:

'I was told by one in a high place:

Your decision was a disaster for the country, which will last till the end of the century.

I was shaken to the core. But I was not downcast. I just thought:

Thank goodness, the judges of the Court of Appeal are independent.

No government dare seek to influence them.'

(Lord Denning *The Closing Chapter* (Butterworths: London, 1983), p. 177)

CONTEXT

Take note offers advice that can save you time and trouble in your studies.

Take note

The United Kingdom has a dualist as opposed to monist legal system. This means that in English law there is a distinction between domestic and international law.

2. Making and ratifying treaties

Because of the UK's dualist legal system once a treaty has been ratified by the executive, it must then be enacted into English law by an Act of Parliament. An example is the Hague-Visby Rules 1968 which were enacted into domestic law by the Carriage of Goods by Sea Act 1971.

Foreign policy and the making and ratifying of treaties are the functions of the executive (see Locke's *Second Treatise on Government*), and the government uses the prerogative to undertake these.

Key points lists the main things to know about each topic.

KEY POINTS

- The United Kingdom was created in 1801 and is a constitutional monarchy.
- Great Britain was created in 1707. Previously, England and Scotland were two independent kingdoms.
- Academics have questioned whether the United Kingdom actually has a constitution.
- There are a number of characteristics of a constitution, which can be used to describe a particular

Core cases and statutes summarises the major case law and legislation in the topic.

CORE CASES AND STATUTES

Case	About	Importance
British Railway Board v. *Pickin* [1974]	This case involved a challenge to the ownership of land in the middle of a railway track.	The House of Lords held that the courts cannot declare an Act invalid or ineffective because of the manner in which the Act was passed or irregularity in the procedure used.
R (Jackson) v. *Attorney-General*	A Labour MP had introduced a private members bill to ban hunting.	The House of Lords reviewed the legality of the legislation. The

Further reading directs you to select primary and secondary sources as a springboard to further studies.

FURTHER READING

Bogdanor, V. *The New British Constitution* (Hart: Oxford, 2009) This is an authoritative account of the British constitution. It discusses recent changes and offers detailed analysis.

Bogdanor, V. *The Coalition and the Constitution* (Hart: Oxford, 2011) This book provides an authoritative account of the 2010 General Election and the subsequent

discussion of the types of constitutions and comparison is made to the Netherlands.

Leyland, P. *The Constitution of the United Kingdom: A Contextual Analysis* 2nd edn (Hart: Oxford, 2012) An authoritative introduction to the United Kingdom's constitution.

Lyons, A. *Constitutional History of*

A **glossary** provides helpful definitions of key terms.

Alternative Vote In May 2011, there was a referendum on replacing First Past the Post with the Alternative Vote. The Alternative Vote system operates to allow voters to list their candidates by preference. If a candidate achieves 50 per cent he will win outright. If no candidate receives 50 per cent of the votes, then the weakest candidate is eliminated and their votes are given to the voter's second favoured candidate. The process will continue until one candidate achieves the important 50 per cent required.

Bias A decision can be challenged where the

Collective ministerial responsibility The convention of collective ministerial responsibility operates to ensure that what is said during cabinet meetings is not made public.

Commonwealth An organisation comprised of former members of the British Empire. It is headed by Her Majesty, the Queen.

Constitution A constitution is a collection of rules, practices and laws which relate to the political life of a country and the key rights of any citizen. A constitution is intended to

What is a Blueprint?

Blueprints provide a unique plan for studying the law, giving you a visual overview of the fundamental building blocks of each topic, and the academic questions and the various outside influences that converge in the study of law.

At the centre are the 'black-letter' elements, the fundamental building blocks that make up what the law says and how it works.

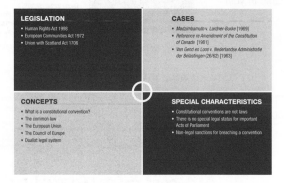

As a law student you will need to learn what questions or problems the law attempts to address, and what sort of issues arise from the way it does this that require critical reflection.

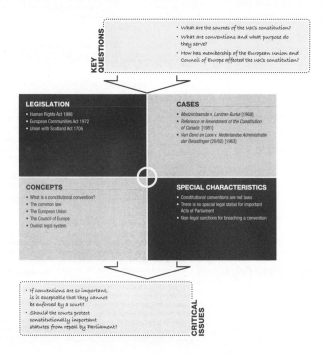

To gain a more complete understanding of the role of law in society you will need to know what influencing factors have shaped the law in the past, and how the law may develop in the near future.

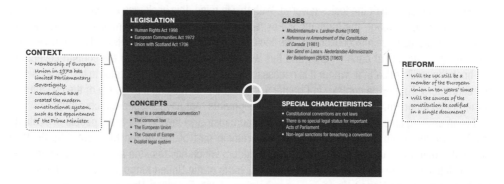

You can use the Blueprint for each topic as a framework for building your knowledge in the subject.

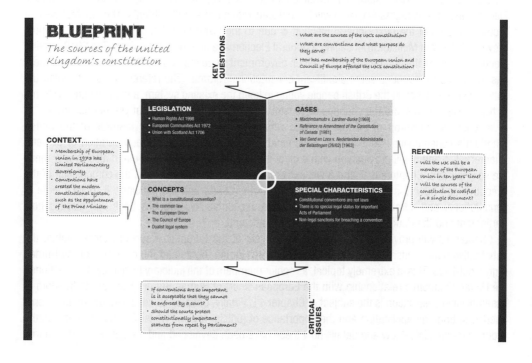

Introduction

Constitutional and administrative law is often viewed with apprehension by students before they begin to study the module. Students think that they are expected to start the module having as a prerequisite an expertise in history, politics and comparative constitutions. You will be relieved to know that this is not the case. As a law student you will be given the tools to acquire the knowledge needed to gain a thorough understanding of the topics covered. With this in mind, this book was written to help students navigate their way through the fundamental aspects of constitutional and administrative law, and to attempt to challenge these misconceptions. This book is only introductory and there is a list of useful secondary reading at the end of each chapter and this will help you to expand upon the content covered in this book. You will notice that, where it is necessary to do so, earlier chapters refer to historical events and characters. To provide context, in Chapter 1 there is a brief historical overview of the constitution of the United Kingdom. This explains the key developments that have shaped the constitution.

It is an exciting time to study constitutional and administrative law. In 2014, the people of Scotland voted in a referendum on whether Scotland will remain part of the United Kingdom. The Scottish electorate voted to remain as part of the United Kingdom which has resulted in more uncertainty over the devolution of more power to Scotland and other parts of the United Kingdom. There is likely to be a referendum on the United Kingdom's membership of the European Union, which could see the United Kingdom leave the European Union.

The United Kingdom's relationship with the European Court of Human Rights and the European Convention on Human Rights has been uneasy, especially given the restrictions placed on deporting the radical Islamic cleric Abu Qatada. It is feasible that depending upon which party wins the 2015 General Election, the Human Rights Act 1998 will be replaced with a British Bill of Rights. The fact that we can predict the date of the next General Election is due to the Fixed-term Parliaments Act 2011, which prevents the Prime Minister from calling a General Election at a time of his choosing. The 2010 General Election produced the first peacetime coalition government since the 1930s. The Coalition government has attempted to introduce some significant constitutional reforms. The referendum on changing the voting system resulted in the British people voting to keep the existing system, and the planned reforms of the House of Lords and the changes to constituency boundaries have, as of yet, not occurred.

Against the backdrop of all this possible reform remain the three key features of the United Kingdom's constitution: Parliamentary Sovereignty, the rule of law and the separation of powers. Chapters 3, 4 and 5 will provide you with a clear introduction to what they are and also to why these are so important. Chapters 6, 7 and 8 will explore the functions of Parliament, the composition of the executive and how it is held to account and finally the courts and the judiciary. A major theme in constitutional and administrative law is executive accountability, and this book will discuss how Parliament and the Courts hold the government to account.

Chapter 10 will provide an introduction to the role of the European Court of Human Rights, the substantive rights under the European Convention on Human Rights and the operation of the Human Rights Act 1998. This is extremely topical, as senior members of the judiciary have recently questioned the United Kingdom's relationship with the European Court of Human Rights. The right to freedom of assembly and association is the subject of Chapter 11. Finally, Chapter 12 considers the requirements needed to bring an application and the importance of judicial review, whilst Chapter 13 outlines the grounds for judicial review and details how these have been developed and are applied by the courts.

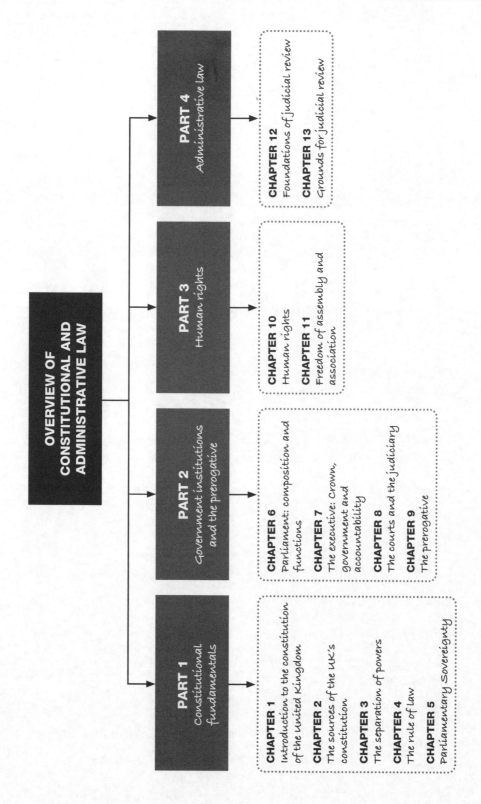

STUDY SKILLS

studying constitutional and administrative law

INTRODUCTION

In this section we will look at the skills required to study constitutional and administrative law. Whilst this book seeks to give you an insight into the subject in terms of content, it is also extremely important that you learn the skills needed to study constitutional and administrative law. We will look at the range of unique sources available and the skills required for writing essays for constitutional and administrative law. We will also look at how to use case law and statutes in assessments. Finally, we will look at how to research a topic for an assessment.

SUBJECT-SPECIFIC RESOURCES

There is a great range of resources available to help you study constitutional and administrative law. Many of these resources are free and can be accessed online.

Useful websites	
United Kingdom Supreme Court. This website is a good source of information about the history of the Supreme Court and new cases.	**http://www.supremecourt.gov.uk/**
United Kingdom Supreme Court blog. This is a useful source that will keep you informed about upcoming Supreme Court cases and recent decisions.	**http://ukscblog.com/**
The website of University College London's Constitutional Unit. This website looks at the constitution from a political viewpoint.	**http://constitution-unit.com/**
The website of University College London's Constitutional Law Group. This website looks at new developments in constitutional law. There will be short articles online which will offer you an interesting insight into the topics which you will cover.	**http://ukconstitutionallaw.org/**
The Ministry of Justice's website. This is useful to learn about the Ministry of Justice and it has many interesting documents such as reports on reforming the prerogative.	**http://www.justice.gov.uk/**

Useful websites	
The UK Human Rights blog. This blog is a great source for news about human rights, both in this country and abroad.	http://ukhumanrightsblog.com/
The Guardian newspaper has a free online section on law. It is regularly updated and will have links to important legal developments, opinion pieces and speeches by important persons such as judges.	http://www.guardian.co.uk/law
The British and Irish Legal Information Institute. This website contains the transcript of all new cases and many older cases. When studying constitutional and administrative law it is useful to look regularly for new cases, especially where the case has been reported in the press.	http://www.bailii.org/
The Institute of Advanced Legal Studies. There are events organised by the institute, many of which are free to attend.	http://www.ials.sas.ac.uk/
Parliament's website is an extremely useful guide to politics, the workings of Parliament and other important information. It offers short and succinct guides which you will find useful to supplement your reading.	http://www.parliament.uk/

Each chapter in this book contains a list of further reading that will give you a range of sources to look at. These include textbooks, journal articles and other academic texts. There are a number of journals that will be relevant to your studies. These include:

- *Public Law* (PL)
- *European Human Rights Law Review* (EHRLR)
- *Human Rights Law Review* (HRLR)
- *Judicial Review* (JR)
- *Cambridge Law Review* (CLR)
- *Law Quarterly Review* (LQR)
- *Modern Law Review* (MLR)

STUDY SKILLS FOR CONSTITUTIONAL AND ADMINISTRATIVE LAW

We will now look at the key skills required for studying constitutional and administrative law, as set out in Figure 1.

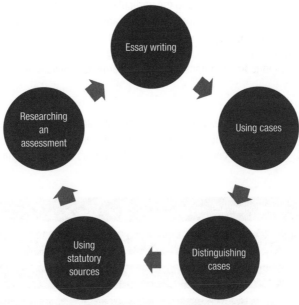

Figure 1 Key study skills

Study skill: When it comes to writing an essay on constitutional and administrative law

Writing an essay is an important study skill and for students studying constitutional and administrative law it is extremely important that you learn the key skills required. Prior to starting your revision you should download previous exam questions from your university's online learning environment. This will give you an example of how the module has been examined in the past. Imagine that you have downloaded your university's previous exam papers and that you have decided to attempt the following question:

'In the 21st century no lawyer can realistically claim that Parliamentary Sovereignty is absolute.'

You should take time to ascertain what the question is about and what the examiner is expecting in an answer. There is often a temptation to write everything you know about the topic, in the hope of impressing the examiner. Unfortunately, this rarely gains students good marks and demonstrates a lack of understanding of what is actually being asked. Questions such as this may appear straightforward and an invitation to write everything you know about Parliamentary Sovereignty, but the examiner will be expecting you to tailor your knowledge to answer the question in the examination booklet. It is helpful to break down the question using bullet points. Once you have done this you should start to plan your structure. This should take no more than a few minutes. In an exam you may only have 60 minutes to answer a question, but time spent planning what you are going to write will mean that you answer the question actually set, your answer is structured, and you do not omit any key points, or repeat yourself unnecessarily.

1. The Introduction

Your introduction should set out what you will be arguing. It should respond to the question set and outline the topic which the question is on, and the particular emphasis of the question. Here you would state that the question is on Parliamentary Sovereignty and whether it is still absolute. You should avoid launching into a narrative about Parliamentary Sovereignty as the examiner expects you to focus on the question. However, you should outline how you are going to approach the question and ideally state how you are going to respond to the proposition that Parliamentary Sovereignty is no longer absolute.

2. The main body

Each of your paragraphs should develop your answer and should follow a logical structure. You must avoid the tendency that many students have which is to write everything they know, or attempt to go into too much detail. Your answer could perhaps be structured as set out in Figure 2.

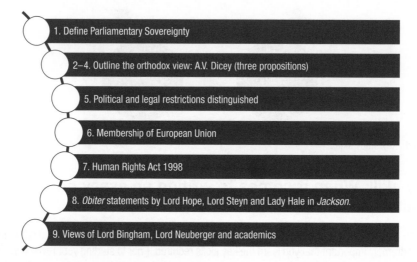

1. Define Parliamentary Sovereignty

2–4. Outline the orthodox view: A.V. Dicey (three propositions)

5. Political and legal restrictions distinguished

6. Membership of European Union

7. Human Rights Act 1998

8. *Obiter* statements by Lord Hope, Lord Steyn and Lady Hale in *Jackson*.

9. Views of Lord Bingham, Lord Neuberger and academics

Figure 2 Planning the main body of your answer

Each paragraph should respond to the question and should demonstrate a clear understanding of the topic and evidence of wider reading. The question will often require you to analyse or evaluate the proposition. You must do this. But what does this actually mean? Put simply, the examiner would expect you to:

- discuss the topic with sufficient clarity of expression and accuracy;
- demonstrate an awareness of the issue being examined;
- explore the controversies which exist and be able to demonstrate your own views on these;
- use your knowledge to see whether the proposition can be supported, or whether you disagree with it;
- contrast different judicial and academic opinions.

3. Conclusion

Your conclusion must not add anything new into your answer, as it should consolidate your answer and give a succinct overview of your argument. It must respond to the question and leave the examiner feeling confident that you have understood the question and have answered it. Many students will leave the analysis and evaluation that was required by the question until the conclusion. You must not do this as otherwise your essay will read like a narrative overview of the topic and you will have not adequately answered the question. Similarly, you must avoid isolated statements such as 'as you can see, Parliament is no longer legally sovereign', because unless you have demonstrated the case for this in your answer, statements such as this could demonstrate a lack of understanding.

IMPROVING YOUR CONSTITUTIONAL AND ADMINISTRATIVE LAW ESSAY-WRITING SKILLS

We have seen how to write and structure an essay on Parliamentary Sovereignty. You will need to develop your essay-writing skills and it is recommended that you follow the steps set out in Figure 3.

Practise under timed conditions

Develop answer plans

Practise past exam questions

Figure 3 Improving your essay-writing skills

Do not forget that you are able to ask your tutor for guidance on essay-writing skills. Your tutor will also be able to look at your practice answers.

STUDY SKILL: WHEN IT COMES TO USING CASES IN ASSESSMENTS

The legal aspects of constitutional and administrative law tend to be based on case law. Whilst there is important legislation such as the Constitutional Reform Act 2005, the Human Rights Act 1998 and the Devolution Acts of 1998 and 2006, there will be considerable focus on case law. For example, judicial review is based on the common law, and therefore it is essential that you are able to use cases effectively in your assessments.

Which cases should you read in full?

It is essential that you read the cases that are highlighted as important in this book and by your tutors. At the end of each chapter there is a list of key cases and it is recommended that you take the time to read these in full. But beware, there is good and bad practice when studying cases, as highlighted in Figure 4.

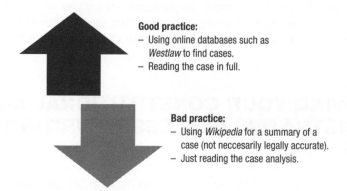

Good practice:
– Using online databases such as *Westlaw* to find cases.
– Reading the case in full.

Bad practice:
– Using *Wikipedia* for a summary of a case (not neccesarily legally accurate).
– Just reading the case analysis.

Figure 4 Good and bad practice when using cases

Let us now consider why you should read a case in full:

1. Different legal opinions – demonstrates depth of knowledge and understanding

The decision *R (Jackson)* v. *Attorney-General* [2005] UKHL 56 is an important case because it considers the Parliament Acts 1911 and 1949. In addition to the *ratio*, there is important *obiter* on Parliamentary Sovereignty. Unless you read the individual judgments then you will not be able to understand the differences in opinion between their Lordships. Some students will just read the textbook and will be able to write a line or two about what Lord Hope and Lord Steyn said in their judgments. However, students who have read the case in full will understand what their Lordships actually meant and will be able to counter this with what Lord Bingham said in his judgment. Equally, the decision in *A* v. *Secretary of State for the Home Department* [2004] UKHL 56 contains a strong dissent from Lord Hoffmann on whether there was an emergency which threatened the life of the nation. This additional detail can be used in an essay question to demonstrate wider knowledge and to assist in your analysis of the question.

2. Particular case facts

Each decision will depend on the background facts. Relying on just a short explanation of a case in your textbook is not sufficient.

3. Gives you the bigger picture

Judgments are often very well written and will set out the law relating to a particular area. By reading the judgment you will often come away with a much clearer understanding of how the law works.

PUTTING WHAT YOU HAVE LEARNT INTO PRACTICE

Imagine that you have been asked by your lecturer to read the case of R (Bancoult) v. Secretary of State for Foreign and Commonwealth Affairs (No.2) [2008] UKHL 61. This is an important House of Lords decision on the use of the prerogative powers to legislate for colonial affairs. By reading the judgment in full you will understand:

- What is meant by the prerogative and how the government uses it today.
- That there was a majority judgment and two dissenting judgments.
- What the legal principles are which can be derived from the case.
- Previous decisions on the use of the prerogative in this area.
- How certain types of decisions are still non-justiciable and why this is the case.

Databases such as Westlaw and Lexis Library will link the cases cited in R (Bancoult) (No.2) and you can then read these should you wish. Importantly, any cases which have subsequently applied, distinguished or criticised the decision will also be highlighted. By going beyond merely reading the case, and researching new cases which are directly relevant, you will demonstrate an awareness of the topic in the assessment.

Distinguishing between legal principle and background facts

In the assessment you will be expected to understand the legal principles which derive from a case. You are not expected to write in detail about the background facts. The facts should only be used to illustrate the legal principle derived from a case, and how it either applies, or does not apply, to the particular facts in a problem question.

For example, consider this problem question on prerogative powers:

Luke is an inhabitant of New Island (NI). NI is a British Overseas Territory that is administered by the Commissioner for NI. The French government has requested to lease NI to build a naval base. The British government enacts an Order in Council, the New Island Constitution Order 2013, which states that no one is allowed to live on NI and all inhabitants must leave.

Student 1's answer

The case of R (Bancoult) (No.2) was an interesting case which concerned the British Indian Ocean Territory. The islanders who had lived on BIOT were known as the Chagossians and had been removed in the 1970s and were prevented by Orders in Council from returning. The case was brought by Mr Oliver Bancoult. It was a very unfair case and the House of Lords in 2008 held that the government had the prerogative power to prevent the islanders from returning. Many academics including Bridget Hadfield have criticised the decision and there is considerable argument over whether the decision was wrong. Also the House of Lords held that prerogative Orders in Council were judicially reviewable. The case also shows that the judges do not all agree, as there was a dissent by Lords Mance and Bingham. This demonstrates how controversial the decision was.

Lord Mance cited Sir William Blackstone, who was a famous legal-writer to support his argument. The majority held that the decision involved non-justiciable areas such as national security and foreign affairs. Luke is a New Island inhabitant and the decision to remove him looks to be very similar. Therefore the government has not acted illegally.

Whilst this answer demonstrates knowledge, there is too much focus on the facts and too little application of the legal principles to the facts. Does your examiner (and in practice, your client) need to know all the background facts and a generic overview of the law?

Student 2's answer

Luke is an inhabitant of New Island, which is a British Overseas territory. On 20 May 2013, the government through an Order in Council enacted the New Island Constitution Order 2013, which stated that all New Island inhabitants had to leave the territory. Luke could attempt to judicially review the decision. In *R (Bancoult) (No.2)*, Orders in Council were held in to be reviewable. The facts here and the decision in *R (Bancoult) (No.2)* are very similar. The decision itself involves the prerogative and Luke could argue that there is no prerogative power to exile the inhabitants of New Island. We know from *R (Bancoult) (No.2)* that Orders in Council are reviewable and so the court here will be able to review the New Island Constitution Order 2013. Looking at whether there is a prerogative power to exile the islanders, we can see that the majority of the House of Lords in *R (Bancoult) (No.2)* held that there was a prerogative power to do this and the Order in Council was not illegal. Therefore, Luke would need to argue that the decision was invalid under one of the grounds for judicial review.

This (very brief) answer is focused on the facts set out in the problem question and applies the legal principles from *R (Bancoult) (No.2)* to the scenario. The legal principles are used to demonstrate how *R (Bancoult) (No.2)* will apply to the facts and what the outcome will be for Luke. There is no irrelevant material cited and the student is not trying to show off their knowledge of information that does not add anything to the answer.

STUDY SKILL: WHEN IT COMES TO DISTINGUISHING CASES IN ASSESSMENTS

We have seen above that you need to be able to identify legal principles and apply these to the facts in the assessment. We have also seen that cases are determined in accordance to the background facts. Therefore, in the assessment you will be expected to distinguish cases and to identify the reasons why different decisions may appear at odds with each other.

Imagine that you are answering a problem question on judicial review:

'Rajah has applied for a fishing licence and his application has been rejected. He has not been given any reasons for why his application has been rejected.'

The issue here is whether fairness requires Rajah to be given reasons for why his application has been refused. If you were simply to cite *R* v. *Secretary of State for the Home Department ex p. Doody* [1994] 1 AC 531 and inform the examiner that at common law there is no general duty for the decision-maker to give reasons, then this would not be sufficient as an answer. You would have to show in what circumstances the courts have held that reasons have to be given. This requires you to distinguish these circumstances from the facts in the question.

Consider the following example answer:

The issue here is whether the decision-maker has to give Rajah reasons for refusing his application. It is clear that what fairness will require will depend on a number of factors and will vary according to each case (*Ex p. Doody*, per Lord Mustill and *Lloyd* v. *McMahon* [1998] AC 625, per Lord Bridge). The fact that this is an application for a licence, rather than a revocation of a licence, will mean that the requirements of fairness will be low (*McInnes* v. *Onslow Fane* [1978] 1 WLR 1520). Whilst at common law there is no general duty to give reasons (*Ex p. Doody*), there are some exceptions which require reasons to be given. It would appear that there is no statutory requirement to give reasons here and so we would have to see whether fairness would require reasons to be given. Unlike *Ex p. Doody* an application for a fishing licence does not involve fundamental issues, such as liberty, where reasons must be given. Nonetheless, if the decision were to appear irrational, such as occurred in *R* v. *Civil Service Appeal Board ex p. Cunningham* [1991] 4 All ER 310, then reasons would have to be given. Here we do not know whether the decision was irrational, as we are unsure of whether Rajah is the only person refused. There are probably administrative explanations for why reasons have not been given (see *R* v. *Higher Education Funding Council ex p. Institute of Dental Surgery* [1994] 1 WLR 242). Therefore, it would appear that fairness does not require that Rajah is given a reason for why his application was refused.

This (brief) answer has used the legal principles established and has distinguished some of the key cases in this area. There has been application of the relevant cases to the facts, and an effort to say, whether they would, or would not, apply on the facts.

STUDY SKILL: WHEN IT COMES TO USING STATUTES IN ASSESSMENTS

Perhaps the most important statute most students will come across when studying constitutional and administrative law is the Human Rights Act 1998 (HRA 1998).

The HRA 1998 incorporates most of the European Convention on Human Rights (ECHR) into domestic law. Schedule 1 lists the Convention rights which have been incorporated. Many students will confuse the HRA 1998 and the ECHR and in an assessment will write that, 'Article 6 of the Human Rights Act 1998 protects the right to a fair trial'. This is wrong as the HRA 1998 incorporates the Convention rights, including Article 6 ECHR, into domestic law and outlines how the Convention rights will operate in the United Kingdom.

You cannot simply rely on legislation in the exam. You must know how the courts have interpreted the legislation. The HRA 1998 issues instructions to the courts on how to give effect to Convention rights.

Looking at section 3 HRA 1998 we can see that the courts are given powers to interpret legislation to give effect to Convention rights:

1. So far as it is possible to do so, primary legislation and subordinate legislation must be read and given effect in a way which is compatible with the Convention rights.

2. This section –

   (a) applies to primary legislation and subordinate legislation whenever enacted;

   (b) does not affect the validity, continuing operation or enforcement of any incompatible primary legislation; and

   (c) does not affect the validity, continuing operation or enforcement of any incompatible subordinate legislation if (disregarding any possibility of revocation) primary legislation prevents removal of the incompatibility.

How would you use section 3 in an assessment? To begin with you must understand how it works. Section 3(1) informs the court that this must read 'primary legislation' (which are Acts of Parliament) and 'subordinate legislation' (which is delegated legislation) 'in a way which is compatible with the Convention rights'. This means that legislation which infringes a Convention right must be interpreted in a way that does not infringe a Convention right.

For example, if Sandra was arrested and detained in a police station cell for a week during which she was not allowed to see a solicitor, then at a minimum there would be a violation of Articles 5 and 6 ECHR. However, if section 5 of the Law and Order Act 2013 (fictitious) stated that 'The police may withhold the right to see a solicitor whilst a suspect is detained', the police could then argue that they have acted legally because they were acting in accordance with the law (see section 6 HRA on the duty of public of authorities to not violate Convention rights).

A court when interpreting section 5 of the Law and Order Act 2013 would be required under section 3(1) to interpret the Act in a manner that is compatible with Convention rights. Clearly, section 5 is incompatible. However, section 3(1) HRA 1998 states that the court can only interpret legislation '[s]o far as it is possible to do so'. This means that the court must not disregard Parliament's intention. To see whether the court could interpret section 5 to make the police's action illegal, we would need to look at case law. Looking at decisions such as *Re S, Re W (Minors)* [2002] UKHL 10, we can see that there are clear limits on the court's use of section 3. Lord Nicholls had stated that, 'a meaning which departs substantially from a fundamental feature of an Act of Parliament is likely to have crossed the boundary between interpretation and amendment' (at [40]). In the assessment you would need to decide whether the courts would be able to use section 3. Considering the facts above, if the court was to use section 3 HRA 1998, then this would depart substantially from the meaning of section 5 and therefore could not be used. Therefore the police have not acted illegally and Sandra was legitimately (albeit in violation of the ECHR) denied access to a solicitor.

You would need to address the following points in your answer:

- Whether a 'Declaration of Incompatibility' could be used by the courts (s.4).
- Whether the police are a public authority (s.6)
- Whether Sandra was a victim for the purposes of the HRA 1998 and whether she had complied with the time limit for bringing her claim (s.7)
- The remedies which are available under the HRA 1998 (s.8).
- The jurisdictional application of the HRA 1998 (Art.1 ECHR).

STUDY SKILL: WHEN IT COMES TO RESEARCHING A TOPIC FOR AN ASSESSMENT

Imagine that you have been asked to write a coursework on whether the United Kingdom conforms to the separation of powers. This is quite a generic question and in order to do well you would have to demonstrate that you have undertaken thorough research.

Using textbooks

Your textbook will have a detailed chapter covering the separation of powers and often students will stop there and rely solely upon the thirty or so pages in their textbook. By doing this you will risk producing a condensed version of the textbook and thus a basic narrative of the position in the United Kingdom. You will need to use other textbooks as each author will explain the separation of powers differently and will offer you a range of further reading to look at. The further reading will direct you to relevant academic articles.

Using articles

Electronic databases such as *Westlaw* and *Lexis Library* offer access to many journals that are relevant to constitutional and administrative law and also have advanced search functions. A quick search of the journal *Public Law* using the keyword 'Supreme Court' would reveal several articles on the Supreme Court, including Masterman, R. 'A Supreme Court for the United Kingdom: two steps forward, but one step back on judicial independence' [2004] *Public Law* 48. You must never use *Wikipedia* in your research, as anyone is able to edit entries on this encyclopaedia.

PUTTING IT ALL TOGETHER

You need to be disciplined when researching for an assessment. You often will have to balance this alongside your studies. Therefore, it is essential that you set aside enough time to research before you start writing. You should avoid getting carried away and risk losing sight of what your lecturer is expecting of you. Always focus on the question and identify the key areas to research. Figure 5 suggests how to research a question on the separation of powers.

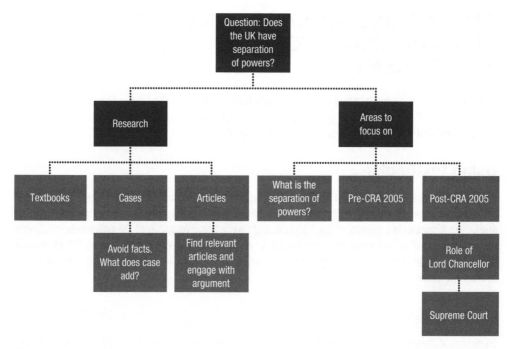

Figure 5 Planning your research

SUMMARY

- There are a variety of resources available when studying constitutional and administrative law. Many of these are specialised and unique to the subject.
- It is important that you use cases and legislation properly as you will be expected to use both in your assessments.
- It is important to know how to research constitutional and administrative law as you are required to use material selectively and identify the key issues being assessed.

PART 1

Constitutional fundamentals

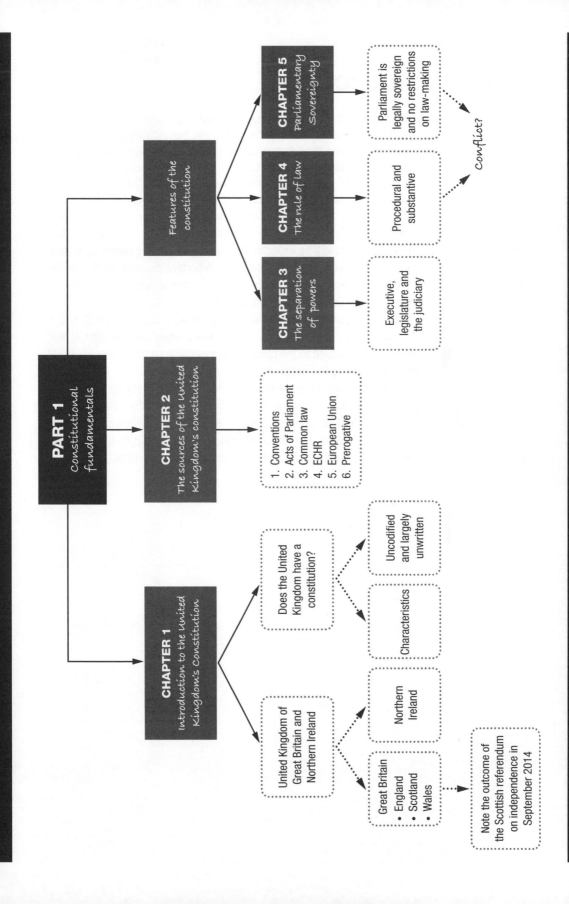

PART 1 INTRODUCTION

Part 1 of Blueprints *Constitutional and Administrative Law* explores the foundations of the United Kingdom's constitution. In Chapter 1 we will begin by looking at the historical development of the United Kingdom, before we then consider the key constitutional reforms introduced by the Labour government (1997–2010) and the Coalition government (2010–). You will be expected to understand what is meant by the term 'constitution', and discuss whether you think that the United Kingdom has a 'written', 'unwritten' or 'codified' constitution, or indeed, whether it has a constitution at all.

The sources of the United Kingdom's constitution will be explored in Chapter 2. This will provide you with a useful overview of the main sources, some of which will be discussed in their own chapters later on in the book. You will be expected to understand what is meant by a 'constitutional convention' and why conventions serve such an important purpose in the United Kingdom's constitution. We will also look at the concept of a constitutional statute and Laws LJ's *obiter* in *Thoburn* v. *Sunderland City Council* [2002] EWHC 195.

The theory of the separation of powers and why it matters is the subject of Chapter 3. This is a controversial topic because many academics would disagree over whether the United Kingdom's constitution has ever conformed to the requirements of the separation of powers. We will look at the arguments surrounding the separation of powers. The rule of law is discussed in Chapter 4 and is an important feature of the constitution. We shall see that the rule of law has an uneasy relationship with the most important feature of the constitution, Parliamentary Sovereignty. In Chapter 5 we will look at what is meant by Parliamentary Sovereignty and the challenges that exist, such as devolution, the United Kingdom's membership of the European Union, the rule of law and judicial activism, and finally the Human Rights Act 1998.

CHAPTER 1

Introduction to the constitution of the United Kingdom

BLUEPRINT

Introduction to the constitution of the United Kingdom

KEY QUESTIONS

LEGISLATION

- Magna Carta 1215
- Bill of Rights 1689
- Devolution Acts 1998
- European Communities Act 1972

CONTEXT

- The UK's constitution has evolved over a long period of time.
- There has been no revolution since 1688. Subsequently, the monarch has voluntarily handed over the running of the country to the Prime Minister and Cabinet Ministers.
- Many people are calling for a modern British Bill of Rights.

CONCEPTS

- What do we mean by a 'constitution'?
- A federal or unitary constitution
- Devolution
- The United Kingdom's constitution is flexible
- Coalition government

- In September 2014 the people of Scotland voted to remain as part of the United Kingdom. Before the vote took place the leaders of the three main political parties promised to devolve more powers to Scotland. The Conservative party also wishes to address the question of English devolution. How this will be addressed remains to be seen.
- Does the absence of a written constitution inadequately protect human rights?
- Does the UK need a codified constitution?

- Does the UK have a constitution?
- What are the characteristics of the UK's constitution?
- Is the UK's constitution unwritten?
- Should the UK have a written constitution?

CASES

SPECIAL CHARACTERISTICS

- Key features of the United Kingdom's constitution are observance of the rule of law, the importance of the separation of powers and the fact that Parliament is legally sovereign
- The United Kingdom has an uncodified consitution
- The United Kingdom's constitution is not wholly unwritten

REFORM

- Devolution has led to the creation of the Scottish Parliament, Welsh Assembly and the Northern Ireland Assembly.
- The decision of the Scottish electorate to remain as part of the United Kingdom will see further powers devolved to Scotland.
- It is likely that more powers will be devolved to Wales and Scotland. It is inevitable that the West Lothian question will need to be addressed (that is Scottish MPs voting on English issues, when English MPs cannot vote on devolved Scottish issues) either through the creation of an English Parliament, restrictions on Scottish MPs voting on English issues, the creation of regional assemblies or increased powers to local authorities.
- There may be a referendum on the UK's membership of the European Union after 2015 (subject to the outcome of the next General Election).

CRITICAL ISSUES

Setting the scene

Many people use the word constitution without really knowing what it means. We will look at what the word constitution means and why every country, organisation or sports club will require a constitution to enable it to work effectively. We will look at the constitution of the United Kingdom. It is important to appreciate just how controversial an area this is. If you ask your lecturers whether the United Kingdom has a constitution, you might receive a number of very different responses. This is because many academics argue that the United Kingdom does not have a constitution. They argue that this so because it is not codified, i.e. written down in a single document such as the constitution of the United States of America. So does this mean that the United Kingdom's constitution is unwritten? Technically large parts of what we consider to be constitutional sources are written down, such as important statutes. However, other sources of the constitution are unwritten, such as constitutional conventions. We will explore whether the United Kingdom has a constitution, and in doing this we will look at the key features of a constitution and see how these apply against the United Kingdom.

We will also look at the history of the United Kingdom and see how the country was created. In September 2014, the Scottish electorate voted to remain as part of the United Kingdom. Prior to the referendum on Scottish independence there was considerable uncertainty over what would happen if Scotland voted to become independent. This included the United Kingdom would require a new flag, whether Scotland be able to join the European Union and would there be a currency union between Scotland and the rest of the United Kingdom. The decision to vote 'no' means that Scotland will now have more powers devolved from the United Kingdom Parliament to the Scottish Parliament. Before the vote took place the leaders of the three main political parties promised to devolve more powers to Scotland. The Conservative party also wishes to address the West Lothian question, which is where Scottish MPs are able to vote on matters that only affect England because this type of decision has been devolved to Scotland. This may lead to the creation of an English Parliament, the exclusion of Scottish MPs from voting on issues that only affect England, the creation of regional assemblies or giving more power to local authorities.

The constitutional history of the United Kingdom is relevant to the modern day and you will need to understand these key events and the impact of devolution to Scotland, Wales and Northern Ireland in 1998.

Chapter overview

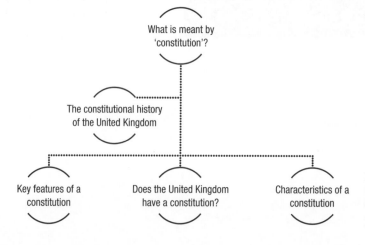

WHAT IS MEANT BY A CONSTITUTION?

What is a **Constitution**? A [handwritten: A set of rules that govern a body] a law society and a company can have a constitution; this word is not used exclusive[ly] [...] ntry. On any level of its use a constitution is the key rules and requirements b[...] [...]ny are governed, and the members, directors and shareholders understand [...] [...]ational level a constitution is a collection of rules, practices, laws which relate [...] [...] of a country and the key rights of any citizen. A constitution is intended to regulate govern[...] [...] it will contain the rules how the courts, the legislature and the executive operate, the rules about elections, the power of the head of [...]e and protection from police and executive oppression.

CORNERSTONE

What do we mean by a 'constitution'?

Professor Anthony King questioned whether the United Kingdom has a constitution and sta[...] [handwritten: Professor Anthony King (2001)]

> 'A constitution is the set of the most important rules that regula[...] [handwritten: Viscount Bolingbroke (1753)]
> different parts of the government of a given country and also r[...]
> parts of the government and the people of the country' (King [...]

Viscount Bolingbroke (who was an important eighteenth-century politician) provides another definition of what is meant by a constitution (*On Parties* (1735), p. 108):

> 'By Constitution we mean, whenever we speak with propri[...] [handwritten: F.F. Ridley (1998)] s, that assemblage of laws, institutions, and customs, derived from [...] of reason . . . that compose the general system, according to w[...] [...] agreed to be governed.'

There are difficulties in defining what exactly [...] [...]tional law and the academic writer F.F. Ridley noted that constitutional law textboo[...] [...] a selection of laws that appear important to the author, together with important conventions [...] often a reduced version of the topics treated by institutionally-oriented political scientists' (Ridley 1998, p. 341). There is some truth in this, as we shall see when we look at the sources of the constitution in Chapter 2.

Many people equate a constitution with a written document, which is codified and protected by the law. An example of this is the United States constitution, where the constitution is protected by a special status of constitutional law and cannot be amended unless through a special procedure. If the federal government or Congress acts in a way that is incompatible with the constitution [...] they are said to be acting unconstitutionally and the United States Supreme Court can cha[...] their a[c]tions. Importantly, the United States Supreme Court can declare an Act of Congress [...] [...]ingdom does not have a written codified constitution, and there is no [...] [...] w. This means that any legal features of the constitution, suc[...] [...] Parliament. [handwritten: Constitution does not have to be written, UK is unwritten and uncodified]

INTERSECTION

The United Kingdom Supreme Court has limite[...] [...]tates Supreme Court, and cannot declare an Act of Parl[...] [...] for this in Chapter 5, where we will consider what is n[...]

Take note

If the United Kingdom does not afford 'constitutional law' a special status, then why do lawyers need to study constitutional and administrative law? The answer is that much of what is covered in this book is of a legal nature, and the political material is essential to understanding how this law works. It is worth remembering that the law of the constitution (i.e. key statutes such as the Human Rights Act 1998) have the same legal status as any other law, despite their importance to our rights and political system.

Now that is not to say that the United Kingdom does not have a constitution, instead the sources of the constitution need to be identified from a range of sources (see below).

The two types of constitutions

Whether the United Kingdom can be said to have a constitution will be discussed below, with reference to the features of constitutions generally. At this point that we can identify the feature if there were a written constitution then as Anthony King has argued ...u be unlikely that this formal document would contain the *entire* constitution. King identified two types of constitution, the written Constitution (capital 'C'), and the unwritten constitution (small 'c'). King argued that there was an overlap between these two types of constitution in each state. King observed that a written constitution will cover much irrelevant material such as where the President must live, but will contain important omissions, such as how the electoral system would operate. However, these omissions are not left out of an unwritten constitution, 'No small-c constitution is, or could possibly be, silent on the subject: every democratic country has, and must have, some kind of electoral system' (King 2001, pp. 4–5). King observed that the United States capital-C constitution makes no reference to the power of the United States Supreme Court to declare an Act of Congress void (ibid, p. 5).

Written /
Unwritten ... Library,

The key features of the United Kingdom's constitution

CORNERSTONE

Key features of the United Kingdom's constitution

The key features of the United Kingdom's constitution are the observance of the rule of law, the importance of the separation of powers and the fact that Parliament is legally sovereign.

We shall briefly look at the key features of the United Kingdom's constitution:

- Parliamentary Sovereignty – Parliament is the highest source of law and can make or change any law that it wishes. The courts must give effect to an Act of Parliament and cannot declare it to be void (Chapter 5).
- Observance of the **rule of law** – the executive cannot act unless their powers are derived from law or the prerogative powers. Acting beyond their powers makes executive action illegal (Chapter 4).

Although there is a debate over whether a government is permitted to do anything, so long as it is not expressly prohibited

- The **separation of po**... with the French writer Montesquieu, th... h is responsible for carrying out gove... (which in the United Kir... for making laws) and t... **judicial** functions) mus... comprised of different p... adhered to a strict version...

- **Constitutional monarc**... but the personal **prero**... regulated by **constituti**... legal rules.

As we will see these key fea... constitution, rather they hav... United Kingdom's constitutio...

Handwritten note (Key features):

Key features;
- Parliamentary Sovereignty - Parliament is highest source of law, courts must listen
- Observance of Rule of law - Executive cannot act unless powers derived from law or prerogative
- Separation of Powers - 3 branches of government; executive (carry out government functions), & legislature (Parliament, make laws), Judiciary (courts perform judicial function
- Constitutional monarchial - Prerogative powers ← Regulated by Constitutional conventions

Handwritten note (right side, partly obscured):

...ote ...ant that you ...r with the ...y used in this ...ingdoms of ...d Scotland only ...rm Great Britain ...ior to this they ...e countries, ...ng the same ...ce 1603. In ...1801, the Kingdom of ...d and Great Britain ...the United ...at Britain ...1927, the name was ...ged to the United Kingdom of Great Britain and Northern Ireland, to reflect Irish independence.

CONSTITUTIONAL HISTORY OF THE UNITED KINGDOM

In order to understand the evolution of the constitution it is important to appreciate the historical origins of the United Kingdom. The events discussed below will be relevant to the topics covered in this book, and so it is helpful to briefly consider some of the key constitutional events of the last thousand years (see Figure 1.1).

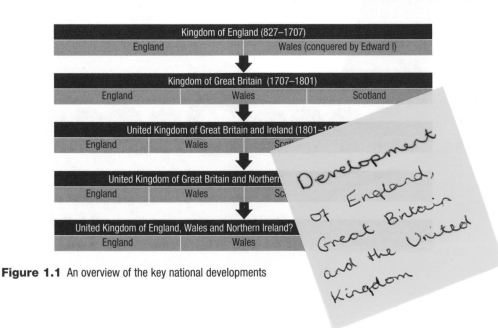

Figure 1.1 An overview of the key national developments

The Kingdom of England

England's first king was Egbert in 827. Prior to this England had been comprised of a number of rival kingdoms ruled by Saxons and Vikings. Saxon and Danish kings ruled England until 1066, when Duke William of Normandy invaded England and seized the English throne.

> The Normans inherited a quite sophisticated English legal system, which did not exist in their Norman homeland. The Normans spoke French, whilst the native English spoke English and resented being ruled by a foreign power. The Plantagenet dynasty followed the Normans and the kingdom of Henry I included much of France, England and parts of Ireland. His son John managed to lose most of his French territory and from then onwards the focus of the kingdom was England. John was unpopular with his barons and faced a major revolt, which led to England being invaded by the French.

CONTEXT

The Magna Carta

CORNERSTONE

Magna Carta 1215 ← *Regarded as first constitutional document*

King John was forced to sign th[e] ...agna Carta at R[un]ymede in 1215. The rebel barons wanted to prevent the king from abusing his pow[er] and stated th[at] the king could not raise taxation without the barons' consent.

Magna Carta signed in 1215
↓
Annulled by the pope
↓
Reissued by John's grandson, Edward I

The Magna Carta was [annulled by the pope and John died] whilst campaigning against the rebel barons. The Magna Carta w[as reissued by John's grandson] Edward I, and is regarded as the first quasi-constitutional document [in medieval England. John had a reputa]tion as a 'bad king' and was viewed by later historians as oppres[sive ...]

Norman Conquest 1066

Magna Carta 1215

First Parliament 1258

The English Civil War 1640/50s

The Glorious Revolution 1688

Act of Un[ion] Scotland 17[0...]

Establishment of Cabinet Government

Irish Independence

Membership of the European Union

Impact of devolution in 1998 and the consequences of Scotland voting to stay as part of the United Kingdom in 2014

Figure 1.2 Key historical events

The First Parliament

The first Parliament met in 1258 at Oxford and, as we will see in Chapter 6, the composition, freedoms and power of Parliament would gradually develop, so that soon no king could rule his country without the assent of Parliament.

The Tudors

Henry VIII merged Wales with England in the 1540s, and crowned himself as King of Ireland. This created a formal union between England and Wales, and a personal union with Ireland. Henry VIII created the Church of England when he broke with the Roman Catholic Church in the 1530s.

The Stuarts

After the death of Elizabeth I in 1603, the English Crown passed to James VI of Scotland. James I ruled as King of England and King of Scotland. The kings of Scotland had successfully repelled English invasions and had maintained an independent nation. James I founded the **Stuart** dynasty in England and believed in the divine right of kings. This meant that the king believed he received his authority to rule directly from God and was thus superior to all laws.

Under James' son Charles I, the Crown and the king's use of the prerogative clashed with Parliament and the supremacy of an Act of Parliament. Unable to work with Parliament, Charles I ruled without calling a Parliament for over a decade. During this time Charles relied on his prerogative powers to raise money, as direct taxation could only be raised with Parliamentary approval. This led to three **English Civil Wars** in the 1640s and '50s, and the execution of Charles I in 1649.

The Commonwealth and the Restoration

The monarchy was abolished and Oliver Cromwell and Parliament ruled England and Scotland as one state during the **Commonwealth**. Cromwell was known as the Lord Protector and refused to be crowned as king. After Cromwell's death the monarchy was restored in 1660. Charles II ruled until 1685 and had an uncomfortable relationship with Parliament. Charles II was succeeded by his Catholic brother, James II, who then attempted to repeal the Test Acts which discriminated against Catholics and used his prerogative powers to dispense with Acts of Parliament.

The Glorious Revolution

James II was forced to flee to France in 1688 when Parliament invited his son-in-law William of Orange to invade. This is known as the **Glorious Revolution** and marks the supremacy of Parliament over the monarchy. In 1689, Parliament offered the throne to William and his wife Mary. From then on Parliament has determined the issue of royal succession. The 1689 Bill of Rights protected the right of Parliament and protected parliamentary privilege, which permits freedom of expression in Parliament. This means that an MP can speak in the House of Commons without fear of being prosecuted or sued.

CORNERSTONE

Bill of Rights 1689

The 1689 Bill of Rights protected the right of Parliament and established legal protection for parliamentary privilege, which permits freedom of expression in Parliament. This means that an MP can speak in the House of Commons without fear of being prosecuted or sued.

The Kingdom of Great Britain

Great Britain was created by the English Union with Scotland Act in 1706, and the Scottish Union with England Act 1707 (this had been agreed under the Treaty of Union 1706). These Acts are collectively known as the Acts of Union 1707. England and Scotland were to be joined to create one country, with a shared Parliament and monarch. Anne I of England (who was also Anne I of Scotland), became Anne I of Great Britain. The Scottish and English Parliaments voted to abolish themselves and a new Parliament would meet at Westminster. It would be comprised of members from England and Scotland. Scotland and England were to have separate legal systems, but would be ruled as one country. Many Scots were unhappy and there were claims that Scottish parliamentarians had to be bribed to vote in favour. The union was important to prevent the kingdoms of England and Scotland from having different monarchs in the future.

The Hanoverians and the development of cabinet government

After Anne died, the throne passed to a distant relative, George of Hanover. George I spoke limited English and left the business of government to his cabinet. Sir Robert Walpole presided over the cabinet meetings and is generally known as the first **Prime Minister**. Under George II and III, there was the development of **cabinet government** with the business of state being run by the government, rather than under the monarch's direction. The political system which operated in the 1740s was admired by the French writer Montesquieu, and influenced his writings on the separation of powers.

The Kingdom of the United Kingdom of Great Britain and Ireland

The Union with Ireland Act 1800 created the United Kingdom of Great Britain and Ireland. The Irish Parliament was abolished and Irish members were to join the Westminster Parliament. Many Irish nationalists were to resent being ruled from London and argued for Home Rule throughout the nineteenth and early twentieth centuries.

During the nineteenth century there was a reform of the electoral system under the Reform Acts, which increased the electoral franchise and abolished the rotten boroughs. There was the development of the constitutional monarchy and the dominance of the political executive in governing the country. The legal system was transformed by the Judicature Acts 1873 and 1875, which merged the common law and equitable system. The Appellate Jurisdiction Act 1876 established the Appellate Committee of the House of Lords and created the Lords of Appeal in Ordinary, or the **Law Lords**. During this period the British Empire expanded to include one quarter of the world, and eventually Canada, New Zealand, Australia and South Africa received their independence as self-governing dominions.

INTERSECTION

The enlargement of the electoral franchise has resulted in all men and women over the age of 18 (subject to limited restrictions) being able to vote. The legislation passed to achieve this will be discussed in Chapter 6.

The Kingdom of the United Kingdom of Great Britain and Northern Ireland

Irish independence

In 1922, the Irish Free State received independence and in 1927 the Royal and Parliamentary Titles Act changed the name of the United Kingdom to the United Kingdom of Great Britain and Northern Ireland. Southern Ireland was independent and only Northern Ireland remained part of the United Kingdom.

Membership of the European Union

CORNERSTONE

European Communities Act

Parliament passed the European Communities Act 1972 to facilitate the United Kingdom's membership of the European Economic Community.

UK joined EU in 1973

After Parliament passed European Communities Act 1972

The United Kingdom finally became a member of the European Communities (now the European Union) in 1973, which was as a result of Parliament passing the European Communities Act 1972. Membership of the European Union has had an important impact on the United Kingdom's law and constitution. We shall see the significance of this in Chapter 5, when we discuss Parliamentary Sovereignty.

DEVOLUTION AND THE REFERENDUM ON SCOTTISH INDEPENDENCE

CORNERSTONE

Devolution

In 1998, Scotland and Wales received devolved powers. In Northern Ireland, the Northern Ireland Act 1998 returned devolved powers, which had been suspended in 1974 as a consequence of the 'Troubles', to Stormont.

The Scotland Act 1998 created a Scottish Parliament with the power to make legislation for Scotland, and a Scottish government which would govern Scotland using the powers devolved from **Westminster**. The Government of Wales Act 1998 created the National Assembly of Wales and a Welsh government. **Devolution** did not affect the integrity of the United Kingdom, as Scotland and Wales did not become independent. Rather, powers were being devolved from Westminster to a local level. However, post 1998, more powers have been devolved and there are calls for increased powers to be given to the Scottish Parliament.

In the 2011 elections for the Scottish Parliament, the Scottish National Party won a majority and called for a referendum on Scottish independence in 2014. In 2012, the United Kingdom and Scottish governments agreed that a referendum on Scottish independence would be held in 2014. In September 2014 the people of Scotland voted to remain as part of the United Kingdom. The leaders of the three main political parties (Conservatives, Labour and Liberal Democrats) have promised to devolve more powers to the Scottish Parliament.

Devolution for England?

England has not been affected by devolution and does not have a devolved Parliament. The West Lothian question remains unanswered and this means that every MP can vote on matters that affect England and many regard this as unfair, since English MPs cannot vote on devolved matters in Scotland or Wales. Many commentators have argued for the creation of an English Parliament to decide exclusively English matters. The decision of the Scottish electorate to remain part of the United Kingdom will inevitably lead to the West Lothian question being addressed. The creation of a devolved English Parliament may be one solution, however, it, like the other proposed solutions, remains controversial.

> If the Scottish people had voted in support of independence, then an Act of Parliament would have been required to grant Scotland its independence. Scottish independence would have created an independent Scotland and a fully sovereign Scottish Parliament at **Holyrood**. The Scottish executive would have governed and the Queen would have become Elizabeth I of Scotland. Civil servants working in Scotland would have been transferred from the United Kingdom's civil service to the Scottish civil service. The military would transfer assets and personnel to Scotland and the Queen would have become the head of the Scottish armed forces. Independence would not affect the judiciary (with the exception of the Supreme Court's current role), as Scotland has a distinct legal system to that of England and Wales. Scotland would either by default, or upon a formal application, have become a member of the European Union.
>
> However, many opponents of Scottish independence warned that Scotland may have found it difficult to become a member of the European Union as the other 28 members would have to formally approve Scotland's membership. Scotland could have become a member of the Council of Europe (and, if it wished to, have the European Convention on Human Rights (ECHR) incorporated into domestic Scottish law).

CONTEXT

RECENT CONSTITUTIONAL DEVELOPMENTS

The Labour government (1997–2010) embarked on a series of important constitutional reforms. Academics have commented on the significance of the reforms. Leyland observed that:

> 'The radical constitutional reform embarked upon by the Blair government elected in 1997 changed the complexion of the UK constitution. In many respects it has come to look much more like a codified constitution' (Leyland 2012, p. 296).

Brazier rejected the idea that the reforms have brought the United Kingdom towards a codified constitution, as many key areas of the constitution were left untouched by the reforms ('How near is a written constitution' [2001] 52(1) *Northern Ireland Legal Quarterly* 1). Instead Brazier regarded the constitution as becoming more written:

(handwritten note, top) Changed aspects of constitution

(handwritten note) Reforms

'In impl... ...the Labour Gov... ...caused Parliament to enact an additional and substantial corpus of statute law... ...racter. While, therefore, the United King... ...acks a codified con... ...ther more of a written consti... ...ion of sixteen Act... ...t, add to th...

(handwritten note) House of Lords Act 1999 removed many aspects of the... 92 hereditary peers from second chamber

...in the... ...rs from the

- ...s... ...d many of the p... ...t the ind... ...made the Lord Ch... ...Act did much... ...ration of powers.

(handwritten note) Constitutional Reform Act 2005 created Supreme Court and removed many powers from Lord Chancellor

- The... Act 1998 and Government o... Wales Act 1998). These Acts introd... devolution and... ated the Scottish Parliament and the Nation... Assembly of Wales. The N... Act 1998 reintroduced devolved po... ...these d... ou powe... had been removed during the troubl... ...governed from West...

(handwritten note) Devolution Acts 1998 introduced devolution and created 'Scottish Parliament' and 'National Assembly of Wales'

(handwritten note) Human Rights Act 1998 – much of ECHR directly incorporated into domestic law

- The Human Rights... ...the... ...pean Conv... ...incorporated into... ...Since... 2000... indi... European Court... ...e th... ...good... intended to...

- The Freedom... ...inter... ...increase exec...

The Coa...

(handwritten note) Freedom of Information Act 2000 – intended to create open government to increase executive accountability

CORNERSTONE

Coalitio...

(handwritten note) October 2000 – no longer have to go to European Court of Human Rights in Strasbourg to enforce their convention rights

...to form a g... ...ments a... ...y are... ...the... a **coalition** ...d Germany. ...servative and ...ce the Second

In the 2... ...ical party secured a majority of seats in the House of Commons. The incu... ...rnment was unable to form a coalition with the Liberal Democrats, and instead th... ...atives and Liberal Democrats decided to form a coalition government. The Prime Minister, Gordon Brown resigned and the Queen invited the leader of the Conservative Party, David Cameron, to form the next government. The Coalition government consists of Conservative and Liberal Democrats ministers and is the first peacetime coalition government since the 1930s.

Both the Liberal Democrats and Conservatives had their own party political manifestos and subsequently agreed on a common set of policies that are contained in the **Coalition Agreement**. This means that ministers from both political parties will have agreed legislation introduced by the government. If politicians from one particular political party wish to introduce non-coalition legislation then this will have to be in the form of a **Private Members' Bill**.

CONTEXT

The Coalition government (2010–) has proposed some important changes to the constitution:

- In 2011, there was a referendum on the voting system. The referendum asked voters if they wished to replace **First Past the Post** with the **Alternative Vote**. A majority of voters voted against changing the voting system.
- The government's 2011 White Paper laid out the plans to reform the House of Lords. It was proposed that the House of Lords will either be wholly elected, or consist of partly appointed and partly elected members. However, due to opposition from within the Conservative Party the reforms will not take place during the 2010–15 Parliament. This was criticised as a breach of the Coalition Agreement by the Conservative's coalition partners, the Liberal Democrats.

INTERSECTION ....

The gradual reform of the House of Lords and the Coalition government's aborted reforms will be discussed in Chapter 6. The House of Lords reform was abandoned by the Coalition government in 2012.

- In 2011, the Coalition government established a Commission on a Bill of Rights. This commission sought views as to whether the United Kingdom requires a Bill of Rights which would expand upon the European Convention on Human Rights (ECHR). This could lead to additional rights to those that exist at the moment. The Commission's final report was inconclusive, although it stated that a Bill of Rights could be introduced in the future.
- The government introduced the Fixed Term Parliaments Act 2011 which subject to exceptions prevents a general election from being called until May 2015. This restricts the Prime Minister's ability to ask the Queen to use her prerogative powers to dissolve Parliament and call a General Election.
- The Coalition Agreement contained plans to change the constituency boundaries in the House of Commons and reduce the number of MPs. This is unlikely to be achieved during the lifetime of this Parliament.

Possible changes beyond 2015

- In 2012, the Prime Minister promised that a referendum on membership of the European Union would be held in the lifetime of the next Parliament. There is a possibility that the United Kingdom may no longer be a full member of the European Union.

- The Human Rights Act 1998 has proved controversial and there is a possibility that the United Kingdom may decide to change its relationship with the European Court of Human Rights. In 2013, the difficulties on deporting Abu Qatada to Jordan led to senior figures in the government to discuss the possibility of temporarily withdrawing from the ECHR. In September 2014, the Prime Minister, David Cameron, announced that a future Conservative government would repeal the Human Rights Act 1998 and replace it with a British Bill of Rights.

KEY FEATURES OF A CONSTITUTION

We will now look at some key features of constitutions (see Figure 1.3). It is important to note that every country has its own unique constitution. For example, the United Kingdom's constitution is similar to Australia because there is a fusion between the executive and the legislature. However, there is also a key difference as, unlike the United Kingdom, Australi... a ...en constitution.

According to F.F. Ridley the characteristics of a con...

'(1) It establishes, or constitutes, the sy... ...rior to the system of government, not part of it, and its ru... ...system.

'(2) It therefore involves an authority outs... ...blishes. This is the notion of the constituent power .. ..uted to the people, on whose ratification the legitimac... ...with it, the legitimacy of the governmental system.

'(3) It is a form of law superior to other l... ...an authority higher than the legislature which makes ... ...ty of the legislature derives from it and is thus bound by ... ...w generally (but not always) leads to the possibility of ju... ...

'(4) It is entrenched – (i) because its pu... ...ers of government, but also (ii) again because of its orig... ...utside the system. It can thus only be changed by special procedur... ...and certainly for major change) requiring reference back to the constituent ... ...er' (Ridley 1988, pp. 342–43)

[Handwritten annotations:]
① Establishes a system of government
② Involves authority outside and above – the order is established
③ Form of law superior to other laws
④ It is entrenched

REFLECTION

Having read the quote from F.F. Ridley above, it is clear that he identified four necessary requirements for a constitution to exist. We shall see below that the United Kingdom does not meet all four requirements. Whether Ridley's four requirements are authoritative on what is essential for a constitution to exist has been vigorously debated. Ridley was dismissive of the United Kingdom having a constitution. He noted that the United Kingdom's Parliament created by the Acts of Union in 1707 'appears to have taken a sovereign power it was not given by the Act which constituted it' (p. 349). Therefore the United Kingdom's constitution does not establish the system of government, nor given Parliamentary Sovereignty can it be entrenched. We shall see in Chapter 5 that Ridley's third characteristic does not exist, as Parliamentary Sovereignty negates the existence of superior form of constitutional law. After you have read this chapter it might be worthwhile considering whether you believe that Ridley's requirements must be met in order for there to be a constitution?

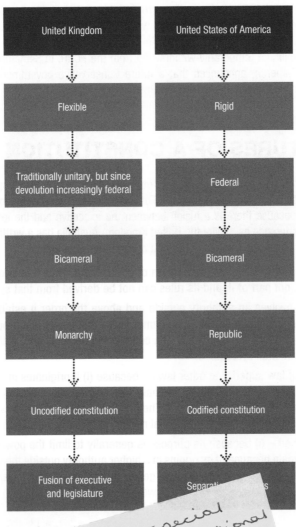

United Kingdom	United States of America
Flexible	Rigid
Traditionally unitary, but since devolution increasingly federal	Federal
Bicameral	Bicameral
Monarchy	Republic
Uncodified constitution	Codified constitution
Fusion of executive and legislature	Separation of powers

Figure 1.3 Key features of a cons...

Rigid or fle...

CORNER...

The United Ki...

The United Kingdom's ... rs. This flexibility can be viewed as a ... op to meet the requirements of a demo ... us because of the lack of safeguards to ...

Handwritten note:

Flexible — no special status of constitutional law within UK;
• Legal aspects can be repealed by ordinary Act of Parliament
• Political rules can be ignored without legal sanction
• Limited legal protection as Parliament is legally sovereign

A constitution can be rigid or flexible. A written constitution will more likely to be rigid, as the key provisions will often be 'entrenched'. This is less likely to be the case where the constitution is unwritten. Importantly, where the constitution is entrenched it will be harder to amend the constitution. This is because the constitution will often have a special legal status and cannot be amended by an Act of the legislature. The constitution will often lay down the requirements needed to amend the constitution. There might be a requirement for a referendum, where the electorate must vote in order to change the constitution. The referendum requirement is used in the Swiss constitution. Alternatively, there may be a requirement that there needs to a vote in the legislature of say 75 per cent to amend the constitution. Where such requirements exist, the constitution may not be amended unless these are complied with.

The constitution may give the judiciary the power to ensure that the requirements are met and to prevent the legislature and executive acting in breach of the constitution. The Israeli Supreme Court and the United States Supreme Court have given themselves the power to declare Acts of the legislature void. In *Marbury* v. *Madison* (1803) 5 US 137, the United States Supreme Court claimed the power to declare an Act of Congress void, which is important as no such power had been conferred by the United States constitution.

Federal or unitary

CORNERSTO⬤⬤

A federal or unitar⬤

A constitution may be **feder** ... one level of government and that is at ... wer is not controlled by the national gov ... ween the national state and the federal ... n where these powers can be abolished ... s powers under the constitution.

Handwritten note:
Unitary - increasingly quasi-federal
- Devolution settlement of 1998 - Scotland, Wales, Northern Ireland
- English Votes of for English Laws
- Increased devolution for Scotland post 2014

In the United Kingdom there has tra ... tion of Northern Ireland), with power bein ... gional government for Scotland, Wales and ... 1707, some commentators had argued for ... r and Edinburgh.

The Labour government (1997–20 ... powers to Scotland, Wales, Northern Ireland and London. This has created a devolved system where Scotland, Wales and Northern Ireland have a legislature with devolved law-making powers. They each have a government to implement policy; however the powers conferred are determined by Westminster. London has a directly elected mayor, although elected mayors have not proved entirely positive elsewhere. The Mayor of London has been given devolved powers and there is an assembly with devolved legislative powers.

Labour had intended to devolve powers to the English regions, but there was little public appetite for this idea. Brigid Hadfield has written that, 'A consideration of the devolved UK constitution may be placed within the perspective of the UK as a unitary state; this is, one in which popular power flows to and political power from the centrally located Parliament and government in London' (Hadfield

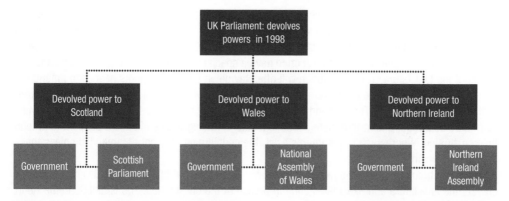

Figure 1.4 Devolution in the United Kingdom

2011, p. 211). Devolution has not created a federal system in the United Kingdom, as the powers are given and can be removed by Parliament (see Figure 1.4). This occurred in 1974 in Northern Ireland, and so legally the Scottish Parliament and government could be abolished by an Act of Parliament. However, the impact of devolution is that it might be more appropriate to describe the United Kingdom as somewhere between being a unitary and a federal state. In light of the outcome of the Scottish referendum in 2014, it is likely that there will be significant changes to the United Kingdom's constitution, which could possibly create a federal system and see powers devolved from the Westminster Parliament to England.

The United States of America is a federal state

The United States of America has a federal constitution and each of the fifty states (California, New Jersey, etc.) has their own constitution (see Figure 1.5). The United States constitution is based on power sharing between the federal and state government.

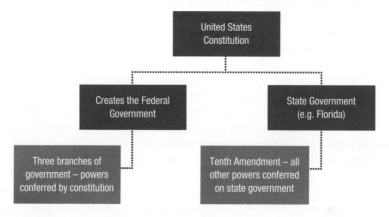

Figure 1.5 The federal structure of the United States of America

CONTEXT

Before the American War of Independence (1776–83) each of the thirteen American colonies had their own form of government. After gaining independence from Great Britain there were many people who wanted each colony to remain independent and not to create a federal state. They were known as anti-federalists, and consequentially, those who favoured unifying the thirteen colonies were known as federalists. The United States constitution created a federal government with three distinct branches: the legislature, the executive and the judiciary.

Article I of the constitution conferred legislative powers to Congress and limited the areas where Congress can make laws. Article II created the executive branch and the position of President. The President has powers conferred on him by the constitution. Article III created the judicial branch and the Supreme Court. The Tenth Amendment of the United States constitution states that all the remaining powers are conferred on individual states. Every state has its own constitution, with its own government, legislature and judiciary. Therefore, unlike the United Kingdom's system, it is the constitution that confers powers and has organised power sharing between state and federal government. Each state has its own legal system and can make its own laws. Therefore a state can abolish the death penalty, legalise same-sex marriage and impose its own immigration laws (see the controversy in Arizona in 2011).

Bicameral or unicameral

The legislature can either be bicameral, that is consisting of two chambers, or unicameral, that is consisting of only one chamber. The United Kingdom and United States both have bicameral legislatures. The two chambers in the United Kingdom are the House of Commons and the House of Lords.

Monarchy or a republic

The United Kingdom has a constitutional monarchy. Queen Elizabeth II is the head of state. A constitution can be republican, that is where there is no monarchy and a President will be the head of state. The United States is a republic and the President is the head of state.

Codified or uncodified constitution

Constitutions can be **codified** or uncodified. If a constitution is codified then the main features of the constitution are brought together in one document.

CORNERST

UK constitution is unwritten and uncodified

Codified = one document

The United Kingd□ stitution

Although it would be incorrec ... ving a wholly unwritten constitution, the constitution is no ... visions have not been consolidated into one document, ir ... onstitutions have.

The Separation of powers or fusion of powers

A constitution can be based on the separation of powers or upon a fusion between the different branches of government. The United States constitution formally creates the separation of powers between the three branches of government. The United Kingdom's constitution is based on a fusion between the legislature and the executive, with the Constitutional Reform Act 2005 reinforcing the separation between the judiciary and the other two branches of government.

> The German constitution of 1949 establishes the power of the German Federal Government. In order to see how the German constitution operates, look at the following link:
>
> http://www.bundesregierung.de/Content/EN/StatischeSeiten/breg/federal-government-function-and-constitutional-basis-acting-in-accordance.html?nn=393254

CONTEXT

DOES THE UNITED KINGDOM HAVE A CONSTITUTION?

We have looked at the important historical and recent developments as well as the key features of the United Kingdom's constitution. The question remains whether the United Kingdom can truly be said to have a constitution. A constitution in the newer sense of the word is more than just a description of how the government works; rather it is the system that decides h   ntry will be governed, and as such will be established via a written document. T   g area and we shall see the arguments for and against whether the U   .

Says no constitution

Thomas Paine's critique ✓

Thomas Paine was a radical writer and politician who wrote   of Independence. In *The Rights of Man* Paine criticised the Britis   s no British constitution. Paine believed that government w   he rulers and governed, and that this compact was the consti   nt on the existence of a constitution. Paine was critical of the   t it was based on the oppressive Norman Conquest, with the   wer without the consent of the people.

Due to no founding document upon which government was based as Normans created Government

Many academics have questioned whether the United   Paine in *The Rights of Man* did not believe that the United Kingdom had a

REFLECTION

> 'We have now to review the governments which arise out of society. If we trace government to its origin, we discover that governments must have arisen either out of the people or over the people. In those which have arisen out of the people, the individuals themselves, each in his own personal and sovereign right, have entered into a compact with each other to produce a government; and this is the only mode in which governments have a right to arise.

> 'This compact is the constitution, and a constitution is not a thing in name only, but in fact. Wherever it cannot be produced in a visible form, there is none. A constitution is a thing antecedent to government, and a government is only its creature. The constitution of a country is not the act of its government, but of the people constituting its government.'

Paine stated that as the Norman Conquest had created the government, there had been no founding document upon which the government was based. Therefore, there could be no constitution.

It must be remembered that Paine was writing in support of the American republic and the new constitution that had created the United States of America. Paine thought that there needed to be a constitution on which the powers of government were based. Therefore, the government must not act unless in accordance with the powers conferred on it under the constitution.

It is interesting to look at Paine's argument:

* Paine argued that: 'A constitution is a thing antecedent to government, and a government is only its creature.' This suggests that there needs to be a formal constitution upon which the legitimacy of the government is based. However, the United States of America was a new country constructed out of the thirteen distinctly unique former British colonies, which needed to be fused into one unified state, whereas the British state had developed its system of governance incrementally.

* Paine argued that: 'Wherever [a constitution] cannot be produced in a visible form, there is none.' Obviously his opponents could not produce a written document which contained the British constitution. However, the absence of a written document does not negate the fact that Britain in the 1790s had some sort of constitution. For instance the behaviour of George III in the 1780s over his treatment of the Fox–North coalition government was attacked as unconstitutional. Even George III was restrained from vetoing an Act of Parliament because it was recognised as unconstitutional to do so. Paine himself noted that England had a republican tradition (such as the power of the House of Commons), but declared, '[m]y is the constitution of England sickly, but because monarchy hath poisoned the republic, the crown hath engrossed the commons?' (*Common Sense*, 1776).

The absence of a written constitution

Does the fact that the United Kingdom's constitutional system is largely unwritten and uncodified mean that the United Kingdom does not have a constitution? Considering Anthony King's definition of a constitution we can see that the United Kingdom 'has a set of rules that regulate the relations' between the executive, the legislature and judiciary. There are also rules which regulate these branches of the government. However, some of these rules are unwritten or are non-legal.

> *[handwritten note:] Not written constitution but has some written sources*

The United Kingdom. is one of the few countries which do not have a written constitution.

The Scottish government has proposed that if Scotland were to become independent that it would have a written constitution.

Many people have argued that the United Kingdom requires a written constitution. Some of the reasons for this are that:

- Parliamentary Sovereignty is incompatible with human rights and the rule of law. In the United Kingdom, Parliament can legislate to create any law it wishes and can act in a manner that is deemed unconstitutional or abolish key features of the constitution. Academics such as Vernon Bogdanor do not see Parliamentary Sovereignty as an obstacle to creating a codified constitution if the former is no longer the dominant principle of the constitution (Bogdanor 2009, p. 215).

- There is no clarity and certainty as to the operation of the United Kingdom's constitution. Too many features depend on non-legal rules being followed, or the executive and Parliament acting with restraint.

- The absence of a written constitution means that there is no special status of constitutional law. The judiciary cannot protect key features of the constitution from repeal by Parliament, or ensure that the executive does not act in a manner that is incompatible with the constitution.

- Human rights are not adequately protected as the Human Rights Act 1998 could be repealed.

- The powers of the monarch, the office and powers of the Prime Minister and government are not defined in law and rely on unwr *Argued there is no british constitution*

F.F. Ridley's critique

F.F. Ridley was dismissive of claims that the United Kingdom has a constitution. He argued that there was in fact no British constitution because there was not a wholly written constitution. He was sceptical of the view the United Kingdom had a constitution:

> 'Not to be left out of the world of constitutional democracies, British writers define constitution in a way which appears to give us one too, even though there is no document to prove it. The argument is that a constitution need not be embodied in a single document or, indeed, wholly written. We say instead that a country's constitution is a body of rules – some laws, some conventions – which regulate its system of government. Such a definition does not, however, bridge the gap between Britain and the rest of the world by providing us with a substitute for a documentary constitution: it simply shifts the ground, by using the word in an entirely different way' (Ridley 1988, p. 340).

Ridley noted that the characteristics of a constitution required that there is a superior type of constitutional law and that this law was entrenched, both of which did not apply in the United Kingdom (ibid, p. 351). He notes that many people regard this as a sign of the flexibility of the British constitution, which he dismisses. Ridley looked at the importance of conventions in the British system, observing that: '[c]onventions are considered binding so long as they are considered binding. That seems just another way of saying the British "constitution" is what people do, how the system works' (ibid, p. 358). Ridley states that conventions are not constitutional and therefore could not form part of a constitution.

INTERSECTION

We shall look at the sources of the United Kingdom's constitution in Chapter 2, including what is meant by constitutional conventions and why they serve an important purpose.

Ridley was critical that the misuse of the word constitution to describe the United Kingdom's collection of conventions and other sources, might cause people to mislead 'themselves into thinking that there are parts of the system to which a special sanctity attaches. But in that normative sense the term is equally meaningless' (ibid, p. 359). What Ridley is emphasising is that Parliamentary Sovereignty results in the ability of Parliament to amend what is regarded as constitutional. It is certainly a persuasive argument.

> However, it could be argued that the British c̶ _____ over time to create a modern democracy. As Sir Ivor Jennings _____ has not been made but has grown'. The powers of the monarch _____ the Prime Minister and cabinet without the need for a writ_____ the British system has survived two world wars _____ countries that do have written constitutions are n_____ the rule of law. A written constitution does not guara_____ governance; instead the government of the country _____ hat is com-patible with a democracy. The British s_____ e a radical government could use the flexibility of the_____.

Handwritten margin note: "Sir Ivor Jennings — Can be argued British constitution has not been made but grown"

REFLECTION

Why do most countries have _____ tion?

If most countries have written constitutions then _____ understand why this is so. We can see that new written constitutions come about _____ a number of reasons, including military defeat, independence and political instability.

Country with a written constitution	The reason for having a written constitution
France	France was defeated by Germany in the Second World War and southern France (Vichy France) became an ally of Nazi Germany. The Fourth Republic was established in 1946 and it had a new constitution. The Fourth Republic collapsed as a result of the French province of Algeria's fight for independence, and the Fifth Republic was established in 1958. The new constitution was aimed at strengthening the power of the executive.
Germany	Germany was defeated by the allied powers in the Second World War. The western occupied zones were merged to create West Germany in 1949. The Germans wanted to prevent another dictatorship and therefore struck a balance between the federal government and the individual states.
Russia	The break-up of the USSR in 1991 and the creation of the Russian Federation led to the creation of a new constitution.
Kenya	Kenya was granted independence by the United Kingdom in 1963.

→

Country with a written constitution	The reason for having a written constitution
United States of America	Drafted in 1787, the constitution created the United States. The thirteen colonies had fought a war of independence against Great Britain. Under the constitution power is shared between federal and individual states.
Australia	The 1901 Commonwealth Constitution of Australia created Australia and united the separate states into a unified federal state. The constitution strikes a balance between federal government and the rights of the individual states.

APPLICATION

Imagine that Port Louis (fictitious) was until recently a province of the Republic of the East Coast. After twenty years of popular protests, the government of East Coast agreed that Port Louis could receive its independence. There are now a number of questions, namely will Port Louis be a democracy, who can vote, will it have a President, or will a senior member of the old royal family be declared king? If Port Louis will have a Parliament, would this be unicameral or bicameral? These are important questions and it is likely that Port Louis will draft a written constitution which will create the system of government. The constitution will attempt to answer these big questions and will aim to avoid any future uncertainties over how the new country will operate. For example, if there is a relatively strong democratic tradition then the constitution need not focus on ensuring democratic safeguards; whereas a tradition of oppression and abuse of power would require entrenching the need to hold democratic elections and limiting the power of Parliament and the President.

Why the United Kingdom does not have a written constitution?

CORNERSTONE

The United Kingdom's constitution is not wholly unwritten

The United Kingdom's constitution is not wholly unwritten. There are written sources of the constitution, which include the common law and Acts of Parliament. It is important to appreciate that to say the United Kingdom's constitution is written, unwritten, codified or uncodified means very different things.

Parts of the constitution are written down, such as key statutes, the common law, the rules of Parliament and the Ministerial Code. The United Kingdom would be capable of drafting a constitution, as Parliament has previously drafted constitutions for former colonies when they have been granted independence. However, determining what should be included as part of a written constitution would be problematic. Professor Conor Gearty has proposed a written constitution. In 2013–14, Gearty invited members of the public to contribute to the proposed written constitution through the project 'Crowdsourcing the UK's constitution'.

Looking at the history, the only time of political crisis significant enough to trigger a written constitution has been the abolition of the monarchy in 1649 and the Glorious Revolution in 1688. During 1649–1660, England was a republic and for much of this period there was a written constitution known as the Institutes of Government. In 1689, the Bill of Rights rebalanced the relationship between the monarch and Parliament. Whilst it guaranteed parliamentary privilege (granting MPs the freedom of speech inside Parliament), it could not be described as a written constitution.

Referendums as a way of protecting the constitution

Many constitutions such as Switzerland's require referendums to change parts of the constitution. In the United Kingdom there is no requirement that a referendum is used to introduce key constitutional changes. However, Professor Vernon Bogandor has noted that many of the key constitutional changes were preceded by a referendum (e.g. devolution and membership of the European Union).

> **REFLECTION**
>
> The European Union Act 2011 establishes a legal requirement for a referendum to be held before the government can agree to any significant changes to the United Kingdom's membership of the European Union. Whilst this offers a legal guarantee that there will be a popular vote, it would be perfectly possible for a future government to repeal the referendum requirement by introducing a new Act of Parliament. This would abolish the legal requirement to hold a referendum. The doctrine of Parliamentary Sovereignty states that Parliament has the ability to repeal any existing Act of Parliament. We shall see in Chapter 5, that Baroness Hale in the case of *R (Jackson)* v. *Attorney-General* [2005] UKHL 56, made an *obiter* statement which indicated that the courts could potentially enforce a referendum requirement (this was not in the context of the European Union).

British Bill of Rights

Before the 2010 General Election, the Human Rights Act 1998 featured in the main parties political manifestos. In particular, the Conservative Party had wanted to introduce a British Bill of Rights to replace the Human Rights Act 1998. The Coalition government established the Commission on a Bill of Rights, which considered the views of those who took part ̶ ̶ ̶ ̶ ̶ ̶ ̶ ̶ ation on whether to introduce a British Bill

> **Take note**
>
> The political motivation to replace the Human Rights Act 1998 is due in part to the controversy surrounding the application of the Act by judges.

Advant ADVANTAGES ...g an unwritten constitution

An unwritten constitution has ̶ ̶ ̶ ̶ ̶ ̶ ̶ ̶ ̶ ̶ ̶ ̶ ̶ ̶ ̶ ̶ ̶ l can develop over time. Therefore the constitution is not entrenc ̶ ̶ ̶ ̶ ̶ ̶ ̶ ̶ ̶ ̶ ̶ ̶ ion has seen the creation of a new state in 1707, 1801 and ̶ ̶ ̶ ̶ ̶ ̶ ̶ ̶ ̶ ̶ ̶ ̶ The creation of the office of Prime Minister and its importa ̶ ̶ ̶ ̶ ̶ ̶ developed over the past 300 years.

Flexible

Can develop over time

P.T.O

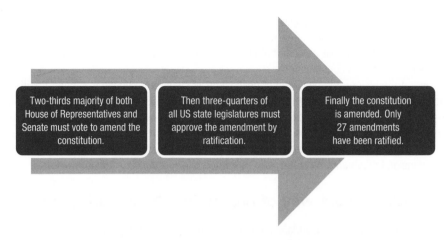

Two-thirds majority of both House of Representatives and Senate must vote to amend the constitution.

Then three-quarters of all US state legislatures must approve the amendment by ratification.

Finally the constitution is amended. Only 27 amendments have been ratified.

Figure 1.6 The procedure for amending the United States constitution

In order to amend the United States constitution a complex procedure must be complied with (see Figure 1.6). Failure to comply with this procedure will mean that the amendment is ineffective.

> An example of such an amendment is the twenty-second, which turned a constitutional convention into a legally enforceable part of the constitution. The convention had prevented Presidents from seeking to serve more than two four-year terms in office. President Franklin D. Roosevelt had breached this convention in 1941 and 1945. Consequently, since the passing of the twenty-second amendment, even popular Presidents are unable to serve more than two terms.

CONTEXT

Flexibility is important and an unwritten constitution can develop without the need of either popular referendums or majority votes in the legislature. Even the constitution of the United States of America relies on other rules apart from those contained in the written constitution, such as the requirement that durin............ on each state's Electoral College .... e in accordance with their state's

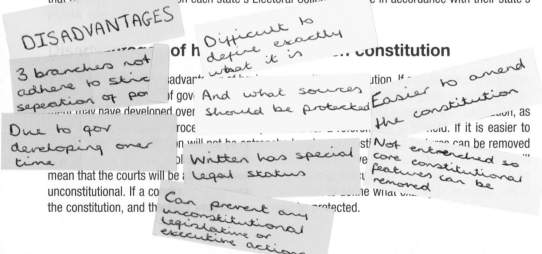

DISADVANTAGES

3 branches not adhere to stic sepeation of po .... may have developed over

Due to gov developing over time

Difficult to define exactly what it is

And what sources should be protected

Written has special legal status

Can prevent any unconstitutional legislative or executive action

of h .... constitution

....ition If ..... Easier to amend the constitution

.....on, as .....ld. If it is easier to sti Not entrenched so core constitutional features can be removed

mean that the courts will be ..... unconstitutional. If a co .... the constitution, and th ....le what ....rotected.

The United Kingdom's constitution?

CORNERSTONE

The United Kingdom does have a constitution

Professor Munro has written on whether the United Kingdom has a constitution. Munro takes the view that it does:

'Does the United Kingdom have a constitution, in the original sense of the word? Yes. Does the United Kingdom have a constitution, in the newer sense of the word? Perhaps not one as we know it, but up to a point' (Munro 2005).

Munro's position is interesting, as whilst the traditional meaning of constitution means a system of rules, the newer meaning equates to a written constitution. Munro has identified that much of the British constitutional system is written. Anthony King has questioned whether the United Kingdom still has a constitution and has concluded that it does, although the traditional constitution has been replaced by a more modern constitution. King notes that the new constitution is based on power sharing and power hoarding by the executive, with the Labour government having devolved powers to Northern Ireland, Wales, Scotland, London and the Bank of England (King 2001, pp. 99–100). King concluded by describing the United Kingdom's constitution as descriptive, that is a list of rules, practices and laws (ibid, p. 101).

Take note

Students will be required to engage with the academic debate on whether the United Kingdom has a constitution. You should be able to present a balanced view, but ultimately your tutor will expect you to form your own informed opinion.

KEY POINTS

- The United Kingdom was created in 1801 and is a constitutional monarchy.
- Great Britain was created in 1707. Previously, England and Scotland were two independent kingdoms.
- Academics have questioned whether the United Kingdom actually has a constitution.
- There are a number of characteristics of a constitution, which can be used to describe a particular country's constitution.
- Whilst the United Kingdom's constitution is uncodified, it would be wrong to describe it as wholly unwritten.
- Parliamentary Sovereignty, the Separation of Powers and the Rule of Law are three of the key features of the United Kingdom's constitution.
- The United States of America serves as a useful comparison to the constitutional arrangements of the United Kingdom.

CORE STATUTES

Statute	About	Importance
Magna Carta 1215	The Magna Carta was signed by King John in 1215. The king's barons had forced him to sign the greater charter and subsequently it was annulled by the pope. However, later monarchs reissued the Magna Carta.	Much of the Magna Carta is no longer in force. Its historic importance as a charter granting rights, and offering protection to individuals from the arbitary rule of the king, means that it has an international reputation and is celebrated in countries such as the United States.
Bill of Rights 1689	The Bill of Rights was presented to William of Orange and his wife Mary by those parliamentarians who had invited the ruler of the Netherlands to invade England in 1688.	The Bill of Rights is really important as it restricted the prerogative powers of the Crown, gave more powers to Parliament and confirmed the privileges of Parliament.
European Communities Act 1972	The United Kingdom required the enactment of the European Communities Act 1972 before it could give effect to its treaty obligations. The United Kingdom became a member of the now European Union in 1973.	The European Communities Act 1972 enables the British courts to give effect to the United Kingdom's treaty obligations. The Act allowed all previous, current and future European Union law to apply in the United Kingdom. This is significant as no additional legislation was required to give effect to regulations, new treaties and decisions of the Court of Justice of the European Union.
Devolution Acts 1998 (Scotland Act 1998 and the Government of Wales Act 1998)	These Acts devolved powers to the Scottish Parliament and the National Assembly of Wales. Powers were also retransferred back to Northern Ireland.	Devolution in 1998 led to increasingly more powers being devolved to Scotland and Wales and to the referendum on Scottish independence in 2014.

FURTHER READING

Bogdanor, V. *The New British Constitution* (Hart: Oxford, 2009)
This is an authoritative account of the British constitution. It discusses recent changes and offers detailed analysis.

Bogdanor, V. *The Coalition and the Constitution* (Hart: Oxford, 2011)
This book provides an authoritative account of the 2010 General Election and the subsequent creation of a Coalition government.

Bradly, A.W. and Ewing, K.D. *Constitutional and Administrative Law* 15th edn (Pearson: Harlow, 2011)
A very detailed textbook which will offer additional information to this book. Refer to this to expand your knowledge of the law.

Dicey, A.V. *Introduction to the Study of the Law of the Constitution* (Liberty Fund: Minneapolis, 1982)
Dicey is an important academic and this is his most important book. It is very readable and it is recommended that you refer to this.

Hadfield, B. 'Devolution a national conversation?' in Jowell, J. and Oliver, D. (eds) *The Changing Constitution* (Oxford University Press: Oxford, 2011)
This chapter offers a detailed look at devolution.

King, A. *Does the United Kingdom still have a constitution? Hamlyn Lecture 2000* (Sweet & Maxwell: London, 2001)
A short and interesting discussion on the United Kingdom's constitution. There is an interesting discussion of the types of constitutions and comparison is made to the Netherlands.

Leyland, P. *The Constitution of the United Kingdom: A Contextual Analysis* 2nd edn (Hart: Oxford, 2012)
An authoritative introduction to the United Kingdom's constitution.

Lyons, A. *Constitutional History of the United Kingdom* (Cavendish: London, 2003)
This book is essential reading for those who wish to have a more in-depth understanding of the key events that have created the modern United Kingdom.

Maitland, F.W. *The Constitutional History of England* (Cambridge University Press: Cambridge, 1965)
A classic text on the history of the United Kingdom's constitution, which is written in a lively and accessible style.

Munro, C. *Studies in Constitutional Law* (Oxford University Press: Oxford, 2005)
This book is highly recommended as a way to further your understanding of the law.

Ridley, F.F. 'There is no British constitution: A dangerous case the Emperor's clothes' (1988) *Parliamentary Affairs* 340
An interesting article that argues that the United Kingdom does not have a constitution.

CHAPTER 2

The sources of the United Kingdom's constitution

BLUEPRINT

The sources of the United Kingdom's constitution

KEY QUESTIONS

LEGISLATION

- Human Rights Act 1998
- European Communities Act 1972
- Union with Scotland Act 1706

CONTEXT

- Membership of European Union in 1973 has limited Parliamentary Sovereignty.
- Conventions have created the modern constitutional system, such as the appointment of the Prime Minister.

CONCEPTS

- What is a constitutional convention?
- The common law
- The European Union
- The Council of Europe
- Dualist legal system

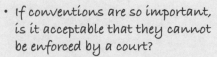

- If conventions are so important, is it acceptable that they cannot be enforced by a court?
- Should the courts protect constitutionally important statutes from repeal by Parliament?

- What are the sources of the UK's constitution?
- What are conventions and what purpose do they serve?
- How has membership of the European Union and Council of Europe affected the UK's constitution?

CASES

- *Madzimbamuto* v. *Lardner-Burke* [1969]
- *Reference re Amendment of the Constitution of Canada* [1981]
- *Van Gend en Loos* v. *Nederlandse Administratie der Belastingen* (26/62) [1963]

REFORM

- Will the UK still be a member of the European Union in ten years' time?
- Will the sources of the constitution be codified in a single document?

SPECIAL CHARACTERISTICS

- Constitutional conventions are not laws
- There is no special legal status for important Acts of Parliament
- Non-legal sanctions for breaching a convention

CRITICAL ISSUES

Setting the scene

We have seen that the question of whether the United Kingdom has as constitution is a controversial issue. But if we accept that the United Kingdom does have a constitution, then what are the sources of the constitution? We shall see that it is not possible to locate just a single source of the constitution, or indeed to go to the British Library and view the 'United Kingdom Constitution' as you can do in many other countries. The question this chapter will address is what exactly are the sources of the constitution? Are the sources written or unwritten? Are the sources legal or non-legal, and if some of the sources are non-legal, then what are the penalties for their breach? Ultimately, can the constitution be protected by the courts? The sources of the United Kingdom's constitution include key statutes, the common law, membership of the European Union, membership of the Council of Europe, constitutional conventions and the prerogative. We shall look at these in turn and explore why they are features of the constitution, and why these are so important.

Chapter overview

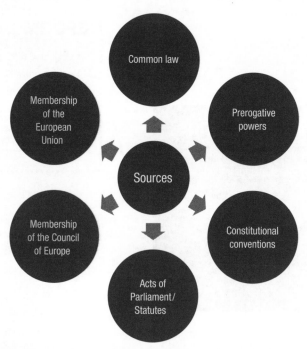

It is important to note that the sources are both legal and political. The constitution is starting to resemble more of a legal than political constitution, with key aspects of the constitution transferred from political practices into legal form. This means that the court can review whether there has been compliance with the legal rules.

ACTS OF PARLIAMENT

Acts of Parliament are an important source of the United Kingdom's constitution. There is no special status of constitutional law in the United Kingdom (see Figure 2.1).

Constitutional statutes

CORNERSTONE

There is no special legal status for important Acts of Parliament

It needs to be remembered that there is no special status of constitutional law. According to the doctrine of Parliamentary Sovereignty, all Acts of Parliament, regardless of their constitutional importance, have the same legal status and can be repealed in the future. In *Thoburn* v. *Sunderland City Council* [2002] EWHC 195 (Admin) Laws LJ identified a list of constitutional statutes and in *obiter* stated that such statutes were superior to other statutes, as they could not be impliedly repealed (see Chapter 5). However, in any event all statutes can be expressly repealed by Parliament, because Parliament is legally sovereign. This means that the Human Rights Act 1998 has the same legal status as the Highways Act 1980.

Professor David Feldman considered constitutional legislation in his article 'The nature and significance of "constitutional" legislation' ([2013] *Law Quarterly Review* 343) and observed that Laws LJ's approach in *Thoburn* of '(t)ying the "constitutional" status of legislation to fundamental rights' was problematic for three reasons:

1. 'First, the category of fundamental rights is not closed'.
2. Constitutional legislation is not 'always concerned with fundamental rights' and this includes legislation concerning state institutions and their relationships with each other.
3. Laws LJ's test is 'over-inclusive' as '(m)ost legislation is concerned with the relationship between the state and the citizen'.

Human Rights Act 1998	Highways Act 1980
• Special constitutional significance – **YES**	• Special constitutional significance – **NO**
• Key rights – Liberty, Fair Trial etc	• Regulates use of highways
• Special legal status – **NO**	• Special legal status – **NO**

Figure 2.1 Acts which are of constitutional significance have no special status

The Magna Carta 1215

In 1215, King John was forced by his own barons to sign the Magna Carta at Runnymede. The Magna Carta was promptly annulled by the pope and John reneged on its terms. The Magna Carta was reissued by Henry III and finally by Edward I in 1297. The Magna Carta is important, as it is regarded as establishing important protection for the subject from the arbitrary power of the monarch. It has also been argued that the Magna Carta established the right to trial by jury (such a right has been dismissed by Lord Justice Auld in 2001, 'Review of the Criminal Courts in England and Wales').

Much of the Magna Carta has been repealed. The most important remaining clause is clause 29, which states that:

> 'No Freeman shall be taken or imprisoned, or be disseised of his Freehold, or Liberties, or free Customs, or be outlawed, or exiled, or any other wise destroyed; nor will We not pass upon him, nor condemn him, but by lawful judgment of his Peers, or by the Law of the Land. We will sell to no man, we will not deny or defer to any man either Justice or Right.'

From reading clause 29 it is clear why at the time it was so significant, as it restricted the power of the monarch to act outside of the law of England.

The Magna Carta is regarded as a constitutionally significant document in many countries, including the United States of America and Australia. Max Radin has written that the Magna Carta 'since at least 1297 . . . has been something more than a statute; it has been an assertion of the existence of fundamental rights of free men, however differently they might have been listed at different periods' ('The Myth of the Magna Carta' (1947) 60(7) *Harvard Law Review* 1060).

CONTEXT

Protect rights and liberties of subject

Bill of Rights 1689

The Bill of Rights 1689 was intended to protect the rights and liberties of the subject and to settle the matter of royal succession. The Bill of Rights was the result of the Glorious Revolution in 1688. The Bill of Rights covered the freedom of elections to the House of Commons, guaranteed MPs the freedom of speech in Parliamentary debates and proceedings, without fear of prosecution or impeachment. Importantly, the Bill of Rights protected individuals by stating that, 'excessive Baile ought not to be required nor excessive Fines imposed nor cruell and unusuall Punishments inflicted'.

Before the Glorious Revolution, the monarch and Parliament had clashed over the raising of money without the consent of Parliament. The Bill of Rights stated that the monarch could no longer raise money through his prerogative powers. The power of the monarch to keep an army was restricted by the need for Parliament's consent.

Controls the succession of the monarchy

Act of Settlement 1701

The Act of Settlement 1701 is important, as it is controls the succession of the monarchy. Under the Act of Settlement a Roman Catholic cannot become the monarch nor can a member of the royal family marry a Roman Catholic without giving up their place in the line of royal succession. Note however the changes introduced by the Succession to the Crown Act 2013.

The Act also ensured judicial independence, as senior judges enjoy security of tenure and can only be removed as a judge by Parliament.

The Coalition government introduced the Succession to the Crown Act 2013 which has changed the rules of royal succession and has removed the preference in favour of men over women. The Act also permits a member of the royal family to marry someone who is a Roman Catholic, without having to give up their place in the royal succession.

CONTEXT

Union with Scotland Act 1706

CORNERSTONE

Created Great Britain

Union with Scotland Act 1706

The Union with Scotland Act 1706 created Great Britain. The Kingdoms of England and Scotland were unified into a single country.

The Union with Scotland Act 1706 may have created Great Britain, but many parts of the Act have been subsequently repealed.

Union with Ireland Act 1800   *Created the UK*

This Act created the United Kingdom, as Article 1 states 'Great Britain and Ireland to be united for ever from 1 Jan. 1801'. Southern Ireland is no longer part of the United Kingdom. However, Northern Ireland remains part of the United Kingdom.

Representation of the People, 1884, 1918, 1928 and 1969)

Increased franchise

This series of Acts has gradually increased the franchise (i.e. those people who are entitled to vote at a general election). Today, men and women aged 18 and over can vote (subject to limited restrictions).

INTERSECTION

For a detailed overview of the effect of each of the Representation of the People Acts see Chapter 6. It might be interesting to work out in what year someone of your age and gender first became eligible to vote.

Parliament Acts 1911 and 1949

[handwritten note: Transformed relationship of HoC and HoL]

The Parliament Acts 1911 and 19 *[handwritten: HoL]* ...formed the relationship between the Houses of Commons and Lords. The House of *[handwritten: now cannot block legislation]* ...r House, and the ability of the House of Lords to block legislation has b...

European Communities Act 1972

The United Kingdom became a member of the European Economic Community (now the European Union) in 1973, and the European Communities Act 1972 gave legal effect to the United Kingdom's membership. The Act is very important as European law would apply in the United Kingdom and the judiciary must interpret domestic law in line with European law.

CORNERSTONE

Dualist legal system and the European Communities Act 1972

The European Communities Act 1972 was needed before the United Kingdom would be able to fulfil its legal obligations as a member of the European Economic Community. This is because the United Kingdom has a dualist legal system and an Act of Parliament was required before European law could be enforceable in a domestic court.

Take note

The limitation imposed on the number of MPs who can become ministers serves an important purpose. If you become a minister you will receive additional remuneration on top of your salary as an MP. You will also have a role within the government and this will help your political career. Therefore, ministerial office is used as a way to encourage MPs to support the government and, consequentially, is lost if the minister does not support the government.

House of Commons Disqualification Act 1975

[handwritten note: Limit number of MP's who become 95]

In order to prevent the gover... ...osition as patronage (i.e. an incentive to s... ...the House of Commons Disqualification Act 1... ...to... MPs who can become ministers to 95.

Police and Criminal Evid... Act 1984

[handwritten note: Provides code of practice for police]

The Police and Crim... ...own as 'PACE') was enacted in response ...an's report into the Brixton riots which occurred in 1981. PACE governs police powers and the admissibility of evidence. It provides a code of practice which offers guidance on how the police should use their powers. These codes cover stop and search, the search of vehicles and property, the interview of suspects, the treatment of suspects and how identification procedures should be conducted.

Human Rights Act 1998

The Human Rights Act 1998 incorpor... most of the European Convention on Human Rights into domestic law. The Convention ... enforceable in domestic law against a public authority. The Act has increased the po... ... Act of Parliament and section 4 permits a court (High Court or ab... ...atibility. It is important to note that section 4 does not permit a court to ... ... be void.

In September 2014, the Prime Minister, David Cameron, p... ... that a future Conservative government would repeal the Human Rights Act 1998 and replace it with a British Bill of Rights.

CORNERSTONE

The Human Rights Act 1998

Most of the European Convention on Human Rights is incorporated into domestic law by the Human Rights Act 1998. The Convention rights are now enforceable in domestic law against a public authority.

Scotland Act 1998

The Scotland Act 1998 devolved powers from Westminster to Scotland. It created the Scottish Parliament and the Scottish government.

Government of Wales Act 1998

The Government of Wales Act 1998 devolved powers from Westminster to Wales. It created the National Assembly of Wales and a Welsh government. The Government of Wales Act 2006 further increased the legislative powers of the National Assembly of Wales.

Northern Ireland Act 1998

The Northern Ireland Act 1998 devolved powers to the Northern Ireland Assembly, after powers had been transferred back to Westminster in 1974. Devolved power is shared between the different political parties at Stormont, where the Northern Ireland Assembly meets.

House of Lords Act 1999

The House of Lords Act 1999 reformed the second chamber, by removing all but ninety-two of the hereditary peers. The reform of the House of Lords remains incomplete (see Chapter 6).

Constitutional Reform Act 2005

The Constitutional Reform Act 2005 created the Supreme Court and removed many of the responsibilities and powers from the office of Lord Chancellor. The Act is very important as it reinforces the separation of powers between the judiciary and the other branches of government. The Lord Chancellor has been replaced as the head of the judiciary by the Lord Chief Justice, with whom he shares the power to discipline judges. The judicial appointment process has been transferred to the Judicial Appointment Commission, which is an independent body.

Equality Act 2010

[handwritten note: Defines prohibited conduct]

The Equality Act 2010 defines pro... characteristics (such as race, religion or belief sex and disability) and lists a range of prohibited conduct which will amount to discrimina... Equality Act 2010 has consolidated the previous legislation covering discrimination ... re equality.

Constitutional Reform and Gove...

[handwritten note: Places civil service on a statutory basis]

This Act places the civil service on a statutory basis, a... ... ... me civil service being regulated under the prerogative. Also there is now a statutory re...irement that treaties entered into by the government under their prerogative powers must be laid before Parliament. This pl... ...e Ponsonby Rule on a statutory basis. These are two very important limitations...

Fixed-term Parliaments Act 2011

[handwritten note: Lifetime of current Parliament fixed until May 2015]

This Act states that the lifetime of the current Parliament will be fixed until May 2015. The Prime Minister is unable to use his discretion to ask the monarch to use her prerogative powers and to dissolve Parliament before May 2015. Prior to the introduction of this Act a Prime Minister could ask the monarch to dissolve Parliament at a date which benefited his party.

> Gordon Brown became Prime Minister in 2007 (after the resignation of Tony Blair) two years into the lifetime of the 2005 Parliament. Brown decided to call a General Election to take advantage of his popularity with the electorate in 2007, however he eventually decided against it. The General Election finally took place in 2010 (as by law a General Election had to occur at least every five years, and the lifetime of the 2005 Parliament had nearly expired). Gordon Brown and the Labour Party failed to secure a majority in the House of Commons.

CONTEXT

European Union Act 2011

[handwritten note: States referendum must be held before any new powers can be transferred to the EU]

This Act states that a referendum ... be transferred to the European Union. However, accordi... ...rendum requirement would not bind a future Parliament, w... ...ling a referendum.

COMMON LAW

CORNERSTONE

The common law

[handwritten note: Common law = case law]

[handwritten note: Judges not meant to make law but interpret Acts of Parliament]

The common law (or case l... ... . to make law, as their duty is to interp... ...ave been created by judges.

The common law is an important source of the constitution. The courts have limited the powers of the monarch and government, by restricting and reviewing the use of the prerogative powers (see Chapter 9). The courts have acknowledged the importance of the separation of powers, by deferring to the executive on matters of policy.

The courts have checked the power of the executive to act outside the law (see *Entick* v. *Carrington* (1765) 19 State Tr 1029, where the court upheld the rule of law). The courts are under a duty to prevent the executive breaching the European Convention on Human Rights (see the Human Rights Act 1998 and *A* v. *Secretary of State for the Home Department* [2004] UKHL 56).

The judges play an important role in interpreting statutes and, despite the doctrine of Parliamentary Sovereignty, the courts have considerable power to interpret an Act of Parliament in the way that the court presumes that Parliament would have intended (see Lord Hoffmann in *R* v. *Secretary of State for the Home Department ex p. Simms* [2000] 2 AC 115).

The common law has developed judicial review as a way of reviewing executive action. Judicial review provides an incredibly important check on the executive at a national and local level (see Chapters 12–13).

MEMBERSHIP OF THE EUROPEAN UNION

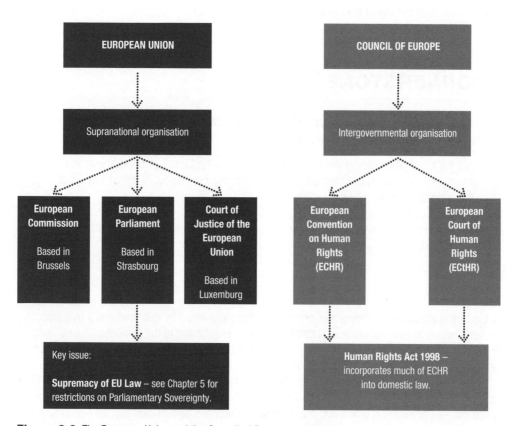

Figure 2.2 The European Union and the Council of Europe distinguished

CORNERSTONE

The European Union

The European Union is a supranational organisation which was originally created after the Second World War (1939–45). It is separate from the Council of Europe, which is an intergovernmental organisation responsible for the European Convention on Human Rights (see Figure 2.2). Today, there are 28 countries which are members of the European Union and its key institutions include the European Commission based in Brussels, the European Parliament based in Strasbourg and the Court of Justice of the European Union (CJEU) which is based in Luxembourg.

The United Kingdom joined the European Economic Community (now the European Union) in 1973. The European Communities Act 1972 gave effect to the United Kingdom's membership and made all present and future European law enforceable in domestic courts. The law of the European Union is an important source of the constitution, as citizens of member states are now also citizens of the European Union (see Article 20, The Treaty on the Functioning of the European Union). Citizens are entitled to travel and reside within any member state. Importantly, where the European Union has competence, then the law of the European Union has supremacy.

CORNERSTONE

Van Gend en Loos v. *Nederlandse Administratie der Belastingen* (26/62) [1963] ECR 1

It was the Court of Justice of the European Union (then the European Court of Justice) that held that European law had supremacy over the domestic law of member states in *Van Gend en Loos* v. *Nederlandse Administratie der Belastingen* (26/62) [1963] ECR 1.

This was confirmed in *Costa* v. *ENEL* (6/64) [1964] ECR 585. The consequence of this is that the constitutional courts of many member states have had to give way to the supremacy of the European law.

In the United Kingdom the European Communities Act gives effect to this supremacy by instructing domestic courts to take into account European law and the decisions of the European Court of Justice. In *R* v. *Secretary of State for Transport ex p. Factortame Ltd (No.2)* [1991] 1 AC 603 the House of Lords set aside an Act of Parliament, where the Act was inconsistent with European law.

There are a number of sources of European Union law. These include primary legislation, which includes the treaties which established and developed the European Union, and secondary legislation, which includes regulations, directives, decisions of the European Commission and the decisions of the Court of Justice of the European Union.

MEMBERSHIP OF THE COUNCIL OF EUROPE

CORNERSTONE

The Council of Europe

The Council of Europe is an intergovernmental organisation that is responsible for the European Convention on Human Rights. Member states agree to allow their nationals to enforce their Convention rights at the European Court of Human Rights, which is based in Strasbourg.

The United Kingdom's membership of the Council of Europe is important as it provides for the protection of human rights. The Council of Europe has 47 members and is separate from the European Union. The Council of Europe promotes human rights, democracy and the rule of law. It was founded in 1949 as a direct consequence of the horrors of the Second World War, where gross human rights violations took place and six million Jews were murdered by Germany.

The United Kingdom was an original member and helped to draft the European Convention on Human Rights. The convention outlined the key rights. The European Court of Human Rights (ECtHR) was established at Strasbourg in 1959 in order to rule on alleged breaches by member states. It was not until the 1960s that British citizens were able to sue the United Kingdom at the European Court of Human Rights, and even then it was not until October 2000 that the Convention rights were directly incorporated into domestic law when the Human Rights Act 1998 came into effect.

Today the Convention rights are directly enforceable in domestic courts against public authorities. Under section 2 of the Human Rights Act 1998 the decisions and opinions of the European Court of Human Rights must be taken into account, although the jurisprudence of the ECtHR is not binding on domestic courts.

CONSTITUTIONAL CONVENTIONS

CORNERSTONE

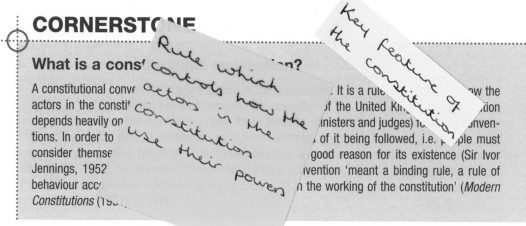

What is a cons' ...n?

A constitutional conv... . It is a rul... w the actors in the consti... f the United Ki... ...tion depends heavily on ...inisters and judges) ... ...nven-tions. In order to ... of it being followed, i.e. ...ple must consider thems... good reason for its existence (Sir Ivor Jennings, 1952 ...vention 'meant a binding rule, a rule of behaviour acc... n the working of the constitution' (*Modern Constitutions* (1...

[Handwritten notes overlaying text:] Rule which controls how the actors in the Constitution use their powers

[Handwritten note:] Key feature of the Constitution

Constitutional conventions are an important source of the constitution and are crucial for the effective operation of the United Kingdom's constitutional system. Without the existence and observance of these conventions, the United Kingdom's uncodified constitution could not work. Conventions regulate the conduct of the monarch, the government, individual minsters, Parliament and judges. Unlike the United States where there is a codified constitution which sets out how their constitutional system works and imposes legal restraints and obligation, the United Kingdom is heavily dependent on conventions, which are a non-legal part of the constitution.

> That is not to say that conventions are not a source of the United States constitution, even if they are not part of the codified constitution. For example, the way the President is elected in the United States is heavily dependent on a constitutional convention, which requires each state's Electoral College to vote in accordance with the popular vote of their state.

CONTEXT

It is necessary to understand the i~ ~~~~~~~~ the United Kingdom's constitution, how they are created and wh~ ~~~~~~~~~~~~~~~~ all, it is necessary to define what we mean by a convention.

Dicey's definition

Dicey's definition of constitutional conventions

Dicey argued that conventions were not law. He argued that: '[w]ith conventions or understandings [the lawyer] has no direct concern. They vary from generation to generation, almost year to year . . . The subject . . . is not one of law but of politics, and need trouble no lawyer or the class of any professor of law' (Dicey 1982, p. cxlv). However, a constitutional lawyer needs to be concerned with conventions, because they are an important source of the constitution.

CORNERSTONE

Constitutional conventions are not laws

Many academics have debated whether conventions can become law and therefore whether they can be enforced in a court. A.V. Dicey (1982) argued that conventions were not law. His reasoning for this view was that:

> '[There is an] essential distinction between the "law of the constitution", which consisting (as it does) of rules enforced by the Courts, makes up a body of "laws" in the proper sense of that term, and the "conventions of the constitution", which consisting (as they do) of customs, practices, maxims, or precepts which are not enforced or recognised by the Courts, make up a body not of laws, but of constitutional or political ethics.'

We can see from Dicey's definition of a convention, that they are 'customs, practices, maxims or precepts' which have developed, rather than laws which are capable of being enforced in courts. Although Dicey wrote that breaches of a convention could lead to breaches of the law, we can see that a breach of a convention may lead to a law being introduced to prevent its breach in the future. One example of this is the Parliament Act 1911 which restricted the House of Lords' power to veto legislation.

The distinction between conventions and law is important for two reasons:

1. There is no legal sanction for breaching a convention, as a breach cannot be enforced in a court.
2. Conventions develop over time to respond to changing social and political circumstances.

Why are conventions important?

Conventions are a flexible way of changing the way the constitution operates, without the need to introduce laws to achieve this. The use of conventions has:

- created modern cabinet government;
- created the office of the Prime Minister;
- reduced the power of the monarch; and
- made the governing party accountable to the House of Commons and the electorate.

Dicey noted that conventions developed 'without any change in the law . . . because they meet the wants of a new time' (ibid, p. ixvi). Jaconelli argued that their existence is important as '(t)he "reasons" which animate many a constitutional convention are among the highest value of political theory'. Jaconelli gives the example of non-judicial members of the House of Lords not taking part in the judicial function of the Lords (prior to the creation of the Supreme Court in 2009), or the Law Lords not taking part in politically consensus matters, and the House of Lords not challenging the House of Commons because of the importance of democracy (Jaconelli 1999, p. 29).

> The resignation of a government is regulated by convention. It is a matter of convention that a government that loses a General Election will resign at once (unless they can form a coalition government). Dicey noted how this convention developed over the nineteenth century and argued that it was important, as it acknowledged the electorate as the political sovereign. When Gordon Brown delayed resigning for a few days after the 2010 General Election, many people argued that this was unconstitutional. There was a popular expectation that a government must resign, and so we can see that the existence of this convention has created an expectation amongst the electorate. A government must also resign on a vote of no confidence in the House of Commons.

REFLECTION

Conventions regulate the United Kingdom's constitution. Jennings famously described conventions as 'the flesh which clothes the dry bones of the law; they make the legal constitution work; they keep it in touch with the growth of ideas' (*The Law and the Constitution* 4th edn, University of London Press: London, 1952), pp. 80–1). This is important, as conventions enable the constitution to change with the time, without the necessity of complex reform. At no point since the Bill of Rights in 1689 has Parliament had to legislate in order to limit the powers of the monarch, instead conventions have developed to control the monarch's use of the prerogative. Equally, the office of Prime Minister has evolved over time and is regulated by convention. Conventions are created to deal with new situations, such as devolution in 1998. Geoffrey Marshall (1984, pp. 8–9) observed that conventions could arise in a number of ways:

1. 'Frequently they arise from a series of precedents that are agreed to have given rise to a binding rule of behaviour'; or

2. 'They might arise quickly, such as a result of an agreement not to do something'; or

3. '[It] may be formulated on the basis of some acknowledged principle of government which provides a reason or justification for it'.

Devolution has made it necessary for the Sewel Convention to be created, which is a promise by Parliament that it will not legislate for Scotland in areas that have been devolved. The Sewel Convention has not imposed a legal restraint, rather a constitutional restraint, which is necessary to ensure that devolution is effective and does not bring the Scottish and Westminster Parliaments into conflict.

CONTEXT

We can see the importance of conventions when we consider that the following are governed by them:

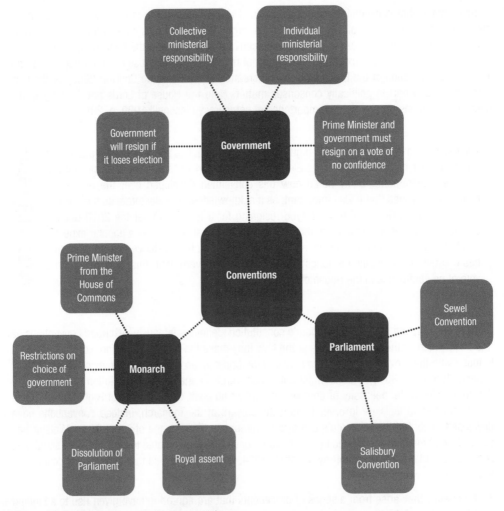

Figure 2.3 Important constitutional conventions

Looking at Figure 2.3 we can see that Parliament, the monarch and the government are restricted in their actions by the existence of constitutional conventions.

Who must follow conventions?

Conventions are only binding on the persons to who.. ~w that a convention exists? The existence of a convention must be accepteu . an important role in the constitution. Jennings argued that we needed to distinguis.. .ons and mere practices and established a test to see if a genuine convention existed (*Law . Constitution* 4th edn, 1952). The test has three stages:

The persons whom they apply

1. What are the precedents for the existence of the convention?
2. Did the actors in the precedents believe they were bound by a rule?
3. Is there a reason for the rule?

All three stages need to be satisfied in order a convention to exist. Look below at Jennings' test and how it is satisfied in practice:

Example 1: The monarch cannot refuse royal assent to legislation

Jennings' Test	The monarch cannot refuse royal assent to legislation
1 What are the precedents?	Yes – there are precedents for the existence of the convention: • The last time a monarch refused royal assent was Queen Anne in 1707. • In 1783, George III did not veto Fox's India Bill, even though the king hated Charles James Fox and the bill.
2 Did the actors in the precedents believe they were bound by a rule?	Yes – the monarchs believe themselves to be bound by the rule: • There has been no refusal of assent in over 300 years, although note that George V considered himself to have the power to veto the Irish Home Rule Bill.
3 Is there a reason for the rule?	Yes – there appears to be very good reasons for the rule to exist: • It is needed to give effect to democracy and to restrict the monarch's use of the prerogative powers.

Example 2: The government must resign if it loses a General Election, without waiting for the next Parliament

Jennings' Test	The government must resign if it loses a General Election, without waiting for the next Parliament
1 What are the precedents?	Yes – there are precedents for the existence of the convention: • Every government that has lost a General Election has resigned during this and the twentieth century. There was some controversy when Gordon Brown waited several days after 'losing' the 2010 General Election before resigning.
2 Did the actors in the precedents believe they were bound by a rule?	Yes – the Prime Minister and government believe themselves to be bound by the rule: • The Prime Minister and the government were expected to resign.
3 Is there a reason for the rule?	Yes – there appears to be very good reasons for the rule to exist: • It is needed to give effect to the will of the electorate. It would be undemocratic to govern having lost a General Election.

We will look in detail at the following conventions later on in this book:

• Choice of Prime Minister (Chapter 6)
• Individual ministerial responsibility (Chapter 7)
• Collective ministerial responsibility (Chapter 7)
• Royal assent (Chapter 6)
• Resignation upon being defeated in a vote of no confidence (Chapter 7)

APPLICATION

Imagine that the highly popular Lord Petersfield (fictitious) held a senior cabinet position and after several of his colleagues were forced to resign, including the Prime Minister, he wishes to stand as party leader and to become the new Prime Minister. Could a member of the House of Lords become Prime Minister? In order to see whether he could, we would need to see how Jennings' test works in practice and whether the convention that the Prime Minister must be a member of the House of Commons would prevent him from becoming Prime Minister.

Applying the three stages as identified by Jennings above, we can see that:

1. There is a precedent for the convention, as the last Prime Minister not to be from the House of Commons, was the Marquis of Salisbury in 1902. Since then all other Prime Ministers have been MPs.

2. There are examples of people believing that they were bound by the rule. In order to become Prime Minister, the Earl of Hume renounced his peerage in 1965. Previously, George V believed that he had to choose Stanley Baldwin MP over Lord Curzon, because of the convention.

3. The reason for the rule is that the House of Commons is elected and it must hold the Prime Minister to account. The Prime Minister must be regarded as accountable to the House of Commons and the electorate, which is something that a member of the House of Lords is not.

Therefore, although there is no legal restriction on Lord Petersfield becoming Prime Minister, there is a rule established by convention, that a member of the House of Lords cannot be the Prime Minister. Lord Petersfield will need to renounce his peerage and stand as a MP as soon as possible in order to become Prime Minister. Which is exactly what the Earl of H------ d in 1965.

Are conventions enforceable?

No as not laws

Considering the constitutional importance of conventions, it might appear disconcerting that the monarch, Parliament or the government might choose not to follow a convention. The significance of the monarch refusing royal assent would be momentous and would have considerable constitutional implications. Conventions are not laws and a breach of a convention will not be enforceable in the courts. This was a point observed by Lord Reid in *Madzimbamuto* v. *Lardner-Burke* [1969] 1 AC 645.

CORNERSTONE

Madzimbamuto v. *Lardner-Burke* [1969] 1 AC 645

In this case the Privy Council held that there was nothing illegal about the United Kingdom passing legislation for Southern Rhodesia, despite the existence of a convention that Parliament could not legislate without the consent of the colony. The legislation had been enacted in response to Southern Rhodesia's unilateral declaration of independence. Lord Reid held that the court was not concerned whether something was unconstitutional as this was not a matter of law.

Likewise in *Attorney-General* v. *Jonathan Cape Ltd* [1976] QB 752, Lord ~~~~~~ considered that a convention was 'binding in cons------ only'. This confirms Dicey's ~~~~~~ are not law and are not enforceable in a ~~~~~~

Confirms Dicey's view

So not enforceable in the courts

"Binding in conscience only"

Canadian perspective

CORNERSTONE

Reference re Amendment of the Constitution of Canada [1981] 1 SCR 753

The United Kingdom is not the only country which uses constitutional conventions. The Canadian Supreme Court considered the legal force of a convention in *Reference re Amendment of the Constitution of Canada* [1981] 1 SCR 753.

When the Canadian government sought to change its constitution it asked the United Kingdom's Parliament to enact legislation to achieve this. The Statute of Westminster 1931 had codified the convention that the Westminster Parliament would not pass legislation for the dominions (self-governing territories such as Canada, New Zealand and Australia), unless asked to do so. In Canada there was a complex procedure to change the constitution, with conventions governing the procedure. It was argued that there was a constitutional convention that the Canadian provinces would have to give their consent before the Canadian constitution could be amended. The question reached the Canadian Supreme Court in *Reference re Amendment of the Constitution of Canada* [1981] 1 SCR 753. The Supreme Court considered Jennings' test for establishing a constitutional convention. The court considered the three-stage test and found that:

1. there was a precedent for the convention that the consent of the provinces was required;
2. the actors treated the rule as binding on them; and
3. finally there was a reason for the rule.

Therefore, a valid constitutional convention existed and the Canadian government would be acting unconstitutionally if it didn't obtain the consent of the provinces. However, the Supreme Court held that there was no legal sanction against the Canadian government for failing to act in accordance with the conventions. The Supreme Court also considered whether a convention could become crystallised, so that it became law. This argument was rejected by the Supreme Court:

> 'This conflict between convention and law which prevents the courts from enforcing conventions also prevents conventions from crystallising into laws, unless it be by statutory adoption. It is because the sanctions of convention rest with institutions of government other than courts, such as the Governor General or the Lieutenant Governor, or the Houses of Parliament, or with public opinion and ultimately, with the electorate, that it is generally said that they are political.'

The Court of Appeal in *Manuel* v. *Attorney-General* [1983] 1 Ch. 77 rejected the argument that a convention could restrict the Canadian government from asking the United Kingdom's Parliament to legislate to create a new constitution. The court held that Parliament could legislate for Canada under section 4 of the Statute of Westminster 1931. Slade LJ dismissed the argument that a convention could restrict this:

> 'The sole condition precedent which has to be satisfied if a law made by the United Kingdom Parliament is to extend to a Dominion as part of its law is to be found stated in the body of the Statute of 1931 itself (section 4). This court would run counter to all principles of statutory interpretation if it were to purport to vary or supplement the terms of this stated condition precedent by reference to some supposed convention, which, though referred to in the preamble, is not incorporated in the body of the Statute' [107].

Nonetheless, the existence of a convention can be relevant to support legal action. In *Attorney-General* v. *Jonathan Cape Ltd* the convention of collective ministerial responsibility was used as evidence to support the argument that information discussed during cabinet meetings, was protected by the tort of confidence. The convention had demonstrated the importance of cabinet discussions remaining confidential.

Non-legal consequences for breaching a convention

CORNERSTONE

Non-legal sanctions for breaching a convention

Despite conventions not be regarded as law, there can be politic̶ ̶ ̶ ̶ ̶ for breaching a convention. One example of this is the Parliament Act 1911, wh̶ ̶ ̶ ̶ ̶ ̶ ̶ ̶ ̶ of the House of Lords breaching the convention not to veto money̶ ̶ ̶

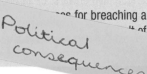

Political consequences

Dicey acknowledged that despite conventions not being law, there could still be sanctions for breaching a convention. Dicey expressly referred to the passing of the Parliament Act 1911, when he noted the possibility of a non-legal sanction. There had been a convention that the House of Lords would not veto money bills. This was breached when the Liberal Chancellor of the Exchequer David Lloyd George presented his budget to Parliament and the Conservative majority in the House of Lords rejected the budget. The government requested that the monarch create a large number of Liberal peers so that the Liberals would have a majority in the House of Lords. The threat worked and the Conservative peers voted in favour of the budget. By way of sanction, the Parliament Act 1911 was passed to restrict the ability of the House of Lords to veto money bills. Failure to follow a convention had resulted in the convention becoming law. Other conventions have become law, such as the convention that Parliament would not legislate for the dominions without their consent. This convention was established by 1926 and was given legal effect by the Statute of Westminster 1931.

Failure to follow some conventions such as individual ministerial responsibility will result in no sanction, especially where the minister at fault has the support of the Prime Minister. However, a minister who refuses to resign may face dismissal. Dicey noted that some conventions were not always followed, but that many were enforced by public opinion.

Given the importance of conventions it is unhelpful that each convention cannot be precisely defined. The conventions develop over time in order to respond to current issues (e.g. devolution resulted in the Sewel Convention). In the 1970s the Australian government attempted the codification of conventions and this proved problematic. This was because conventions are flexible and develop over time in order to respond to new situations, whereas a code does not develop under its own violation and will become incomplete (see Jaconelli 1999). Andrew Blick has recently explored the impact of the publication of the Cabinet Manual in 2011 and its impact on conventions. The Cabinet Manual sets out many important conventions, although it also excludes others. Blick observes that '[c]onstitutional conventions do not lend themselves readily to codification' and notes the possible effects of having certain conventions set out in such a document. These include strengthening those included and weakening those which were excluded, preventing conventions from evolving to meet new situations and interestingly, the Cabinet Manual being used in judicial review proceedings to challenge ministerial behaviour (Blick 2014, p. 191).

REFLECTION

PREROGATIVE POWERS

The prerogative powers will be covered in detail in Chapter 9. The [...] important source of the constitution because it forms the remainder of the [...] powers. That is, powers which are recognised by the common l[...] monarch by statute. Prerogative powers are largely exercised today b[...] although the monarch still possesses her personal prerogative powers. The prero[...] cover:

What the monarchy can do

- the deployment of British armed forces and the decision to declare war;
- foreign policy and dealings with other countries;
- the appointment of the Prime Minister, royal assent and the decision to dissolve Parliament (now covered by the Fixed-term Parliaments Act 2011) and trigger a General Election.

Importantly the prerogative powers exist independently of Parliament and are subjected to limited parliamentary review.

KEY POINTS

Constitution comprised of different sources

Conventions play important role in constitution

No special status of constitutional law

- The United Kingdom's cons[...] nt sources.
- Constitutional conventions pla[...] he United Kingdom's constitution.
- There are a number of important stat[...] 8. However, there is no special status of constitutional law.

CORE CASES AND STATUTES

Case	About	Importance
Van Gend en Loos v. *Nederlandse Administratie der Belastingen* (26/62) [1963]	This was a decision of the European Court of Justice.	It was the Court of Justice of the European Union (then the European Court of Justice) that held that European law had supremacy over the domestic law of member states.
Madzimbamuto v. *Lardner-Burke* [1969]	The decision involved the unilateral declaration of independence by the British colony of South Rhodesia and the subsequent attempt by the United Kingdom to legislate for this colony.	This case is important as it demonstrates that a convention preventing legislation without a colony's consent does not prevent Parliament from enacting legislation for that colony.

Case	About	Importance
Reference re Amendment of the Constitution of Canada [1981]	The Canadian Supreme Court held that there was no legal requirement for the Canadian government to consult with the provinces before amending the constitution.	The Canadian Supreme Court held that conventions were not laws and would not become a law just because they were important and had existed for a long time. The court had applied the test established by Professor Jennings to determine whether there was indeed a convention which required consultation to take place.

Statute	About	Importance
Union with Scotland Act 1706	Prior to the creation of Great Britain in 1707 Scotland and England were separate countries which shared only a monarch. This was a personal union and not a political union. The Union with Scotland Act 1706 was an English Act of Parliament which enabled the creation of Great Britain.	This Act and its Scottish equivalent are referred to as the Acts of Union. From his accession in 1603, James I of England and James VI of Scotland had wanted to unite his two kingdoms. It took over a hundred years for this to be achieved and was spurred on by English concerns about who would succed to the Scottish throne after the death of Queen Anne.
European Communities Act 1972	The United Kingdom required the enacting of the European Communities Act 1972 before it could give effect to its treaty obligations. The United Kingdom became a member of the now European Union in 1973.	The European Communities Act 1972 enables the British courts to give effect to the United Kingdom's treaty obligations. The Act allowed all previous, current and future European Union law to apply in the United Kingdom. This is significant as no additional legislation was required to give effect to regulations, new treaties and decisions of the Court of Justice of the European Union.
Human Rights Act 1998	Most of the ECHR was directly incorporated into domestic law by the Human Rights Act 1998.	The Convention rights are directly enforceable in domestic courts.

FURTHER READING

Blick, A. 'The Cabinet Manual and the Codification of Conventions' [2014] (67) 1 *Parliamentary Affairs* **191**
This is an interesting article on the Cabinet Manual and the effect of codifying conventions.

Bradly, A.W. and Ewing, K.D. *Constitutional and Administrative Law* **(Pearson: Harlow, 2011)**
A very detailed textbook which will offer additional information to this book. Refer to this to expand your knowledge of the law.

Dicey, A.V. *Introduction to the Study of the Law of the Constitution* **(Liberty Fund: Minneapolis, 1982)**
Dicey was an important academic and this is his most important book. It is very readable and it is recommended that you refer to this.

Feldman, D. 'The nature and significance of "constitutional" legislation' [2013] *Law Quarterly Review* **343**
Refer to this article for academic commentary on constitutional legislation.

Horspool, M. and Humphreys, M. *European Union Law* **(Oxford University Press: Oxford, 2010)**
This book provides an introduction to European law.

Jaconelli, J. 'The nature of constitutional convention' (1999) 19(1) *Legal Studies* **24**
The article looks at conventions and makes comparisons with their use in the United States of America.

Jaconelli, J. 'Do constitutional conventions bind?' (2005) *Cambridge Law Journal* **149**
This article looks at whether conventions are binding and offers a chance to engage in a discussion on legal theory.

Jennings, I. *Law and the Constitution* **4th edn (University of London Press: London, 1952)**
This book provides an authoritative approach to constitutional conventions.

Marshall, G. *Constitutional Conventions: The Rules and Forms of Political Accountability* **(Oxford University Press: Oxford, 1984)**
This book is the leading work on constitutional conventions. Refer to this for more details on each of the important conventions.

Munro, C. *Studies in Constitutional Law* **(Oxford University Press: Oxford, 2005)**
This book is highly recommended as a way to further your understanding of the law.

Wheare, K. *Modern Constitutions* **(Oxford University Press: Oxford, 1951)**
This is an interesting text which explores areas such as constitutional conventions.

CHAPTER 3

The separation of powers

BLUEPRINT

The separation of powers

KEY QUESTIONS

LEGISLATION

- Constitutional Reform Act 2005
- House of Commons Disqualification Act 1975

CONTEXT

- The Glorious Revolution 1688 and the impact it had on the constitution.
- The development of Cabinet government.
- The impact of the Constitutional Reform Act 2005.

CONCEPTS

- The separation of powers
- Checks and balances
- The executive
- The legislature
- The Prerogative of Mercy
- Vote of no confidence
- Prime Minister's Questions
- Security of tenure for senior judges
- The purpose of judicial review

- Is it necessary to have strict separation of powers?
- Does the United States have strict separation of powers?

- What is the separation of powers?
- Why should the functions of government be carried out by different branches?
- Does the United Kingdom have the separation of powers?

CASES

- *R v. R (Rape: Marital Exemption)* [1992]

REFORM

- Should the UK reform the fusion between the executive and legislature? Could this be achieved by stopping the Prime Minister from sitting in Parliament?
- Reforms to the House of Commons and House of Lords, such as boundary changes.

SPECIAL CHARACTERISTICS

- Fusion between the legislature and the executive
- The Supreme Court
- The United Kingdom does not have a written constitution

CRITICAL ISSUES

Setting the scene

We will look at the importance of the separation of powers as a constitutional theory. The powers that we are concerned with are the power to make law, the power to govern the country and the power to administer justice. Every country needs these three powers to be exercised in order for it to function. We shall see that academics and judges have argued that the three powers, or functions of government, should be exercised separately and that a different branch of government, which is comprised of different people, should carry out each function.

Why should a country's governmental system conform to the theory of the separation of powers? Is it necessary for the legislative, executive and judicial branches of government to be comprised of different groups of people and should each branch exercise distinctive functions? These are some of the questions which we will address. We will focus on the United Kingdom and ask whether the United Kingdom conforms to the separation of powers. This is a controversial issue as many academics dispute whether the United Kingdom actually does have separation of powers. However, as we shall see this is far from a simple yes or no answer. Therefore, for examination purposes it is essential that you understand the way that the United Kingdom's government operates. We will also explore the impact of the Constitutional Reform Act 2005 and whether further reform is needed.

Chapter overview

What is meant by the separation of powers?

Does the UK have separation of powers? Views of academics and members of the judiciary.

The overlaps of personnel and functions.

Does the UK have adequate checks and balances?

The impact of the CRA 2005 and further reform.

WHAT IS THE SEPARATION OF POWERS?

CORNERSTONE

The separation of powers

The separation of powers requires that the powers or functions of government (law-making, governing and administration of justice), must be exercised by the three distinct branches of government: the executive, the legislature and the judiciary.

The separation of powers can be explained as the division of the three key functions of any state between different groups of individuals. This, as we shall see below, could be set out in a written constitution, such as the constitution of the United States of America. The separation of powers has considerable constitutional importance and should not be seen as irrelevant or too dependent on theory. It serves a practical purpose, namely to prevent tyranny and the abuse of power by an individual or group of individuals.

Several years ago in Pakistan, members of the judiciary and lawyers protested against the government of General Musharraf. The Chief Justice of Pakistan and other members of the judiciary were arrested. The protest symbolised the importance of the separation of powers in Pakistan.

CONTEXT

We shall see that English judges have stated that there exists a form of separation of powers in the United Kingdom. However, until recently there were very few academics that would support this view.

THE THREE FUNCTIONS OF GOVERNMENT

In any state there are three identifiable functions of government which need to be carried out to ensure that the state operates effectively. The executive, the legislature and the judiciary should exercise these functions.

INTERSECTION

It is important to understand the composition and function of the executive, legislature and the judiciary in the United Kingdom. In order to have a detailed understanding of this you may wish to refer to Chapters 6–8:

- Parliament (see Chapter 6)
- The executive (see Chapter 7)
- The judiciary (see Chapter 8)

The executive

In the United Kingdom the executive is comprised of the monarch, the government (the Prime Minister, ministers who attend cabinet and junior ministers), the emergency services, the armed forces, local government, government departments and the **Civil Service**. Additionally as a result of devolution, there are separate governments in Scotland, Wales and Northern Ireland. Each of these governments has responsibility for administering the powers which have been devolved since 1998.

The legislature

CORNERSTONE

The United Kingdom's Parliament

The legislative function of creating laws is carried out by the United Kingdom's Parliament. Parliament is comprised of the House of Commons, the House of Lords and the Queen in Parliament.

The United Kingdom's Parliament is based at Westminster and is bicameral. This means that there are two chambers, the House of Commons and the House of Lords. Because of the Parliament Acts 1911 and 1949, the House of Lords has limited power to prevent legislation from being passed. According to the constitution the United Kingdom's Parliament has legislative sovereignty (see Chapter 5).

Members of the House of Commons are directly elected by their constituents. The system used is **First Past the Post**, i.e. the candidate with the most votes becomes that consistency's Member of Parliament. Members of the House of Lords are not elected. Most members of the House of Lords are appointed by the three main political parties. Additionally there are 92 hereditary peers (who are members because they have inherited a title) and 26 Church of England Bishops. The House of Lords Reform Act 1999 removed the vast majority of hereditary peers. However, the Act did not decide whether members of the House of Lords should be elected, appointed or a mixture of both. In Chapter 6 we will look in more detail at House of Lords reform.

Devolution

As a result of devolution the United Kingdom's Parliament has devolved law-making powers to the Scottish Parliament and the National Assembly of Wales (see Figure 3.1). Both of these legislative bodies have significant law-making powers, however, both are calling for further powers. The Northern Ireland Assembly has been reinstated having been suspended during the period known as the 'Troubles'. Today there is power sharing between political parties representing Protestants and Catholics at Stormont.

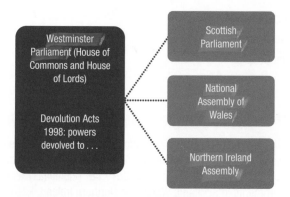

Figure 3.1 The effect of devolution

The judiciary

CORNERSTONE

The Supreme Court

The United Kingdom's Supreme Court was created by the Constitutional Reform Act 2005. It opened in October 2009 and replaced the Appellate Committee of the House of Lords.

The judiciary is comprised of different courts and tribunals (see Figure 3.2). The senior court is the Supreme Court. This is the ultimate appeal court within the United Kingdom. However, Scotland and Northern Ireland have their own separate legal systems and so are outside the jurisdiction of England and Wales. They also have their own court structure and judiciary. However, the jurisdiction of the Supreme Court to hear appeals in criminal cases is controversial in Scotland. Prior to the Constitutional Reform Act 2005 the Supreme Court was known as the Appellate Committee of the House of Lords, and its members were commonly known as the Law Lords (Lords of Appeal in Ordinary). They are now known as Justices of the Supreme Court. We will see below that the Supreme Court must not be confused with the United States Supreme Court. The Judicial Committee of the Privy Council sits in the same building as the Supreme Court and is the highest court of appeal for British overseas territories, Crown dependencies (such as Jersey), and several countries in the **Commonwealth**, including Jamaica. You will come across many Privy Council decisions in your studies and whilst they are not binding in England and Wales, they are nonetheless persuasive.

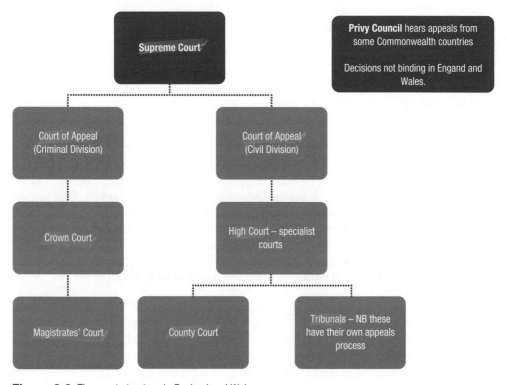

Figure 3.2 The court structure in England and Wales

The next senior court is the Court of Appeal. The Court of Appeal has a separate criminal and civil division. The head of criminal justice is the Lord Chief Justice and the head of civil justice is the Master of the Rolls. The Lord Chief Justice is the head of the judiciary. Then there is the High Court. The High Court is comprised of a number of specialised courts which deal with different areas of law. The High Court was created by the Judicature Acts 1873 and 1875, which merged the common law courts and the equitable Court of Chancery. In Chapters 12 and 13 you will see that applications for **judicial review** will be made at the High Court. The Crown Court hears serious criminal cases and the judge will preside over the case to determine questions of law, although the jury will determine questions of fact.

The courts which most people will have contact with are the County Courts and Magistrates' Courts. County Courts are located in most large towns and deal with smaller civil cases (usually under £50,000). Magistrates' Courts (which try summary only and triable either way offences) will hear over 95 per cent of criminal cases. Magistrates are volunteers and do not have legal training, although they are assisted by a legally trained advisor. Additionally, there are a number of tribunals which are concerned with specific areas such as employment law, social security and immigration.

WHAT DO THE THREE BRANCHES OF GOVERNMENT DO?

The executive

CORNERSTONE

The executive

The executive is used to describe the function of governing a country. The executive includes the monarch, the government and the Civil Service.

The government of the day sets the legislative agenda of the new Parliament, which is set out in the Queen's Speech. The government uses the powers granted by Parliament to govern the country. The government will make decisions such as deploying British military personnel overseas and the budget. The government represents the **Crown**, hence it is 'Her Majesty's Government'. Each minister is responsible for a government department, such as defence, health and education. Senior ministers who are in charge of a government department attend cabinet. The Prime Minister is not elected directly by the electorate. Instead, the political party who can command the support of the House of Commons (i.e. with the most MPs or able to form a coalition) is invited by the monarch to form a government. The Prime Minister is usually the leader of the political party which has the most MPs in the House of Commons.

The monarch's role in our constitutional monarchy is largely ceremonial. The important decisions which the monarch must make, such as choosing a Prime Minister, approving ministerial appointments, dissolving Parliament (note the Fixed-term Parliaments Act 2011) and giving **royal assent** to legislation so that it becomes law, are regulated by constitutional conventions.

At a local level the executive powers are used by local authorities to run local services such as schools, retirement homes and transportation.

The legislature

The legislature makes law and exercises the legislative function. In the United Kingdom a bill does not become law before it receives royal assent. An Act of Parliament gives the executive the power to govern the country. The legislature will then hold the executive accountable by using committees to overview government policy and the way that the laws are administered. The legislature will also allow the executive to make legislation known as secondary or delegated legislation. Unlike an Act of Parliament this delegated legislation can be reviewed by the courts.

The judiciary

The judiciary applies the law. There are two different types of law, case law and statute law. Judges will interpret an Act of Parliament and will apply it to a particular set of facts. There are a number of ways that judges can interpret legislation. However, judges must avoid going beyond what Parliament intended when it created the statute. Since the decision in *Pepper* v. *Hart* [1992] UKHL 3, the courts, when confronted with an ambiguous statutory provision, have been permitted to refer to **Hansard** to look at the record of parliamentary debate, in order to ascertain Parliament's intention.

Judges will create case law by interpreting the statute in accordance with different sets of facts. Additionally, large parts of the law of tort and contract law are judge-made with little influence from statute. There is a hierarchy known as precedent, which means that lower courts are bound by the decisions of the higher courts. This means that a lower court such as the High Court must apply the decision of a higher court, such as the Court of Appeal, unless it is possible to distinguish the two cases. The doctrine of precedent will ensure judicial certainty. Since the *1966 Practice Statement* [1966] 3 All ER 77, the House of Lords (now the Supreme Court) is no longer bound by the previous decisions of the House of Lords.

WHO IDENTIFIED THE CLASSIC DOCTRINE OF THE SEPARATION OF POWERS?

Aristotle

The Greek philosopher Aristotle in his book *Politics* identified the importance of having different people control the functions of the state. Having different people control each function is essential to the separation of powers. Aristotle wrote: '[a]ll states have three elements . . . When they are well-ordered, the state is well-ordered' (1297b, 1–1298a, 150). Aristotle defined the three elements as (i) deliberating over public affairs (which would be the executive), (ii) choosing the magistrates and how to elect them and (iii) the judiciary. Aristotle had reached this conclusion after exploring the different systems of government in the Greek world.

Aristotle taught Alexander the Great, and Aristotle himself had been taught by the philosopher Plato, who had in turn had been taught by Socrates. Aristotle eventually fell out with both Alexander the Great and Plato.

CONTEXT

Montesquieu

CORNERSTONE

Montesquieu and the separation of powers

The modern doctrine of the separation of powers comes from the French philosopher Charles, Baron De Montesquieu. Montesquieu, in his book *The Spirit of the Laws* (1748), defined the separation of powers.

Montesquieu was heavily influenced by John Locke's book, the *Two Treatises of Government* (1689). Locke argued that whilst the legislature should be the most important body in the state, the executive and the legislature should each exercise separate powers. It is important to note that for much of the seventeenth century, the conflict between the legislature and the executive had dominated English politics.

Two civil wars were fought between Parliament and the Crown in the 1640s, and another between Parliament and royalists in the 1650s. Parliament triumphed and the monarchy was abolished. The combination of the legislative and the executive functions in Parliament was not a success. Eventually the monarchy was restored in 1660; however Parliament and the Crown continued to have an uneasy relationship and James II was forced to flee to France in 1688. Parliament invited William and Mary to become joint monarchs. However, Parliament was now superior to the executive, as the Crown was conferred on candidates of Parliament's own choosing.

CONTEXT

Montesquieu based his theory on the constitution of England. It should be remembered that Montesquieu was writing before the rise of cabinet government (i.e. before the monarch surrendered the day-to-day executive powers to his Prime Minister). Montesquieu admired the constitutional settlement in England, as in France there was not yet a national parliament. Montesquieu famously stated that:

'In every government there are three sorts of power: the legislative; the executive in respect to things dependant on the laws of nations [this would be the executive]; and the executive in regard to matters that depend on the civil law [the judiciary].'

The separation of powers is not simply an idea as to how the three branches of a state should be organised. There are very good reasons as to why there needs to be the separation of powers. Montesquieu believed that it was important for the liberty of the individual that these powers were not in the hands of one person or individual body. Montesquieu believed that where the executive and legislative powers were not separated, then there could be no liberty as a 'monarch or senate could enact tyrannical laws, to execute them in a tyrannical manner'. Equally, Montesquieu believed that were the judicial and legislative powers were not separated, then peoples' lives 'would be subject to arbitrary control'. If the judicial and executive powers were not separated then 'the judge might behave with violence and oppression'.

REFLECTION

The requirement of 'checks and balances'

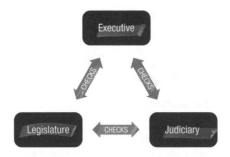

Figure 3.3 Checks and balances

CORNERSTONE

Checks and balances

Montesquieu did not believe that there needed to be a strict separation of powers. This was because if each person or branch of government was left to use their power unchecked by the other branches, then there could be misuse of that power, which would result in oppression. Therefore, it is important that each branch is accountable to the others. This accountability is known as checks and balances.

Having **checks and balances** means that one branch of government will review the activities of the other branches to ensure that the power given to them is used properly (see Figure 3.3). This makes sense as supervision ensures that there is accountability and good government. Arguably, too much interference is a bad thing, as interference in judicial decision-making by the government or Parliament, or parliamentary involvement in judicial appointments, might undermine the independence of the judiciary. However, the judiciary should respect Parliament's role in making law and should not seek to usurp that function. Montesquieu argued that the legislature should not have the power to summon itself, but instead should be summoned by the executive, which would regulate its meetings. Equally the executive should be able to check the legislature's power. Montesquieu argued that, '[w]ere the executive power not to have a right of restraining the encroachment of the legislative body, that latter would become despotic; for as it might arrogate to itself what authority it pleased, it would soon destroy all the other powers.'

The influence of Montesquieu on the drafters of the United States constitution

Montesquieu influenced the drafters of the United States constitution. The 'founding fathers' of the United States of America were former British subjects who wished to be independent of the British Parliament and eventually the Crown. The constitution creates strong separation of powers in the United States (see Figure 3.4).

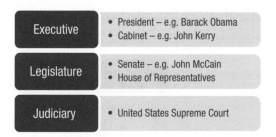

Figure 3.4 Separation of power in the United States

The new capital, Washington, was built after the American War of Independence and it was designed to emphasise the importance of the separation of powers. There is a presidential palace, which is now known as the White House, there is Congress which houses the House of Representatives and the Senate, and a distinct Supreme Court building. It is clear that symbolically, as well as legally, a different body of people exercises each power.

The composition of the legislature and its functions are set out in Article I. The powers of the House of Representatives and Senate are clearly defined. There are strict term limits, with Representatives serving two years and Senators six years before having to seek re-election. The composition of the executive and its functions are set out in Article II. The office of President and the powers of the presidency are set out clearly, with a strict four-year term limit. The composition of the judiciary and its functions are set out in Article III. The Supreme Court is the superior court and the judges enjoy security of tenure.

Take note

The United States Supreme Court has the power to strike down legislation which is unconstitutional. This power was decided in the case of Marbury v. Madison [1803] 5 US 137, where the court held that '[a] law repugnant to the Constitution is void'. Note that the United States constitution did not give such a power to the courts. The English courts cannot do this, as this would offend the constitutional principle of Parliamentary Sovereignty. Judicial review in England and Wales is limited to checking the validity of decisions made by the executive.

If you read the United States constitution it is clear that the drafters intended there to be a separation of function between each branch of the state. Additionally, there is no overlap of personnel. In order to join the executive a member of the legislature must resign, such as when Hilary Clinton resigned as a Senator in order to become Secretary of State (i.e. Foreign Secretary).

Checks and balances

The United States constitution does not follow the strict separation of powers as there are checks and balances. This means that each branch can legitimately exercise a limited review of the power of the other branches. This prevents each branch from having a monopoly of power. For example, the legislature's function is to make law, but it is restrained from making any law it likes by the limited power of the presidential veto (contained in the codified constitution) and the power of the judiciary to strike down unconstitutional law (developed by case law). The President is not immune and can be impeached by the legislature, with the House of Representatives voting on whether there are grounds to impeach and the Senate acting as the court. The last President to be successfully impeached was Andrew Johnson in 1867, whilst Bill Clinton was unsuccessfully impeached in the late 1990s (President Nixon resigned before facing impeachment charges).

The President has the power to veto legislation. However, unlike the United Kingdom (with refusal of royal assent), the legislature can override the President's veto with a two-thirds majority in both Houses of Congress.

Historical support for the separation of powers

The classic quote used to justify the separation of powers is that of Lord Acton, who wrote in 1887 that: '[p]ower tends to corrupt, and absolute power corrupts absolutely. Great men are almost always bad men.' A classic example is the first British Prime Minister, Sir Robert Walpole, who was notoriously corrupt and amassed a considerable personal fortune. Walpole famously remarked that '[e]very man has his price'. Unsurprisingly, corruption was associated with the politics of the eighteenth century.

The Instrument of Government 1653

The Commonwealth was established after English Civil Wars. In 1653 the **Protectorate**, was established and Oliver Cromwell ruled England, Scotland and Ireland (1653–58). The Protectorate was established by the Instrument of Government, which formed the basis of a constitution, outlining the powers of the Lord Protector and Parliament. It listed the functions of the state and who was responsible for carrying these out, with the executive power being in the hands of the Lord Protector (Art. II) and the legislative power being in the hands of both Parliament and the Lord Protector (Art. I). Marchamont Needham observed that 'placing the legislative and executive powers in the same persons is a marvellous in-let of corruption and tyranny' (*A True State of the Case of the Commonwealth* (1654), p. 10).

However, in the United Kingdom is there a need to adhere to the theory of the separation of powers? The United States was a new country and could create a new system of government. The United Kingdom has evolved as a democracy with an independent judiciary, an elected House of Commons that enjoys universal suffrage and a constitutional monarchy. We shall see below that many academics have doubted whether the United Kingdom has ever had separation of powers.

DOES THE UK HAVE SEPARATION OF POWERS?

CORNERSTONE

The United Kingdom does not have a written constitution

Unlike most other countries the United Kingdom does not have a written constitution (although some of the constitutional sources are written). This is not to say that the United Kingdom does not have a constitution, but rather that there is no document that contains the key constitutional arrangements.

Consequentially, the United Kingdom's constitution is far more fluid than a country that has a rigid codified constitution. The constitution existed prior to the imposition of a rigid set of rules which could incorporate the theory of the separation of powers.

INTERSECTION

There is much debate over whether the United Kingdom has a constitution. Writers such as F.F. Ridley have argued that there is no constitution, whereas Munro refutes this view. You may wish to refer back to Chapter 1 for more detail on the debate as to whether the United Kingdom has a constitution.

The United Kingdom has evolved constitutionally since Montesquieu

The country that Montesquieu observed in the 1720s is very different to the United Kingdom of today. The House of Lords dominated Parliament and the franchise was limited. Cities such as Manchester had no MPs, whilst many small villages had two MPs. The monarch dominated the executive, although it was in the reign of George I that the position of First Minister (or Prime Minister) developed under Sir Robert Walpole. Gradually the system of cabinet government developed and the everyday running of the state was left to parliamentarians who could gain enough support in the House of Commons to form a government. The arrangement where parliamentarians carried out the executive function may offend the theory of the separation of powers, but it has proved constitutionally expedient. Academics have criticised Montesquieu, arguing that he wrongly described the British political system and that the United Kingdom has never conformed to the separation of powers.

> **Take note**
>
> The United Kingdom's constitutional system has changed since the 1720s–40s. You will need to be familiar with these changes and how these have impacted on whether the United Kingdom has separation of powers.

OVERLAPS OF FUNCTION AND PERSONNEL

CORNERSTONE

Fusion between the legislature and the executive

In the United Kingdom there is a fusion between the legislature and the executive. As a matter of convention the government must be comprised of parliamentarians and the Prime Minister must be a member of the House of Commons.

In this section we will be exploring the overlaps of function and personnel in the United Kingdom. It is important to understand the extent of the overlaps and to be able to assess whether the United Kingdom has the separation of powers (see Figure 3.5).

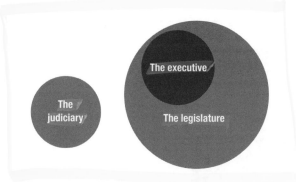

Figure 3.5 Fusion between the three branches of government

Executive and legislature

An overlap of personnel

The government is part of the executive. The government is comprised of the Prime Minister, the cabinet (e.g. Foreign Secretary), junior ministers, parliamentary private secretaries and government whips who must ensure that MPs vote in support of government-sponsored bills, known as **public bills**. By convention the government is comprised of parliamentarians from both Houses of Parliament (see Figure 3.6). This means that there must be an overlap, as to have people in cabinet who are not members of either House would be unconstitutional. The senior positions in government (such as the Chancellor of the Exchequer) are usually occupied by MPs. Although, Lord Mandelson, who is a member of the House of Lords, served as the First Secretary of State and the Secretary of State for Business, Innovation and Skills between 2008 and 2010.

The Prime Minister by convention is a member of the House of Commons. The last Prime Minister from the House of Lords was the Marquis of Salisbury in 1902. Similarly, by convention the government is comprised solely of parliamentarians. If the Prime Minister wishes to appoint an individual who is not a member of either House of Parliament, then this individual must then seek election as a MP, or more commonly will be appointed a life peer (as in the case of Peter Mandelson in 2008). This means that there is an overlap between the personnel in the legislature and the executive. For example, prior to the Constitutional Reform Act 2005, the Lord Chancellor who is a senior government minister, and sits in cabinet and is a member of the legislature was also the speaker of the House of Lords.

At the moment there are 650 MPs. This means that any government requires at least 326 MPs to have a majority. The government can use ministerial offices as patronage, to ensure support from an MP in return for a position in government. The House of Commons Disqualification Act 1975 was

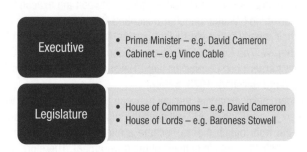

Figure 3.6 Overlap in personnel between Parliament and the executive

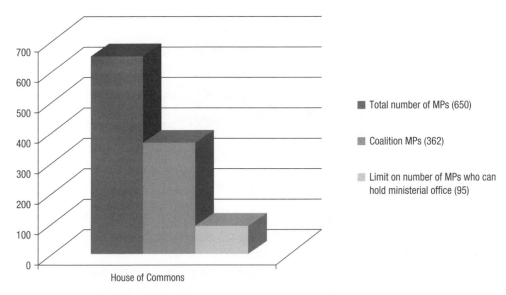

Figure 3.7 2010 General Election: the effect of the House of Commons Disqualification Act 1975 on the number of MPs who can hold ministerial office

introduced to restrict the number of ministers which a government may create (see Figure 3.7). Section 2 of the Act limits the number of ministerial office holders to 95. This still gives the government guaranteed support of 95 MPs, which is nearly one-sixth of the House of Commons.

CORNERSTONE

House of Commons Disqualification Act 1975

The House of Commons Disqualification Act 1975 was introduced to restrict the number of ministers which a government may create. Section 2 of the Act limits the number of ministerial office holders to 95. This still gives the government guaranteed support of 95 MPs, which is nearly one-sixth of the House of Commons.

An important question for people looking at how politics and the constitution operate is whether the fusion which exists in the United Kingdom between the executive and legislature is a good or bad thing? Walter Bagehot described the close union of the executive and legislature in their 'nearly complete fusion' as the 'The efficient secret of the English constitution'. (Bagehot, W. *The English Constitution* (Oxford University Press: Oxford, 2001), p. 11). Whereas, the former Lord Chancellor, Lord Hailsham, referred to this fusion as an elected dictatorship (Lord Hailsham 1976, p. 693).

As a result of modern political parties, the link between the government and MPs is strong. In order to build a career in politics, an MP will need the support of the Prime Minister in order to be promoted to the front bench (i.e. to become a minister). The government relies on whips to ensure that their MPs vote in support of the government. Therefore, a government that has won a large majority in the House of Commons effectively controls the legislative

REFLECTION

process. The other parties are unable to prevent legislation from being approved or propose alternative legislation. This means that a government with a majority can legislate (in the House of Commons at least) as it wishes, free from any legal limitations, as the courts cannot question the validity of an Act of Parliament. That is not to say that a government with a majority is entirely safe, as there is always a risk of a backbench revolt, whereby MPs in the government's own party will vote against its legislation.

Many critics have argued that Parliament is rendered powerless under the current system. However, Conor Gearty has observed that whilst '(t)here is certainly some truth in the deep-seated and frequently repeated criticism that Parliament has over many decades become the poodle of the executive', he denies that 'things are not nearly so bad as is sometimes believed, particularly by lawyers and by advocates of strong human rights measures' (*Principles of Human Rights Adjudication* (Oxford University Press: Oxford, 2004), p. 210).

The Queen in Parliament

The monarch appoints the government, although this prerogative power is restricted by convention. The power of Parliament to legislate is known as the **Queen in Parliament**. As a matter of convention the monarch must give her royal assent to legislation before a bill becomes law.

Ministers can create law

As a matter of expediency, ministers are given powers by the legislature to create law. This secondary legislation is known as delegated legislation. The minister is effectively allowed to create legislation within the remit of the powers given to him by Parliament.

Additionally ministers have non-statutory power under the prerogative. The prerogative is recognised by the common law. There is very little parliamentary scrutiny on ministerial use of the prerogative. We will look at the limitations of parliamentary scrutiny of the prerogative in Chapter 9. Where the prerogative and an Act of Parliament cover the same subject matter, then the court will give effect to the Act.

Executive and judiciary

An overlap of personnel

Prior to the Constitutional Reform Act 2005 the **Lord Chancellor** was the head of the judiciary. This meant that the Lord Chancellor could appoint judges, discipline judges and determine which judges could hear certain cases. Lord Hailsham argued that this overlap was necessary, as the Lord Chancellor 'is in the business of defending and preserving the independence and integrity of the judiciary . . . To discharge this function it is necessary that he should be a member of all three traditional branches of government.' Lord Hailsham regarded his role as 'the judges' friend at court, whether he is acting as their public defender in Parliament or as their private representative in **Whitehall**. For this purpose he is to be regarded as the representative of the judicial body and not simply as a member of the executive' (Lord Hailsham 1989, 308). The Lord Chancellor was regarded as protecting judicial independence from Parliament as well as his colleagues in government. According to Professor Drewry, under the old system, '[j]udges got on with their task of judging; parliamentarians looked nervously at a frontier guard-house marked "judicial-independence", occupied by the formidable figure of the Lord Chancellor, and kept their distance.' (Drewry 2013, p. 359).

This system was problematic, as if a senior member of the executive was in charge of the judiciary, then the executive could be accused of undermining the independence of the judiciary. Furthermore, the Lord Chancellor could sit as a judge and took precedence in the House of Lords. According to Colin Munro, 'it has not been suggested that the executive has tried to interfere with the independence of judges trying cases. What has been in contention is the extent to which judges, rather than the executive, should have control over the administration of courts and legal processes' (Munro 2005, p. 316). Lord Steyn argued extra-judicially in favour of the creation of a Supreme Court. His Lordship stated, '[t]he practice of the Lord Chancellor and his predecessors of sitting in the Appellate Committee is not consistent with even the weakest principle of separation of powers or the most tolerant interpretation of the constitutional principles of judicial independence or rule of law' (Lord Steyn 2002, p. 382).

The problem was that a defendant who has breached a law made by the legislature (of which the Lord Chancellor was a member), enforced by the executive (of which the Lord Chancellor was a senior member) and applied by the judiciary (which the Lord Chancellor headed and could sit as a judge), could argue that he has not had a fair trial.

The Home Secretary's sentencing powers

Lord Steyn had criticised the Home Secretary's sentencing powers (Lord Steyn 1997). Writing extra-judicially, His Lordship stated that:

> 'The Home Secretary still retains the power to set the tariff of the term of imprisonment to be served in the case of mandatory sentences of life imprisonment for murder. Sentencing for any crime is a judicial function. The function of determining the tariff in the case of mandatory life sentences ought to be performed in public by neutral judges. That function ought not to be performed by the Home Secretary. The present opaque arrangements are in conflict with the principle of the separation of powers and with open justice. It ought to be brought into line with the position in regard to discretionary life sentences which is recognised to be a judicial function. I would hope that we can put our own house in order in this respect rather than await a further ruling from the European Court of Human Rights.'

The Home Secretary as a result of section 269 of the Criminal Justice Act 2003 no longer has the power to set minimum tariffs for life sentences in cases involving an adult defendant. Section 269 has introduced a new scheme where the courts, instead of the Home Secretary, will determine the minimum term. Section 269 was introduced because of the judgments of the European Court of Human Rights in *Stafford* v. *UK* [2002] 35 EHRR 32 and the House of Lords in *R* v. *Secretary of State for the Home Department ex p. Anderson* [2002] 3 WLR 1800. Previously, the Home Secretary had lost the power to set the tariff for defendants under the age of eighteen.

CORNERSTONE

The Prerogative of Mercy

This prerogative power is used to give full pardons, partial pardons and to release prisoners early on compassionate grounds.

The Prerogative of Mercy is exercised by the monarch on the advice of the Secretary of State for Justice. Previously, it was the Home Secretary who advised the monarch. The last pardon was that of the Liverpool Football Club fan, Michael Shields, in 2009. This enables the executive to quash the sentence given by the courts. (See 'The Governance of Britain Review of the Executive Prerogative Powers: Final Report' (2009)).

The Attorney-General

The Attorney-General is a member of the executive and sometimes attends cabinet. The Attorney-General is the government's chief legal advisor. Crucially, where a judge has given a sentence which is considered unduly lenient the Attorney-General has limited power to refer the matter to the Court of Appeal. The Attorney-General has the power to prosecute for breach of the Contempt of Court Act 1981. The Attorney-General can also stop a prosecution on indictment, this is known as *nolle prosequi*. Additionally, if there has been an acquittal, he can refer a point of law to the Court of Appeal. The Attorney-General is assisted by the Solicitor-General.

By convention the Attorney-General must be able to exercise his powers to prosecute independently of his colleagues in cabinet. According to Geoffrey Marshall, 'since 1924 the holders of the Attorney-General's office . . . have asserted that by convention in matters related to the institution and withdrawal of prosecutions the Attorney-General exercises his function independently of the Cabinet' (*Constitutional Conventions*, p. 113).

Legislature and judiciary

The legislature's judicial function

Prior to the Constitutional Reform Act 2005 Parliament had a judicial function which was carried out by the Appellate Committee of the House of Lords. This arrangement was created by the Appellate Jurisdiction Act 1876. The Lords of Appeal in Ordinary (informally known as the **Law Lords**) were appointed by the Crown and performed this judicial function. The Law Lords were able to sit in the legislative chamber of the House of Lords and could take part in political debates. During passing of the Human Rights Act 1998, Lord Brown-Wilkinson, actively took part in debates and rejected the proposition that the jurisprudence of the European Court of Human Rights should be binding on the House of Lords. Thus, the Law Lords were members of the legislature and the highest court in the United Kingdom.

Since the 1840s the other members of the House of Lords did not take part in the House's judicial function. The issue of who could hear an appeal arose during the trial of Daniel O'Conner, when the Prime Minister's supporters encouraged the non-judges to leave the chamber. The Court had its own rooms to hear cases, although it delivered its decision in the legislative chamber. Nonetheless, such an arrangement was quite confusing and did little to demonstrate the separation of powers.

Parliament could also issue Acts of Attainder which carried the death penalty, the last being passed in 1715. This was a legislative act. Alternatively, Parliament could impeach an individual.

> The House of Commons would vote on whether to impeach and the House of Lords would vote on whether the defendant was guilty. This was a trial and required an offence to have been committed. The usual laws of evidence applied. The last impeachment trial was that of Henry Dundas in 1806. Impeachment had been used as a way of making the executive accountable to Parliament.

CONTEXT

Overlap of personnel

Prior to the Constitutional Reform Act 2005 judges could take part in parliamentary debates and the Lord Chancellor was a member of the legislature and the head of the judiciary. This was confusing and raised questions about the independence of the judiciary from the legislature. Lord Steyn supported reforming these arrangements and argued that for many people it was difficult to appreciate the distinction between the Parliamentary House of Lords and the Law Lords (2002, p. 382). His Lordship stated:

'In 2002 the highest court in the land is still a committee of the legislature . . . It has the appearance of a subordinate part of the Upper House. The sittings of the Appellate Committee therefore take place in a Committee room in the Palace of Westminster, and the Law Lords work on the Law Lords' Corridor . . . A regular reminder of its status is also the theatrical performance in the chamber of Law Lords making speeches when they give their opinions after prayers with the mace on the woolsack. When judgments were delivered in *Pinochet No.1* the crowded benches of the chamber apparently led foreign television viewers to believe that Lady Thatcher was part of the dissenting minority who opposed the extradition of General Pinochet!'

We can see that the Law Lords delivered their judgments in the chamber of the House of Lords, and sitting in the same chamber were the non-judicial members of the House of Lords, which included Baroness Thatcher. Thatcher was a friend of General Pinochet, who was facing extradition to Spain to face charges of crimes against humanity. So to the casual observer it would appear that Thatcher *might* have been able to vote in the case before the Appellate Committee of the House of Lords – which we know was not the case.

Judges make law

According to the doctrine of the separation of powers the legislature should create law whilst the judiciary apply the law. However, the courts do create law. The law that the courts have made is known as the common law. Before Parliament began to create the vast number of laws that it does today, it was the decisions of the courts that were recorded and used to create a system of precedent. In your studies you will find that the vast majority of contract law and tort law was created by judges and is still relevant. However, many judges argue that the courts do not create law, rather they just discover it. This can be criticised as a myth. We must distinguish between the common law (judge-made law) and the role of the judiciary today in interpreting statutes. Today the courts' role is to interpret legislation and to give effect to the intention of Parliament.

According to the theory of the separation of powers, judges should not make laws. However, in reality judges have been accused of law-making. In the past it was regarded as acceptable for judges to state and refine our law, but today this is the role of Parliament. The orthodox view that judges do not make the law was stated by Lord Esher MR in *Willis* v. *Baddeley* [1892] 2 QB 324 at 326, where His Lordship stated:

> 'This is not a case, as has been suggested, of what is sometime called judge-made law. There is, in fact, no such thing as judge-made law, for the judges do not make the law, though they frequently have to apply existing law to circumstances as to which it has not previously been authoritatively laid down that such law is applicable.'

However, many judges have pointed out that the judiciary does make law. The common law is judge-made and the judges are not merely finding law. This was the view of Lord Reid (1972, p. 23) who argued:

> 'There was a time when it was thought almost indecent to suggest that judges make law . . . Those with a taste for fairytales seem to have thought that in some Aladdin's cave there is hidden the Common Law in all its splendour and that on a judge's appointment there descends on him knowledge of the magic words Open Sesame. Bad decisions are given when the judge has muddled the password and the wrong door opens. But we do not believe in fairytales any more.'

We can see that Lord Reid was critical of the view that judges just discover the law.

Marital rape and the courts

CORNERSTONE

R v. R (Rape: Marital Exemption) [1992] 1 AC 599

There are a number of very important cases where judges have controversially made law. In *R* v. *R (Rape: Marital Exemption)* [1992] 1 AC 599, the House of Lords held that the Sexual Offences (Amendment) Act 1976 could be interpreted as to make marital rape unlawful. In *R* v. *R* the victim and the defendant were separated but were not yet divorced.

Marianne Giles is critical of the decision and argued that the court went beyond the 'bounds of their legitimate law-making powers' and that it would be better for Parliament to reform the law, rather than a piecemeal development by judges. Giles also criticised judicial law-making in '[t]he law relating to recklessness . . . [which is] another prime example of judicial law-making effecting major changes, and resulting in a state of confusion and disagreement for many years' (Giles 1992, p. 407).

Example of judicial law-making: Tort law

Lord Atkins in *Donoghue* v. *Stevenson* [1932] AC 562 created the modern tort of negligence. Previously there was not a general duty to avoid causing another loss. Victorian judges had restricted civil liability to contract law. Modern negligence is a branch of law that has been created by judges. So too is the law relating to psychiatric injury in tort, which has been developed and restricted by case law. One example is the decision in *Alcock* v. *Chief Constable of South Yorkshire* [1992] 1 AC 310. The House of Lords were motivated by public policy concerns, i.e. the risk that too many claimants might sue after a large-scale disaster. Parliament has yet to reform this area of the law.

DOES THE UNITED KINGDOM'S SYSTEM HAVE SUITABLE CHECKS AND BALANCES?

Executive and legislature

Given that over the past thirty years most governments have enjoyed a majority in the House of Commons, there is scope for the executive to dominate the legislature. It is important that the legislature is able to check the power of the executive and review its actions.

Vote of no confidence in a government

CORNERSTONE

Vote of no confidence

The government is accountable to the House of Commons. If the Prime Minister loses a vote of no confidence then the government will resign and this will trigger a General Election.

The government must command the support of the majority of the House of Commons. In this respect the government owes its survival to the continual support of the House of Commons. A vote of no confidence will as a matter of convention force the Prime Minister to resign or to request that Parliament is dissolved and this will trigger a General Election. The Fixed-term Parliaments Act 2011 which introduced fixed-term parliaments which will last five years, has nonetheless preserved the ability of a vote of no confidence to trigger a General Election. Given that apart from the last General Election in 2010, recent elections have seen the government gain a large majority, it is unlikely that a vote would succeed in bringing down the current Coalition government. This is because the development of the modern political party has made it more difficult for this to happen. The last vote of no confidence was in 1979, which brought down the Callaghan government and triggered a General Election. Therefore a vote of no confidence is only a risk to a government without a majority in the House of Commons.

Prime Minister's Questions

CORNERSTONE

Prime Minister's Questions

When Parliament is in session Prime Minister's Questions (PMQs) take place every Wednesday at 12pm. The Prime Minister faces thirty minutes of questions from the Leader of the Opposition and from backbench MPs.

Prime Minister's Questions (PMQs) is televised and the performance of the Prime Minister and the Leader of the Opposition is scrutinised by politicians and the media. Commentators will critique their performance and a weak speaker might face a backbench revolt from within their own party. However, success during PMQs does not necessarily secure victory at the ballot box for the Leader of the Opposition (see William Hague's performance as leader of the Conservative Party). Critics regard PMQs as nothing more than a televised Punch and Judy show.

The question which must be asked, is just how effective is PMQs in holding the government to account? The answer is that it depends. The Prime Minister must make himself available for questions and this is televised, although in 2013 David Cameron frequently missed PMQs and the Deputy Prime Minister, Nick Clegg, stood in for him. The performance of the Prime Minister matters, as it is reported in the media and ultimately may influence voters. PMQs give Parliament the opportunity to question the government's proposals and the Prime Minister is expected to defend his government's policies.

Critics accuse PMQs of being just a platform for sound bites and that it offers little in terms of accountability. However, the former Prime Minister Tony Blair revealed in his memoirs that he found PMQs to be a terrifying experience.

Tony Blair, *A Journey* (Arrow Books: London, 2010)

'PMQs was the most nerve-racking, discombobulating, nail-biting, bowel-moving, terror-inspiring, courage-draining experience in my prime ministerial life, without question. You know that scene in *Marathon Man* where the evil Nazi doctor played by Laurence Olivier drills through Dustin Hoffman's teeth? At around 11.45 on Wednesday mornings, I would have swapped 30 minutes of PMQs for 30 minutes of that.'

CONTEXT

Ministerial Question Time

Senior government ministers have an opportunity to answer questions in Parliament. This takes place during ministerial question time.

Select and general/standing committees

INTERSECTION

> Please refer to Chapter 6 for a more detailed discussion on select committees in the House of Commons and their strengths and weaknesses in holding the executive to account.

In the House of Commons, **select committees** oversee the work of government departments. The committees have no power to compel ministers to attend. Ministers are not allowed to sit on the committees. This is important as the committees serve to review executive action and to scrutinise policies. This means that Parliament can exercise independent scrutiny of the executive. The committees focus on that department's policies, spending and administration. The work of the committee is published. The House of Lords has five select committees that focus on the Constitution, the European Union, Communications, Science and Technology and Economic Affairs. The general or standing committees are involved with the progress through Parliament of particular pieces of legislation.

Executive and judiciary

Security of tenure

CORNERSTONE

Security of tenure for senior judges

The judiciary enjoys security of tenure and guaranteed payment under the Act of Settlement of 1701. This means that judges cannot be removed unless they misbehave.

Prior to the Act of Settlement monarchs such as Charles II (1660–85) and James II (1685–88) had dismissed judges so that the courts would find in their favour. The result is that the judiciary do not owe their continued employment to the support of the executive. This prevents the executive from dismissing judges who reach politically controversial decisions.

Lord Denning has recounted that after the decision in *Heatons Transport (St Helens) Ltd* v. *Transport and General Workers Union* [1972] 3 WLR 73:

'I was told by one in a high place:

Your decision was a disaster for the country, which will last till the end of the century.

I was shaken to the core. But I was not downcast. I just thought:

Thank goodness, the judges of the Court of Appeal are independent.

No government dare seek to influence them.'

(Lord Denning *The Closing Chapter* (Butterworths: London, 1983), p. 177)

CONTEXT

The Lord Chancellor traditionally appointed judges and notwithstanding the Constitutional Reform Act 2005 and the creation of the Judicial Appointments Commission, the Lord Chancellor still has an important role in the appointment of members of the judiciary.

Judicial review

CORNERSTONE

The purpose of judicial review

The judiciary can review the actions of the executive. This is known as judicial review. Judicial review allows the court to decide whether the executive's actions were unreasonable, **irrational**, or illegal or gave rise to a **legitimate expectation** and whether there was procedural impropriety. This means that where Parliament has given a minister the power to make secondary legislation or make decisions, that the minister must use the power for the intended purposes, must not make an unreasonable decision and must not be biased.

Judicial review is extremely important as it is a key check on the use of statutory powers by the executive. Judicial review is not an appeal and the courts should not substitute its own opinion for that of the decision-maker. The courts can quash the original decision and order the decision-maker to make the decision again.

As discussed above the executive can make Orders using the royal prerogative. Traditionally it was held that the manner in which the prerogative was used was not reviewable. However, in the case of *Council of Civil Service Unions* v. *Minister of State for Civil Service* [1985] AC 374 [known as *GCHQ*] the House of Lords held that the prerogative was reviewable. According to Lord Roskill there were certain areas which were non-justiciable. This was because the court was aware that the executive had the expertise and function of determining these issues, i.e. the decision to go to war. We will see in Chapter 9 that the list of non-justiciable prerogative powers has been reduced by subsequent judicial decisions.

Judicial review is an important check and balance by the judiciary. Where the executive is accused of breaching the European Convention on Human Rights the court may apply a higher standard of review to see whether the decision was proportionate. This risks substituting the decision of the decision maker for that of the court. Arguably this offends the theory of separation of powers. We shall look at this in more detail in Chapter 13.

Royal prerogative

As well as being reviewable, the prerogative's scope and existence can be determined by the courts. Parliamentary control of the prerogative is limited as the executive has refused to disclose the full extent of its prerogative powers. Where an Act of Parliament and the prerogative cover the same area the courts will apply the Act and the prerogative will go into abeyance (see *Attorney-General* v. *De Keyser's Royal Hotel Ltd* [1920] AC 508). The courts have restricted the use of new prerogatives, as Diplock LJ stated in *British Broadcasting Corporation* v. *Johns* [1964] WLR 1071 that 'it is 350 years and a civil war too late for the Queen's courts to broaden the prerogative'. However, the degree of judicial scrutiny depends upon the composition of the court.

Legislature and judiciary

No power to review the validity of an Act of Parliament

The United Kingdom's judiciary cannot set aside an Act of Parliament which is considered to be unconstitutional. Some members of the judiciary have questioned whether the courts could do this. The *obiter* in *R (Jackson)* v. *Attorney-General* [2005] UKHL 56 demonstrates differing judicial attitudes to Parliamentary Sovereignty. Lord Steyn had argued that if Parliament should legislate to do the unthinkable, then the courts might have to reconsider the Judicial Rule of Recognition. This rule recognises that parliament is legally sovereign and as a consequence no one can question an Act of Parliament.

INTERSECTION

To understand why judges have no power to review the validity of an Act of Parliament, please refer to Chapter 5 on Parliamentary Sovereignty.

Human Rights Act 1998

Section 3 of the Human Rights Act 1998 allows the court to read down and interpret an Act so that it complies with the Convention rights. However, the power to do this is restricted as the courts must not go beyond what Parliament intended when enacting legislation. This is a controversial power as some judges have been accused of going against what Parliament intended. Section 4 allows courts (High Court and above) to issue a **declaration of incompatibility** where an Act of Parliament breaches a Convention right that has been incorporated under the HRA 1998. A declaration of incompatibility does not allow the court to set aside an Act, however Parliament will usually amend the Act to remove the incompatibility with the Convention right. The importance of the HRA 1998 is that it allows the judiciary to challenge an Act of Parliament in a way that was impossible before. Whilst it may be argued that these powers are given by Parliament and can be removed by Parliament, nonetheless the judiciary have successfully challenged the previous government's controversial terrorism legislation in *A* v. *Home Secretary* [2004] UKHL 56. The Anti-Terrorism, Crime and Security Act 2001 allowed for indefinite detention of suspected terrorists without trial. The House of Lords issued a declaration of incompatibility and the Parliament eventually responded by amending the offending legislation and introduced control orders.

Ouster clauses

The courts have refused to allow the legislature to prevent judicial review of executive actions. Where an Act of Parliament attempts to restrict judicial review the courts have managed to review the executive's use of the powers conferred by the statute. In *Anisminic Ltd* v. *Foreign Compensation Commission* [1969] 2 AC 147 the courts interpreted an **ouster clause** which prevented review of a decision made by the Commission as inapplicable. This was because the decision reached was interpreted as a purported determination and not a proper determination. It was clear what Parliament had intended; nonetheless, the courts had construed the words of the statute to enable judicial review.

Parliamentary scrutiny

If a judge is accused of misconduct, then both Houses of Parliament can pass a resolution calling for that judge to be dismissed. According to the Subjudice Rule, Parliament cannot discuss forthcoming and current cases. There is a constitutional convention that states that members of the legislature should not criticise individual judicial decisions. However, Parliament can criticise judicial sentencing policy. This convention is repeatedly broken, such as when Margaret Thatcher in 1979 criticised the leniency of sentence for a defendant convicted of molesting a child.

IMPACT OF THE CONSTITUTIONAL REFORM ACT 2005

CORNERSTONE

The Constitutional Reform Act 2005

The office of the Lord Chancellor has been reformed by the Constitutional Reform Act 2005. This Act changed the way that judges are appointed and has created the United Kingdom's Supreme Court.

The Constitutional Reform Act 2005 (CRA) has changed the United Kingdom's constitutional arrangements in a number of ways (see Table 3.1). The impact on the separation of powers is considerable, although the Act does not attempt to reform the fusion between the legislature and executive in terms of the overlap of personnel.

The main provisions of the Act will be discussed below with reference to the overlaps that existed previously.

Judicial independence

Section 3 states that the executive must uphold judicial independence:

'The Lord Chancellor, other Ministers of the Crown and all with responsibility for matters relating to the judiciary or otherwise to the administration of justice must uphold the continued independence of the judiciary'

Take note

The Constitutional Reform Act 2005 does nothing to empower the Supreme Court to strike down legislation that is considered unconstitutional or offends the rule of law. This is because of the doctrine of Parliamentary Sovereignty.

The creation of a Supreme Court

Section 23 creates the Supreme Court. The Supreme Court is housed in the former Middlesex Guildhall. The building has been renovated and proceedings are televised. The judges are now known as Justices of the Supreme Court. Crucially section 137 prevents serving judges from sitting or voting in the House of Lords. This prevents a blurring of the distinction between the Justices in their capacity as judge and politician. The creation of the Supreme Court is extremely symbolic.

The reform of the role of Lord Chancellor

The position of Lord Chancellor has been reformed. The Lord Chancellor is now also the Secretary of State for Justice.

Table 3.1 A comparison of the situation before and after the Constitutional Reform Act 2005

Who sits in Parliament?	Prior to CRA 2005	Post CRA 2005
Legislature	Yes	Yes
Executive	Yes (Government)	Yes (Government)
Judiciary	Yes, in the House of Lords	No

Who makes laws?	Prior to CRA 2005	Post CRA 2005
Legislature	Yes	Yes
Executive	Yes, through delegated legislation	Yes, through delegated legislation
Judiciary	Yes, through case law	Yes, through case law

Nonetheless, the Lord Chancellor still has a role in all three branches of government. Section 7 states that the Lord Chief Justice is now the head of the judiciary in England and Wales and is responsible for welfare, training and guidance. He takes over these duties from the Lord Chancellor. Section 2 states that the Lord Chancellor must be qualified by experience but need not be a lawyer. Chris Grayling was the first non-lawyer to act as Lord Chancellor. The Lord Chancellor no longer has any judicial functions and will no longer sit as a judge. This is very important as this removes the potential for breaching Article 6 of the European Convention on Human Rights, which guarantees a fair and impartial tribunal. Although Lord Falconer (2003–2007), who replaced Lord Irvine (1997–2003) as Lord Chancellor, promised not to sit as a judge, it is important that the judiciary are seen to be independent of the executive. We have seen that Lord Hailsham had defended the role of the Lord Chancellor as the judiciary's friend in government. This role of representing the judiciary falls to the Lord Chief Justice, who under section 5 of the CRA 2005 is permitted to make representations to Parliament. Lord Judge, the former Lord Chief Justice, has commented that the CRA 2005 has removed a valuable link between the judiciary and the government:

> 'There's nobody in the cabinet who is responsible for representing – to those members of the cabinet who may need advice on an issue – how a particular proposal may impact on the judiciary.'

Lord Judge also commented that there were political restrictions on the ability to make representations under section 5 to Parliament, as this risked being seen to take sides against the government (see Rozenberg, J. *The Guardian*, 30 January 2013).

The appointment of the judiciary has been reformed. Section 14 transfers the right of appointment of High Court Judges and District Judges from the Lord Chancellor to the Queen. This is very important. Equally, the establishment of the Judicial Appointments Commission under section 61 opens up the judicial appointment process. The Lord Chancellor no longer appoints candidates and under section 29 can only reject the nominees presented by the Judicial Appointments Commission. The Crime and Courts Act 2013 will transfer the Lord Chancellor's role in the appointment process for a large number of judges to the Lord Chief Justice (s.20). This reduces the role of the Lord Chancellor in judicial appointments. Section 27 states how the Judicial Appointments Commission will select the Supreme Court Justices. The Lord Chancellor and the Lord Chief Justice are both responsible for disciplining judges (ss.108 and 109).

Section 18 removes the Lord Chancellor as speaker of the House of Lords. The Lord Chancellor is still a member of the legislature. Since 2007 all Lord Chancellors have been members of the House of Commons.

....**APPLICATION**

Imagine that a barrister was appointed to the judiciary. Prior to the CRA 2005 her appointment would have been managed by the Lord Chancellor and was not a transparent process. Post the CRA 2005 judicial appointments are managed by the Judicial Appointments Commission. The Lord Chancellor still has a limited power to veto the barrister's appointment. Once appointed the new judge would be managed by the Lord Chief Justice who is the head of the judiciary in England and Wales. If she misbehaves in office she will be disciplined by both the Lord Chancellor and the Lord Chief Justice. Eventually, she might become a member of the Supreme Court. As a Justice of the Supreme Court she would no longer have the right to sit in the House of Lords. As a Justice of the Supreme Court she would not have the power to strike down Acts of Parliament, however repugnant the Act may be.

UK SEPARATION OF POWERS? WHAT ACADEMICS THINK

It is important to appreciate that academics have different views as to whether the United Kingdom's constitution conforms to the requirements of the separation of powers. Barendt (2005) argued that Montesquieu's understanding of the British constitution was flawed. This view is supported by Lord Hailsham. Barendt stated that:

'The truth is that there is no effective separation of powers between legislature and executive in the United Kingdom in the sense of a system of "checks and balances". The advent of mass political parties has destroyed the semblance of such a system which existed a century ago'.

Barendt argued that, '[t]here is, however, an effective separation of the judicial power from the other branches. Judges may not sit in the House of Commons and they are protected from summary removal under the Act of Settlement 1701.' Barendt continued to state that the role of the Lord Chancellor and the Law Lords involvement with the House of Lords 'contravene the principle, albeit moderately and perhaps acceptably'. Barendt argued that, '[w]hile there is in practice a fusion of legislative and executive *powers*, there is in principle a distinction between the two *functions*.'

Munro observed that the separation of powers 'have shaped constitutional arrangements and influenced our constitutional thinking . . . The separation in the British Constitution, although not absolute, ought not to be lightly dismissed' (2005, p. 332).

Other academics such as Griffith and Street were critical and argued 'the doctrine is so remote from the facts that it is better to disregard it altogether' (Griffith J.A.G. and Street H. *Principles of Administrative Law* 5th edn (Pitman: London, 1973), p. 16). Equally hostile are S.A. De Smith and R. Brazier who argued that 'no writer of repute would claim that it is a central feature of the modern British constitution' (*Constitutional and Administrative Law*, 8th edn (Penguin: London, 1998), p. 18).

UK SEPARATION OF POWERS? WHAT JUDGES THINK

Lord Steyn (1997) writing extra-judicially considered the separation of powers and observed:

'in *Duport Steels Ltd* v. *Sirs*, Lord Diplock repeated that "it cannot be too strongly emphasised that the British Constitution, though largely unwritten, is firmly based on the separation of powers". I respectfully agree with those observations. But, given that all members of the political executive are members of the legislature, the concept applies in a qualified form in this country.'

Lord Bingham observed that:

'While the British constitution does not, quite obviously, provide for the separation of legislative and executive authority, it does . . . [Lord Bingham noted that prior to the CRA 2005 there were two exceptions: the Lord Chancellor and the House of Lords] provide for an absolute separation of judicial from legislative and executive authority' (2011, pp. 71–72).

Other members of the judiciary have highlighted the importance of judicial independence and the fact that judiciary and legislature both have different functions. Lord Donaldson stated in *R* v. *HM Treasury, ex p. Smedley* [1985] QB 657 at 666 that it is:

'[O]f the highest importance that the legislature and the judicature are separate and independent of one another . . . It therefore behoves the courts to be ever sensitive to the paramount need to refrain from trespassing on the province of Parliament.'

CONCLUSION

Does the United Kingdom have separation of powers? It is important that after reading this chapter you feel confident to answer this question. We have seen that the separation of powers has been acknowledged as important to prevent tyranny and abuse of power. Historically, the legislature and the executive have struggled for mastery. Since the seventeenth century the law-making powers of the executive have been checked by Parliament. What does the separation of powers actually mean? Does the existence of checks and balances, which necessitate interference by the other branches of government into the workings of a particular branch, prevent there being separation of powers? Can the United Kingdom's system of government be regarded as conforming to what is required by the separation of powers, or does the overlap of personnel and function prevent this?

The Constitutional Reform Act 2005 has created the Supreme Court and reformed the role of Lord Chancellor. However, the fusion of the executive and legislature has not been reformed by the CRA 2005.

Should the fusion between the executive and legislature be reformed and would the United Kingdom benefit from an executive that is not comprised of members of the legislature? Such reform might result in a US-style President and cabinet which are not part of the legislature, and who are not questioned directly in the legislature on a weekly basis. This raises the questions as to whether the President would be directly elected, or whether it would be dependent on the number of seats a party has in the House of Commons.

REFLECTION

It is important to understand the key areas of the separation of powers as detailed in Figure 3.8.

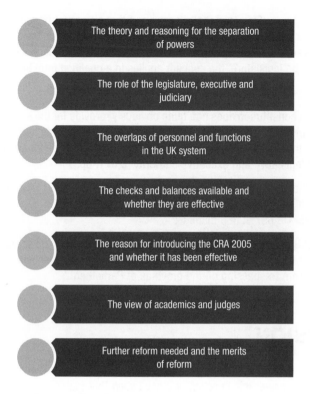

Figure 3.8 Key areas of the separation of powers

KEY POINTS

- The separation of powers is regarded as important to ensure the effective running of a country and to avoid the risk of tyranny and the abuse of power.
- The separation of powers requires the three powers, making laws, governing the country and the administration of justice, to be exercised by three distinct bodies, each of which is comprised of different people.
- Strict separation of powers without checks and balances would risk good government and would permit the abuse of power.
- The classic account was written by Montesquieu, whose writings influenced the drafters of the United States constitution.
- It is controversial as to whether the United Kingdom's system has the separation of powers. Although the Constitutional Reform Act 2005 has changed the relationship between the judiciary and the other branches of government.

CORE CASES AND STATUTES

Case	About	Importance
R v. R (Rape: marital exemption) [1992]	This case concerned whether forcing your wife to have intercourse was a criminal offence.	The House of Lords held that forced intercourse within a marriage amounted to rape. The case has been criticised as judicial law-making.

Statute	About	Importance
House of Commons Disqualification Act 1975	This Act limits the number of ministerial office holders to 95.	The Act restricts the ability of the executive to dominate the House of Commons by creating an excessive number of ministers.
Constitutional Reform Act 2005	Introduced key constitutional reforms and helped to strengthen the separation of powers between the judiciary and the two other branches of government.	This Act created the Supreme Court and reformed the office of Lord Chancellor. The Lord Chief Justice is now the head of the judiciary in England and Wales. The Act also introduced changes in the way judges are appointed.

FURTHER READING

Barendt, E. 'Separation of powers and constitutional government' [2005] *Public Law* **599**
Refer to this article to understand why the separation of powers is so important.

Bingham, T. *The Lives of the Law: Selected Essays and Speeches 2000–2010* **(Oxford University Press: Oxford, 2011)**
Parts of this book refer to the separation of powers and the constitution generally.

Bradley, A.W. and Ewing, K.D. *Constitutional and Administrative Law* **15th edn (Pearson: Harlow, 2011)**
An interesting and detailed textbook. Refer to this to develop your understanding of this topic.

Claus, L. 'Montesquieu's mistakes and the true meaning of separation' [2005] *Oxford Journal of Legal Studies* **419**
An interesting critique of Montesquieu's writings.

Drewry, G. 'Parliamentary accountability for the administration of justice' in Horne, A., Drewry, G. and Oliver, D. (eds) *Parliament and the Law* **(Hart: Oxford, 2013)**
Provides an overview of the reforms to the office of Lord Chancellor.

Giles, M. 'Judicial law-making in the criminal courts: the case of marital rape' [1992] *Criminal Law Review* **407**
A critique of judicial law-making in the criminal law. There are some interesting arguments raised here.

**Hailsham, Lord 'Elective dictatorship'
(1976) 120 *Solicitors Journal* 693**
The classic article on the dangers of a fusion
between the executive and the legislature.

**Hailsham, Lord 'The office of Lord
Chancellor and the separation
of powers' [1989] *Civil Justice
Quarterly* 308**
Written by a Lord Chancellor, this article seeks
to explain why the position prior to the CRA
2005 could be justified.

**Lester, A. 'English judges as law
makers' [1993] *Public Law* 269**
An interesting article on judicial law-making.

**Munro, C. *Studies in Constitutional
Law* (Oxford University Press:
Oxford, 2005)**
Refer to this book for a series of interesting
chapters on the constitution. It is highly
recommended that you refer to this book
during your studies.

**Reid, Lord 'The judge as
lawmaker' (1972) 12 *Journal
of the Society of Public Teachers
of Law* 23**
Refer to this for a judge's opinion as to
whether judges are law-makers.

**Steyn, Lord 'The case for a Supreme
Court' [2002] *Law Quarterly Review*
382**
An interesting and persuasive argument in
favour of a Supreme Court.

**Steyn, Lord 'The weakest and
least dangerous department of
government' [1997] *Public Law* 84**
This article looks at the role of the judiciary.

**Windlesham, Lord 'The Constitutional
Reform Act 2005: ministers, judges
and constitutional change: part 1'
[2005] *Public Law* 806**
An interesting article on constitutional reform.

CHAPTER 4
The rule of law

BLUEPRINT

The rule of law

LEGISLATION

- Act of Settlement 1701

CONTEXT

- Judicial willingness to hold the government to account.

CONCEPTS

- Defining the rule of law
- The procedural rule of law
- The substantive rule of law
- The thick and thin versions of the rule of law
- Retrospective laws

- Can a dictatorship be regarded as having the rule of law?
- Can a bad law ever be regarded as conforming to the requirements identified by Raz or Bingham?

- What is meant by the term 'the rule of law'?
- What purpose does the rule of law serve?
- What are the different versions of the rule of law and how are they distinct?

CASES

- *Entick* v. *Carrington* [1965]
- *R (Jackson)* v. *Attorney-General* [2005]

REFORM

- Will judicial observance of the rule of law place limitations on Parliamentary Sovereignty?
- Impact of legal aid reforms on the rule of law, i.e. access to the courts by ordinary people.

SPECIAL CHARACTERISTICS

- Historical independence of the judiciary
- Dicey's version of the rule of law
- A bad law is not compatible with the substantive version of the rule of law

CRITICAL
ISSUES

Setting the scene

The observance of the rule of law is an important characteristic of the United Kingdom's constitution. Although, as we have discussed in Chapter 1, the United Kingdom does not have a fully written constitution, the rule of law is an integral concept to the operation of the constitutional system and plays an important part in the English legal system.

The rule of law means that the government and its agencies must act in accordance to the law, that the government is not above the law, and that the law should be sufficiently certain and accessible. There can be no action by the executive unless there is legal authority to do so. The laws created by the courts and Parliament must meet certain conditions, otherwise they do not comply with the rule of law. The government cannot decide the extent of its own authority, otherwise the government would wield arbitrary power and there would be no certainty. The rule of law holds that the state is governed in accordance with the law, not the arbitrary whim of its current rulers. The rule of law is not just a public law issue, it is important to other branches of the law from criminal to commercial law. We will look at the definition and different versions of the rule of law, and see why it matters that the United Kingdom's laws are compatible with this important characteristic of the constitution.

Chapter overview

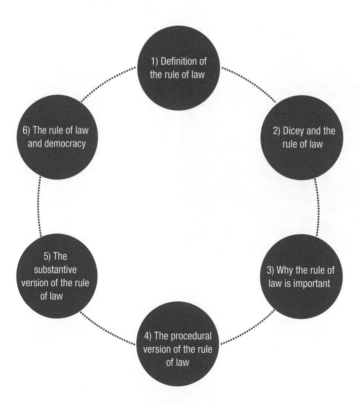

DEFINITION OF THE RULE OF LAW

How do we define the rule of law? This is problematic as we shall see below, as the rule of law can mean different things to different people. F.A. Hayek's definition of the rule of law provides a useful start.

CORNERSTONE

Defining the rule of law

F.A. Hayek in *The Road to Serfdom* (1944, p. 54) gave a very famous and authoritative definition of the rule of law. Hayek stated:

'[the rule of law] stripped of all technical formalities . . . means that government in all its actions is bound by rules fixed and announced beforehand – rules which make it possible to foresee with fair certainty how the authority will use its coercive powers in given circumstances, and to plan one's individual affairs on the basis of this knowledge.'

We will see below that there are two versions of the rule of law:

1. Formal/procedural as defined by Joseph Raz.
2. Substantive as defined amongst others by Lord Bingham.

These two versions are different. It is important as you read this chapter to understand the difference.

DEVELOPMENT OF THE RULE OF LAW IN ENGLAND

The Magna Carta of 1215 was forced on King John by his barons (see Chapter 1). Although the Magna Carta was annulled by the Pope at John's request, it was reissued by John's son and grandson. The most important clause is clause 29 which stated that the king did not have the arbitrary power to condemn a man, the only way a man could be condemned was by lawful judgment. The monarch's power was limited by the developing criminal law and the existing legal system. There is a story that when King James I succeeded to the English throne in 1603, while on his way to London his men caught a thief. The king wanted the man killed straight away and the thief was hanged. Subsequently the king was informed that in England a man could only be condemned if he was found guilty after a trial.

CORNERSTONE

Entick v. *Carrington* (1765) 19 State Tr 1029

The rule of law is an important feature of the constitution. The courts have held the executive could not act outside the law. An important example is the decision of Lord Camden CJ in *Entick* v. *Carrington* (1765) 19 State Tr 1029.

In *Entick* v. *Carrington* the Home Secretary had sent his agents to search the house of John Entick, who was a supporter of the radical John Wilkes. Entick was accused of producing libellous material which criticised the government. The agents broke into his house and searched his papers for four hours. Entick sued them for trespass. The agents had entered and searched the property under a warrant authorised by the Home Secretary. Lord Camden CJ found in favour of Entick and held that the Home Secretary was not a magistrate and therefore did not have the authority to issue a warrant. Consequentially, the actions of the agents were illegal. Lord Camden's judgment supports the rule of law, as the executive may only act in accordance to the powers given to them under the law: '[i]f any such power in a Secretary of State, or a Privy Counsellor, had ever existed, it would appear from our law-books; all the ancient books are silent on this head.'

Lord Camden made the following points:

- There was no authority that the government could search a house of a person accused of libel. The consequences of such a power would be that anyone suspected could have their house searched.

- Such a general power would give the Home Secretary arbitrary and discretionary power to decide whose house to search.

- Lord Camden noted that if there was a need to seize libellous material before it was published, then this decision should be taken by Parliament: 'if the Legislature be of that opinion they will make it lawful'.

- The government should prosecute Entick for libel and let a jury try him.

It is interesting to note that Lord Camden CJ indicated that if Entick were guilty, then he was a dangerous man; but nonetheless, the government could not act illegally – even if it they were acting to prevent anarchy. Today, the courts prevent the government from acting illegally (i.e. by violating the European Convention on Human Rights), even where the government considers a group, or an individual, to be a danger to national security. Examples of this include the attempts to deport the radical cleric Abu Qatada (*Othman* v. *Secretary of State for the Home Department* [2013] EWCA Civ 277) and the Belmarsh case, where suspected terrorist suspects were detained without trial (*A* v. *Secretary of State for the Home Department* [2004] UKHL 56).

....**APPLICATION**

In light of the decision in *Entick* v. *Carrington*, imagine that the Home Secretary had received permission from the king to issue the warrant. Would this have made a difference? The answer would be no. However, had the Home Secretary received the authority to issue the warrant from an Act of Parliament then he could have lawfully issued the warrant and no trespass would have been committed.

Illegality

The government must act in accordance with the law. It is not above the law, should the Prime Minister commit a criminal offence then he will be arrested. The Crown Prosecution Service and the police cannot refuse to prosecute, unless they are legally allowed to do so. An example of this is Chris Huhne, who was a senior cabinet minister and was convicted of conspiracy to pervert the course of justice. Despite his position, Huhne was not immune from being prosecuted.

When ministers exceed the powers given to them by acting illegally or use those powers for an improper purpose, then it is possible to bring an application for judicial review. This enables the courts to quash an illegal decision (see Chapter 13). A minister who ignores a court order can be held to be in contempt of court. In *M* v. *Home Office* [1994] 1 AC 377 the Home Secretary was found to be in contempt of court. This was because the Home Office had deported a Zimbabwean national, notwithstanding a court order preventing him from being deported.

DICEY AND THE RULE OF LAW

CORNERSTONE

Dicey and the rule of law

Dicey claimed that the rule of law or the supremacy of law had been a key feature of English law and politics since 1066. The concept of the rule of law existed before Dicey, but it was Dicey who, if not responsible for inventing the phrase, was responsible for ensuring that it is recognised as a key part of the constitution.

Dicey defined the rule of law as meaning 'at least three distinct though kindred concepts'. The first meaning of the rule of law was that no one could be punished or deprived of their goods unless they had breached a law, which has been established in an ordinary way and applied by an ordinary court. This meant that the state could not act in an arbitrary manner which was unlawful.

The second meaning of the rule of law was that no man is above the law, and that anyone (the Prime Minister or a billionaire) 'is subject to the ordinary law of the realm and amenable to the jurisdiction of the ordinary tribunals'. This means that no one is above the law and that anyone can be tried by the courts. So for example, the Prime Minister could be prosecuted for shoplifting and could not prevent himself from being tried before a court. The law is supreme and no one is immune from their legal obligations. Dicey was critical of the French use of administrative courts, and believed that administrative issues should be tried by ordinary courts. Today the English law has developed administrative law, with judicial review as a key part of administrative law, which enables citizens to challenge the executive's decisions.

The third meaning of the rule of law is that 'the general principles of the constitution (as for example the right to personal liberty, or the right of public meeting) are with us the result of judicial decisions determining the rights of private persons in particular cases brought before the courts'. This means that the constitutional principles which safeguard our freedoms have been created by the common law (i.e. previous judicial decisions). The rule of law requires the law to protect our key liberties and prevent tyranny.

TWO VERSIONS OF THE RULE OF LAW

Academics have attempted to define the rule of law and we will look at two versions which have received particular attention and have proved influential (see Figure 4.1).

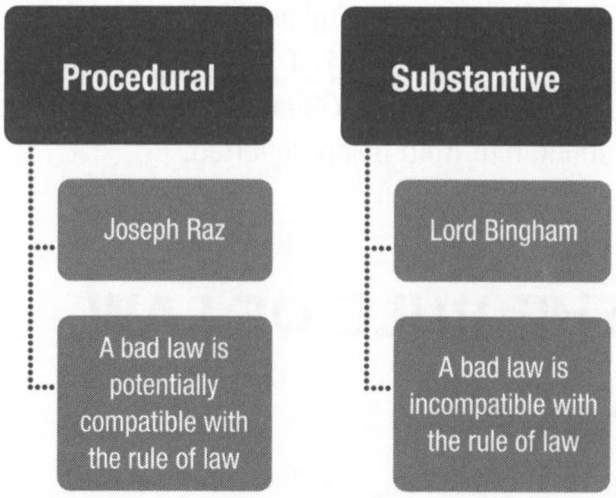

Figure 4.1 Different versions of the rule of law

Joseph Raz and the formal (procedural) version of the rule of law

CORNERSTONE

The procedural rule of law

This version of the rule of law is concerned with how the law is made, how it is applied and the procedure used. It is not concerned with whether a law is good or bad.

Joseph Raz in 'The Rule of Law and its virtue' (1977) 93 *Law Quarterly Review* 195 outlined what was meant by the rule of law. Raz stated:

'"The rule of law" means literally what it says: the rule of the law. Taken in its broadest sense this means that people should obey the law and be ruled by it. But in political and legal theory it has come to be read in a narrower sense, that the government shall be ruled by the law and subject to it (which is expressed as) "government by law and not by men".'

Raz outlined the rule of law as a formal concept. The procedure must be certain, the law accessible and capable of being understood. Raz argued that the rule of law had nothing to do with democracy, the protection of human rights, justice or equality. Instead it was a political idea.

An important question to consider is whether a country ruled by a dictator could be regarded as having the rule of law. Joseph Raz (1977) considered whether a dictatorship could be considered as having the rule of law:

'A non-democratic legal system, based on the denial of human rights, on extensive poverty, on racial segregation, sexual inequalities and religious persecution may, in principle, conform to the requirements of the rule of law better than any of the legal systems of the more enlightened western democracies.'

REFLECTION

This is interesting as Raz is arguing that potentially a dictatorship might conform to the rule of law better than a democracy:

> 'It is evident that this conception of the rule of law is a formal one. It says nothing about how the law is to be made: by tyrants, democratic majorities or any other way. It says nothing about fundamental rights, about equality or justice. It may even by thought that this version of the doctrine is formal to the extent that it is almost devoid of content. This is far from the truth.'

Raz believed that the formal version of the rule of law does have content, namely the important procedural requirements which he identified. These requirements are necessary to ensure that people are able to follow the law, as set out in Figure 4.2.

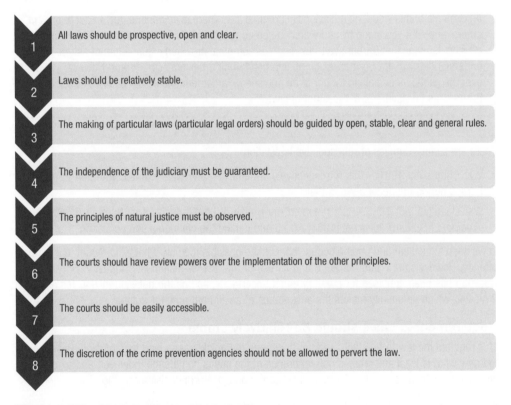

1 All laws should be prospective, open and clear.

2 Laws should be relatively stable.

3 The making of particular laws (particular legal orders) should be guided by open, stable, clear and general rules.

4 The independence of the judiciary must be guaranteed.

5 The principles of natural justice must be observed.

6 The courts should have review powers over the implementation of the other principles.

7 The courts should be easily accessible.

8 The discretion of the crime prevention agencies should not be allowed to pervert the law.

Figure 4.2 Requirements of the procedural rule of law

We will now consider these requirements in turn.

Requirement 1: All laws should be prospective, open and clear

CORNERSTONE

Retrospective laws

This requirement prohibits the use of retrospective laws. This means that Parliament cannot make laws criminalising actions you did yesterday. If this was the case, then your lawful actions on Monday would on Tuesday be considered a criminal offence; and therefore, you could then be prosecuted for what you did on Monday.

APPLICATION

An example of this would be omissions in criminal law. There is no general duty to act to protect others, and so if you stood by and watched someone drown you have not committed a criminal offence. Imagine that Barbara were to watch as someone drowned in just a foot of water. There understandably might be a press campaign condemning her omission to act. However, whatever the public mood calling for her to be punished, Parliament should not pass a law to punish Barbara, as her failure to act was not unlawful.

There are some examples of retrospective legislation:

- War Crimes Act 1991 – this retrospectively criminalised any war crimes committed in mainland Europe during the Second World War.
- War Damages Act 1965 – this reversed the House of Lords' decision in *Burmah Oil Co (Burma Trading) Ltd* v. *Lord Advocate* [1965] AC 75 and denied the claimants compensation.

Laws need to be clear and unambiguous. It should be possible to know what will amount to a criminal offence. However, the Fraud Act 2006 and its use of the test for dishonesty from *R* v. *Ghosh* [1982] QB 1053 has been criticised for creating much uncertainty, as has the decision in *R* v. *Hinks* [2001] 2 AC 241 which potentially makes the acceptance of a valid gift amount to theft.

Requirement 2: Laws should be relatively stable

This requires the law to be stable and not to change too quickly as to lead to confusion. People need to know what is legal and what is not. Ignorance of the law is no defence; however, as Raz observes we need knowledge of the law for both short-term and long-term decision-making.

Requirement 3: The making of particular laws (particular legal orders) should be guided by open, stable, clear and general rules

Raz identifies the use of orders made by the executive and its agencies, such as the police. These laws are designed to be flexible, but must be made in accordance with a general framework which is laid down by the law.

Requirement 4: The independence of the judiciary must be guaranteed

CORNERSTONE

The independence of the judiciary and the Act of Settlement 1701

The Act of Settlement 1701 guaranteed judicial independence. This has been reinforced by the Constitutional Reform Act 2005.

The judiciary must be independent and capable of applying the law consistently. Raz argued that people rely on case law to understand how the law will apply to them. Raz also argued that judicial independence was 'essential for the preservation of the rule of law'. The Act of Settlement 1701 and the Constitutional Reform Act 2005 guarantee judicial independence and provide judges with a salary and security of tenure, meaning that the judiciary are independent of the executive. Certainty of the law is important, and English commercial law has a good reputation because of this legal certainty. Lord Mansfield first identified this in *Vallejo* v. *Wheeler* (1774) 1 Cowp 143. Ralf Dahrendorf, stated that the independence of the judiciary was vital for the existence of the rule of law: 'independence of the "judicial department" may indeed be regarded as the very definition of the "rule of law"; it is certainly an important part of it . . . the partisan administration [under the control of the government or Parliament] is in fact the prevision of the law, and the denial of the rule of law' (Dahrendorf 1977, p. 1).

Requirement 5: The principles of natural justice must be observed

Raz argued that for **natural justice** to be observed meant that there needed to be an '[o]pen and fair hearing [and the] absence of **bias**'. In the United Kingdom any decision taken by a public body must be procedurally proper and that the decision-maker, whether administrative or judicial, should not be biased. We shall see in Chapter 13 that if this is not the case then a decision can be judicially reviewed.

Requirement 6: The courts should have review powers over the implementation of the other principles

Raz stated the courts should have 'a very limited review – merely to ensure the conformity to the rule of law' over primary and secondary legislation, as well as executive administrative action. This is interesting as the court:

- can judicially review secondary legislation and executive administrative action;
- cannot judicially review primary legislation. Parliamentary Sovereignty states that the courts cannot review an Act of Parliament;
- can interpret an Act of Parliament to ascertain Parliament's intention where there is confusion as to the Act's meaning.

Requirement 7: The courts should be easily accessible

Raz stated that the courts needed to be accessible. There should not be long delays and the costs should not be excessive. The legal system can be expensive and, especially with the reduction of legal aid, many people cannot afford to bring claims or to defend themselves. On 5 March 2013, *The Times* had an article on its front page which read 'Top judge warns of risk to rule of law' (written by Francis Gibbs). This article explored the government's reduction of the legal aid budget and the 'top judge' referred to in the headline was Lord Neuberger, the President of the Supreme Court. Lord Neuberger warned that the reform to legal aid could undermine the rule of law.

Lord Woolf's reforms of the civil justice system resulted in the introduction of the Civil Procedure Rules in 1998. These rules were intended to reduce delays, reduce costs and introduce fairness as an overriding objective.

Requirement 8: The discretion of the crime prevention agencies should not be allowed to pervert the law

This requirement demands that the prosecution does not have the discretion to refuse to prosecute certain offences or offenders. Equally, the police should not decide which crimes to investigate or to enforce. The Attorney-General does have the power to initiate or stop prosecutions, and the Director of Public Prosecutions, who manages the Crown Prosecution Service (CPS), can offer guidance on which offences to prosecute (e.g. assisted suicide). The CPS, under the Code of Practice for Prosecutors, has the discretion to refuse to prosecute where it is not in the public interest to do so.

APPLICATION

Imagine that Parliament passes the Inequality Act (fictitious) which gives public bodies and private companies the right to discriminate on the grounds of race, religion, sex and age. The Act stipulates that anyone who is unemployed and aged over forty can face compulsory euthanasia. Would such a law meet the eight requirements above? Potentially this Act of Parliament would satisfy Raz's eight requirements.

The substantive version of the rule of law

CORNERSTONE

The substantive rule of law

This version of the rule of law is concerned with the quality of the law, rather than just the procedural requirements. The law must be a good law.

Andrei Marmor has argued that, '[t]he most common mistake about the rule of law is to confuse it with the ideal of the rule of good law, the kind of law, for instance, that respects freedom and human dignity' (Marmor 2004, p. 1). According to the procedural version, the rule of law has nothing to do with whether the law is considered to be a good one; instead it is concerned with the procedural requirements. Parliament could enact laws that we would consider repugnant and this law could still qualify as being compatible with the rule of law. There have been many academics who have argued that the rule of law should relate to the quality of the law, i.e. the rule of law should mean more than the narrower version that was defined by Raz. Instead they argue that the rule of law should have a wider meaning and that a law must be considered a good law in order to qualify. Therefore, a country's law must not just meet the procedural requirements, but must be viewed objectively as a good law.

Lord Bingham (2007) outlined the sub-rules which he believed comprised the rule of law. It is interesting to see that His Lordship's sub-rules initially seem familiar to those proposed by Raz. However, there are fundamental differences between the two:

- Sub-rule 1: The law needs to be accessible, 'intelligible, clear and predictable'.
- Sub-rule 2: Questions of law and liability need to be decided by application of law and not discretion.
- Sub-rule 3: The law must apply to everyone, unless differences can be justified.
- Sub-rule 4: There must be adequate protection of fundamental human rights.
- Sub-rule 5: People must be able to resolve legal disputes without facing a huge legal cost or excessive delays.
- Sub-rule 6: The executive must use the powers given to them reasonably, with good faith, for the proper purpose and must not exceed these powers.
- Sub-rule 7: There must be procedural fairness.
- Sub-rule 8: The state must comply with the obligations of international law.

Sub-rule 4 is interesting as Lord Bingham is rejecting the procedural version of the rule of law. This is important as a 'state which savagely repressed or persecuted sections of its people could not in my view be regarded as observing the rule of law, even if the transport of the persecuted minority to the concentration camp . . . were the subject of detailed laws duly enacted and scrupulously observed'. This raises the question, such as what do fundamental human rights mean? Lord Bingham acknowledged this and noted that the definition is vague.

The compliance with international law in sub-rule 8 raises some important questions. Governments who act illegally in times of war may try and justify their actions on the grounds of necessity; however, if they breach international law then they are acting in violation of the rule of law. Lord Bingham refused to say whether the United Kingdom had breached the rule of law when it invaded Iraq in 2003. However, His Lordship would later state in his 2010 book *The Rule of Law* that there was no legal justification for the invasion.

Parliamentary Sovereignty and the rule of law

CORNERSTONE

A bad law is not compatible with the substantive version of the rule of law

A law which violates human rights such as religious freedom and prohibits marriages between people of different racial groups is a bad law. As such it would not be compatible with the substantive version of the rule of law. However, in some countries mixed-faith marriages might be considered detrimental to the society and there might be an attempt to justify this restriction. Therefore, whether a law is good or bad is subjective.

The United Kingdom's Parliament is legally sovereign and can make any law it wishes. There are no legal restraints to prevent Parliament from violating human rights, as the Human Rights Act 1998 gives the courts no power to declare an Act void, as this would be impossible under the traditional doctrine of Parliamentary Sovereignty (see Chapter 5). According to Lord Hoffmann, 'Parliamentary sovereignty means that Parliament can, if it chooses, legislate contrary to fundamental principles of human rights. The Human Rights Act 1998 will not detract from this power' (*R* v. *Secretary of State for the Home Department ex p. Simms* [2000] 2 AC 115 at 131). The present constitutional system may not be sufficient to protect human rights and prevent bad laws from being passed as was noted by Ralf Dahrendorf (1977) who stated, '[i]n Britain, some greater emphasis on the rule of law may not come amiss, including possibly the explicit recognition that the sovereignty of parliament is not a sufficient guarantee of human rights.'

So is Parliamentary Sovereignty compatible with observance of the rule of law?

CORNERSTONE

R (Jackson) v. *Attorney-General* [2005] UKHL 56

In this case the House of Lords made some interesting *obiter* comments about the relationship between the rule of law and Parliamentary Sovereignty. In Chapter 5 we will look at the impact of the rule of law on Parliamentary Sovereignty.

Lord Hope stated that '[t]he rule of law enforced by the courts is the ultimate controlling factor on which our constitution is based' [107]. Baroness Hale commented that '[t]he courts will treat with particular suspicion (and might even reject) any attempt to subvert the rule of law by removing governmental action affecting the rights of the individual from all judicial scrutiny' [159]. Whilst Lord Steyn stated that if Parliament did the unthinkable then the courts would be forced to qualify the principle of Parliamentary Sovereignty [102]. Such judicial comments would suggest that Parliamentary Sovereignty and the substantive version of the rule of law are incompatible. Lord Steyn writing extra-judicially went further and argued that a sufficiently serious violation of the rule of law, would result in the courts qualifying the principle of Parliamentary Sovereignty:

'For my part the dicta in *Jackson* are likely to prevail if the government tried to tamper with the fundamental principles of our constitutional democracy, such as five-year Parliaments, the role of the ordinary courts, the rule of law, and other such fundamentals. In such exceptional cases the rule of law may trump parliamentary supremacy' (Lord Steyn 2006, p. 243).

Can a 'bad law' be compatible with the rule of law? What is a bad law? Section 23 of the Anti-terrorism, Crime and Security Act 2001 permitted the government to detain suspected terrorists without trial for an indefinite period of time. This violated Articles 5 and 6 of the European Convention on Human Rights [ECHR]. However, it was possible to derogate under Article 15. The government had been given these powers by Parliament under the Act. The powers were justified on the grounds of national security. Was this a bad law, even if it was purporting to defend the lives of citizens? The House of Lords ruled in *A* v. *Secretary of State for the Home Department* [2004] UKHL 56 that section 23 breached the ECHR, as no derogation was permitted in the circumstances.

REFLECTION

In South Africa during apartheid, the White African ruling elite discriminated against the Black and Asian population. Those in power and the majority of the electorate (albeit with most of the population prohibited from voting) considered that the apartheid laws were good laws. It would appear that South Africa met the procedural requirements of the rule of law. Lord Steyn (2006) stated that:

'In the apartheid era millions of black people in South Africa were subjected to institutionalised tyranny and cruelty in the richest and most developed country in Africa. What is not always sufficiently appreciated is that by and large the Nationalist Government achieved its oppressive purposes by a scrupulous observance of legality. If the judges applied the oppressive laws, the Nationalist Government attained all it set out to do. That is, however, not the whole picture. In the 1980s during successive emergencies . . . almost every case before the highest court was heard by a so-called "emergency team" which in the result decided nearly every case in favour of the Government. Safe hands were the motto. In the result the highest court determinedly recast South African jurisprudence so as to grant the greatest possible latitude to the executive to act outside conventional legal controls.'

It is clear that a 'bad law', which does not protect fundamental human rights, will violate the substantive version of the rule of law that was advocated by Lord Bingham.

It is important to contrast how the two versions of the rule of law operate. We can do this by demonstrating whether in the following scenarios a given country would conform to the rule of law:

Country	The relevant law	Violation of the procedural version of the rule of law?	Violation of the substantive version of the rule of law?
South Africa	There were apartheid laws until the early 1990s, which separated people of different racial groups. There were no voting rights for Black Africans, etc. Today apartheid has ended and there is equality for people of all racial groups.	No violation.	Yes there is a violation.
United States of America	In the southern states there was segregation until the 1960s. This led to restrictions on the rights of African Americans.	No violation.	Yes there is a violation.
Arizona	There have been extremely controversial laws aimed at reducing illegal immigration.	No violation.	Debatable.

→

Country	The relevant law	Violation of the procedural version of the rule of law?	Violation of the substantive version of the rule of law?
China	There are restrictions on political freedoms, religious freedoms and human rights violations.	Yes. The judiciary are not independent.	Yes there is a violation.
United Kingdom	Detention without trial was introduced by the Anti-terrorism, Crime and Security Act 2001. This has now been repealed.	Initially no. The government was legally able to derogate from Article 5 of the ECHR, however, the House of Lords in *A* v. *Secretary of State for the Home Department* [2004] UKHL 56 held that it was not proportionate to detain only foreign terrorist suspects.	Yes there is a violation.

IMPORTANCE OF THE RULE OF LAW IN A DEMOCRACY

Does a democracy need to adhere to the rule of law? Does adherence to the rule of law make a country democratic? In the United Kingdom the courts have at times shown considerable deference to the government and have held that in the absence of a law against doing something, the government would be legally allowed to do it. The decision in *Malone* v. *Metropolitan Police Commissioner (No.2)* [1979] 2 All ER 620 is an example of this. In *Malone* the government was allowed to tap people's phones.

CORNERSTONE

The thick and thin versions of the rule of law

K.D. Ewing, *Bonfire of the Liberties: New Labour, Human Rights, and the Rule of Law* (2010)

'The principle is, however, impossible to define in a way that commands universal agreements, with "thin" and "thick" versions . . . There is no thinner a version of the rule of law than that expressed by Vice Chancellor Sir Robert Megarry in *Malone* v. *Metropolitan Police Commissioner*, where he said that England (sic) is not a country where everything done by government is prohibited unless expressly permitted; rather England is a country where everything done by government is permitted unless formerly prohibited.'

As we have seen, Raz's version of the rule of law permits an authoritarian state to have the rule of law, providing that it abides by the procedural requirements.

Ralf Dahrendorf (1977) noted that: '[d]emocracy is precious, but the rule of law is indispensable, and the two often do not go together . . . However, at no time can it be acceptable to cross the boundary between expediency and morality, and suspend the rule in the sense of leaving elementary human rights in the partisan and often soiled hands of government.' Dahrendorf noted that a country can have the rule of law but that does not mean that it is a democracy. The rule of law is important as it prevents a government from abusing human rights. Dahrendorf looked at Germany and noted that Bismarck's Germany (late nineteenth century) was not a democracy, but abided by the rule of law, whereas Hitler's Germany (1933–1945) was also not a democracy, but it violated fundamental human rights.

Take note

When people use the term 'the rule of law' they often mean different things. Therefore, in defining the rule of law you must be aware of the many different versions which we have discussed above.

KEY POINTS

- The rule of law is an important feature of the United Kingdom's constitution.
- There can be many different definitions of the rule of law, with Raz's procedural or formal version, and Lord Bingham's substantive version.
- Dicey is credited with coming up with the phrase 'the rule of law' and he identified three meanings of the rule of law.
- There is a potential for conflict between parliamentary sovereignty and the rule of law.

CORE CASES

Case	About	Importance
Entick v. *Carrington* [1765]	The lawfulness of executive action.	The executive could not act without lawful authority. The Home Secretary's agent had acted without lawful authority.
R (Jackson) v. *Attorney-General* [2005]	A Labour MP had introduced a private members bill to ban hunting. This bill was supported by the Labour government and was approved by the House of Commons. It was rejected by the House of Lords and the government reintroduced the bill and used the Parliament Acts 1911 and 1949 to overcome the opposition in the House of Lords. The Hunting Act 2004 and the validity of the Parliament Act 1949 were challenged by opponents of the ban.	The House of Lords reviewed the legislation on a point of law. The Parliament Act 1949 was held to be valid and the Hunting Act 2004 was held to be primary legislation. Their Lordships made some interesting *obiter* comments about Parliamentary Sovereignty and the relationship between it and the rule of law.

FURTHER READING

Bingham, Lord 'The rule of law' [2007] (67) Cambridge Law Journal 1
This article explores the rule of law.

Bingham, Lord The Rule of Law (Allan Lane: London, 2010)
This book is a good introduction to the rule of law and comments on the evolution of the rule of law and the war against terror.

Bradly, A.W. and Ewing, K.D. Constitutional and Administrative Law 15th edn (Pearson: Harlow, 2011)
Refer to this textbook for a more detailed look at the rule of law.

Dicey, A.V. Introduction to the Study of the Law of the Constitution (Liberty Fund: Minneapolis, 1982)
Refer to this book for Dicey's definition of the rule of law.

Dahrendorf, R. 'Confusion of powers: politics and the rule of law' [1977] 40(1) Modern Law Review 1
This paper looks at the rule of law in the 1970s.

Ewing, K.D. Bonfire of the Liberties: New Labour, Human Rights, and the Rule of Law (Oxford University Press: Oxford, 2010)
An interesting and provocative book. Refer to this to broaden your understanding of constitutional and administrative law.

Marmor, A. 'The rule of law and its limits' [2004] Law & Philosophy 1
This is a detailed exploration of the rule of law.

Raz, J. 'The rule of law and its virtue' (1977) 93 Law Quarterly Review 195
This article is recommended reading as it discusses the eight key requirements of the rule of law.

Steyn, Lord 'Democracy, the rule of law and the role of judges' [2006] European Human Rights Law Review 243
An interesting article which looks at the relationship between Parliamentary Sovereignty and the rule of law.

CHAPTER 5
Parliamentary Sovereignty

BLUEPRINT

Parliamentary Sovereignty

LEGISLATION

- European Communities Act 1972
- Statute of Westminster 1931
- Human Rights Act 1998

CONTEXT

- Origins of Parliamentary Sovereignty.
- Impact of the Glorious Revolution in 1688.
- Impact of UK's membership of the European Union.

CONCEPTS

- Parliamentary Sovereignty
- Implied and express repeal
- Rule of recognition
- Constitutional statutes
- Devolution
- Manner and form

- Should constitutional statutes be protected from implied repeal?
- Will judicial observance of the rule of law place limitations on Parliamentary Sovereignty?

- What is meant by the term 'Parliamentary Sovereignty'?
- Why must the courts apply an Act of Parliament?
- Are there any limitations on Parliamentary Sovereignty?

CASES

- *British Railway Board* v. *Pickin* [1974]
- *Thoburn* v. *Sunderland City Council* [2002]
- *R* v. *Secretary of State for Transport ex p. Factortame Ltd (No 2)* [1991]
- *Vauxhall Estates Ltd* v. *Liverpool Corporation* [1932]
- *R (Jackson)* v. *Attorney-General* [2005]
- *R* v. *A (Complainant's Sexual History)* [2001] UKHL 25

REFORM

- Can Parliament entrench legislation and impose manner and form requirements?
- See Baroness Hale's *obiter* comments in *Jackson* on referendum requirements.
- Will there actually be a referendum on the UK's membership of the EU?
- What impact will the 2014 referendum on Scottish independence have on Parliamentary Sovereignty?

SPECIAL CHARACTERISTICS

- The prerogative does not make law and neither can it impose any new legal obligations
- Dicey and Parliamentary Sovereignty
- Only an Act of Parliament is legally sovereign
- An Act ordering the death of blue-eyed babies is perfectly valid
- No one can question the validity of an Act of Parliament
- The courts cannot question the way in which the Act was made
- The courts must apply an Act of Parliament
- The interpretation of legislation – section 3 Human Rights Act 1998
- Should judges use section 3 or section 4 of the Human Rights Act 1998?
- Would a referendum requirement ever be enforceable?

CRITICAL ISSUES

Setting the scene

Parliamentary Sovereignty is the most important doctrine in the United Kingdom's constitution. The United Kingdom's constitution is mainly unwritten and, as we saw in Chapter 1, unlike the United States of America, the United Kingdom's constitution is uncodified and there is no special status of constitutional law. Why is this important? The answer is that Parliament is the highest law-making body in the United Kingdom and each Parliament has the ability to make or unmake any law that it wishes. What is crucial is that there is no restriction on the subject matter of an Act of Parliament: an Act that would impose compulsory euthanasia on people aged over thirty would be legal and could not be challenged by the courts.

In reality, Parliament does not legislate to impose compulsory euthanasia or kill all babies with blue eyes, and so it might be tempting to dismiss the full effect of the doctrine as somewhat academic. However, we shall see that according to the traditional doctrine as championed by A.V. Dicey, there are no legal limits to what Parliament could do. Importantly, in recent cases leading judges have rejected this argument and have stated in *obiter* that Parliament's sovereignty is not unlimited.

As we saw in Chapter 3 in the United Kingdom the executive dominates the legislature and so a government with a majority can decide what laws will be passed by Parliament. This means that the government through their control of the legislature has considerable legislative powers. It is clear that whilst a government with a large majority could be defeated by a majority of MPs voting against its legislation, this seldom happens and backbench MPs will only rebel against their own party where legislation is particularly controversial.

We shall discuss the traditional doctrine and then address the challenges to Parliamentary Sovereignty. These challenges are membership of the European Union, the Human Rights Act 1998, devolution and the rule of law. It is important that you understand the classic doctrine in order to appreciate the effect of these challenges.

Chapter overview

ORIGINS

CORNERSTONE

Definition of Parliament

It is important to define what is meant by Parliament. According to Dicey: 'Parliament means . . . the King, the House of Lords, and the House of Commons; these three bodies acting together may be aptly described as the "King in Parliament,"' (Dicey 1982, ch.1, p. 3).

Lawyers and politicians will tell you that Parliament is legally sovereign. But what does this mean? It means that Parliament can legislate in any way that it wishes. There are no limitations on the Acts that Parliament can pass, save the requirement that the Queen needs to give royal assent in order for a bill to become an Act. Importantly, a bill is not sovereign as it is not law, neither is a resolution by both Houses of Parliament. This seems unproblematic, especially if Parliament enacts legislation that is not considered to be bad or immoral. But there would be nothing to stop Parliament from passing a piece of legislation which would ban freedom of religion and the wearing of religious symbols and clothing. Legislation effectively banning certain religious clothing has already been passed by the French legislature and has proved to be controversial. See Figure 5.1 for a look at the challenges facing Parliamentary Sovereignty.

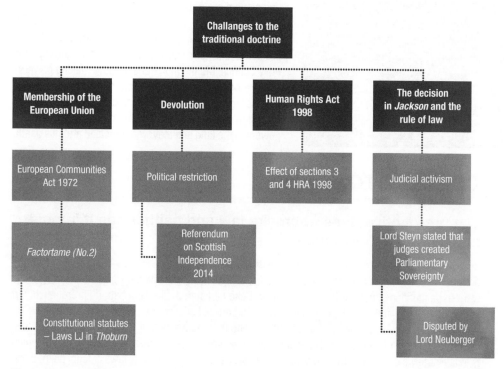

Figure 5.1 Challenges facing Parliamentary Sovereignty

APPLICATION

Imagine that a law were to be passed by the United Kingdom's Parliament which banned the wearing of all religious clothing in public. Arguably this would be considered by many to be a bad law. However, what about the courts? Surely in light of the Human Rights Act 1998 the judges would refuse to apply such a law? The answer would be no. This is because Parliamentary Sovereignty prevents judges from refusing to apply an Act of Parliament. We shall see that membership of the European Union has imposed restrictions on Parliamentary Sovereignty, but legally it would still be possible for Parliament to enact legislation such as this.

Take note

It is important to consider whether Parliament actually enacts bad laws? Is the Identification Card Act 2006 an example of a 'bad law'? This Act would have introduced compulsory identification card and did introduce the National Identity Register. Professor K.D. Ewing criticised identification cards as the 'nasty offspring' of the 2006 Act and would permit 'a bewildering amount of personal information to be recorded by a State authority (for what purpose?)' (Bonfire of the Liberties (2010), p. 9). The Act was passed with the aim to benefit the state. However, its opponents argued that it would have a negative impact on civil liberties.

Some groups in society may regard an Act of Parliament as a bad law because of what the Act intends to do, or because of the possible consequences it may have. Whether a law is good or bad can be subjective, as is it depends on a particular individual's point of view.

Who decided that Parliament was sovereign?

Parliament is not the only law-making body in the United Kingdom. Firstly, the monarch historically used prerogative powers to govern the country. Whilst today the prerogative powers are not a law-making power, i.e. capable of passing legislation, there was a time when the monarch did claim law-making powers. The monarch could issue proclamations and still can create orders through the Privy Council. Did the monarch have law-making powers? The prerogative powers were last treated as being able to pass legislation equivalent to that of Parliament during the reign of Henry VIII. Parliament had granted these powers to the king and they were repealed after his death.

CORNERSTONE

The prerogative does not make law and neither can it impose any new legal obligations

However, Sir Edward Coke CJ in *Case of Proclamations* (1611) 12 Co. Rep 74 had declared that the prerogative could not be used to impose new legal obligations upon subjects, unless these obligations were to be found in statute or the common law. Coke had stated, 'the king hath no prerogative, but that which the law of the land allows him'. This is important because the prerogative is viewed as the remaining discretionary powers of the monarch. The prerogative cannot be used in new situations, i.e. where there is no precedent of it being used in the past. This means that the prerogative, which is today largely exercised by the government, cannot be used to create new laws or legal obligations.

Secondly, the judges have created the common law. According to Dicey, '[a] large proportion of English law is in reality made by the judges' (1982, p. 18).

So why then is Parliament viewed as legally sovereign? Parliament is the supreme law-making body in the United Kingdom and no other body can question or declare an Act of Parliament to be invalid (see Figure 5.2).

The common law in the early seventeenth century maintained that an Act of Parliament could not be applied by the courts if it went against a fundamental right of the common law. Sir Edward Coke CJ (in *Dr Bonham's Case* (1609) 8 Coke Reports 113b at 118a) was willing to impose limitations on Parliament:

> 'And it appears in our books, that in many cases, the common law will controul Acts of Parliament, and sometimes adjudge them to be utterly void: for when an Act of Parliament is against common right and reason, or repugnant, or impossible to be performed, the common law will controul it, and adjudge such Act to be void'.

Sir Edward Coke's views of the power of Parliament were considered by Sir William Blackstone, who observed '[t]he power and jurisdiction of parliament, says Sir Edward Coke, is so transcendent and absolute, that it cannot be confined, either for causes or persons, within any bounds' (*Commentaries on the Laws of England* (University of Chicago Press: Chicago, 1979)).

The seventeenth century was dominated by a series of conflicts between the Stuart kings and Parliament. For over a decade Charles I ruled the country without summoning Parliament. This meant that the king sought to use his prerogative power to impose new obligations, such as taxation upon his subjects, without parliamentary approval. According to Jeffrey Goldsworthy, '[e]ven before the 1640s, many . . . lawyers described Parliament's legislative authority as legally unlimited.' Goldsworthy continued to argue that during the English Civil War, Royalists and Parliamentarians disagreed on whether it was the King in Parliament (i.e. the king giving royal assent) or only both Houses of Parliament acting on their own that was legally sovereign (Goldsworthy 1999, p. 231).

The dispute between Parliament and King Charles I led to three civil wars in the 1640s and 50s. Parliament won the first (1640–46) and second (1647–49) civil wars and Charles I was beheaded in 1649. Royalist supporters of Charles' son were defeated in the third civil war (1649–51).

Oliver Cromwell ruled as the Lord Protector during the Protectorate. After Cromwell's death the monarchy was restored and Charles II became king. He was succeeded by his brother James II who

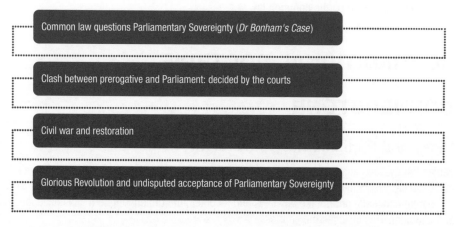

Figure 5.2 The important development of Parliamentary Sovereignty in the seventeenth century

quarrelled with Parliament and eventually fled abroad to France. As Parliament had been dissolved (that is suspended by James II) a group of former parliamentarians invited James' son-in-law William of Orange and his wife Mary to become joint monarchs in 1688. This was known as the Glorious Revolution and Parliament passed the Bill of Rights in 1689.

Since the Glorious Revolution, the monarch has ruled at the bequest of Parliament as it has been Parliament who has decided Royal Succession. The Act of Settlement 1701 established the requirement that the monarch must be a protestant. From 1688 Parliament has been regarded as legally sovereign. According to Jeffrey Goldsworthy, '[a]fter the Revolution of 1688, Parliament's sovereign power was used to control both the royal succession and the prerogatives of the Crown, which some royalists had previously deemed sacrosanct. Parliamentary sovereignty was central to the ideology of . . . Whigs, and . . . (most) Tories as well' (p. 23).

> It has not always been accepted that there are no restrictions on Parliament's legislative sovereignty. Even after 1688 the courts observed that there were some restrictions. In *City of London* v. *Wood* (1701) 12 Mod.Rep. 669, 687–688, Holt CJ stated, '[a]nd what my Lord Coke says in *Dr. Bonham's case* in his 8 Co. is far from any extravagancy, for it is a very reasonable and true saying, that if an Act of Parliament should ordain that the same person should be party and Judge, or, which is the same thing, Judge in his own cause, it would be a void Act of Parliament . . . An Act of Parliament may not make adultery lawful, that is, it cannot make it lawful for A. to lie with the wife of B. but it may make the wife of A. to be the wife of B. and dissolve her marriage with A.'
>
> In 1701, the common law was still maintaining that common law principles of natural justice, i.e. a man cannot be a judge in his own cause, would be protected from parliamentary legislation. Equally, adultery was deemed immoral and could not be legalised by Parliament. This as we shall see is no longer the case.

REFLECTION

Given that the United Kingdom lacks a codified constitution it is unsurprising that there is no statute which declares Parliament to be legally sovereign. In 1688 it was political fact that Parliament had defeated the Crown. Over the past three hundred years the courts have recognised and given effect to this political fact. As we shall see in Chapter 9 when the prerogative and an Act of Parliament cover the same subject matter, it will be the prerogative which must make way for the Act (*Attorney-General De Keyser's Royal Hotel Ltd* [1920] AC 508). An Act of Parliament can also invalidate important rights that have been developed by the common law.

THE TRADITIONAL DOCTRINE

CORNERSTONE

Dicey and Parliamentary Sovereignty

Parliamentary Sovereignty has been undisputed since 1688. Professor A.V. Dicey is the academic most closely associated with the view that Parliament is legally sovereign. According to Dicey Parliament can make or unmake any laws and no one in the United Kingdom can challenge an Act of Parliament. This includes the courts.

We shall consider what Dicey meant and explore the traditional account of Parliamentary Sovereignty. According to Dicey there were three principles:

1. Parliament is the supreme law-making body and could make or unmake any law it wished, no matter what the subject-matter was;

2. no person or court could question the validity of an Act of Parliament; and

3. Parliament is not bound by its predecessors, nor can it bind its successors.

First requirement: Parliament is the supreme law-making body

CORNERSTONE

Only an Act of Parliament is legally sovereign

Parliament is the supreme law-making body, whereas according to Dicey the political sovereign is the electorate. It is important to note that only a valid Act of Parliament is sovereign and not a bill. The bill must receive royal assent before it becomes an Act. The monarch has the prerogative power to decide whether to give her assent. By convention the monarch will give her assent, as the last time that royal assent was refused was in 1707 (the Scottish Militia Bill).

Considering Dicey's definition of Parliament it is clear that one House acting on its own, such as the House of Commons, is not legally sovereign unless the Parliament Act 1911 and 1949 apply. In *Stockdale* v. *Hansard* (1839) 112 ER 1112 the High Court held that a resolution of the House of Commons (and indeed both Houses) was not law. The case involved an action for defamation and a defence that the House of Commons had authorised the publication of documents via a resolution. In dismissing the defence, Lord Denman CJ stated that, 'the House of Commons is not the Parliament, but only a co-ordinate and component part of the Parliament . . . the resolution of any one of them cannot alter the law, or place any one beyond its control.'

There is no special status of constitutional law

In the United Kingdom there is no special status of constitutional law. This means that the Highways Act 1980 and the Constitutional Reform Act 2005 are treated the same by the courts; they are both normal Acts of Parliament and it is irrelevant the Constitutional Reform Act 2005 has any special constitutional significance. In a twenty-first-century democracy it is concerning that statutes which establish or preserve fundamental constitutional rights hold no special legal status and could be repealed in the same manner as any other statute.

> ### Take note
>
> An Act of Parliament is superior to the common law and Parliament can legislate to reverse decisions of even the Supreme Court. The controversial House of Lords decisions in *YL* v. *Birmingham City Council* [2007] 3 All ER 957 and *Malcolm* v. *Lewisham LBC* [2008] UKHL 43 were both specifically reversed by two Acts of Parliament. An Act of Parliament is superior to the prerogative and Parliament could legislate to abolish certain prerogative powers. An Act of Parliament according to the doctrine is superior to international obligations and other sources of law, such as European law.

There are no restrictions on the areas on which Parliament can legislate

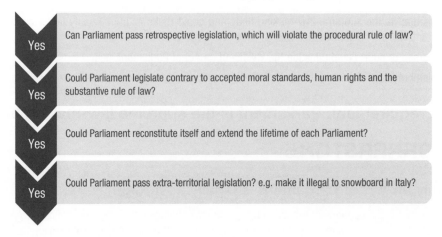

Figure 5.3 No restrictions on Parliament's legislative ability

According to Sir William Blackstone, '[Parliament] can, in short, do everything that is not naturally impossible; and therefore some have [called] . . . its power the omnipotence of Parliament' (Blackstone, *Commentaries*, i. pp. 160, 161). The traditional doctrine of Parliamentary Sovereignty claims that there are no legal restrictions on Parliament's ability to legislate. This is not to say that there might be political or practical restrictions on the ability of Parliament to legislate in any way it chooses.

Lord Steyn had written extra-judicially that, '[t]he courts acknowledge the sovereignty of Parliament. And in countless decisions the courts have declared the unqualified supremacy of Parliament. There are no exceptions' (see Lord Steyn 'The Weakest and Least Dangerous Department of Government' [1997] *Public Law* 84 at 85). This is at odds with His Lordships' *obiter* comments in *Jackson* which suggest the opposite (see below).

The courts have no discretion to prefer their own interpretation over that which Parliament intended. Lord Edmund-Davies in *Duport Steel Ltd* advised judges to avoid the urge to do the following:

'My Lords, a judge's sworn duty to "do right by all manner of people after the laws and usages of this realm" sometimes puts him in difficulty, for certain of those laws and usages may be repugnant to him. When that situation arises, he may meet it in one of two ways. First, where the law appears clear, he can shrug his shoulders, bow to what he regards as the inevitable, and apply it . . . Alternatively, a judge may be bold and deliberately set out to make new law if he thinks the existing legal situation unsatisfactory. But he risks trouble if he goes about it too blatantly, and if the law has been declared in statutory form it may prove too much for him, dislike it though he may . . . From time to time some judges have been chafed by this supremacy of Parliament, whose enactments, however questionable, must be applied.'

i. Parliament can legislate to pass retrospective legislation which offends the procedural requirements of the rule of law

INTERSECTION

The rule of law is an important feature of the constitution. For more detail on what is meant by the rule of law please refer to Chapter 4.

According to Professor Raz the procedural version of the rule of law requires there to be no retrospective legislation ('The Rule of Law and its virtue' (1977) 93 *Law Quarterly Review* 195). However, Parliament has enacted retrospective legislation. Retrospective legislation is where an Act of Parliament is enacted to change the law as it applied before the Act was created. It criminalises actions that were not regarded as criminal offences at the time that they took place.

REFLECTION

Why would Parliament need to pass retrospective legislation and can it be justified? There are a few examples of retrospective legislation. The War Crimes Act 1991 allowed the prosecution for 'murder, manslaughter or culpable homicide' which was 'committed during the period beginning with 1st September 1939 and ending with 5th June 1945 in a place which at the time was part of Germany or under German occupation [which] . . . constituted a violation of the laws and customs of war'. The Act only applied to individuals who later became British citizens or a resident of the United Kingdom, the Isle of Man or the Channel Islands. Michael Hirst commented that, '[The War Crimes Act 1991] is unusual in that it has retrospective effect, creating offences under English law in respect of conduct that, when originally committed, was incapable of amounting to any such offence' (*Jurisdiction and the Ambit of the Criminal Law*, (Oxford University Press: Oxford, 2003), p. 241). We can see that there was a need to prosecute war criminals who otherwise might have escaped justice.

Controversially, the War Damage Act 1965 reversed the decision of the House of Lords in *Burmah Oil Co Ltd* v. *Lord Advocate* [1965] AC 75. The House of Lords were asked to rule on whether compensation was payable where the prerogative had been used to destroy private property, in order to prevent it falling into the hands of the enemy. In 1942, the oil wells belonging to Burmah Oil had been destroyed to prevent these being captured by the Japanese Army. A majority of the House of Lords ruled that compensation was payable. The War Damage Act 1965 reversed this decision and held that compensation was not payable. Recently there has been debate over whether the Fraud Act 2006 has introduced an element of retrospective criminalisation into the criminal law.

ii. Parliament can legislate against accepted moral standards and violate human rights (which offends the substantive version of the rule of law)

CORNERSTONE

An Act ordering the death of blue-eyed babies is perfectly valid

According to Dicey: '[t]here is no legal basis for the theory that judges, as exponents of morality, may overrule Acts of Parliament . . . A modern judge would never listen to a barrister who argued that an Act of Parliament was invalid because it was immoral, or because it went beyond the limits of Parliamentary authority' (pp. 19–20). This means that Parliament can legislate contrary to acceptable moral standards. The most drastic statement to this effect is from Leslie Stephens who wrote that, '[i]f a legislature decided that all blue-eyed babies should be murdered, the preservation of blue-eyed babies would be illegal' (*The Science of Ethics*, 1882).

Over a hundred years later in *R* v. *Secretary of State for the Home Department ex p. Simms* [2000] 2 AC 115, Lord Hoffmann reiterated that the unfettered legislative ability of Parliament remained unchanged by the passing of the Human Rights Act 1998:

> 'Parliamentary sovereignty means that Parliament can, if it chooses, legislate contrary to fundamental principles of human rights. The Human Rights Act 1998 will not detract from this power. The constraints upon its exercise by Parliament are ultimately political, not legal. But the principle of legality means that Parliament must squarely confront what it is doing and accept the political cost' (at 132).

Lord Hoffmann noted that the restraints on Parliament are political and not legal. Would a government remain in power for long if Parliament enacted legislation that was repugnant to the majority of the population? However, as Dicey (1982, p. 9) observed, Parliament is not limited in its actions as an agent of the electorate or by the idea of trusteeship, rather it is sovereign in its own right. Even if Parliament does not owe a duty to the electorate there is still a risk that an MP might be voted out of office by her constituents.

iii. Parliament could legislate to remove key constitutional rights

In the United States the Supreme Court can declare legislation to be void if it is held to be unconstitutional. In the United Kingdom Parliament has the ability to legislate to remove key constitutional rights and could for example repeal the Human Rights Act 1998. Equally, Parliament would be able to pass legislation which would restrict the categories of people who could vote, such as those who are over a certain age.

iv. Parliament can reconstitute itself, extend its own duration and the procedural requirements for passing a bill

Parliament has the ability to reconstitute itself and change the procedures for enacting legislation. The courts will look to the parliamentary roll and are only concerned with whether the legislation has received royal assent.

It is possible for Parliament to legislate to extend the lifetime of each Parliament. The Triennial Act of 1694 limited the life of each Parliament to three years. The Septennial Act 1716 extended the lifetime of each Parliament to six years. This was very controversial as Parliament was viewed as usurping the power of the electors. Today, the lifetime of Parliament is five years. Subject to a number of exceptions, the Fixed-term Parliaments Act 2011 restricts the Prime Minister from requesting that the monarch dissolves Parliament before the expiry of the five-year fixed term. Therefore we know that the next General Election will take place in May 2015.

v. Parliament can pass extra-territorial legislation

Parliament can pass legislation that will apply beyond the territory of the United Kingdom.

> ### Take note
>
> The House of Lords Act 1999 has changed the composition of the House of Lords. Most of the hereditary peers have been removed. Parliament could legislate to abolish the House of Lords and replace to it with an elected Senate or with nothing at all. As we have seen above, the Parliament Acts 1911 and 1949 have reduced the power of the House of Lords to prevent a bill from becoming law.

APPLICATION

Imagine that Parliament decides that it is an offence to drive on the right-hand side of the road and enacts legislation which expressly states that it will apply throughout the world. A British citizen who goes on holiday to the United States and abides by the local and drives on the right-hand side of the road, could upon her return home face prosecution. An American citizen who travels on holiday to the United Kingdom could also be prosecuted.

In English law there is a presumption that when Parliament creates a criminal statute that its application is limited to England (see Lord Reid in *Treacy* v. *DPP* [1971] AC 537, 551). The War Crimes Act 1991 criminalised acts that took place in continental Europe.

CONTEXT

Sir Ivor Jennings famously stated that Parliament could legislate to make it an offence to smoke on the streets of Paris. The obvious answer to this is that a French court would not uphold an Act of Parliament nor would it prosecute anyone who did smoke on the streets of Paris. But this is not a legal restriction on the ability of Parliament to legislate beyond the United Kingdom; rather it is a political or practical restriction.

Parliament has granted independence to the former colonies of the British Empire. In doing this it has lost the ability to legislate for over a quarter of the world. Years ago an Act of Parliament could be applied from Vancouver to Auckland, and from Toronto to Cape Town. These countries have gained political and legislative independence and even if Parliament expressly stated that an Act should apply to, say, South Africa, the South African courts would refuse to apply it. The granting of independence is a political and diplomatic restriction, rather than a legal one.

CORNERSTONE

The Statute of Westminster 1931

The Statute of Westminster 1931 granted the Dominions of the British Empire (such as the Irish Free State and Canada) legislative independence from the Westminster Parliament.

Section 4 of the Statute of Westminster 1931 prevented an Act of Parliament from applying to a Dominion:

'No Act of Parliament of the United Kingdom passed after the commencement of this Act shall extend, or be deemed to extend, to a Dominion as part of the law of that Dominion, unless it is expressly declared in that Act that that Dominion has requested, and consented to, the enactment thereof.'

In *British Coal Corporation* v. *The King* [1935] AC 500, Viscount Sankey L.C. observed that section 4 did not prevent Parliament from choosing to legislate for a Dominion in the future (at 520). His Lordship stated that:

'It is doubtless true that the power of the Imperial Parliament to pass on its own initiative any legislation that it thought fit extending to Canada remains in theory unimpaired: indeed, the Imperial Parliament could, as a matter of abstract law, repeal or disregard section 4 of the Statute.'

It was argued in *Manuel* v. *Attorney General* [1983] 3 WLR 821 that by 1931 there was a constitutional convention that Parliament would not legislate for Canada. Despite the convention, Parliament could still legislate to change the Canadian constitution. The case concerned a request by the Canadian government for the Westminster Parliament to change the Canadian constitution.

CONTEXT

The decision in *Madzimbamuto* v. *Lardner-Burke* [1969] 1 AC 645 concerned the unilateral declaration of independence by Southern Rhodesia in 1965. The United Kingdom responded by passing the Southern Rhodesia Act 1965, which declared that Southern Rhodesia was still part of the British Empire and that Acts of Parliament still applied. Lord Reid held that despite the existence of a convention that the United Kingdom would not legislate for Southern Rhodesia, Parliament could still legislate as although it 'was a very important convention . . . it had no legal effect in limiting the legal power of Parliament'. Lord Reid stated that:

'It is often said that it would be unconstitutional for the United Kingdom Parliament to do certain things, meaning that the moral, political and other reasons against doing them are so strong that most people would regard it as highly improper if Parliament did these things. But that does not mean that it is beyond the power of Parliament to do such things, If Parliament chose to do any of them the courts could not hold the Act of Parliament invalid' (at 723).

vi. Each Parliament is legally sovereign and it can make or unmake any law

Each Parliament is legally sovereign and therefore can repeal any laws which have been passed by its predecessors.

Second requirement: no one can question the validity of an Act of Parliament

CORNERSTONE

No one can question the validity of an Act of Parliament

No person or body can question the validity of an Act of Parliament. Once a bill has received royal assent then the Act of Parliament must be applied by the courts. The courts cannot question the Act with regards to the procedure which Parliament followed to pass the bill, nor whether Parliament may have been misled by a party who had an interest in seeing the bill passed.

This was acknowledged by Sir William Blackstone who had argued that, '[t]rue it is, that what the Parliament doth, no authority upon earth can undo.' Under the traditional doctrine of Parliamentary Sovereignty neither the courts nor the monarch's prerogative powers can set aside an Act of Parliament. This is important as it gives Parliament considerable freedom to legislate without being restricted by the other key constitutional principle which is the rule of law. Crucially Parliament can change its composition, for example it could pass legislation to abolish the House of Lords which would mean that Parliament would no longer be bicameral.

i. No one can question the way that an Act of Parliament was made, in terms of procedure or whether Parliament was misled

CORNERSTONE

The courts cannot question the way in which the Act was made

The courts cannot question the validity of an Act of Parliament, nor can they enquire into the way in which the bill was passed by Parliament. The courts according to Lord Campbell in *Edinburgh and Dalkeith Railway Company* v. *Wauchope* [1842] 8 Cl & Fin 710 are restricted to looking at the parliamentary roll. As long as a bill has passed both Houses (however, note the effect of the Parliament Acts 1911 and 1949) and has received royal assent, then the courts cannot investigate further.

In *Edinburgh and Dalkeith Railway Company* v. *Wauchope* [1842] Lord Campbell stated '[a]ll that a court of justice can look to is the parliamentary roll; they see that an Act has passed both Houses of Parliament, and that it has received the royal assent, and no court of justice can inquire into the manner in which it was introduced into Parliament, what was done previously to its being introduced, or what passed in Parliament during the various stages of its progress through both Houses of Parliament'. This means that the courts are restricted from questioning the background of an Act.

ii. The decision in *Pickin*

CORNERSTONE

British Railway Board v. *Pickin* [1974] AC 765

In *British Railway Board* v. *Pickin* [1974] AC 765 the House of Lords restated a key constitutional principle that the courts cannot declare an Act invalid or ineffective because of the manner in which the Act was passed or any irregularity in the procedure used.

Pickin concerned ownership of land. Pickin claimed that he owned the land in the middle of the track because of the Bristol and Exeter Railway Act 1836. This Act was repealed by the British Railways Act 1968, which was a private Act. The claimant alleged that the Act was ineffective because the British Railway Board had misled Parliament. The House of Lords held that courts could not investigate this allegation, because they could not examine the procedure by which Parliament passed the Act. Lord Wilberforce famously declared that an Act of Parliament could not be declared invalid because of an alleged irregularity in the procedure used. According to Lord Wilberforce, '[t]he remedy for a Parliamentary wrong, if one has been committed, must be sought from Parliament, and cannot be gained from the courts' (pp. 792–3).

Lord Morris stated that the courts can only resolve issues such as the correct interpretation of a statute. Once an Act of Parliament is on the statute book it cannot be questioned by the courts:

'It is the function of the courts to administer the laws which Parliament has enacted. In the processes of Parliament there will be much consideration whether a Bill should or should not in one form or another become an enactment. When an enactment is passed there is finality unless and until it is amended or repealed by Parliament. In the courts there may be argument as to the correct interpretation of an enactment: there must be none as to whether it should be on the Statute Book at all' (p. 789).

iii. The decision in *Jackson*

CORNERSTONE

R (Jackson) v. *Attorney-General* [2005] UKHL 56

In this case the House of Lords was asked to consider the validity of the Hunting Act 2004. The Hunting Act 2004 was extremely controversial as it banned hunting in the United Kingdom.

The House of Lords (the legislative chamber, not the court) had opposed the Hunting Bill and had rejected it on two occasions. The Parliament Act 1911 as amended by the Parliament Act 1949, allowed the House of Commons after one year to pass a bill without the consent of the House of Lords.

The applicants argued that the Hunting Act 2004 was invalid because it had been passed under the procedures established by the Parliament Act 1949. The applicants argued that the Parliament Act 1949 was an invalid Act. They also argued that legislation passed under the Parliament Act 1911 was delegated and not primary legislation, thus it could be reviewed by the courts. Finally, they argued that the legislative power under the Parliament Act 1911 was not unlimited.

The House of Lords dismissed the appeal. The House held that legislation passed under the 1911 Act would be an Act of Parliament. The 1911 Act did not create delegation legislation; rather it was a new way of enacting primary legislation, whereby the House of Commons could legislate without the consent of the House of Lords. The House held that the 1911 Act could be amended by the 1949 Act, and therefore the Hunting Act 2004 was a perfectly valid Act of Parliament. Therefore, the House had rejected the argument that the provisions under section 2 of the 1911 Act could not be used to enlarge the power of the House of Commons.

iv. Why did the House of Lords find *Jackson* distinguishable from *Pickin*?

Lord Bingham justified the review of the 1949 Act and the Hunting Act 2004, distinguishing the facts of *Jackson* from *Pickin*. This was because unlike in *Pickin*, the courts were not investigating 'the internal workings and procedures of Parliament to demonstrate that it had been misled and so had proceeded on a false basis' (para 27), and in the present case it involved a question of law, which only the court and not Parliament could resolve. Lord Bingham agreed with the Attorney-General that the Parliament Act 1911 could be amended to enable Parliament to legislate to extend the life of Parliament (para 32).

Lord Nicholls noted the constitutional principle from *Pickin* and upheld the House of Lords decision to review the legislation:

> 'Their challenge to the lawfulness of the 1949 Act is founded on a different and prior ground: the proper interpretation of section 2(1) of the 1911 Act. On this issue the court's jurisdiction cannot be doubted. This question of statutory interpretation is properly cognisable by a court of law even though it relates to the legislative process. Statutes create law. The proper interpretation of a statute is a matter for the courts, not Parliament. This principle is as fundamental in this country's constitution as the principle that Parliament has exclusive cognisance (jurisdiction) over its own affairs.'

The House of Lords rejected the appeal and refused to declare that the Hunting Act 2004 was invalid. However, it was the *obiter* comments of the Law Lords that proved controversial with regards to parliamentary sovereignty. We shall look at the impact of *Jackson* on Parliamentary Sovereignty below.

APPLICATION

Imagine that Parliament passed the Squirrel Culling Act 2014 (fictitious) to respond to the threat posed by grey squirrels to native red squirrels. Because of opposition in the House of Lords, the government uses the procedure under the Parliament Acts 1911 and 1949 to pass the bill without the support of the House of Lords. The Act states that all local councils in England must actively take steps to eliminate all grey squirrels. Friends of Grey Squirrels, which is a pressure group, attempt to challenge the validity of the Act. They argue that the Parliament Act 1949 is invalid and therefore the Squirrel Culling Act 2014 is also invalid. They also argue that the procedure used to pass the bill was flawed. Their arguments would be rejected. We know from *Jackson* that the Parliament Act 1949 is valid and from *Pickin* that the courts cannot question parliamentary procedure.

v. The courts must apply an Act of Parliament

CORNERSTONE

The courts must apply an Act of Parliament

The court has no discretion under the doctrine of Parliamentary Sovereignty to declare an Act to be invalid or to ignore the intention of Parliament.

In *City of London* v. *Wood* (1701) 12 Mod. Rep. 669, 687–688, Holt CJ stated that '. . . an Act of Parliament can do no wrong, though it may do several things that look pretty odd'. The courts are tasked with interpreting Acts of Parliament and rely upon a number of rules to do this. What is crucial is that the courts when interpreting an Act must not go against what Parliament intended when it passed the Act. This is a delicate balancing act and as we shall see when we look at section 3 of the Human Rights Act 1998, the court must be careful not to usurp Parliament's legislative function.

The courts have often reiterated the different roles of the judiciary and Parliament. Lord Diplock in *Duport Steels Ltd* v. *Sirs* [1980] 1 WLR 142 considered the relationship between Parliament and the courts. The House of Lords had to decide the correct interpretation of section 13 of the Trade Union and Labour Relations Acts 1974 and 1976. Lord Diplock was clear that Parliament makes the law and that the court must interpret the law:

> 'My Lords, at a time when more and more cases involve the application of legislation which gives effect to policies that are the subject of bitter public and parliamentary controversy, it cannot be too strongly emphasised that the British constitution, though largely unwritten, is firmly based upon the separation of powers; Parliament makes the laws, the judiciary interpret them . . .'

REFLECTION

His Lordship warned that judges must not be tempted to use their powers of interpretation to refuse to give effect to Parliament's intention, no matter how controversial the Act may be:

> 'Where the meaning of the statutory words is plain and unambiguous it is not for the judges to invent fancied ambiguities as an excuse for failing to give effect to its plain meaning because they themselves consider that the consequences of doing so would be inexpedient, or even unjust or immoral. In controversial matters such as are involved in industrial relations there is room for differences of opinion as to what is expedient, what is just and what is morally justifiable. Under our constitution it is Parliament's opinion on these matters that is paramount.'

vi. The courts cannot review an Act of Parliament

The courts can review delegated legislation and the prerogative. If for example the Welfare Reform Act 2014 (fictitious) gave ministers the power to make delegated legislation to help relieve fuel poverty, and the minister made delegated legislation under the Act to help tackle obesity, then the courts could review the delegated legislation and hold it to be ***ultra vires*** and quash the delegated legislation.

Judicial review is an important check on the executive's power. The courts cannot judicially review an Act of Parliament and nor can they hold it to be void on the grounds of irrationality and *ultra vires*. This is because there is an important distinction between primary and secondary legislation. Primary legislation cannot be reviewed by the courts. In contrast, Acts of the Scottish Parliament can be judicially reviewed as the power to legislate has been devolved from the Westminster Parliament under the Scotland Act 1998.

This can be contrasted with the position in the United States. Although the United States constitution does not permit the Supreme Court to do this, the United States Supreme Court has claimed the right to review primary legislation. In the key case of *Marbury* v. *Madison* [1803] 1 Cr 137 the court held that it could declare an Act of Congress to be unconstitutional.

CONTEXT

Third requirement: Parliament cannot be bound by its predecessors, nor can Parliament bind its successors

i. The requirement of express repeal

CORNERSTONE

Express repeal

Express repeal means that each Parliament must have the ability to expressly repeal legislation enacted by previous Parliaments. By using express words Parliament can repeal existing legislation (see Figure 5.4).

Figure 5.4 An example of express repeal

According to Dicey, Parliament is prevented from 'entrenching' a particular piece of legislation. This means that Parliament cannot prevent future Parliaments from expressly repealing legislation that it has enacted.

ii. The requirement of implied repeal

CORNERSTONE

Implied repeal

Implied repeal means that where there are two Acts of Parliament which cover the same subject matter, the courts must apply the later Act of Parliament. Implied repeal does not require there to be express words in the newer Act of Parliament. Implied repeal is important, as in order to be legally sovereign the current Parliament must be able to impliedly repeal legislation enacted by a previous Parliament (see Figure 5.5).

Figure 5.5 An example of implied repeal

CORNERSTONE

Vauxhall Estates Ltd v. *Liverpool Corporation* [1932] 1 KB 733

In this case landowners were seeking compensation and they sought to argue that the higher measure of compensation payable by the Land (Assessment of Compensation) Act 1919 should apply, rather the lower measure of compensation available under the Housing Act 1925.

The landowners argued that the 1919 Act should apply because of section 7(1), which stated that:

'The provisions of the Act or order by which the land is authorised to be acquired, or of any Act incorporated therewith, shall, in relation to the matters dealt with in this Act, have effect subject to this Act, and so far as inconsistent with this Act those provisions shall cease to have or shall not have effect.'

The owners argued that:

1. the 1925 Act was inconsistent with the 1919 Act;
2. the 1919 Act had not been impliedly repealed by the 1925 Act (this was because section 7(1) stated that where a later Act was inconsistent with the 1919 Act, the 1919 Act would still have effect and the newer provisions would be ineffective);
3. the 1919 Act had been entrenched by Parliament and required express repeal; and
4. the 1919 Act had not been expressly repealed.

Their argument was dismissed by the High Court. Mr Justice Avory stated that there could be no restrictions on Parliament's ability to impliedly repeal an earlier Act of Parliament, no matter what the language of the previous Act suggested:

'[W]e are asked to say that by a provision of this Act of 1919 the hands of Parliament were tied in such a way that it could not by any subsequent Act enact anything which was inconsistent with the provisions of the Act of 1919. It must be admitted that such a suggestion as that is inconsistent with the principle of the constitution of this country . . . I should certainly hold, until the contrary were decided, that no Act of Parliament can effectively provide that no future Act shall interfere with its provisions . . . if they are inconsistent to that extent, then the earlier Act is impliedly repealed by the later.'

Reference was made to the decision in *Brown* v. *The Great Western Railway Company* (1882) 9 QBD 744, where implied repeal was used to give effect to a later Act of Parliament. In *Brown* Field J had observed that implied repeal existed as part of statutory interpretation:

'If an Act of Parliament is passed containing clauses which are repugnant to and inconsistent with prior legislation, the legislature cannot have two minds at one and the same time, and therefore the subsequent mind must alter the first mind. Therefore, if even in an affirmative Act there is a clause which is repugnant to and inconsistent with a previous Act, the two cannot stand together; the subsequent Act repeals the prior Act, and, à fortiori, when it is negative.'

Ellen Street Estates Ltd v. *Minister of Health* [1934] 1 KB 590 involved an attempt by a local authority to compulsory purchase land in Stepney, London. An argument similar to *Vauxhall Estates Ltd* was submitted on behalf of the landowner. The landowner argued that the 1925 Act could not impliedly repeal the 1919 Act and that Parliament was required to use express words in order to repeal 1919 Act. The Court of Appeal rejected the proposition that Parliament could bind a successor as to the form of subsequent legislation. Maugham LJ held that an Act of Parliament could not bind a previous Parliament as to the manner and form of future legislation:

'The Legislature cannot, according to our constitution, bind itself as to the form of subsequent legislation, and it is impossible for Parliament to enact that in a subsequent statute dealing with the same subject-matter there can be no implied repeal. If in a subsequent Act Parliament chooses to make it plain that the earlier statute is being to some extent repealed, effect must be given to that intention just because it is the will of the Legislature. This second point also fails.'

iii. The manner and form debate

The decisions in *Ellen Street Estates Ltd* and *Vauxhall Estates Ltd* are important as they support Dicey's third principle that it is not possible for Parliament to bind future Parliaments. Based on Dicey's third principle, an Act cannot be entrenched by requiring (i) only express repeal, or (ii) that it cannot be repealed at all.

CORNERSTONE

Manner and form

Academics have debated whether Parliament could be bound to comply with manner and form requirements. This means that an Act of Parliament cannot restrict its future repeal, i.e. by requiring a particular percentage of the House of Commons to vote for repeal, or the holding of a national referendum. It has been argued that if Parliament has the ability to redefine the requirements for passing a bill under the Parliament Acts 1911 and 1949, which exclude the House of Lords, it would be able to set further requirements which require additional requirements to be met before particular legislation could be amended or enacted.

All that is required to repeal existing legislation is a simple majority in both Houses of Parliament. Adopting an orthodox approach, where there is a referendum requirement in a statute this would not prevent a subsequent Parliament from passing an Act to change the law, without first having held a referendum. The only limitation on Parliament legislating without first having held a referendum would be political.

Section 2 of the European Union Act 2011 states that the United Kingdom cannot ratify a treaty which amends or replaces either the Treaty of the European Union or the Treaty for the European Union, unless:

1. Parliament has approved such this by passing an Act of Parliament; and

2. there has been a referendum.

iv. It is not possible to entrench legislation

As we have seen above, according to Dicey's orthodox account legislation cannot be entrenched. Parliament must have the ability to repeal any previously enacted legislation. Unlike the United States, there is no special status of constitutional law in the United Kingdom. Therefore, even if an Act of Parliament concerned the constitution, an attempt to entrench such an Act would be invalid. The Statute of Westminster 1931 could not prevent a later Parliament from legislating for a Dominion without its consent. The decision in *Manuel* v. *Attorney General* [1983] 3 WLR 821 concerned Parliament legislating to change the Canadian constitution (albeit at the request of the Canadian government). Slade LJ reiterated that Parliament could not bind its successors by enacting legislation such as the Statute of Westminster in 1931.

There have been attempts by Parliament to prevent future Parliaments from amending legislation. Dicey gave the Acts of Union as one example, where Parliament had 'endeavoured to pass Acts which should tie the hands of their successors'. However, Dicey noted that 'the endeavour has always ended in failure'. Prior to the Acts of Union, England and Scotland had been separate nations. The Acts had intended to lay down the future workings of Great Britain. Yet key provisions of the Acts that created the United Kingdom have been repealed. If the Act which founded Parliament (since the English and Scottish Parliaments had ceased to exist) could be repealed, despite the clear intention of an earlier Parliament, then it is clear entrenchment will be ineffective.

Scottish lawyers have argued that Parliament was not born unfree and that there are restrictions on its legislative freedom. In *MacCormick* v. *Lord Advocate* [1953] SC 396, Lord Cooper had stated '[t]he principle of the unlimited sovereignty of Parliament is a distinctively English principle which has no counterpart in Scottish constitutional law'. His Lordship did not rule on whether the Act of Union could bind Parliament, but it is interesting to question whether we should assume that English constitutional principles, rather than Scottish ones, should apply as of right to a new British Parliament.

REFLECTION

LIMITATIONS ON THE TRADITIONAL DOCTRINE

1. Membership of the European Union

The United Kingdom joined the European Economic Community (now the European Union) in 1973. As the United Kingdom is a dualist state (that is a state which makes a distinction between national and international law) an Act of Parliament was required to give legal effect to membership of the EEC. The European Communities Act 1972 (ECA) was passed to facilitate the United Kingdom's membership. The UK's membership of the EU opened up possible limitations on Parliamentary Sovereignty and Figure 5.6 sets out other potential areas of conflict.

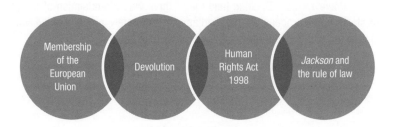

Figure 5.6 Possible limitations on Parliamentary Sovereignty

CORNERSTONE

The European Communities Act 1972

The European Communities Act 1972 is an important statute as it states how domestic courts should apply European Union law.

Section 2, General Implementation of Treaties states:

'(1) All such rights, powers, liabilities, obligations and restrictions from time to time created or arising by or under the Treaties, and all such remedies and procedures from time to time provided for by or under the Treaties, as in accordance with the Treaties are without further enactment to be given legal effect or used in the United Kingdom shall be recognised and available in law, and be enforced, allowed and followed accordingly; and the expression and similar expressions shall be read as referring to one to which this subsection applies. Similar expressions shall be read as referring to one to which this subsection applies.

'(4) The provision that may be made under subsection (2) . . . includes, subject to Schedule 2 to this Act, any such provision (of any such extent) as might be made by Act of Parliament, and any enactment passed or to be passed, other than one contained in this part of this Act, shall be construed and have effect subject to the foregoing provisions of this section; but, except as may be provided by any Act passed after this Act.'

The European Union now has twenty-eight member states and has ever increasing competence to legislate over new areas. The Court of Justice of the European Union (the CJEU) formerly the European Court of Justice (the ECJ) is the highest court and is tasked with ensuring compliance, enforcement and the uniformity of European law. The CJEU will ensure that individuals can enforce their rights under European law and that member states meet their obligations.

It was the ECJ and not a Treaty that established that where the European Union has competence, that it will be European law and not national law that will be supreme. Where there is a conflict between the two then it will be European law that must be applied (see the decisions in *Van Gend en Loos* v. *Nederlandse Administratie der Belastingen* (26/62) [1963] ECR 1 and *Costa* v. *ENEL* (6/64) [1964] ECR 585). This has led to conflict with the constitutional courts in other member states.

The position prior to *Factortame (No.2)*

In *McCarthys Ltd* v. *Smith* [1979] 1 WLR 1189 Lord Denning MR held that it was the duty of the national court to give priority to European law where the national law was inconsistent. Lord Denning stated that in doing this the courts were having regard to Parliament's intentions under section 2(1) and (4) ECA 1972. However, Lord Denning held that if there was a repudiation of the ECA 1972, or express inconsistency with European law (i.e. Parliament deliberately intended to legislate contrary to European law) then the courts were under a duty to apply national law.

The controversial decision in *Factortame (No.2)*

CORNERSTONE

R v. Secretary of State for Transport ex p. Factortame Ltd (No.2) **[1991] 1 AC 603**

The decision in *Factortame Ltd (No.2)* has been regarded as limiting Parliamentary Sovereignty. The decision concerned Spanish fishermen who sought to exploit the fishing quota that had been granted to British fisherman by the EEC (see Figure 5.7). The fishermen established a company that was registered in the United Kingdom. The company was majority owned by the Spanish fishermen and had a fleet of 95 vessels. The UK government enacted the Merchant Shipping Act 1988 to prevent the fishermen from exploiting the quota.

The Merchant Shipping Act 1988 imposed conditions and the 95 vessels failed these since they were owned by a majority of Spanish nationals and were controlled by Spanish nationals. The Act required that at least 75 per cent of the ownership of the company's shares and its directors had to be British. The fisherman alleged that the Act contravened their EEC rights, which were given effect in English law by the European Communities Act 1972.

The case reached the House of Lords. In *R v. Secretary of State for Transport ex p. Factortame Ltd (No.1)* [1990] 2 AC 85 the House was asked by the fishermen to grant interim relief. This was whilst

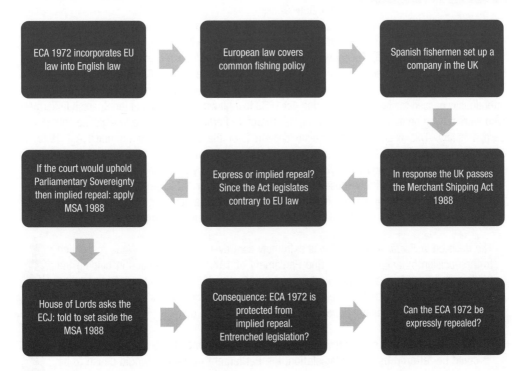

Figure 5.7 The decision in *Factortame (No.2)*

a decision of the ECJ was pending on the matter. The House ruled that it could not grant interim relief, as this would mean overturning an Act of Parliament. According to Lord Bridge:

> 'The effect of the interim relief granted would be to have conferred upon them rights directly contrary to Parliament's sovereign will and correspondingly to have deprived British fishing vessels, as defined by Parliament, of the enjoyment of a substantial proportion of the United Kingdom quota of stocks of fish protected by the common fisheries policy. I am clearly of the opinion that, as a matter of English law, the court has no power to make an order which has these consequences' (pp. 142–143).

Take note

In *Factortame (No.2)* Lord Bridge viewed any limitation on Parliamentary Sovereignty as voluntary. This was because Parliament understood that EU law was supreme and the 1972 Act gave effect to this. The courts were following the instructions of Parliament when giving supremacy to EU law.

The House asked the ECJ by way of preliminary reference whether it must set aside the Act. The ECJ ruled that the Act must be set aside, because it was the only obstacle to granting interim relief (*R* v. *Secretary of State for Transport ex p. Factortame Ltd and Others* (C-213/89) [1991] 1 All ER 70). The House of Lords ruled in *Factortame (No.2)* that section 2 of the European Communities Act 1972 gave the court the authority to disapply an Act of Parliament. Lord Bridge noted that Parliament in 1972 had accepted that European law was supreme over national law, 'whatever limitation of its sovereignty Parliament accepted when it enacted the European Communities Act 1972 was entirely voluntary'. The Act made it clear that 'the duty of a United Kingdom court, when delivering final judgment, to override any rule of national law found to be in conflict with any directly enforceable rule of Community law' (pp. 658–9).

Lord Bridge justified the House of Lords' decision by reference to Parliament enacting the European Communities Act 1972. It is important to note that if there was a limitation of sovereignty, then it was Parliament that had ordered the courts to give supremacy to European Union law (where it had competence). His Lordship specifically referred to the jurisprudence of the ECJ which (as stated above) has consistently held European law to be supreme. The decision was controversial. Parliament had intentionally passed the Merchant Shipping Act 1988 to deal with the actions of the Spanish fishermen who were relying on their European law rights. Therefore Parliament intended to legislate contrary to European law. This was inconsistent with section 2 of the European Communities Act 1972. If Parliament was sovereign then the House of Lords must apply the doctrine of implied repeal. In that case the House of Lords, no matter what answer the ECJ gave by way of preliminary reference, must apply the later Act. Instead the House of Lords applied the older Act to set aside the newer Act. The ECA 1972 appears to be protected from implied repeal. This is novel and therefore the Act would appear to have been entrenched and is *the* exception to the doctrine of implied repeal.

REFLECTION

The decision in *Factortame (No.2)* was extremely controversial. Professor Wade responded to the decision by asserting that '[t]he Parliament of 1972 had succeeded in binding the Parliament of 1988 and restricting its sovereignty, something that was supposed to be constitutionally impossible' (Wade, 1996). This was, Professor Wade stated, 'at least in a technical sense . . . a constitutional revolution'. Wade argued that:

> 'It is obvious that sovereignty belongs to the Parliament of the day and that, if it could be fettered by earlier legislation, the Parliament of the day would cease to be sovereign . . . Nothing in Lord Bridge's language suggests that he regarded the issue

as one of statutory construction. He takes it for granted that Parliament can "accept" a limitation of its sovereignty which will be effective both for the present and for the future. It is a statement which could hardly be clearer: Parliament can bind its successors. If that is not revolutionary, constitutional lawyers are Dutchmen'.

Professor Wade regarded this as a political rather than legal revolution brought about by membership of a new political order which is the European Union. It is the courts and Parliament which can change this rule of recognition and decide whether a future Parliament can be fettered. It is clear that Wade believes that the judges are able to adapt Parliamentary sovereignty to deal with a new political reality. Wade viewed the decision as a legal revolution. The recognition of legal sovereignty is 'a political fact which the judges themselves are able to change when they are confronted with a new situation which so demands'.

Responding to Wade's article, Professor TRS Allan questioned the argument that *Factortame (No.2)* had brought about a legal revolution and that the 1972 Act had bound newer Acts of Parliament ('Parliamentary sovereignty: law, politics, and revolution' [1997] *Law Quarterly Review* 443). Allan observed that Wade had rejected as implausible the argument that 'the 1972 Act creates only a *rule of construction* for subsequent statutes, requiring such statutes to be read as compatible with rights arising under European Community law in the absence of express words to the contrary'. Allan questions whether Parliamentary Sovereignty is a matter for the judges, i.e. legal, as opposed to politicians, i.e. political. Allan remarked that to '[t]alk of revolution falsely implies that the courts' role is merely to accept, on grounds of expediency, whatever the politicians decide'.

What does this mean? It can be argued that *Factortame (No.2)* was based on political expediency. The House of Lords had no choice other than to follow the 1972 Act whilst (i) the United Kingdom was a member of the European Union and (ii) unless the 1972 Act was expressly repealed. Putting aside academic arguments, Allan stated that '[f]or all practical purposes . . . it is certainly true that the sovereignty of Parliament has been curtailed during continued membership of the European Community.'

Can the common law modify Parliamentary Sovereignty to restrict implied repeal and as a consequence protect constitutional statutes?

It would appear that one Parliament can be bound by a decision of a previous Act of Parliament. However, the only decision which supports this is *Factortame (No.2)* and the ECA 1972 is the only Act which is protected from implied repeal.

The decision in *Thoburn* v. *Sunderland City Council* [2002] EWHC 195 involved the so-called Metric Martyrs, who were convicted of breaking the law by selling goods in imperial weights rather than by metric. The sellers were obliged by law to indicate the price of the food per kilogram; however their machines were not calibrated to do this.

Laws LJ dismissed the sellers' appeal. However, Laws LJ's *obiter* statements concerning Parliamentary Sovereignty after *Factortame (No.2)* were interesting. Laws LJ's stated that Parliament cannot bind its successors by restricting implied repeal or express repeal. This is because the law will not allow them to do it. Neither can the European Union bind future Parliaments. Parliament is unable to abandon its legal sovereignty. Laws LJ stated that Parliamentary Sovereignty was still controlled by the United Kingdom, but it was not the politicians but rather the common law which can modify it. It is the common law that has created the exceptions to implied repeal and can decide whether an Act has succeeded in binding future Parliaments. Addressing the problems created by membership of the European Union, the courts have resolved the problem by creating two supremacies, that of Parliament and the European law where it has competence. Laws LJ took the view that the decision in *Factortame (No.2)* demonstrates that, '[t]he conditions of Parliament's legislative supremacy in the United Kingdom necessarily remain in the United Kingdom's hands. But the traditional doctrine has in my judgment been modified. It has been done by the common law, wholly consistently with constitutional principle.' Laws LJ noted that 'Parliament cannot bind its successors by stipulating against repeal, wholly or partly, of the 1972 Act. It cannot stipulate as to the manner and form of any subsequent legislation. It cannot stipulate against implied repeal any more than it can stipulate against express repeal.'

His Lordship clearly regarded the decision in *Factortame (No.2)* as holding that section 2(4) cannot be impliedly repealed. What is interesting is that Laws LJ extends the effect of the decision, by stating that where the common law recognises rights as constitutional or fundamental then implied repealed could be modified to protect Acts which are of a constitutional significance. This is a bold statement. Firstly, according to Parliamentary Sovereignty all Acts are the same and should be capable of being impliedly repealed by a later Act; secondly, there is no special status of constitutional law in the United Kingdom; and thirdly, the common law cannot impose limitations on Parliament's legislative ability. Therefore Laws LJ's *obiter* comments are a radical reconsideration of the traditional doctrine of Parliamentary Sovereignty.

CORNERSTONE

Constitutional statutes and *Thoburn* v. *Sunderland City Council* [2002] EWHC 195

Laws LJ in *Thoburn* v. *Sunderland City Council* [2002] EWHC 195 was of the opinion that constitutional statutes should be protected from implied repeal:

> 'In the present state of its maturity the common law has come to recognise that there exist rights which should properly be classified as constitutional or fundamental and from this a further insight follows. We should recognise a hierarchy of Acts of Parliament: as it were "ordinary" statutes and "constitutional" statutes. The two categories must be distinguished on a principled basis. In my opinion a constitutional statute is one which (a) conditions the legal relationship between citizen and state in some general, overarching manner, or (b) enlarges or diminishes the scope of what we would now regard as fundamental constitutional rights . . . Ordinary statutes may be impliedly repealed. Constitutional statutes may not . . . A constitutional statute can only be repealed, or amended in a way which significantly affects its provisions touching fundamental rights or otherwise the relation between citizen and state, by unambiguous words on the face of the later statute . . . (This) preserves the sovereignty of the legislature and the flexibility of our uncodified constitution . . . the courts (in interpreting statutes and, now, applying the Human Rights Act 1998) will pay more or less deference to the legislature, or other public decision-maker, according to the subject in hand.'

Laws LJ observed that, '[t]he common law has in recent years allowed, or rather created, exceptions to the doctrine of implied repeal, a doctrine which was always the common law's own creature.' Laws LJ acknowledges that Parliament could expressly repeal an Act that was protected by implied repeal. This can be seen as common law constitutionalism. It must be restated that Laws LJ's distinction between normal and constitutional legislation is *obiter* and is not binding.

INTERSECTION

> Please refer to Chapter 2 for a discussion on what is meant by a constitutional statute.

Has Parliament voluntarily surrendered part of its sovereignty?

Lord Justice Laws argued that Parliament cannot surrender its sovereignty; the only limitations can be imposed by the common law. In *Jackson* Baroness Hale stated that 'Parliament has . . . for the time being at least, limited its own powers by the European Communities Act 1972'. Lord Neuberger writing extra-judicially has argued that, '[w]hen the courts scrutinise the validity of Acts of Parliament, and refuse to apply them where they are in conflict with European Union law, as happened in *Factortame (No.2)*, they do not so in the teeth of Parliament. They do so precisely because that is what Parliament has chosen to give the courts the power to do.' His Lordship said that the decision was not 'a refutation of Parliamentary sovereignty: on the contrary, it is an instance of its operation'.

Could Parliament expressly repeal the European Communities Act 1972?

Parliament could expressly repeal the European Communities Act 1972. This, however, is a legal question. We know that membership of the European Union is controversial, e.g. intra-party divisions within the Conservative Party over membership in the early 1990s and 2010s. Many politicians, lawyers and members of the public favour leaving or renegotiating the United Kingdom's membership. There would be political, economic and diplomatic problems in leaving the European Union as it is one of the United Kingdom's largest trading partners. The Prime Minister, David Cameron, has promised that if the Conservatives win the next General Election, there will be a referendum on the future of the United Kingdom's membership of the European Union. In 2013 a private members' bill was introduced and if enacted there will be a legal requirement to hold such a referendum by 2017 at the latest.

It could be argued that membership of the European Union has affected sovereignty, as although Parliament may have voluntarily surrendered its sovereignty, the European Union will have increased competence over many new areas. Therefore, sovereignty for practical purposes may be regarded as having been permanently surrendered.

Referendum requirement before the UK ratifies a new EU Treaty

The European Union Act 2011 (EUA 2011) states that there must be a national referendum before the United Kingdom ratifies a new treaty replacing the existing European treaties (s.2 EUA 2011). Whilst the EUA 2011 is on the statute book there is a legal requirement that a referendum is held. However, in the future could the referendum requirement become entrenched with the courts requiring any future Parliament to comply with its provisions? If so, this would protect the referendum requirement from both express and implied repeal.

2. Devolution Acts 1998

CORNERSTONE

Devolution

When legislative powers have been transferred from the national Parliament and given to a regional legislative assembly this is referred to as devolution. The Labour government wanted to devolve power from Westminster and to allow the regions have a say over local issues.

The Devolution Acts 1998 refer to the Scotland Act 1998, the Government of Wales Act 1998 and the Northern Ireland Act 1998. These acts created the Scottish Parliament and the National Assembly of Wales. Additionally, powers were returned to Northern Ireland and the Northern Ireland Assembly was re-established (see Figure 5.8).

Not all legislative powers have been transferred, as otherwise the United Kingdom would cease to function if different laws applied to key areas of national life, such as the economy, foreign affairs and defence. The United Kingdom remains a unitary state as power is devolved from Westminster and could be revoked. However, in reality devolution has created more of a quasi-unitary system, with the appearance of an increasingly federal structure.

However, the reforms in 1998 and 2006 allowed the Scottish Parliament and National Assembly of Wales to legislate over a certain number of areas. Despite being able to create legislation, these new

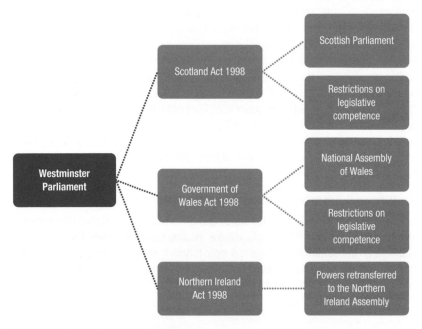

Figure 5.8 Devolution in the United Kingdom

legislative bodies cannot legislate where they have no competence to do so as the Westminster Parliament has restricted their legislative capability. Brigid Hadfield noted that:

'Devolution has been presented by successive Labour Governments in terms of the needs to preserve the union, on the one hand, and, on the other, to enhance accountability, responsiveness, inclusiveness and transparency as reflected in new forms of governance for the devolved nation' ('Devolution and the changing constitution: evolution in Wales and the unanswered English question' in Jowell J. and Oliver D. (eds) *The Changing Constitution* 6th edn (Oxford University Press: Oxford, 2007), p. 272).

Scotland Act 1998

Section 1 of the Scotland Act 1998 created the Scottish Parliament, which sits at Holyrood. Section 28 concerns legislation passed by the Scottish Parliament which are known as Acts of the Scottish Parliament. As with Acts of the Westminster Parliament, section 28(5) states that, '[t]he validity of an Act of the Scottish Parliament is not affected by any invalidity in the proceedings of the Parliament leading to its enactment.' Crucially, Section 28(7) states that, '[t]his section does not affect the power of the Parliament of the United Kingdom to make laws for Scotland.'

Section 29(1) clearly states that, '[a]n Act of the Scottish Parliament is not law so far as any provision of the Act is outside the legislative competence of the Parliament.' If an Act of the Scottish Parliament legislates for section 29(1)(b) reserved matters, or breaches the restrictions in schedule 4 (s.20(1)(c)), or importantly is 'incompatible with any of the Convention rights or with Community law' (s.29(1)(d)), then the Act will be invalid. As we shall see below, unlike an Act of the Westminster Parliament, the Scottish Parliament cannot legislate contrary to the Convention rights which are incorporated into domestic law by the Human Rights Act 1998. The task of reviewing Scottish legislation will fall to the courts.

> **Take note**
>
> An Act of the Scottish Parliament is not legally sovereign. The Scottish Parliament can only legislate where Westminster holds that it has competence to do so. The Westminster Parliament could still legislate for areas where the Scottish Parliament has been given competence.

The courts can judicially review an Act of the Scottish Parliament. This means that unlike Acts of the Westminster Parliament, which cannot be reviewed, the courts can declare the Acts illegal (*ultra vires*). Although as Craig and Walters have observed, there is authority that Acts of the Scottish Parliament cannot be judicially reviewed on the grounds of irrationality ('The courts, devolution and judicial review' [1999] *Public Law* 274).

As with Westminster, the party with a majority in the Scottish Parliament will form a government (although there have been coalition governments). Barry Winetrobe observed that the United Kingdom government wanted the Scottish government to be based on the Westminster model, and that 'the relationship between the Scottish Executive and the Scottish Parliament will be similar to the relationship between the UK Government and the UK Parliament' ('Scottish devolution: developing practice in multi-layered governance' in Jowell J. and Oliver D. (eds) *The Changing Constitution* 6th edn (Oxford University Press: Oxford, 2007), p. 213).

What effect does Scottish devolution have on Parliamentary Sovereignty? Parliament is still the superior law-making body in the United Kingdom. The Scotland Act 1998 does not prevent Parliament from legislating for Scotland. Even if it did, Parliament could still expressly repeal the Act at a later date. There is a convention established known as the Sewel Motion, which states that the Westminster Parliament would not legislate for devolved matters. Would Parliament legislate contrary to the

Scotland Act 1998? This not a legal question but rather a political one. The consequence of such legislation might ultimately result in Scottish independence. If there were to be a violation of the powers devolved to Scotland, then this would lead to calls for a second referendum to be held on Scottish independence. Any government will be wary of introducing legislation that would seek to legislate for devolved matters.

Professor McEldowney has observed that '[t]he legal sovereignty of the UK Parliament has not been diminished by devolution, but democratically and politically the devolved institutions have rival and strong claims to legitimacy within their areas and these affect the politics of UK parliamentary sovereignty' ('The Impact of Devolution on the UK Parliament', in Horne, A., Drewry, G. and Oliver, D. *Parliament and the Law* (Hart Publishing: Oxford, 2013), p. 219). Therefore, whilst Scotland remains part of the United Kingdom this will lead to more powers being devolved to Holyrood from Westminster.

The Scottish National Party is currently in government in Scotland. The SNP won an overwhelming majority in the elections for the Scottish Parliament and argued that they had secured a mandate for holding a referendum on Scottish independence. The referendum took place on 18 September 2014 and asked '[s]hould Scotland be an independent country?' For the first time, young adults aged between 16–17 were permitted to vote.

If there had been a 'yes' vote, legally it would have been the Westminster Parliament which would have had to give Scotland its independence. This would have been achieved by repealing the Act of Union with Scotland.

The Scotland Act 1998 reserves all constitutional matters to the Westminster Parliament. Therefore, the Scottish government and Scottish Parliament, as devolved bodies, would be acting illegally if they attempted to hold their own referendum. If Scotland had pressed ahead and held a referendum and subsequently declared unilateral independence, then this would be legally ineffective. However, this would demonstrate a practical limit to the sovereignty of the Westminster Parliament. In order to hold a referendum there needed to be an agreement between the British and Scottish governments. This is known as the Edinburgh Agreement and increased the legislative competence of the Scottish Parliament to hold a referendum (see s.30 Scotland Act 1998). However, the only way Scotland can receive its independence is through an Act of Parliament.

Government of Wales Acts 1998 and 2006

The Government of Wales Act 1998 created the National Assembly of Wales. The National Assembly of Wales sits in Cardiff and the party who can command the support of the Assembly will form a government. The Government of Wales Act 2006 devolved more powers to the Assembly. According to section 81 the Assembly cannot legislate contrary to Convention rights, which are now incorporated under the Human Rights Act 1998. Similarly, section 82 reiterates this restriction with regards to international obligations (such as international law). Therefore the National Assembly of Wales is not a sovereign legislative body. The Government of Wales Acts have not legally restricted Parliamentary Sovereignty, but rather have placed political restrictions on areas that Parliament can legislate on.

Northern Ireland Act 1998

The Northern Ireland Assembly is based at Stormont and is not based on the Westminster model. The parties are required to share power, rather than the largest party forming a government. During the troubles in Northern Ireland the powers of the Assembly were revoked and the province was ruled from Westminster. Powers were devolved in 1998 as a result of the Good Friday peace agreement that brought the troubles to a close.

3. Human Rights Act 1998

CORNERSTONE

Human Rights Act 1998

On 10 October 2000 the Human Rights Act 1998 (HRA 1998) came into force. It had the effect of directly incorporating most of the European Convention on Human Rights (ECHR) into English law. The HRA 1998 allows Convention rights to be directly enforced by domestic courts where there has been a breach of these rights by a public authority (s.6 HRA 1998).

Prior to 2000, Convention rights were not enforceable in domestic courts and British citizens had to take their case to the European Court of Human Rights (ECtHR), which is based at Strasbourg. If the party were successful at Strasbourg the United Kingdom would be under an obligation to pay damages.

INTERSECTION

For more details on the HRA 1998 and the ECHR please refer to Chapter 10.

The rights contained in the ECHR are very important. The HRA 1998 is an important statute. Does the HRA 1998 restrict Parliamentary Sovereignty? The HRA 1998 was never intended to limit Parliamentary Sovereignty. Unlike the fundamental rights protected by the Canadian constitution (see the Canadian Charter of Rights and Freedoms), the domestic courts do not have the power to strike down or dissapply an Act of Parliament which is held to be incompatible with the HRA 1998. Laws LJ in *Thoburn* had argued that the HRA 1998 should be a constitutional statute which is protected from implied repeal.

If the intention of Parliament was that the HRA 1998 would not limit Parliamentary Sovereignty, then does the effect of the Act in practice impose any limitation? To answer this we need to consider sections 3 and 4 of the HRA 1998.

CORNERSTONE

The interpretation of legislation – section 3, Human Rights Act 1998

Section 3 concerns the interpretation of legislation and gives courts the following instruction: '[s]o far as it is possible to do so, primary legislation and subordinate legislation must be read and given effect in a way which is compatible with the Convention rights.'

Section 3 gives the courts extremely wide interpretive powers to read primary legislation as though it were Convention compliant. This means that the courts can read words into a statute to give effect to Convention rights. This interpretive power is novel (with the exception of ECA 1972) in domestic law and the courts can go beyond the words used by Parliament when it passes an Act. Section 3 'does not affect the validity, continuing operation or enforcement of any incompatible primary legislation', which means that the Act will remain unchanged and it is still valid. The courts can question an Act of Parliament and have considerable scope to amend the effect of an Act.

The use of section 3 raises the problem of judges becoming lawmakers and reading down words into a statute that are contrary to what Parliament intended. The use of section 3 has proved to be controversial in practice. Alison Young questions whether Parliament, as a result of section 3, has given the courts considerable power to restrict Parliamentary Sovereignty:

'Section 3(1) appears to limit the powers of the court, allowing them to interpret statutes in a manner compatible with Convention rights only when it is possible to do so. However, in practice, Parliament has given the judiciary carte blanche to determine when it is impossible to interpret statutes in a manner compatible with Convention rights. The express words of section 3(1) are so vague that they do not provide a clear outline of the limits of possibility . . . Moreover, it raises issues as to the reality of parliamentary supremacy, particularly when delineating the respective roles of the judiciary and the legislature. How can the judiciary respect Parliament's intention with regard to its role under section 3(1) of the Act, if Parliament has made its intentions so unclear as to place the court fully in charge of delineating its own power? Parliamentary sovereignty has given way to judicial sovereignty' (Young 2002, p. 53).

The courts need to ascertain the intention of Parliament and ensure that its interpretation of statutes respects this. Section 3 requires the courts to look for the key intention of Parliament, and not just the natural and ordinary meaning of the words used. Sir Philip Sales explained this approach:

'[t]he limit of the interpretative obligation is whether it is "possible" to construe the domestic legislation compatibly with . . . Convention rights . . . It will not be "possible" to construe domestic legislation in this way if to do so would distort or undermine some important feature of the legislation. Parliamentary sovereignty is thus preserved, but in a somewhat attenuated sense . . . The application of the relevant test calls for a value judgment on the part of the court, to assess whether Parliament has expressed some sort of fundamental intention in the legislation which it must be presumed from the scheme of the legislation and the language it has used it would not have been willing to sacrifice if confronted at the time with objections based on . . . Convention rights. Since the court is required not to confine itself to determining the intention of Parliament simply from the words used and the usual canons of construction, but has to try to assess whether the intention derived from the words of the legislation is of an essential character or not, this is not a straightforward exercise. In effect, the courts have to examine whether some departure from what has hitherto been regarded as the natural meaning of the statute is justified, having regard to the general objective of producing compatibility with Convention rights set by s.3 of the HRA, but balancing that objective against the general long-stop preservation of parliamentary sovereignty inherent in the HRA: can a compatible construction be produced without generating excessive friction or dissonance in terms of the Parliamentary intent to be derived from the words of the legislation to be construed?' (Sales 2009, p. 598).

CORNERSTONE

R v. A (Complainant's Sexual History) [2001] UKHL 25

One of the most controversial uses of section 3 to read down words into a statute was in *R* v. *A*. This case concerned whether the defendant in a rape trial could adduce evidence as to the victim's sexual history. Section 41 of the Youth Justice and Criminal Evidence Act 1999 stated that the defendant was unable to do this unless the court could rely on one of the three narrow exceptions. Parliament had intended to restrict the discretion of the trial judge in controlling when such evidence was admissible.

In *R* v. *A (Complainant's Sexual History)* the House of Lords held that section 41 of the Youth Justice and Criminal Evidence Act 1999 breached Article 6 of the ECHR and deprived the defendant of a fair trial. The House of Lords used section 3 to read down words and interpreted section 41 to allow evidence of the victim's previous sexual history to be admitted.

Aileen Kavanagh contrasted the supposedly different approaches of Lord Hope and Lord Steyn and has argued that the academic criticism ignores the fact that the House of Lords' decision to rely on section 3 was unanimous (Kavanagh 2005, p. 259). In *R* v. *A* it was Lord Steyn's judgment that was the most controversial. As Kavanagh argued, 'Lord Steyn was clear at the outset of his judgment in *A* that the interpretative obligation under s.3 is a strong one, which applies even if there is no ambiguity in the language. This point is uncontroversial. It was endorsed by Lord Hope in *R*. v. *A*, and has been followed in subsequent decisions of the House of Lords and supported by many of the senior judiciary.' What was more controversial was when His Lordship stated that, '[i]n accordance with the will of Parliament as reflected in s.3 it will sometimes be necessary to adopt an interpretation which linguistically may appear strained. The techniques to be used will not only involve the reading down of express language in a statute but also the implication of provisions.' According to Kavanagh this meant that judges could go beyond the text of the statute as the 'primary source of interpretation':

> 'The most prominent reason given by critics of *A* for its illegitimacy is that it went against what Parliament intended when they enacted s.41 YJCEA . . . There is no denying that the interpretation in *A* is contrary to Parliament's intention to control the admissibility of sexual history evidence by way of the narrowly circumscribed gateways alone. Parliament decided against the "safety valve approach" which would allow judges a residual discretion to admit evidence it would be unsafe to exclude, and the judges nonetheless read this discretion into the legislation. Does this render the decision in *R*. v. *A* illegitimate?'

In *Re S, Re W (Minors)* [2002] UKHL 10, Lord Nicholls held that the Court of Appeal had overstepped a constitutional boundary and had disregarded the intention of Parliament. The Court of Appeal had used section 3 to read words into section 31 of the Children Act 1989 in order to make the provision Convention compliant. His Lordship stated that the courts should not ignore Parliament's intention and observed that, 'a meaning which departs substantially from a fundamental feature of an Act of Parliament is likely to have crossed the boundary between interpretation and amendment' (at [40]). Lord Nicholls held that the courts had to have regard to the fundamental purpose of the Act. If the court's interpretation of the statute is different than what Parliament had intended, then the courts will have overstepped the mark, by having used section 3 to amend rather than to interpret the legislation.

His Lordship's approach allows the court to interpret an Act to give the victim a remedy, whilst still upholding the doctrine of Parliamentary Sovereignty.

Lord Nicholls in *Re S, Re W (Minors)* [2002] UKHL 10 had observed:

> 'But the reach of this tool is not unlimited. Section 3 is concerned with interpretation . . . In applying section 3 courts must be ever mindful of this outer limit. The Human Rights Act reserves the amendment of primary legislation to Parliament. By this means the Act seeks to preserve parliamentary sovereignty. The Act maintains the constitutional boundary. Interpretation of statutes is a matter for the courts; the enactment of statutes, and the amendment of statutes, are matters for Parliament' (at [38]–[39]).

The decision in *Ghaidan* v. *Godin-Mendoza* [2004] UKHL 30 concerned whether a homosexual partner fell within the protection afforded by the Rent Act 1977. The defendant's partner had died and he wanted to become a protected assured tenant, which protected 'spouses' in the event of a tenant's death. Did a homosexual partner fall within the definition of spouse? The House of Lords relied on section 3 and interpreted spouse to include homosexual partners. Lord Steyn defended his approach to section 3. His Lordship stated that, '[i]f Parliament disagrees with an interpretation by the courts under section 3(1), it is free to override it by amending the legislation and expressly reinstating the incompatibility.' His Lordship stated that if the Convention rights were to be 'brought home' then UK citizens would need to be able to rely on the courts using section 3, as opposed to section 4.

CORNERSTONE

Should judges use section 3 or section 4 of the Human Rights Act 1998?

In *Ghaidan* v. *Godin-Mendoza* [2004] UKHL 30 Lord Steyn had observed that:

> 'In enacting the 1998 Act Parliament legislated "to bring rights home" from the European Court of Human Rights to be determined in the courts of the United Kingdom . . . That is what Parliament was told. The mischief to be addressed was the fact that Convention rights as set out in the ECHR, which Britain ratified in 1951, could not be vindicated in our courts. Critical to this purpose was the enactment of effective remedial provisions . . . The linch-pin of the legislative scheme to achieve this purpose was section 3(1). Rights could only be effectively brought home if section 3(1) was the prime remedial measure, and section 4 a measure of last resort' (at [42] and [46]).

Where it is not possible to use section 3 to give effect to Convention rights, a court (from the High Court to the Supreme Court) may instead issue a section 4 declaration of incompatibility. A declaration of incompatibility declares to Parliament that the Act violates a Convention right. The courts cannot declare the Act to be invalid and it remains good law. The courts have no power to strike down incompatible legislation. The person whose rights have been violated will not usually have a remedy if the courts are unable to use section 3 and instead issue a section 4 declaration of incompatibility. It is for this reason that Lord Steyn preferred the use of section 3 rather than section 4.

The decision in *R (Jackson)* v. *Attorney-General* [2005] UKHL 56

We have previously discussed the background to the House of Lords decision in *Jackson*. In reaching their decision the members of the House of Lords made some very interesting *obiter* comments on Parliamentary Sovereignty. Lord Bingham reiterated that:

> 'The bedrock of the British constitution is, and in 1911 was, the supremacy of the Crown in Parliament . . . Then, as now, the Crown in Parliament was unconstrained by any entrenched or codified constitution. It could make or unmake any law it wished. Statutes, formally enacted as Acts of Parliament, properly interpreted, enjoyed the highest legal authority' (at [9]).

This is clearly the traditional view of the doctrine. However, there were other very different views expressed (see Figure 5.9).

The potential validity of a manner and form requirement

Lord Steyn challenged the traditional doctrine of Parliamentary Sovereignty. His Lordship did so in a number of ways. According to the traditional doctrine, Parliament is not bound by manner and form, which means that an Act which established special procedural or voting requirements to repeal it,

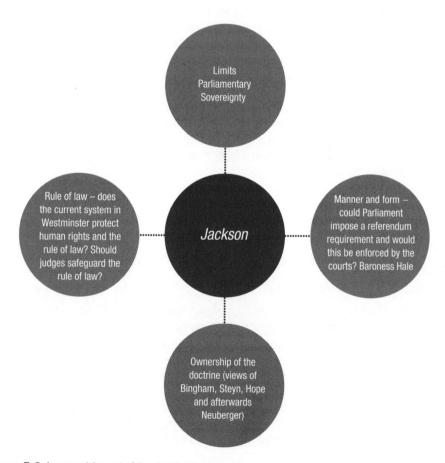

Figure 5.9 Issues arising out of the decision in *Jackson*

could not prevent these requirements from being ignored at a later date. However, Lord Steyn stated that:

'Apart from the traditional method of law making, Parliament acting as ordinarily constituted may functionally redistribute legislative power in different ways. For example, Parliament could for specific purposes provide for a two-thirds majority in the House of Commons and the House of Lords. This would involve a redefinition of Parliament for a specific purpose. Such redefinition could not be disregarded' (at [81]).

This is important as His Lordship is suggesting that a manner and form requirement could bind future Parliaments and that the courts would not disregard such requirements when enquiring into the validity of a future Act. Lord Steyn referred to an article written by Owen Dixon in 1935:

'The very power of constitutional alteration cannot be exercised except in the form and manner which the law for the time being prescribes. Unless the legislature observes that manner and form, its attempt to alter its constitution is void. It may amend or abrogate for the future the law which prescribes that form or that manner. But, in doing so, it must comply with its very requirements.' ('The Law and the Constitution' [1935] 51 *Law Quarterly* 590 at 601)

His Lordship referred to *Attorney General for New South Wales* v. *Trethowan* (1931) 44 CLR 394, where the court had ruled that as legislation required a referendum to abolish the Upper House of the New South Wales Parliament, any Act purporting to do this without having first held a referendum would be invalid. Lord Steyn referred to *Harris* v. *Minister of the Interior* [1952] (2) SA 428 (AD) which was a South African decision. The voting rights of non-white nationals in South Africa were protected by a requirement that any changes to the legislation required a two-thirds majority. The court found that an Act that did not fulfil the requirement was void. It is clear that His Lordship is showing that in other common law jurisdictions manner and form requirements have been held to be effective.

Baroness Hale argued that if Parliament could remove the requirement for the consent of the House of Lords, then a binding manner and form requirement could be possible. If that were so, then a court could require Parliament to comply with such a requirement. However, Her Ladyship does not attempt to provide a definitive answer.

CORNERSTONE

Would a referendum requirement ever be enforceable?

Baroness Hale had observed in *Jackson* at [163]:

'What the Commonwealth cases do suggest, however, is the contrary proposition: that if Parliament is required to pass legislation on particular matters in a particular way, then Parliament is not permitted to ignore those requirements when passing legislation on those matters, nor is it permitted to remove or relax those requirements by passing legislation in the ordinary way . . . If the sovereign Parliament can redefine itself downwards, to remove or modify the requirement for the consent of the Upper House, it may very well be that it can also redefine itself upwards, to require a particular parliamentary majority or a popular referendum for particular types of measure. In each case, the courts would be respecting the will of the sovereign Parliament as constituted when that will had been expressed. But that is for another day.'

Parliamentary Sovereignty is not absolute

Lord Steyn observed that Parliamentary Sovereignty was the general principle of the United Kingdom's constitution, but rejected the view that it was absolute and without restriction. His Lordship believed that the courts can qualify Parliamentary Sovereignty and could potentially declare an Act void. Importantly, His Lordship viewed the doctrine as a common law construct – one that is a common law rule. The consequence of this is important, as if we follow His Lordship's interpretation, then the courts could legitimately modify their own rule. Lord Steyn did not accept that there could be no qualifications on Parliament's legislative sovereignty:

> 'The classic account given by Dicey of the doctrine of the supremacy of Parliament, pure and absolute as it was, can now be seen to be out of place in the modern United Kingdom. Nevertheless, the supremacy of Parliament is still the *general* principle of our constitution. It is a construct of the common law. The judges created this principle. If that is so, it is not unthinkable that circumstances could arise where the courts may have to qualify a principle established on a different hypothesis of constitutionalism. In exceptional circumstances involving an attempt to abolish judicial review or the ordinary role of the courts, the . . . new Supreme Court may have to consider whether this is constitutional fundamental which even a sovereign Parliament acting at the behest of a complaisant House of Commons cannot abolish' (at [102]).

Lord Hope agreed with Lord Steyn and observed that:

> 'Our constitution is dominated by the sovereignty of Parliament. But Parliamentary sovereignty is no longer, if it ever was, absolute . . . It is no longer right to say that its freedom to legislate admits of no qualification whatever. Step by step, gradually but surely, the English principle of absolute legislative sovereignty of Parliament which Dicey derived from Coke and Blackstone is being qualified (at [104]).

His Lordship is describing an incremental process where Parliamentary Sovereignty is being reconsidered and will evolve over time.

The importance of the rule of law

Lord Hope stated that:

> 'The rule of law enforced by the courts is the ultimate controlling factor on which our constitution is based. The fact that your Lordships have been willing to hear this appeal and to give judgment upon it is another indication that the courts have a part to play in defining the limits of Parliament's legislative sovereignty' (at [107]).

Observance of the rule of law may appear to be at odds with the unqualified supremacy of Parliament. This is because the Parliament could legislate contrary to what is required by both the procedural and substantive versions of the rule of law. This raises the possibility that the Supreme Court in the future might be asked to choose between the two.

Putting *Jackson* into context

Lord Carswell struck a note of caution in *Jackson* and observed that:

> 'As a judge I am very conscious of the proper reluctance of the courts to intervene in issues of the validity of Acts of Parliament. I should be most unwilling to decide this or any other case in a way which would endanger that tradition of mutual respect' (at [168]).

Lord Neuberger, writing extra-judicially, rejected Lord Steyn's proposition that the courts created Parliamentary Sovereignty:

'I cannot accept the accuracy of the claim that Parliamentary sovereignty is a product of the common law, or that, because common law existed prior to Parliament's 'legislative supremacy' . . . I am not aware of any authority which supports, let alone establishes, the proposition that the common law created Parliamentary sovereignty. Nor am I aware of any significant authority which suggests that the common law can justify the courts lawfully setting aside or invalidating a statute . . . I doubt that Lord Steyn would suggest that that provides much of a foundation for his doubts about Parliamentary sovereignty' (at [42]).

Lord Bingham in his book *The Rule of Law* rejected the idea that the judges established Parliamentary Sovereignty, stating that they have just accepted its existence: '[t]he judges did not by themselves establish the principle, and they cannot, by themselves, change it.' (at p. 267). Lord Hope (2011) writing extra-judicially disagreed with Lord Neuberger's comments on the decision in *Jackson*:

'[Neuberger] concluded that the doctrine of Parliamentary sovereignty remains as it was declared to be by Dicey. Although he recognised that the judges have a vital role to play in protecting individuals against the abuses and excesses of an increasingly powerful executive, he said that we cannot go against Parliament's will as expressed through a statute. That, with respect, seems to be to a dangerous doctrine unless one can be absolutely confident that the increasingly powerful executive will not abuse the legislative authority of a Parliament which, ex hypothesi, it controls because of the absolute majority that it enjoys in the House of Commons.'

Lord Hope was aware that Parliament could choose to legislate contrary to the rule of law.

'The ultimate safeguard against such abuses of the legislative power of Parliament lies in the power of the judges. After all, other countries such as the USA, Canada and Germany believe that rights are better protected when judges, rather than politicians, have the last word. It does no harm to our unwritten constitution for the judges to indicate to the executive arm of government that it should not assume that the sovereignty of Parliament, over which it has control, is entirely unlimited.'

This is a clear warning that the courts could limit the legislative ability of Parliament. Furthermore, Lord Hope remarked that:

'The absence of a general power to strike down legislation which it has enacted does not mean that the courts could never fashion a remedy for use in an exceptional case where the survival of the rule of law itself was threatened because their role as the ultimate guardians of it was being removed from them.'

This indicates that the courts reserve the right to limit Parliamentary Sovereignty should the need arise. Is Lord Hope correct? Could the United Kingdom's Supreme Court declare an Act of Parliament to be invalid on the grounds that it is repugnant to the rule of law, i.e. unconstitutional? Professor Dawn Oliver considered the outcome of a judicial strike down of an Act of Parliament and noted that such action would prove to be counter-productive ('Parliamentary Sovereignty: A Pragmatic or Principled Doctrine?' (2012), available at http://ukconstitutionallaw.org/2012/05/03/dawn-oliver-parliamentary-sovereignty-a-pragmatic-or-principled-doctrine/). Oliver argued that:

'In my view therefore it could well be extremely unwise, damaging to the authority of the judiciary and the rule of law itself and to the stability of our constitutional arrangements, and counter-productive for the courts to strike down a provision in an Act, however much it is contrary to some of the elements of the rule of law and other constitutional "principles".'

Professor Oliver considered Lord Hope's *obiter* in *Jackson* and argued it would be unworkable in practice:

> 'So in my view a "principle" that the rule of law is *the* controlling principle and might entitle courts to disapply statutory provisions – as Lord Hope indicated in *Jackson* – would come up against the typical, pragmatic and wise English response: that is all very well in principle and theory, but what about the practice? The practice of striking down legislation in our unwritten constitution and constitutional culture would not work.'

Would the potential fallout of a judicial strike-down of an Act of Parliament be enough to prevent the Supreme Court from adopting the approach of Lords Hope and Steyn? Arguably, this could depend on the legislation in question and the political and constitutional climate that existed at the time. For example a judicial strike-down of an Act that imposed draconian press regulation would likely be met with considerable media support.

The *obiter* in *Jackson* explored the conflict between Parliamentary Sovereignty and the rule of law. Lord Neuberger observed that 'Professor Bogdanor has, as noted by Lord Bingham, stated that it is "*clear that there is a conflict between the two constitutional principles, the sovereignty of parliament and the rule of law.*" Might this conflict justify or require the courts to place limits on Parliamentary sovereignty?' Lord Neuberger noted that Lord Hope and Baroness Hale appeared to suggest that 'the courts might reject legislation if it contravened' the rule of law. His Lordship noted that there were two types of rule of law, procedural and substantive. It is the substantive version that is problematic since it protects human rights. Lord Neuberger found such a proposition to be problematic, as 'it cannot be the case that any aspect of a statute which is contrary to an aspect of the rule of law to be overruled by the courts'.

If Lord Steyn is correct then the courts could modify Parliamentary Sovereignty to allow limitations. This is very controversial. Goldsworthy considered whether the judges could repudiate Parliamentary Sovereignty. He argued that judges had no grounds for doing this based upon 'a venerable tradition of English law, a golden age of constitutionalism, in which the judiciary enforced limits to the authority of Parliament imposed by common law or natural law. There never was such an age' (*The Sovereignty of Parliament: History and Philosophy* (Oxford University Press: Oxford, 1999), p. 235).

REFLECTION

CONCLUSION

We have discussed the origins and what Parliamentary Sovereignty means. The challenges faced are not fatal to Parliamentary Sovereignty. Finally, as Vernon Bogdanor has observed: 'the doctrine of parliamentary sovereignty clearly means something very different from what it meant before Britain entered the European Community in 1973. It remains in form, but not substance. In practice, therefore, if not in law, parliamentary sovereignty is no longer the governing principle of the British constitution' (Bogdanor 2009, p. 283).

KEY POINTS

- Parliamentary Sovereignty arose as a consequence of the conflict between the Crown and Parliament in the seventeenth century.
- Dicey is associated with the view that Parliament has unlimited legal sovereignty and can make or unmake whatever law it wishes.
- The courts give effect to Parliamentary Sovereignty through the doctrines of express and implied repeal.
- Devolution is a political restriction on Parliamentary Sovereignty.
- Membership of the European Union and the supremacy of EU law is an important challenge to Parliamentary Sovereignty.
- The rule of law and Parliamentary Sovereignty are ultimately incompatible and the *obiter* in *Jackson* suggests that judges may be willing to place limitations on Parliament's legislative ability in order to safeguard important freedoms and the rule of law.

CORE CASES AND STATUTES

Case	About	Importance
British Railway Board v. *Pickin* [1974]	This case involved a challenge to the ownership of land in the middle of a railway track.	The House of Lords held that the courts cannot declare an Act invalid or ineffective because of the manner in which the Act was passed or irregularity in the procedure used.
R (Jackson) v. *Attorney-General* [2005]	A Labour MP had introduced a private members bill to ban hunting. This bill was supported by the Labour government and was approved by the House of Commons. It was rejected by the House of Lords and the government reintroduced the bill and used the Parliament Acts 1911 and 1949 to overcome the opposition in the House of Lords. The Hunting Act 2004 and the validity of the Parliament Act 1949 were challenged by opponents of the ban.	The House of Lords reviewed the legality of the legislation. The Parliament Act 1949 was held to be valid and the Hunting Act was was held to be primary legislation. Their Lordships made some interesting *obiter* comments about Parliamentary Sovereignty and the relationship between it and the rule of law.
Vauxhall Estates Ltd v. *Liverpool Corporation* [1932]	The case the concerned implied repeal of existing legislation. There were two Acts of Parliament both of which provided different amounts of compensation. The claimant had argued that the earlier Act should apply.	A later Act of Parliament will impliedly repeal a previous Act where the Acts are inconsistent and cover the same subject matter.

Case	About	Importance
R v. *Secretary of State for Transport, ex p. Factortame Ltd (No.2)* [1991]	The United Kingdom Parliament legislated to prevent Spanish fishermen from using the United Kingdom's fishing quota.	The House of Lords ruled that where an Act of Parliament and EU law conflicted, then section 2 of the European Communities Act 1972 gave the court the authority to disapply an Act of Parliament.
Thoburn v. *Sunderland City Council* [2002]	The decision involved a trader who had sold fruit by imperial rather than metric weight.	Laws LJ made some very important *obiter* comments that suggested that there was a special status of constitutional law which was protected from implied repeal.
R v. *A (Complainant's Sexual History)* [2001] UKHL 25	This case concerned whether the defendant in a rape trial could adduce evidence as to the victim's sexual history. Section 41 of the Youth Justice and Criminal Evidence Act 1999 stated that the defendant was unable to do this unless the court could rely on one of the three narrow exceptions.	Lord Steyn's approach to using section 3 of the Human Rights Act 1998 proved to be controversial. Section 3 gives the courts wide interpretive powers and allows it to read down words into an Act of Parliament in order to make it ECHR compliant.

Statute	About	Importance
Statute of Westminster 1931	This gave the Dominions (Canada etc.) legislative independence from the UK Parliament.	This Act limited the ability of the Westminster Parliament to legislate for Dominions of the British Empire.
European Communities Act 1972	The United Kingdom required the enacting of the European Communities Act 1972 before it could give effect to its treaty obligations. The United Kingdom became a member of the now European Union in 1973.	The European Communities Act 1972 enables the British courts to give effect to the United Kingdom's treaty obligations. The Act allowed all previous, current and future European Union law to apply in the United Kingdom. This is significant as no additional legislation was required to give effect to regulations, new treaties and decisions of the Court of Justice of the European Union.
Human Rights Act 1998	The statute that incorporated the European Convention on Human Rights into UK domestic law.	The effect of sections 3 and 4 HRA 1998 have been viewed as a challenge to Parliamentary Sovereignty.

FURTHER READING

Bingham, Lord *The Rule of Law* (Allen Lane: London, 2010)
A straightforward introduction to the rule of law and explores its relationship with Parliamentary Sovereignty.

Bogdanor, V. *The New British Constitution* (Hart: Oxford, 2009)
A modern account of the United Kingdom's constitution.

Bradley, A.W. and Ewing, K.D. *Constitutional and Administrative Law* 15th edn (Pearson: Harlow, 2011)
Refer to this book to develop your understanding of this topic.

Dicey, A.V. *Introduction to the Study of the Law of the Constitution* (Liberty Fund: Minneapolis, 1982)
Refer to this book for Dicey's views on Parliamentary Sovereignty.

Goldsworthy, J. *The Sovereignty of Parliament: History and Philosophy* (Oxford University Press: Oxford, 1999)
An in-depth account of the history and development of Parliamentary Sovereignty.

Hope, Lord 'Sovereignty in question: A view from the bench' delivered at the WG Hart Legal Workshop, 28 June 2011 (available at http://www.supremecourt.gov.uk/docs/speech_110628.pdf)
A thought-provoking and highly relevant judicial exploration of the challenges facing Parliamentary Sovereignty.

Kavanagh, A. 'Unlocking the Human Rights Act: the "radical" approach to section 3(1) revisited' [2005] *European Human Rights Law Review* 259
An interesting article about judicial use of section 3 of the HRA 1998.

Munro, C. *Studies in Constitutional Law* (Oxford University Press: Oxford, 2005)
Refer to this book for a series of interesting chapters on the constitution. It is highly recommended that you refer to this.

Neuberger, Lord 'Who are the masters now?' *Second Lord Alexander of Weedon Lecture*, 6 April 2011 (available at http://www.judiciary.gov.uk/media/speeches/speakers/lord-neuberger-of-abbotsbury)
This is a highly recommended lecture which covers many points raised in this chapter.

Sales, P. 'A comparison of the principle of legality and section 3 of the Human Rights Act 1998' (2009) *Law Quarterly Review* 598
An analysis of the use of section 3 of the HRA 1998.

Wade, H.W.R. 'Sovereignty – revolution or evolution?' (1996) *Law Quarterly Review* 568
Recommended as an academic reaction to the decision in *Factortame (No.2)*.

Young, A. 'Judicial Sovereignty and the Human Rights Act 1998' [2002] *Cambridge Law Journal* 53
This article looks at Parliamentary Sovereignty and the HRA 1998.

PART 2

Government institutions and the prerogative

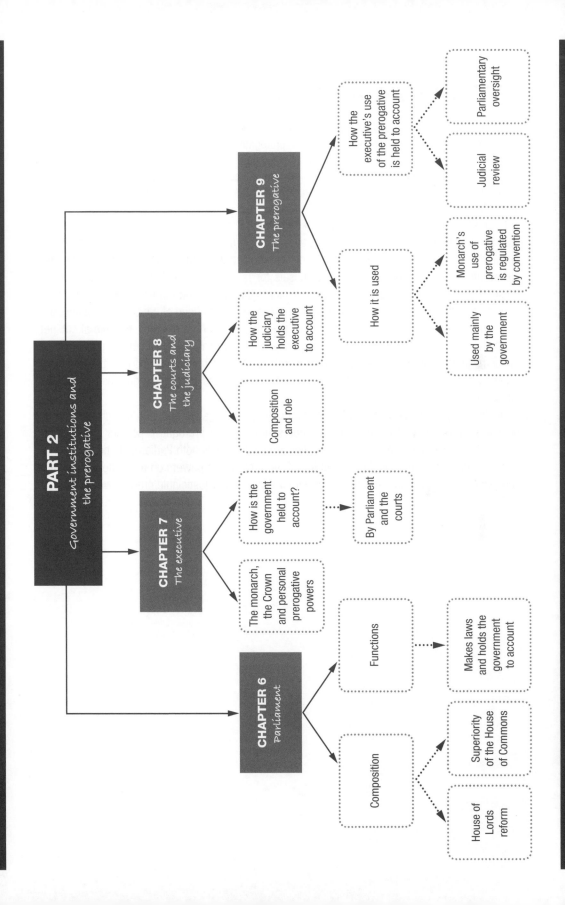

PART 2 INTRODUCTION

Part 2 of Blueprints *Constitutional and Administrative Law* explores the workings of Parliament, the government, the courts and the exercise of the prerogative powers. These four chapters could be summed up as concerning how the executive, or more precisely, the government, is held to account. Accountable government is of fundamental importance, because ministers exercise considerable power and must be accountable to both Parliament and the courts in their exercise of statutory and prerogative powers.

The history, functions and composition of Parliament is explored in Chapter 6. The chapter will look at how Parliament holds the executive to account through select committees, Prime Minister's Questions and debates in both Houses. The reform of the House of Lords will be discussed and we shall see the different proposals for reform and question whether the current House of Lords is fit for purpose. Chapter 7 explores the Crown and the executive. We will look at the role of the present monarch in the United Kingdom and as head of the Commonwealth, the meaning of the term 'Crown', the evolution of the position of Prime Minister, the role of cabinet and the Civil Service. We shall also see how conventions regulate the conduct of ministers. The role of the judiciary is considered in Chapter 8 and we shall see how the courts hold the executive to account, the reasons why the Supreme Court was created and the importance of judicial independence.

Finally, Chapter 9 will explore what is meant by the prerogative and who exercises the prerogative powers today. It is important to understand why the prerogative powers are far from irrelevant and just how important it is that they are controlled by both Parliament and the courts. In the last decade there have been calls to put the prerogative powers on a statutory basis and increased judicial willingness to review certain previously non-justiciable prerogative powers.

CHAPTER 6

Parliament: composition and functions

BLUEPRINT

Parliament: composition and functions

KEY QUESTIONS

LEGISLATION

- Parliament Acts 1911 and 1949
- House of Lords Act 1999
- Representation of the People Act(s)

CONTEXT

- The establishment of Parliamentary Sovereignty over the Crown (prerogative).
- Devolution and the transfer of powers from Westminster.

CONCEPTS

- First Past the Post
- The constituency
- Select committees
- Henry VIII clauses
- The Salisbury Convention
- Parliamentary privilege

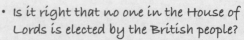

- Is it right that no one in the House of Lords is elected by the British people?
- Is First Past the Post an unfair way of electing our MPs? Is proportional representation a more democratic method?

- Who is responsible for making laws?
- What is the composition of the House of Common and the House of Lords?

CASES

- *R* v. *Chaytor* [2010]

REFORM

- Should the House of Lords be reformed and become 100 per cent elected?
- Should there be an English Parliament?
- Should select committees have more power?

SPECIAL CHARACTERISTICS

- Parliamentary Sovereignty
- Membership of the House of Lords
- The executive dominates Parliament
- Prior to 2009 the House of Lords had a judicial function
- Bicameral Parliament
- Parliamentary procedure for making law

CRITICAL ISSUES

Setting the scene

The United Kingdom's Parliament is known as the Westminster Parliament and sits in the Palace of Westminster. The Palace was rebuilt in the 1830s after a fire destroyed the original medieval complex. It is an imposing gothic building situated on the Thames and its most famous landmark is the clock tower which contains a bell called 'Big Ben'. In 1707 as a result of the Acts of Union the English and Scottish Parliaments were dissolved and the new British Parliament sat at Westminster. The British Parliament was united with the Irish Parliament in 1801, when the personal union between the British and Irish Crown was formalised by the Act of Union. Southern Ireland is no longer part of the United Kingdom and before the referendum on Scottish independence took place in September 2014 there was a chance that Scotland might leave the United Kingdom. We will briefly look at the legislative bodies created by the Devolution Acts in 1998. We will then consider the composition and function of Parliament and at the possibility of further reform. Questions such as how parliamentarians hold the government to account and the role of MPs will be explored.

Chapter overview

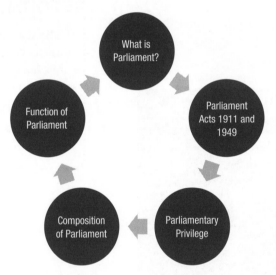

THE UNITED KINGDOM'S PARLIAMENT

CORNERSTONE

Bicameral Parliament

The United Kingdom has a bicameral Parliament. This means that Parliament is comprised of two legislative chambers. These are known as the House of Commons and the House of Lords. They owe their name to their respective historical origins (we will discuss this below).

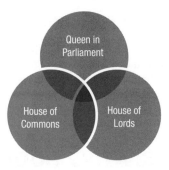

Figure 6.1 The composition of Parliament

Many countries have a bicameral system such as France and the United States. In the United States the legislative body is known collectively as Congress. There are two Houses in Congress, the House of Representatives and the Senate. In the United Kingdom, both Houses are known as the Houses of Parliament. Each House is comprised of different types of members.

Together the House of Commons, the House of Lords and the Queen in Parliament form Parliament (see Figure 6.1). The monarch plays an important role as her approval is required before proposed legislation can become law. Royal assent is one of the personal prerogative powers of the monarch. This means that the law-making power of Parliament is exercised through the legislative supremacy of the Queen in Parliament.

> ### Take note
>
> Parliament is bicameral and is comprised of the:
>
> - House of Commons
> - House of Lords
> - Queen in Parliament
>
> The participation of all three is required in order to make a valid Act of Parliament (subject to the Parliament Acts 1911 and 1949).

Parliament's legislative sovereignty

CORNERSTONE

Parliamentary Sovereignty

The United Kingdom Parliament is the supreme law-making body in the United Kingdom. An Act of Parliament is legally sovereign and cannot be challenged by the courts. Parliamentary Sovereignty is being challenged by the United Kingdom's membership of the European Union, the rule of law, the Human Rights Act 1998 and the political consequences of devolution (see Chapter 5). Nonetheless, Parliamentary Sovereignty is the key principle of the United Kingdom's unwritten constitution.

Parliament is legally sovereign as a result of winning the long-running conflict with the Crown over the issue of legal supremacy. Today, the Crown's remaining discretionary powers, known as the prerogative, are inferior to an Act of Parliament. Equally, the common law is inferior to an Act of Parliament. Unlike in the United States or Canada, the United Kingdom's Supreme Court cannot strike down Acts that are held to be unconstitutional. Indeed, unless Parliament permits otherwise the courts cannot question the validity of an Act of Parliament. If Parliament has legislative sovereignty then, according to Dicey, it is the electorate who has the political sovereignty (*Introduction to the Study of the Law of the Constitution* (Liberty Fund: Minneapolis, 1982)).

The Parliament Acts 1911 and 1949

The House of Commons and the House of Lords fulfil the legislative function of the United Kingdom. The House of Commons is an elected body and the House of Lords is comprised of hereditary and appointed peers. The House of Commons is the most powerful House, as it can pass legislation without the assent of the House of Lords under the Parliament Acts 1911 and 1949.

DEVOLVED LEGISLATIVE BODIES

Take note

The Devolution Acts of 1998 created the National Assembly for Wales (Government of Wales Act 1998) and the Scottish Parliament (Scotland Act 1998). Since their creation, more power has been devolved to these legislative bodies. Following the creation of Northern Ireland in 1922 the Northern Ireland Assembly was abolished and has been reconstituted over the course of the last 90 years. This was as a result of the 'Troubles' in Northern Ireland which saw almost thirty years of sectarian strife and terrorism which was responsible for a great many deaths. Powers have been retransferred to the Northern Ireland Assembly under the Northern Ireland Act 1998.

The devolved legislative bodies in Northern Ireland, Wales and Scotland have been given power to create legislation for their respective area. This legislation does not enjoy legal sovereignty and can be declared invalid by the courts. These devolved legislatures have been given devolved powers to make legislation in certain policy areas, such as education. They may not exceed the powers devolved by the Westminster Parliament.

The Scottish Parliament and the Sewel Convention

In a referendum in 1997, 74.3 per cent of Scottish voters supported devolving powers to Scotland. This was an improvement on the 51.6 per cent who voted in support of devolution in 1979. The Scottish Parliament is responsible for legislating under the devolved powers. The Westminster Parliament legislates for non-devolved matters in Scotland. According to the **Sewel Convention** the Westminster Parliament will not legislate for devolved matters. As noted in Chapter 5 there is nothing legally that could prevent Westminster legislating on devolved matters, or indeed abolishing the Scottish Parliament. The referendum on Scottish independence asked the Scottish electorate whether they wished to leave the United Kingdom. As over 55 per cent of the electorate voted to remain as part of the United Kingdom, the three main political parties will have to honour their promise to devolve more powers to Scotland. This could mean that eventually, if powers are also devolved to an English Parliament or regional assemblies, that the Westminster Parliament will just be responsible for truly national matters such as defence and foreign affairs.

The National Assembly of Wales

A referendum in Wales in 1997 saw a tiny majority of Welsh voters (50.3 per cent) support the creation of the National Assembly of Wales. This was hardly a strong endorsement of devolving powers from Westminster. However, this was a significant improvement on the 20.3 per cent who voted in favour of devolution in 1979. The Government of Wales Act 1998 and the Government of Wales Act 2006 have devolved powers from Westminster to Cardiff.

The West Lothian Question and an English Parliament

As part of its devolution programme, the Labour government had intended to devolve powers to the English regions. There were plans, for instance, to create a North East regional assembly, but this proved unpopular with over three-quarters of voters rejecting the proposals in 2004 and this has not been proceeded with. It is controversial that Scottish, Welsh and Northern Irish MPs can vote on matters that affect England, whereas English MPs cannot vote on devolved matters. This is known as the West Lothian Question. Many people now support the creation of an English Parliament to decide English affairs. If this were to occur, then the Westminster Parliament would have devolved most of its law-making powers. As a consequence of more powers being devolved to Scotland, the Conservative party wishes to address the West Lothian question through some sort of English devolution. This might result in powers being devolved to regional assemblies, non-English MPs being excluded from voting on laws which only concern England or the creation of an English Parliament.

> One example of the key differences between England and Scotland is the cost of healthcare for the elderly and university fees. The Scottish Parliament has voted to make university tuition fees free for Scottish students, whereas Scottish MPs were able to vote on raising English tuition fees to £9,000 per year.

CONTEXT

SECONDARY OR DELEGATED LEGISLATION

An Act of Parliament can delegate law-making powers to individual ministers. This delegated legislation is not primary legislation but rather is secondary legislation, which means that the courts can review ministerial use of their delegated legislative powers (see Chapter 13).

An Act of Parliament will allow a minister to create new law without requiring additional Acts of Parliament. This permits a minister to develop policies in line with the aims set out in the Act, which will just set out a framework and it is for the minister to develop the required legislation to give effect to what Parliament intended. Ministerial use of delegated legislation is controlled by Parliament, with two House of Lords committees reviewing ministerial use of delegated legislation (the House of Lords Delegated Powers Scrutiny Committee and the House of Lords Secondary Legislation Scrutiny Committee).

> **Take note**
>
> Each year far more delegated legislation is created than primary legislation. Delegated legislation is required because it would not be possible for Parliament to spend its time passing all the required legislation. Primary legislation cannot be judicially reviewed by the courts; whereas, secondary legislation can be reviewed. For the constitutional reasons for this distinction see Chapter 5.

CORNERSTONE

Henry VIII clauses

Sometimes a bill will contain a clause which will give the government the power to repeal or amend that bill in the future using delegated legislation. Such a clause is known as a Henry VIII Clause, as Parliament gave Henry VIII the power to legislate using his prerogative by the Statute of Proclamations. Parliament will give a minister the power to create further legislation in a Bill, but if this secondary legislation will impose new legal obligations on people then the consent of Parliament is needed.

Otherwise secondary legislation can be created by a minister using the powers conferred on him by Parliament. Statutory instruments are the most common type of delegated legislation.

HISTORY OF THE UNITED KINGDOM'S PARLIAMENT

Parliament has been called every year since 1689. The Bill of Rights in 1689 stated that the King must summon Parliament every year. The King was restricted from making or unmaking laws without the consent of Parliament. The Bill of Rights asserted the legislative supremacy of Parliament over the monarch. We must remember that the legislative supremacy of Parliament involves the Queen in Parliament and the monarch's assent is required before a bill can become law.

The English Parliament

The Magna Carta, which was presented to King John by his barons in 1215, established the idea that the barons in a representative capacity were needed to consent before the king could raise taxation. This was significant as it restricted the power of the Crown to govern without the consent of the barons and introduced the idea of governing by consensus. Although the Magna Carta was annulled by the pope it was later reissued by Edward I.

> The barons rebelled against John's son, Henry III, who was forced to hold the first meeting of Parliament at Oxford in 1258. Crucially, the barons wanted to advise the king and consent to taxation. This established regular meetings of Parliament, whose role was to consult with the monarch on taxation.
>
> CONTEXT

It was only in 1295 that two distinct groups of representatives were summoned, the Lords and members representing counties and towns. Parliament's consent was required in 1362 for all taxation that the monarch wished to raise. The role of Parliament was soon extended to formally disposing monarchs and finally to consenting to all the laws that the monarch wished to make in 1414. It is clear that medieval monarchs appreciated that they needed to consult with Parliament and a weak monarch, such as Edward III (albeit this was due to illness), could face parliamentary attempts to impeach his advisors and dismiss members of the council. Parliament approved the English reformation and granted considerable law-making powers to Henry VIII.

> Parliamentarians did not enjoy freedom of speech in the chamber and soon clashed with the monarch. During the reign of Charles I the relationship between monarch and Parliament deteriorated and the king ruled without summoning one for twelve years, attempting to govern using his prerogative powers instead. Eventually the king was forced to recall Parliament and this led to civil war. The king raised an army and Parliament did the same. Parliament defeated the king and voted to execute Charles I in 1649. Parliament then ruled without a king, with Oliver Cromwell having dictatorial powers as the Lord Protector. Upon his death the monarchy was restored. The relationship between Parliament and Charles II
>
> CONTEXT

and James II was not a happy one. James II was deposed by Parliament in 1688 and William of Orange and his wife Mary were invited to become joint monarchs.

In 1689 the Bill of Rights helped establish the supremacy of Parliament over the executive as it prohibited the raising of taxes and an army without parliamentary consent. The Bill of Rights also established parliamentary privilege which ensured that parliamentarians enjoyed free speech inside the chamber. The English Parliament was legally sovereign, but this power could only be exercised by the King or Queen in Parliament.

The United Kingdom Parliament

The Acts of Union in 1707 created Great Britain and the new Parliament was comprised of members from England and Scotland. It met at Westminster and continued to enjoy legal sovereignty. The Union with Ireland Act 1800 incorporated Ireland into the new United Kingdom. The Irish Parliament was dissolved and Irish parliamentarians joined the Westminster Parliament.

During the eighteenth century parliamentarians took over the governance of the country from the monarch. The development of cabinet government saw the government being composed of members of the Houses of Commons and Lords. Matters of great importance would be debated in the chambers of both Houses and oratory was an important skill. Speeches were reproduced as pamphlets and sold to the public.

In the eighteenth and nineteenth centuries not everyone could vote. The franchise (i.e. those who could vote) was limited to very wealthy men, and not every town or city had a Member of Parliament. We will see below how the franchise was expanded to include most men and women aged over eighteen.

Parliament Acts 1911 and 1949

CORNERSTONE

Parliament Acts 1911 and 1949

The Parliament Acts 1911 and 1949 altered the relationship between the House of Commons and the House of Lords. The Acts have limited the ability of the House of Lords to prevent bills from becoming law.

The passing of the Parliament Act 1911 was an important development and resulted from the House of Lords rejecting the government's budget. At this time the House of Lords could vote to reject any legislation and there was nothing that the House of Commons could do about this. A constitutional convention regulated money bills and the House of Lords rejected the budget and only relented when the government threatened to create new peers that would vote in their favour. As a consequence of breaching a convention, the Parliament Act 1911 was passed. This Act restricted the House of Lords' ability to delay the passing of a bill by more than two years after the bill's second reading in the House of Commons. This applied to all bills except those to extend the lifetime of Parliament (see Figure 6.2). The House of Lords is unable to veto money bills as these will be automatically passed one month after being introduced to the House of Lords.

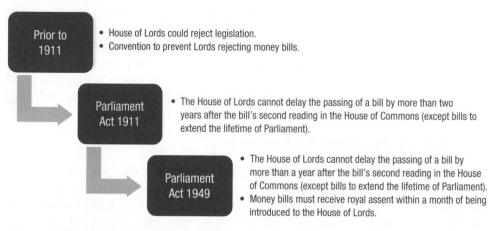

Figure 6.2 The Parliament Acts 1911 and 1949

CORNERSTONE

The Salisbury Convention

The **Salisbury Convention** exists to ensure that the House of Lords does not veto bills which were contained in the government's election manifesto. It came about in 1945 when the Labour government wished to legislate to give effect to its manifesto but were in a minority in the House of Lords. The Labour Leader of the Lords, Viscount Addison, remarked that, 'in the House of Lords the Labour Benches are, as it were, but a tiny atoll in the vast ocean of Tory reaction'. This convention helped to ensure that Labour could introduce key manifesto commitments. For more information see 'The Salisbury Doctrine' House of Lords Library Note (2006).

> **Take note**
>
> The Parliament Acts 1911 and 1949 gave the House of Commons supremacy over the House of Lords. It is important to understand why they were introduced and what the restrictions are on using these Acts today.

The Parliament Act 1949 reduced the ability of the House of Lords to delay the passing of a bill one year after the bill's second reading in the House of Commons. The new Act was needed to introduce key legislation, including the Iron and Steel Bill. This amendment to the Parliament Act 1911 was considered necessary as the House of Lords could still block the Labour government's legislation during the last two years of the lifetime of a Parliament. The House of Lords were acting in breach of the Salisbury Convention. The 1949 Act was passed under the 1911 Act, thus removing the need for the House of Lords to consent.

The House of Lords still has the power to veto bills that will extend the lifetime of Parliament, or bills which were originally introduced in the House of Lords. The validity of the Parliament Acts 1911 and 1949 was questioned in *R (Jackson)* v. *Attorney-General* [2005] UKHL 56 (see Chapter 5). The House of Commons is now the most important House and the power of the Lords is limited. However, the House of Lords can still scrutinise bills and provide important amendments. Lord Bingham observed that, '[t]he Parliament Acts mitigated the affront to democracy inherent in the power of an unelected, unaccountable chamber to thwart the will of the elected chamber answerable to the electorate' (Lord Bingham 2011, p. 113).

The lifetime of each Parliament

The lifetime of each Parliament was shortened from seven to five years by the Parliament Act 1911. Previously, the Septennial Act 1715 had stated that the maximum lifetime of each Parliament was seven years. The Fixed-term Parliaments Act 2011 prevents the calling of a General Election until May 2015. This is unless an exception applies. The monarch will dissolve Parliament and call a General Election. Once dissolved, parliamentarians are prevented from entering Parliament. Parliament will be opened every year by the Queen in a ceremony known as the State Opening of Parliament.

> Today the monarch is not allowed to enter the House of Commons. During the State Opening of Parliament an official known as Black Rod will be sent from the House of Lords to summon MPs in the House of Commons. Black Rod will bang on the door and the MPs will open the door and slam it in Black Rod's face. This rather strange tradition originates from the time when Charles I had entered the chamber of the House of Commons to arrest several MPs.

CONTEXT

Parliamentary privilege

CORNERSTONE

Parliamentary privilege

The Bill of Rights 1689 gave parliamentarians certain privileges. Article 9 of the Bill of Rights 1689 states '[t]hat the Freedome of Speech and Debates or Proceedings in Parlyament ought not to be impeached or questioned in any Court or Place out of Parlyament'.

Parliamentarians enjoy freedom of speech and can speak freely in the Houses of Parliament. This enables parliamentarians to speak without risk of criminal or civil sanction. An example of this privilege being used is when MPs have revealed the names of those persons protected by super injunctions without facing the prospect of being prosecuted under the Contempt of Court Act 1981. Equally, statements can be made which if made outside the chamber could give rise to a claim for defamation in tort. This right of free speech is essential in a modern democracy and parliamentarians should have the freedom to incite debate. However, on the other hand parliamentarians have been criticised by the judiciary for misusing parliamentary privilege. Parliamentary privilege also means that Parliament has exclusive competence over its own proceedings. The courts have determined the extent of parliamentary privilege. One such example is the Supreme Court's decision in *R* v. *Chaytor* [2010] UKSC 52, where the court ruled that parliamentarians could not invoke parliamentary privilege to prevent prosecution for false accounting.

Link with the executive

The Prime Minister by convention must be from the House of Commons. If the Prime Minister wishes to appoint a person to a ministerial position, then that person by convention will have to become a member of either House of Parliament. The commonest method is to appoint that person as a member of the House of Lords. Peter Mandelson was appointed as a member of the House of Lords and became a member of Gordon Brown's cabinet. Lord Mandelson was viewed as one of the most powerful members of cabinet, despite not being an MP.

During the Second World War the Prime Minister wanted Ernest Bevin, who was the leader of a trade union, to join the cabinet. Bevin had to first become an MP before he could take up his ministerial position. Recent examples include the retired admiral, Alan West, who upon being appointed to the House of Lords became Security Minister under the previous government.

CONTEXT

COMPOSITION OF PARLIAMENT

We will now have a look at the composition of Parliament and who exactly the members of both Houses are. The members of both Houses are known as parliamentarians. They all have offices in the parliamentary estate and have access to staff, libraries and other resources.

CORNERSTONE

R v. *Chaytor* [2010] UKSC 52 and the expenses scandal

It is important at this point to highlight the recent controversy surrounding parliamentary expenses. As a result of a newspaper investigation it was revealed that both MPs and Lords had been abusing the expenses system. This revelation resulted in the then Prime Minister, Gordon Brown, and other leading politicians repaying money which they had received, and a new expenses regime being introduced. Both MPs and Lords have been convicted and have served custodial sentences. Initially those parliamentarians accused had argued that they could rely on parliamentary privilege as a defence. The Supreme Court in *R* v. *Chaytor* unsurprisingly rejected this. The result is that the reputation of Parliament has been tarnished.

HOUSE OF COMMONS

We will look first at the composition of the House of Commons and how MPs are elected.

The Member of Parliament

Members of Parliament (MPs) represent their local **constituencies**. There are 650 MPs in the House of Commons from constituencies across the United Kingdom. Out of the 650 MPs elected in the 2010 General Election only 147 are women. The first female MP to take her seat in the House of Commons was Nancy Astor in 1919 (Countess Constance Markievicz was the first woman to be elected to Parliament in 1918 but as a member of Sinn Fein she did not take her seat). There are only 28 MPs from ethnic minorities. The first Asian MP took his seat in the 1890s. All MPs are elected and none are appointed. Everyone is entitled to vote in the constituency where they live (subject to some restrictions). Most MPs are members of a political party and support that party's policies, however, an extremely small number of MPs are independents and do not align themselves to any political grouping.

CORNERSTONE

The constituency

The MP will represent the constituency in Parliament and will serve as a link between the legislature and the electorate. The MP will hold surgeries in their constituency to enable their constituents to raise important issues and to seek their help. The MP will be expected to use their time to benefit their constituency, for example by protesting against plans to build a waste disposal site or the closure of a local factory.

How MPs are elected

MPs are elected at the General Election (or through a special by-election). Candidates will put themselves forward and will pay a deposit. Almost anyone can stand as an MP, with the notable exception of Lords who cannot do so unless they renounce their peerage (see Tony Benn who campaigned to be permitted to renounce his hereditary peerage to stand as a Labour MP). The main political parties field candidates who stand for election. The local party association has power over who is nominated to stand as their party's candidate. The Labour Party and Conservative Party have in some constituencies introduced all-female shortlists for candidates because only a minority of MPs are female. Before the 2010 General Election the Conservative Party decided to change the rules about how candidates were selected. This experiment only applied to two constituencies. Firstly, they allowed anyone to stand as the Conservative candidate, and secondly, they permitted any constituent to vote for who became the local Conservative candidate.

CORNERSTONE

First Past the Post

The method of electing an MP is called First Past the Post. This allows the person with the most votes to become the MP. This system is controversial for many reasons, namely that it permits an MP to be elected without having a majority of the total votes. For example an MP could be elected with just 33 per cent of the vote or a majority of just one vote.

This means that there are a large number of MPs who were not elected by a majority of their constituents. Many people feel that their vote is wasted if they live in a constituency where most people will vote for a particular political party. One example of this is Luton South where the local MP is almost guaranteed to be a member of the Labour Party, or neighbouring Dunstable where the local MP will almost be guaranteed to be a member of the Conservative Party. The Ballot Act 1872 introduced secret voting, which means that you do not need to tell anyone who you voted for. This ensures that people have the freedom to vote without being influenced by the candidate's supporters, or indeed their own friends and family.

As well as voting at a polling station, it is possible to register to vote via the post. Postal voting has led to allegations of election fraud. However, as voter turnout is low in the United Kingdom with only two-thirds of those entitled to vote doing so in 2010, many people see postal voting as a good way to try and encourage more people to vote. In Australia people are obliged by law to vote and every election will see a debate in the press on whether the United Kingdom should introduce compulsory voting.

The need for reform

The First Past the Post system means that the number of MPs a political party has at Westminster does not actually reflect the share of the popular vote that the party received. It must be remembered that voters do not vote for a political party, rather they vote for their local MP. Nonetheless, the United Kingdom's system of modern political parties means that First Past the Post will usually lead to either a Labour or a Conservative government. The 2010 General Election led to the first coalition government since the Second World War, and is the exception rather than the norm. In 2010 the Liberal Democrats received almost seven million votes, but despite their share of the vote (23 per cent), the Liberal Democrats only managed to win 8.8 per cent of the seats (57). The fact that the number of MPs does not reflect the actual percentage of votes is a major criticism of the system used to elect MPs in the United Kingdom. The Liberal Democrats have supported changing the voting system and replacing it with proportional representation.

Table 6.1 The House of Commons after the May 2010 General Election

Party	Seats	Percentage of votes
Conservative	306	36.1%
Labour	258	29%
Liberal Democrat	57	23%
Democratic Unionist	8	0.6%
Scottish National	6	1.7%
Sinn Fein	5	0.6%
Plaid Cymru	3	0.6%
Social Democratic and Labour	3	0.4%
Alliance	1	0.1%
Green	1	1%
Independent	1	
Speaker	1	
Total	**650**	

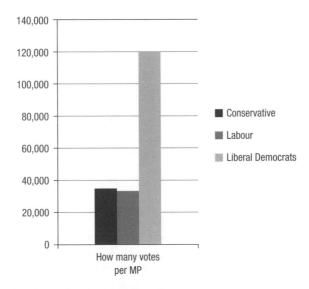

Figure 6.3 How many votes does it take to elect an MP?

It is certainly true that the existing system means that the number of votes does not necessarily reflect the number of seats in the House of Commons. On a breakdown of the 2010 General Election results it took 33,940 votes to elect a Conservative MP, 33,370 to elect a Labour MP and 119,944 votes to elect a Liberal Democrat MP (see Figure 6.3).

> Proportional representation is used in many different countries such as Germany. The number of seats a political party has in the legislature is based on their overall share of the national vote. Whilst proportional representation ensures that the legislature represents the voting intentions of the electorate, many critics allege that introducing this system into the United Kingdom would lead to weak and unstable coalition governments. Italy is often referred to as there have been sixty-one governments since 1945. There is a fear that fringe parties such as the British National Party might gain seats in the House of Commons. Critics also point to the Weimar Republic in Germany during the 1920s and '30s, where proportional representation was blamed for weakening the government of Germany and allowing the NSDAP (Nazis) to take power in 1933.

REFLECTION

The 2011 referendum on changing the method of voting

In May 2011, there was a referendum on proposals to replace First Past the Post with the Alternative Vote (AV). The AV system allows voters to list their candidates by preference. If a candidate achieves 50 per cent he will win outright. If no candidate receives 50 per cent of the votes, then the weakest candidate is eliminated and their votes are given to the voter's second favoured candidate. The process will continue until one candidate achieves the important 50 per cent required. The nation voted in favour of retaining First Past the Post.

Who can vote?

We take it for granted that if we are aged over eighteen then we are entitled to vote and although this is generally true, there are a few exceptions.

Can prisoners vote?

Prisoners are not entitled to vote but the European Court of Human Rights in *Hirst* v. *United Kingdom (No.2)* (2005) 42 EHRR 849 held that a blanket ban on all prisoners voting was unlawful. The UK Supreme Court in *R (Chester)* v. *Secretary of State for Justice* [2013] UKSC 63 applied the decision in *Hirst* but refused to issue a declaration of incompatibility, as the matter was being considered by the UK Parliament and a declaration had been issued on a previous occasion. In 2013 the Joint Committee on the Draft Voting Eligibility (Prisoners) Bill recommended that prisoners should be allowed to vote unless there was a good reason to restrict certain types of prisoners from voting. If the recommendations become law then the UK will no longer be in breach of the European Convention on Human Rights.

Historically only a small number of people could vote at a General Election. Voting rights were restricted to men who owned land and had a certain income. The constituencies were not spread evenly over the United Kingdom so, for example, despite being a large city Manchester did not have any MPs. When the American colonists declared independence because of Britain's attempt to tax them without the Americans being represented by the body that made the law, some commentators could point to Manchester to show that their situation was not unique. On the other hand, small villages might have two MPs. These were known as rotten boroughs.

The universities of Oxford and Cambridge both had their own MP and former students could return to take part and vote (as well as voting in their own constituency). This meant that the nobility controlled a large number of consistencies and could build up their own followings in Parliament. The ability of the nobility to secure patronage through their ownership of these constituencies resulted in placing considerable power in their hands.

The reforms in the nineteenth century increased the number of men who could vote by lowering the income requirement. This happened through the Representation of the People Acts. The most significant was the Great Reform Act of 1832. However, the creation of voting parity between men and women would take almost another hundred years to achieve.

Take note

Looking at Figure 6.4 and taking into account your current age, in what year were you able to vote at your current age? For example, Jasmine who is thirty-four could only vote in 1918, and Delia who is twenty-one could only vote in 1928.

CORNERSTONE

Representation of the People Acts

The first of these was the Great Reform Act 1832 (Representation of the People Act 1832). Most women over the age of thirty only received the vote in 1918. There was only fully voting equality between men and women in 1928. The result of universal franchise saw the creation of the Labour Party and the first Labour government in 1922. There have been calls to reduce the voting age to sixteen and a private members' bill which attempted to achieve this was unsuccessful in 2008.

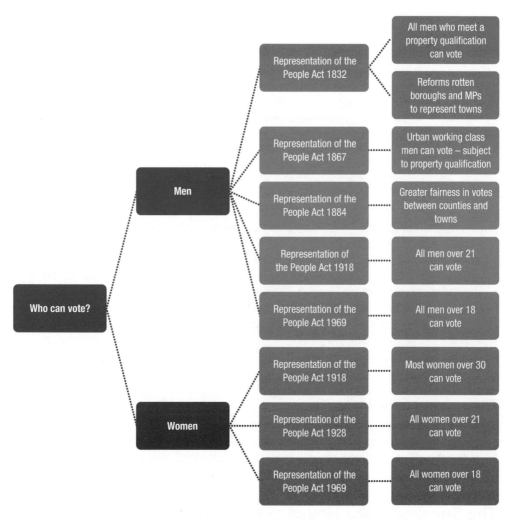

Figure 6.4 The expansion of the franchise

The House of Commons creates the government

A government is created in the House of Commons. The political party or coalition that has the most seats in the House of Commons will form the next government.

Only an MP can become the Prime Minister

By convention only an MP can become the Prime Minister. The last Prime Minister from the House of Lords was the Marquis of Salisbury who resigned in 1902. Had Churchill inherited the family Dukedom of Marlborough then he would not have been able to become Prime Minister in 1940. The convention has been shown to exist because whenever there has been a choice between an MP and a Lord, the monarch has chosen the MP to become Prime Minister. The choice in 1940 was between

Churchill and Lord Halifax. In 1924 it was between Stanley Baldwin MP and Lord Curzon, and the king chose Baldwin.

In 1963, the Prime Minister Harold Macmillan resigned due to ill health. At that time there was no internal way to select the next leader of the Conservative Party, and therefore Macmillan's successor as Prime Minister. This meant that the Queen had to make a choice between two Conservative cabinet ministers, Rab Butler and the Earl of Home. On the advice of Macmillan, the Queen chose the Earl of Home, who after becoming Prime Minister considered himself bound by convention and renounced his peerage. He was able to become an MP as there was a vacant seat and Home won the by-election.

APPLICATION

Lord Poplar (fictitious) sits in the House of Lords and is a member of the Conservative Party. He has been made Foreign Secretary and is very popular with the electorate. The Prime Minister is forced to resign due to ill health. Lord Poplar wishes to put himself forward to become leader of the Conservative Party (and therefore Prime Minister). Would the convention that the Prime Minister must come from the House of Commons prevent him from becoming Prime Minister? Lord Poplar could renounce his peerage, although there is nothing legally which would prevent a member of the House of Lords from becoming Prime Minister. Ultimately, it may well depend on public and press opinion.

The vote of no confidence

Ultimately the House of Commons can vote to bring down the government. The last government to be defeated by a vote of no confidence was that of James Callaghan in 1979. Upon losing the vote the Prime Minister will as a matter of convention ask the monarch to dissolve Parliament. This will trigger a General Election.

The Speaker of the House of Commons

The business of the House of Commons is presided over by the Speaker of the House. The speaker is an MP who is elected by his colleagues to chair debates and run the proceedings in the House. The Speaker is accorded significant respect by the House and can keep order during noisy debates. The Speaker lives in the Palace of Westminster and continues to represent his constituency. The Speaker is a high-profile position and carries significant authority.

Reforming the House of Commons

The Coalition government has introduced plans to reduce the number of MPs and to make the size of constituencies more consistent. This was contained in the 2010 Coalition Agreement. Due to political reasons it is unlikely that this will be achieved during the lifetime of the 2010–2015 Parliament. This is controversial as a number of high-profile MPs will risk losing their seats. However, the House of Commons has arguably too many MPs when contrasted with the House of Representatives in the United States, which has fewer members who represent a larger population.

HOUSE OF LORDS

CORNERSTONE

Membership of the House of Lords

The House of Lords is the upper chamber in the United Kingdom. Its members are all appointed or entitled to seats through their position, and importantly none are elected by the electorate.

The House of Lords is a controversial body as it is seen by many as lacking any democratic legitimacy, because unlike the House of Commons it holds considerable law-making power and yet is not accountable to the British people. According to Alexandra Kelso, '[i]t is perhaps ironic that the House of Lords is, on the one hand, condemned for its undemocratic composition, and, on the other hand, applauded for the important contribution it makes to the broad work of parliament' ('Parliament' in *The Oxford Handbook of British Politics* (Oxford University Press: Oxford, 2011), p. 232). Members of the House of Lords are not paid a salary, but receive expenses. There are 778 members which is a very large number, especially when we consider that the Senate in the United States only has 100 members. The discussion of the different types of members will be looked at alongside the continuing reform of the House of Lords (see Figure 6.5).

The hereditary peers

CORNERSTONE

House of Lords Act 1999

Most of the hereditary peers were removed from the House of Lords under the House of Lords Act 1999. The reform of the House of Lords is considered by many to be incomplete.

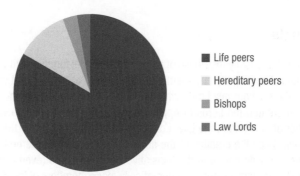

- Life peers
- Hereditary peers
- Bishops
- Law Lords

Figure 6.5 The composition of the House of Lords

Traditionally all hereditary peers were entitled to sit in the House of Lords. The House of Lords Act 1999 has removed this right, and instead only ninety-two peers were allowed to remain. Those ninety-two hereditary peers were selected by their fellow hereditary peers. Hereditary peers had traditionally played an important part in government, as many Prime Ministers were from the nobility.

The life peers

The majority of the members of the House of Lords are life peers. There are 667 in total. Life peers were introduced by the Life Peerages Act 1958. Life peers have no fixed term and are appointed for life. It is not a hereditary peerage and so the peerage ceases to exist upon death. Life peers are appointed via the House of Lords Appointments Commission. The Commission will nominate individuals for life peerages and will vet nominations made by political parties. Life peerages are given to senior politicians upon retiring from the House of Commons, or upon losing their seats, distinguished persons in the arts, sciences, broadcasting and the Civil Service, etc. Distinguished peers include Lord Sugar, star of television's *The Apprentice*, Lord Coe, who was responsible for the London 2012 Olympic Games, and the former Deputy Prime Minister, Lord Prescott.

There is controversy over peerages being given to those who give money to political parties. Tony Blair, the then Prime Minister, was interviewed twice by police in 2006 over allegations that peerages were being given in return for donations to the Labour Party.

CONTEXT

The Bishops

The United Kingdom unlike most other countries gives the leaders of a religious faith seats in its legislative chamber. This is a historical quirk. There are twenty-three Church of England Bishops who are members of the House of Lords. The Bishops play an important role and take part in the legislative process. Other faith groups are not formally represented by such a fixed quota, but religious leaders have been made life peers such as the Chief Rabbi.

The Law Lords

As we shall see below, historically the House of Lords had a judicial function and was the highest court in the United Kingdom. Traditionally any member of the House of Lords could sit and judge a case. This ceased in the 1840s when only Lords who had legal training would try the case. The Appellate Jurisdiction Act 1876 created the Lords of Appeal in Ordinary, commonly known as the Law Lords. However, as a matter of convention the Law Lords would not normally sit in the legislative chamber of the House of Lords. Since the creation of the new United Kingdom Supreme Court in 2009, members of the Supreme Court do not sit in the legislative House of Lords (even if entitled to as peers), whilst new Supreme Court Justices are not automatically made members of the House of Lords. There are still twenty-three members who are/were serving members of the court.

The crossbenchers

Members of the House of Lords (with the exception of the Law Lords and Bishops) can be members of political parties. The Labour Party currently has 220 peers, the Conservatives 221 and the Liberal Democrats 99. Significantly there are 181 crossbench peers who are independent and do not belong to a political party. The crossbenchers are important and play an important role in ensuring that debates are not always dominated by politics.

The Speaker of the House of Lords

Prior to the Constitutional Reform Act 2005, the Speaker of the House of Lords was the Lord Chancellor. The Speaker is now elected by the members of the House.

Further reform of the House of Lords

Reforming the House of Lords was first seriously considered by the Liberal government at the beginning of the twentieth century. In 1999, the Labour government introduced the House of Lords Act 1999 to remove the majority of the hereditary peers. Whilst this removed the vast majority of hereditary peers, it did nothing to introduce an element of democracy into the second chamber. As a result of the Parliament Acts 1911 and 1949 the House of Lords is inferior to the House of Commons. Consequentially, there was a concern that further reform that legitimised the House of Lords as a democratic legislative chamber would change the relationship between the two Houses.

Wakeham Commission Report

The Wakeham Commission delivered its report in 2000. The commission was comprised of senior politicians and academics. The commission suggested that there should be further reform of the House of Lords. The main proposals were:

- The balance of power between the two Houses should be unchanged. The Parliament Acts 1911 and 1949 would remain.
- The House of Lords would have a proportion of regional members who would represent the regions.
- The new chamber should be wholly or substantially elected.
- Those appointed should be chosen by a genuinely independent appointment commission. This would prevent the system from being abused by the government.
- Other religious groups should be represented in the chamber.
- All members would serve fifteen-year terms.

Whilst the Wakeham Commission's recommendation for an independent appointment commission was taken up, no further reform of the House of Lords has been carried out since then.

The 2007 White Paper on House of Lords reform was followed by Parliament having a free vote on how to reform the House of Lords in March 2007. The House of Commons voted against a wholly appointed House of Lords (66 per cent against). The House of Commons voted for an 80 per cent elected and 20 per cent appointed House of Lords (53 per cent in support). The House of Commons also voted to support a wholly elected House of Lords (60 per cent in support). The House of Lords voted overwhelmingly in favour of a fully appointed House of Lords (75 per cent in support).

2008 White Paper

The Labour government's White Paper in 2008 'An Elected Second Chamber: Further reform of the House of Lords' looked at further ways to reform the House of Lords. The government supported the findings of the Wakeham Commission that suggested introducing elections to the House of Lords. Elected members would serve a 12–15-year non-renewable term. The government stated that an appointed element could exist in the reformed House of Lords, whilst the Church of England Bishops would still have a place amongst the appointed members.

In its 2008 White Paper, 'The role of the reformed House of Lords?' [at para 3.1] the Labour government put forward its opinion that:

> 'The reformed second chamber should be confident in challenging both the executive and the House of Commons. The second chamber should be able to make the government pause and reconsider. Ultimately, however, the government should be able to get its business through the legislature, through effective resolution of disagreements between the two Houses and, if necessary in the most exceptional cases, by using the Parliament Acts. This ensures the primacy of the House of Commons and means that, ultimately, any gridlock between the two Houses can be resolved.'

It was clear that the then government was determined to secure the supremacy of the House of Commons and to prevent the House of Lords from having increased powers to veto legislation. The reforms would increase the legitimacy of the House of Lords.

REFLECTION

Lord Bingham argued that appointment 'no matter how enlightened and wise the process of selection, can never yield a House which is either democratic or representative or constituted on a popular basis'. Whereas His Lordship highlighted that an elected House would raise other problems, namely how the members would be elected. If the members were elected by proportional representation then the Lords would feel 'more truly representative of opinion in the country than the Commons'. His Lordship stated that an elected House might see the members being drawn from second rate politicians and the House would lose its current distinguished membership (Lord Bingham 2011, pp. 116–118).

It is interesting to look at House of Lords reform from the viewpoint of a senior member of the judiciary. Lord Bingham proposed that the House should be replaced by a Council of the Realm.

- It would be similar to the House of Lords and wholly appointed.
- Its role would be to review legislative proposals and not law-making. Parliament would be unicameral and the Council would not be a second chamber. It could not recommend the contents of a bill, but could make recommendations to the Commons.
- The Council could not veto legislation and would have fewer powers than the current House of Lords.
- The Council would choose its own members.
- Members could become ministers.
- The Commons would take heed of the recommendations made by the Council.

These proposals would protect the experience, reputation and knowledge of the current House of Lords, which would be lost by having an elected House of Lords.

Recent Coalition proposals

The Coalition government proposed further reform of the House of Lords. The draft bill was presented to the Parliament along with the government's White Paper. These reforms were considered by the Joint

Committee on the Draft House of Lords Reform Bill. However, the Prime Minister, David Cameron, decided not to proceed with House of Lords reform. This was a political decision because of the lack of support from Conservative backbenchers and the amount of time that would have to be spent debating the proposals in the House of Commons. Whether there will be an attempt at further reform of the House of Lords after the 2015 General Election remains to be seen (note the Fixed-term Parliaments Act 2011).

The draft House of Lords Reform Bill 2011 contained the following proposals:

- Initially the name 'The House of Lords' would be retained – although some favour renaming it as the Senate.
- The chamber would contain 300 members. The membership could be wholly elected, or have a majority elected (240) and 60 appointed. There would be 12 Church of England Bishops. Although there would be no hereditary peers in the reformed House. They could stand for election as elected members.
- The supremacy of the House of Commons would be preserved, with the Parliament Acts 1911 and 1949 unchanged. The elections to the House of Lords would be staggered, with a third elected every five years. This is similar to the United States Senate.
- Each member would serve for one fifteen-year term. This would be non-renewable.
- The appointed members would be chosen along a similar process as today.
- A peerage would not be given to members of the House of Lords.
- Unlike the present House of Lords the members would receive a salary.
- Members would be elected by proportional representation. The bill suggested using the single transferable vote.

It is perhaps ironic that the Coalition government intended to reform the House of Lords at the same time that the House proved to be extremely effective at checking the government's reforms. During 2011–2012 the government suffered a number of defeats in the House of Lords. (For more details on government defeats in the House of Lords see the UCL Constitution Unit's ongoing research at: http://www.ucl.ac.uk/silva/constitution-unit/research/parliament/house-of-lords/lords-defeats).

> You have been asked to vote on the future of the House of Lords, please vote for the option that you find most preferential. What were your reasons for choosing this option?
>
> The House of Lords should be abolished as we require only one chamber [ ]
>
> The House of Lords should be 100 per cent elected [ ]
>
> The House of Lords should stay as it is now [ ]
>
> The House of Lords should be 70 per cent elected and 30 per cent appointed [ ]
>
> The House of Lords should be 70 per cent appointed and 30 per cent elected [ ]

REFLECTION

FUNCTION OF PARLIAMENT

We shall now look at the function of Parliament. We will look at the law-making powers of Parliament, the recently reformed judicial function of Parliament and the role of Parliament in providing a check on the power of the executive.

Law-making

The most important function of Parliament is making law. We will look at how laws are made.

Different types of bills

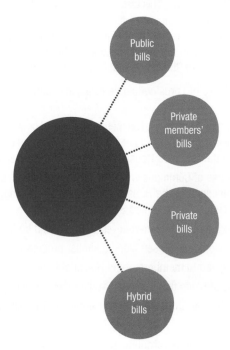

Figure 6.6 Different types of bills

The most common types of bills are public bills (see Figure 6.6 for the different types of bills). Public bills are introduced to Parliament by the government. We shall see below the procedure used for public bills. Examples of public bills include the Constitutional Reform Act 2005.

Private members' bills are unlikely to succeed because being independent of government policy, they are unlikely to attract the support of a majority of parliamentarians. Either an MP, or a member of the House of Lords, can introduce private members' bills. The ways that a private members' bill can be introduced include by ballot, the ten-minute rule and by presentation. The method most likely to be successful is by the ballot procedure. For the 2012–13 parliamentary session MPs were given the chance to put themselves forward to introduce a private members' bill. Twenty MPs were chosen randomly by a ballot and were allowed to put forward a private members' bill.

Alternatively, an MP can use the ten-minute rule which allows parliamentarians a short period of time to raise issues, but this is not enough time to seriously introduce a bill. Equally presentations are unlikely to succeed, as there is insufficient opportunity for the parliamentarian presenting the bill to gain support. Members of the House of Lords can also introduce a private members' bill. An example of a private members' bill introduced in the House of Lords in 2012 is the Airports (Amendment) Bill. Successful examples of private members' bills include the Hunting Act 2004 and the Abortion Act 1967.

Private bills are bills that will only change the law for a particular organisation which will promote the bill. It is not a way of changing the law for the entire country, but only the law in relation to a particular private or public body. An example of a recent private bill is the Canterbury City Council Bill which was introduced in the 2007–2008 parliamentary session. The purpose of this bill was to regulate trading in Canterbury and to increase the powers of the police and council officials to issue enforcement notices.

Finally, there can be a bill which is a hybrid (i.e. part) private and public bill. It is hybrid because it will concern certain groups or individuals (like a private bill), but will also affect the public (like a public bill). Hybrid bills are introduced by the government or a backbencher and will often attempt to undertake a large project, such as the Channel Tunnel Bill. A recent example of a hybrid bill is the Crossrail Bill. Crossrail is a major construction project which will link Essex and Heathrow through a high-speed train and underground link. A bill which is hybrid will undergo a more lengthy procedure than a public bill.

Public bills: procedure and stages

CORNERSTONE

Parliamentary procedure for making law

It is important to consider that before a bill can become law it must be supported by the majority of those voting in the House of Commons and, subject to the Parliament Acts 1911 and 1949, the House of Lords. Finally, before a bill can become an Act it must receive royal assent.

Prior to introducing a bill to Parliament the government will issue a draft bill. This is designed to invite comment from the public. A Green Paper will seek consultation from interested groups and this can influence the bill that will be introduced to Parliament. A White Paper states government policy and is far more precise. The Law Commission will often provide draft bills for the government to consider and many of these have become law, such as the Contracts (Rights of Third Parties) Act 1999 and the Fraud Act 2006.

APPLICATION

How does a bill become law? We have seen the different types of bills and most are introduced as public bills by the government. The government can introduce a bill in either the House of Commons or Lords (see Figure 6.7). Where a bill is introduced in the House of Commons it receives its first reading, which is an opportunity of introducing the bill to the House. The bill will then be debated by the House in the second reading. If the House votes in support of the bill, then it can proceed to the committee stage. The Public Bill Committee will consider whether amendments need to be made to the bill. They will seek the views of experts on the proposed legislation. The amended bill will then proceed to the report stage where MPs can debate whether there should be additional amendments. If the bill is controversial this can be lengthy. Finally, the bill will proceed to its third reading. At this stage no new amendments can be proposed and the House must vote on the amended bill. If the House votes in support of the bill then the bill goes to the House of Lords. The procedure in the House of Lords is very similar to the House of Commons. The role of the House of Lords is to provide an important check on the Commons, as the House is less partisan and there are a considerable number of Lords who are independent (crossbenchers). The quality of the debate is better and more informed. The House of Lords will propose amendments and will often vote against the bill. This has happened on quite a few occasions with the Coalition government's bills over the reform of legal aid, the National Health Service and the benefit system.

Bills introduced in the House of Commons

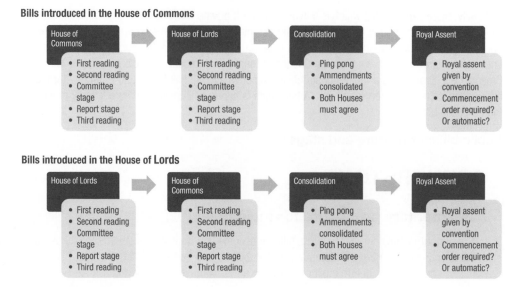

Bills introduced in the House of Lords

Figure 6.7 The procedure for bills in Parliament

What happens if the House of Lords votes against a bill? In this case it must be remembered that the House of Commons is the superior House because of the Parliament Acts 1911 and 1949. The bill will be reintroduced in the Commons and then proceed to the Lords. The bill can be passed after one year despite the House of Lords refusing its consent. However, whilst the Hunting Act 2004 and the War Crimes Act 1991 were passed without the consent of the Lords, the Mode of Trial Bill in 1999/2000 was dropped by the then government after being defeated on many occasions by the House of Lords.

Normally the House will propose amendments and the bill will then proceed to the stage known as consideration of amendments. Both Houses must consider the other's amendments and this is known as the 'ping-pong' stage. Once both Houses have agreed the wording of the bill it will proceed to the monarch for royal assent. Only then will the bill become an Act. As we will see in Chapter 9, the monarch does not have to give her assent to a bill, but assent will be given as a matter of convention. However, the Act must be brought into force by a commencement order made by a government minister, or automatically if there is none. It is not uncommon that sections of an Act will never be introduced.

Resolutions

A resolution of either House of Parliament is not law. Rather it is the House voting to express its opinion on a certain matter.

Executive accountability

An important function of Parliament is to hold the executive to account. In the United Kingdom the executive is very powerful and will dominate Parliament through the governing party controlling a majority of the seats in the House of Commons. Nonetheless, Parliament must hold the executive to account and challenge the bills introduced by the government and secondary legislation made by ministers.

CORNERSTONE

The executive dominates Parliament

In *R (Jackson)* v. *Attorney-General* Lord Steyn observed the government's dominance of the House of Commons:

'My Lords, the power of a government with a large majority in the House of Commons is redoubtable. That has been the pattern for almost 25 years. In 1979, 1983 and 1987 Conservative Governments were elected respectively with majorities of 43, 144 and 100. In 1997, 2001 and 2005 New Labour was elected with majorities of respectively 177, 165 and 67. As Lord Hailsham of St Marylebone explained in *The Dilemma of Democracy* (1978), p 126, the dominance of a government elected with a large majority over Parliament has progressively become greater. This process has continued and strengthened inexorably since Lord Hailsham warned of its dangers in 1978' (at [71]).

The House of Commons and executive accountability

The superior House

The House of Commons is the superior House. Under the Parliament Acts 1911 and 1949 it can pass legislation without the consent of the House of Lords.

Party control and a government majority

Ultimately the House of Commons can make and destroy a government. If defeated in a vote of no confidence a government must resign. However, as noted by Lord Steyn above, the British political system has had a tradition of returning governments with a majority. Even the coalition government enjoys a majority and has been able to pass what has been controversial legislation through the House of Commons. This means that the government can control the House of Commons and pass whatever legislation that is required.

The vast majority of MPs belong to a political party and therefore will owe their loyalty to that party. The government whips (who are MPs that actively encourage other MPs to vote with the party) will try and prevent a MP from abstaining from or voting against government legislation. Therefore, it is fair to say that most MPs will vote according to party allegiances.

The quality of debate

The quality of debate in the House of Commons is inferior to that of the House of Lords. Debate is often political and avoids real discussion of the issues. The purpose of debate is to review legislation and to propose amendments. The debate is recorded in Hansard and is available to read online. Debates are televised and can be watched on BBC Parliament.

Take note

This is not to say that a government with a large majority is immune from being defeated. Although the previous Labour government had enjoyed a large majority in the House of Commons it still suffered defeats in the Commons. An example of this was in 2005, when 49 Labour MPs voted against the government over its proposed anti-terror legislation. This defeat was the first suffered by the then Prime Minister, Tony Blair, in the House of Commons. On other occasions the Labour government had to rely on the support of opposition MPs in order to counter its own backbench MPs. An example of this was in 2003, when 139 Labour MPs supported a rebel amendment to the British government's position on Iraq.

Questioning government policy

Members of Parliament can ask questions of the government. The most well-known is Prime Minister's Question Time [PMQs].

> PMQs take place when Parliament is sitting every Wednesday at midday for thirty minutes. How effective PMQs is at holding the government to account is questionable, but it is important for both the Prime Minister and the Leader of the Opposition to perform well.

Ministerial question time is an opportunity for MPs to question ministers from different government departments. An MP can ask written questions and will send these to the relevant government department. These can be more effective than oral questions. The answer they receive can be given on a particular named day, or received at some point in the future.

There are other ways of MPs raising issues or questioning government policy. Adjournment debates relate to a discussing a particular topic, either chosen by the speaker or by MPs. The MP whose topic is chosen by the ballot procedure can ask a question, and the minister will respond to it. Adjournment debates take place either in the House of Commons or Westminster Hall. Another way of raising an issue is through an Early Day Motion. An Early Day Motion will attract signatures of support from other MPs, although it is very rare for these to be debated in the House of Commons. Nonetheless, they are a way of raising important issues.

The committee system

We will look at the committee system in the House of Commons. We should note that there are different types of committees:

- select committees;
- general or standing committees; and
- joint committees.

CORNERSTONE

Select committees

Select committees in the House of Commons investigate the work of a particular government department. A select committee is comprised of eleven members from across the political parties which are represented at Westminster.

Membership of select committees is based on the number of seats a political party has in the House of Commons, i.e. the bigger parties will have a larger representation on committees. A minister is not allowed to be a member of a select committee. There are different ways to appoint members to committees, but most are elected by fellow MPs. The select committee's main function is to review the work of the relevant government department and will have access to important information. It will seek written and oral evidence and then will publish its recommendations. The government then has sixty days to respond. The work of the committee is important to ensure that the department is accountable to Parliament. The proceedings of the committee are televised and although ministers and civil servants cannot be compelled to attend when summoned by the committee, it is advisable that they do attend to face questioning.

In November 2001, the independence of the select committees was seriously questioned when the Labour government deliberately prevented the reappointment of Gwyneth Dunwoody to a committee, which she had previously chaired in the previous Parliament. Had she been nominated then she would have probably have been elected as the chairperson. Previously in July 2001, Dunwoody had been stripped of her position as the chair of the Transport Select Committee by government whips. Dunwoody was not the only Labour MP to be stripped of such a position. The government's treatment of Dunwoody illustrates the problems MPs face when they attempt to hold their own government to account.

REFLECTION

The House of Commons Reform Committee delivered its first report in 2009, entitled 'Rebuilding the House'. The committee noted that in response to the Dunwoody controversy, 'the Parliamentary Labour Party agreed a procedure for Labour nominations of Chairs and select committee members to be agreed by their backbench Parliamentary Committee'. The committee discussed the strengths and weaknesses of the select committee system:

Strengths	Weaknesses
Party balance in the select committees. This means that the opposition parties can nominate MPs to sit on committees and overview the work of the government.	Power of the whips to control the appointment of chairperson. This should be a matter for the House of Commons. MPs in order to be nominated have to agree to the parties' choice of chair.
Split between the government and opposition parties between the positions of committee chairs. This means that the government will not have a monopoly over the chairs of the committees.	It is wrong that the executive can prevent 'maverick' MPs from becoming members of a committee, or that 'former Ministers, and that favoured candidates are parachuted into committees when a vacancy occurs'.
Some power for committees in theory to choose their chairperson. Although the committee noted that this is limited in practice.	Lack of transparency as all political parties will decide on how to divide up position of chairs and whips will decide who to nominate as members.
Full membership of committees. There are many MPs willing to serve.	The committee system is used as a source of party political patronage. Membership of committees is 'largely controlled and influenced by the whips [and] might on occasion be less an "alternative career path" and more of an extension of the massive patronage that already exists through the appointment of ministers'.

The committee proposed that chairs of select committees should be elected by MPs. This was adopted and today the chairperson for most select committees is elected by MPs. This takes place through the use of a secret ballot.

We can see why it is very important that the select committees are able to exercise independently from government. The committees need to review the executive and hold ministers to account. The committee noted that the use of committee membership as patronage meant that committee membership would not be regarded as an 'alternative career path'. This means that unlike in the United States where committee membership and ultimately chairing that committee is considered as a valid and important political career, in the United Kingdom it could be regarded as a stepping stone to a ministerial position.

In the United States, committees exercise considerably more power than they do in the United Kingdom. Serving on a committee is attractive to senior politicians. For example, John Kerry chaired the Senate Foreign Relations Committee after losing the 2004 presidential election against George W. Bush. In 2012 Kerry succeeded Hillary Clinton as US Secretary of State.

CONTEXT

General committees are focused around particular bills that are going through Parliament. They play an important part in a bill becoming law. The task of members of a general or standing committee is to consider the merits of a bill and then to write a report which is then presented to Parliament. In order to do this the committee will seek written and oral evidence from civil servants and third parties. The House of Commons will consider the report and any amendments which the committee has proposed.

Joint committees are comprised of members from both Houses of Parliament. They will focus on an area such as House of Lords reform, human rights and the ongoing review of delegated legislation.

Accountability?

Lord Sumption (2011) has written extra-judicially that the House of Commons does hold the government to account. His Lordship was rejecting the view raised by Lord Steyn in *Jackson* (see above):

'There is a widespread perception that Parliament is no longer capable of holding ministers or officials to account, because party discipline enables ministers with a majority in the House of Commons to control it . . . [However] the degree of ministerial control over the House of Commons has if anything declined in recent years. Departmental committees of the House of Commons have proved to be a moderately effective method of holding ministers and public officials to account, and a highly effective method of exposing their inadequacies to politically damaging publicity. Even on the floor of the House, where proceedings are naturally more partisan, MPs have defied the party whip more often and in greater numbers in the last two decades than at any time since the war. Individual ministers are vulnerable to Parliamentary sentiment, however large the government's majority.'

Do you think that the House of Commons effectively holds the government to account? Do MPs have sufficient freedom to raise matters and start debates in the House?

REFLECTION

The House of Lords and executive accountability

Limited power to veto/delay legislation: the Parliament Acts and the Salisbury Convention

As noted above, the House of Lords has a limited power to veto legislation and the House of Commons can pass legislation under the Parliament Acts 1911 and 1949 without the consent of the House of Lords. The **Salisbury Convention** has further limited the House of Lords' ability to vote against governmental policy that was in its election manifesto. Whilst it may appear correct that the House of Lords has limited powers, it must be remembered that the House of Commons is dominated by a government that enjoys a majority of MPs. The House of Lords has voted against many bills and has successfully forced the government to change its policy on occasion. However, even if the Lords cannot prevent a bill from becoming law, their opposition can highlight flaws in the bill and offer amendments, which can be incorporated into the final bill. In 2011 and 2012, the House of Lords voted against bills (legal aid, welfare benefits and the National Health Service) and as a consequence the government made a considerable number of amendments.

The independent crossbenchers, the experience of members and informed debate

The crossbenchers play an important role in preserving the non-partisan environment of the House of Lords. In the House of Commons there are very few members who are not members of a political party. The ability to have a large a number of independent Lords which are not members of either the government, or the opposition, is important as it offers a non-political perspective on proposed legislation. The members of the Lords tend to have a lot of experience in different areas of society, as a debate on a particular topic will benefit from having Lords with experience in that area. This mixture of highly qualified and respected people in the House of Lords has built a reputation of experience and high-quality debate. Debate in the Lords tends to be better and more considered than in the House of Commons. The crossbenchers serve to make debate less partisan. Any reform of the House of Lords would need to preserve this important strength. Ultimately, the House of Lords does serve as an important and vocal check on the government's legislative agenda.

Questioning government policy

Just as in the House of Commons, government ministers in the House of Lords are questioned during ministerial question time.

The committee system

The House of Lords select committees each focus on a particular area of economics, sciences, the United Kingdom's constitution and the European Union. The committee's proceedings are televised. The role of the general committee is conducted in the chamber of the House of Lords by all members, rather than a distinct group of members as happens in the Commons.

Judicial function

CORNERSTONE

Prior to 2009 the House of Lords had a judicial function

Prior to 2009, Parliament (or more specifically the House of Lords) was the highest court in the United Kingdom (see the Constitutional Reform Act 2005). Over time the Judicial House of Lords had developed into a separate court, and only specially appointed Lords could hear appeals (Lords of Appeal in Ordinary). The United Kingdom Supreme Court is now distinct both in location and name from the legislative House of Lords.

The creation of the Supreme Court was seen as an important way of helping to create the separation of powers in the United Kingdom. Importantly, it was confusing if not questionable to have the highest court and the legislative chamber sharing the same name, members (as the Law Lords could take part in debates and vote) and building.

Historically, Parliament used impeachment to hold the executive to account. The House of Commons would vote on whether there were sufficient charges to impeach and the trial would take place before the House of Lords. The last impeachment took place in 1806. Impeachment still takes place in the United States of America and President Clinton was unsuccessfully impeached in the late 1990s.

CONTEXT

KEY POINTS

- Parliament is comprised of the House of Commons, the House of Lords and the Queen in Parliament.
- Reform of the House of Lords has been proposed since the beginning of the twentieth century. The House of Lords Act 1999 left considerable scope for further reform.
- The Parliament Acts 1911 and 1949 have limited the power of the House of Lords to veto legislation.
- Members of Parliament who represent their constituents in the House of Commons are elected by a system known as First Past the Post. Members of the House of Lords are not elected by the electorate.
- Parliament is the supreme law-maker in the United Kingdom and is responsible for holding the executive to account.

CORE CASES AND STATUTES

Case	About	Importance
R v. *Chaytor* [2010]	This decision concerned the recent parliamentary expenses scandal.	Several of the parliamentarians who had been accused of committing a criminal offence had argued that the expenses scandal fell within parliamentary privilege. Therefore it was not a matter for the ordinary criminal courts.

Statute	About	Importance
Parliament Acts 1911 and 1949	These Acts changed the relationship between the House of Commons and the House of Lords.	The Acts removed the ability of the House of Lords to veto certain types of legislation. The House of Lords have been unable to prevent the passing of Acts including the Hunting Act 2004.
Representation of the People Act(s)	Since 1832 a series of Acts have expanded the franchise.	These Acts now allow both men and women who are aged eighteen or over to vote.
House of Lords Act 1999	The Act removed most of the hereditary peers from the House of Lords.	This Act started the process of reforming the House of Lords. Many commentators regard the reform of the House of Lords as incomplete.

FURTHER READING

Bingham, T. *Lives of the Law: Selected Essays and Speeches 2000–2010* (Oxford University Press: Oxford, 2011)
This book provides comment on the House of Lords reforms as well as an alternative proposal.

Bradley, A. and Ewing, K. *Constitutional and Administrative Law* 15th edn (Pearson: Harlow, 2011)
A detailed textbook which provides students with additional content to this book.

Gay, O. and Tomlinson, H. 'Parliamentary privilege and freedom of speech' in Horne, A., Drewry, G. and Oliver, D. *Parliament and the Law* (Hart: Oxford, 2013)
Refer to this chapter for a discussion on parliamentary privilege and freedom of speech.

Hadfield, B. 'Devolution and the changing constitution: evolution in Wales and the unanswered English question' in Jowell, J. and Oliver, D. (eds) *The Changing Constitution* (Oxford University Press: Oxford, 2007) →

This chapter offers a detailed look at devolution and the absence of devolved powers to England.

House of Lords Briefing (2006) 'Reform and proposals for reform since 1900' (available at http://www. parliament.uk/documents/lords-information-office/hoflbpreform.pdf)
This document provides an overview of the key reforms of the House of Lords in the twentieth century.

Leyland, P. *The Constitution of the United Kingdom: A Contextual Analysis* **(Hart: Oxford, 2007)**
See the chapters on the UK Parliament and devolution.

Lipscombe S. and Horne, A. 'Parliamentary privilege and criminal law' in Horne, A., Drewry, G. and Oliver, D. *Parliament and the Law* **(Hart: Oxford, 2013)**
Refer to this chapter for details on the parliamentary expenses scandal.

Oliver, D. 'The Parliament Acts, the constitution, the rule of law, and the second chamber' (2012) 33(1) *Statute Law Review* **1**

An interesting article looking at the most recent reforms to the House of Lords.

Sumption, J. 'Judicial and political decision-making: The uncertain boundary', The F.A. Mann Lecture, 2011
An interesting paper that looks at the role of the judiciary and also the argument that Parliament cannot hold the government to account.

Wakeham, Lord (Chairman) *A House for the Future: Royal Commission on the Reform of the House of Lords* **(The Stationery Office: London, 2000)**
Refer to this to understand the reforms proposed by the Wakeham Commission.

White Paper (2008) 'An elected second chamber: Further reform of the House of Lords'; White Paper (2011) 'The House of Lords Reform Draft Bill'
Refer to the 2011 document for the most recent proposed reforms.

www.parliament.uk
A useful website that provides details on the workings and functions of Parliament.

CHAPTER 7

The executive: Crown, government and accountability

BLUEPRINT

The executive: Crown, government and accountability

KEY QUESTIONS

LEGISLATION

- Freedom of Information Act 2000

CONTEXT

- Transformation from absolute monarchy to cabinet government.
- The creation of the office of Prime Minister.

CONCEPTS

- The convention of individual ministerial responsibility
- The convention of collective ministerial responsibility
- The Crichel Down affair
- Cabinet government
- The Civil Service
- The Ministerial Code

- Has the 2010–15 Coalition government changed the operation of government in the United Kingdom?
- Are existing forms of accountability effective?

- What role does the monarch have?
- How did the modern form of cabinet government arise?
- Who holds the government to account?

CASES

- *Attorney-General* v. *Jonathan Cape Ltd* [1976]

REFORM

- Will the United Kingdom still have a monarchy in 50 years?
- Will there be more coalition governments in the future? What impact will this have on the Westminster model of government?

SPECIAL CHARACTERISTICS

- The 'Crown' is a misleading term
- The monarch's right to be consulted, to encourage and to warn
- Parliament must hold the executive to account
- The Queen's role in the Commonwealth
- The Prime Minister must be a member of the House of Commons

CRITICAL ISSUES

Setting the scene

The executive is responsible for the governance of the United Kingdom. When we talk about the executive we could mean the government, the cabinet, the Prime Minister or the Crown. Equally we could be referring to the civil servants who run the government departments, local authorities, government agencies such as the Crown Prosecution Service or the Highways Agency, or the armed forces. The growth of the executive in the twentieth century has been considerable, with the executive now responsible for many areas of our lives. We will all encounter the state and its agencies on a daily basis, and our day-to-day freedoms are monitored and in some ways restricted by the state. For example, our telephone calls may be tapped, our journey to work recorded by CCTV cameras, our private information collated and until recently it was likely that we would all require a compulsory identity card.

We will focus on the roles of the monarch, the government, the cabinet, the Prime Minister and government departments. Consideration will also be given to the executive bodies which have been created by devolution in Wales, Scotland and Northern Ireland, as well as a directly elected mayor in London. Given that the executive is responsible for the running of the United Kingdom and will make important decisions, such as the closing of hospitals, the decision to invade a foreign country and indeed which schools will receive funding to replace existing buildings, we will look at how the executive is held to account. Accountability is important to prevent the executive from dominating public life and taking arbitrary decisions. We will look at how the executive is held to account, politically by Parliament, and legally by the courts.

Chapter overview

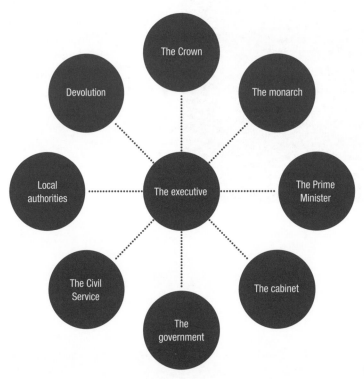

THE CROWN

CORNERSTONE

The 'Crown' is a misleading term

The Crown is a term which is misleading, as Maitland famously wrote '[t]here is one term against which I wish to warn you, and that term is "the crown". You will certainly read that the crown does this and the crown does that. As a matter of fact we know that the crown does nothing but lie in the Tower of London to be gazed at by sight-seers' (*The Constitutional History of England* (Cambridge University Press: Cambridge, 1965), p. 418).

The Crown is an important symbol of the state, as during the State of Opening of Parliament by the Queen, the Crown will be brought to Parliament in its own carriage and will be accompanied by an escort of the Household Cavalry.

Maitland observed that in order to see who exercises the power we needed to look at whether the power was being exercised under the prerogative or statute. The Crown is shorthand for the power which is exercised by the government, though prerogative and statutory powers. The Crown can be used to describe the monarch's powers or those powers which are exercised by the government.

THE MONARCH

The head of state of the United Kingdom is the monarch. The monarchy is a constitutional one, meaning that the monarchy's role is regulated by the constitution. The monarch's power is restricted by the constitution. We need to appreciate that the restrictions are not written down nor are they legal, instead constitutional conventions regulate the monarch's role within the United Kingdom's constitution.

Over the last several hundred years the monarch's power has been reduced. The monarch's ability to make laws was challenged by Parliament and the courts during the seventeenth century. Today the monarch plays a largely ceremonial role carrying out duties such as opening Parliament, receiving ambassadors and giving formal assent to legislation. The monarch is also head of the Commonwealth and is still head of state of many Commonwealth nations including Australia, Canada and Jamaica.

The current monarch is Elizabeth II who has reigned since 1952. Elizabeth II is Queen of the United Kingdom (although to be accurate she should be Elizabeth I). The heir to the throne is Prince Charles, Prince of Wales (see Figure 7.1 for a list of monarchs since 1714).

Take note

The monarch has personal prerogative powers and could theoretically refuse to give her assent to legislation, to choose her government and Prime Minister. Legally the monarch could do these things. However, the monarch will follow constitutional conventions which state that her power will be controlled by established constitutional principles. The existence of the monarchy is owed to the monarch's voluntary surrender of power.

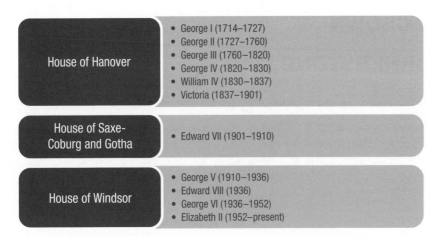

Figure 7.1 The monarchs of the United Kingdom since 1714

CORNERSTONE

The Queen's role in the Commonwealth

The Queen is also the monarch of those Commonwealth countries where she is also head of state. For example, Elizabeth II is Queen of Australia and is represented by a governor-general who gives formal assent to legislation. The Queen of Australia has prerogative powers and these are regulated by constitutional conventions.

A constitutional monarchy

The United Kingdom is a constitutional monarchy and over time the monarch's actual power has been gradually eroded.

The fact that the monarchy still exists is a remarkable achievement. Most other European monarchies were swept away at the end of the First World War. Germany, France, Russia, Italy and Poland are republics, while Spain and several other northern European countries, such as Denmark and Norway, are monarchies.

CONTEXT

The monarchy under the Stuarts was one of absolute monarchs who claimed to have the divine right of kings. James I and Charles I believed themselves to have superior law-making powers to Parliament and Charles I ruled for much of his reign without there being a Parliament. Charles I fought a civil war against Parliament, but was defeated and executed. Eventually the monarchy was restored under Charles II, who clashed with Parliament, as did his brother James II, who eventually fled to

France. Parliament gave the crown to William III and Mary II and from then on Parliament was acknowledged as legally sovereign, and was superior to the executive. The monarchy retained considerable power, however, until the succession of the German-speaking George I in the eighteenth century and the creation of cabinet government. Then George I handed over the day-to-day running of the country to his first minister, Sir Robert Walpole, who is regarded as the first Prime Minister. Thenceforth, it was parliamentarians who dominated the executive and exercised most of the monarch's prerogative powers.

REFLECTION

The monarchy has been good at evolving to survive. The modern House of Windsor was created by George V in 1917 to distance himself from his German relatives. George V was determined that the monarchy would be connected to the British people and he recorded the first Christmas Day broadcast which continues today. Commenting on how the monarchy has survived as a legitimate system in a democracy, Vernon Bogdanor wrote:

> 'The most remarkable feature in the history of the monarchy remains the skill with which it has adapted itself to changing conditions. In Britain, the monarchy has been an institution which, behind unchanging forms, has seemed almost infinitely adaptable, even if at times this adaption seemed somewhat unwilling' (Bogdanor 1995, p. 302).

Recently, Parliament has enacted legislation that will permit the first-born child of the monarch to succeed to the throne regardless of gender. This is important as it shows that the monarchy as an institution is not sexist. The monarchy must be relevant if it is to survive and it must serve its important purpose that according to Bogdanor is to represent the United Kingdom (p. 307). The present monarch, Elizabeth II, has represented the United Kingdom abroad and serves as an important symbol of continuity with the past, and as a head of state the monarch is above party politics.

Walter Bagehot in *The English Constitution* (1867) noted:

> 'A *family* on the throne is an interesting idea . . . [it] brings the pride of sovereignty to the level of petty life. No feeling could seem more childish than the enthusiasm of the English at the marriage of the Prince of Wales' (p. 85).

Bagehot was writing in the 1860s, but this surely applies to the royal wedding of Prince William and Catharine Middleton in 2011?

The personal power of the monarch

The monarch exercises those prerogative powers which are personal to her (see Chapter 9). The monarch has the power to refuse assent to legislation, to choose her next government and Prime Minister and to dissolve Parliament (subject to the Fixed-term Parliaments Act 2011). These powers are very important and it might seem strange that in a democracy, a person who is unelected would exercise these. However, the constitution controls the exercise of these powers through the existence of conventions. The last monarch to refuse to give her assent to a bill was Queen Anne in 1707, and George III understood that in the early 1780s that he could not refuse assent to legislation which he disliked.

The monarch cannot exercise her prerogative powers unless acting upon the advice of her ministers. Obviously, she could act without such advice, but this would mean that the monarch would be acting unconstitutionally.

> Exceptionally, there may be times that the monarch will exercise her powers without the advice of her ministers. Elizabeth II in her capacity as Queen of Fiji sent two messages in 1987; these messages were sent without the advice of her Fijian ministers who had been deposed by a military coup.

CONTEXT

This means that the choosing of a government, the dissolution of Parliament and the giving of royal assent is decided for the monarch by the electorate, the Prime Minister and Parliament. Where the monarch has exercised her powers to make a choice without first having received advice, then such an exercise of choice might prove controversial. An example of this is where the monarch had to choose between two leading members of the Conservative Party to become Prime Minister in 1957 and 1963. Today the internal rules of the Conservative Party would decide the leadership of the party, so that the monarch would not be required to make such a choice again.

Bagehot noted that the monarch had the prerogative power to veto legislation, but in reality '[s]he must sign her own death-warrant if the two Houses unanimously send it up to her', and that the monarch no longer controlled the executive, as ministers pursue policies independently of the monarch (pp. 98–99). Bagehot defined the rights of the monarch as being the right to be consulted, the right to encourage and the right to warn. The monarch today still has weekly meetings with the Prime Minister and offers advice and encouragement, and may well warn against particular government proposals. These meetings are private and so we do not know what is said.

CORNERSTONE

The monarch's right to be consulted, to encourage and to warn

Walter Bagehot, *The English Constitution* (1867), p. 111
'To state the matter shortly, the sovereign has, under a constitutional monarchy such as ours, three rights – the right to be consulted, the right to encourage, the right to warn. And a king of great sense and sagacity would want no others. He would find that his having no others would enable him to use these with singular effect. He would say to his Minister: "The responsibility of these measures is upon you. Whatever you think best must be done. Whatever you think best shall have my full and effectual support. BUT you will observe that for this reason and that reason what you propose to do is bad; for this reason and that reason what you do not propose is better. I do not oppose, it is my duty not to oppose; but observe that I WARN." Supposing the king to be right, and to have what kings often have, the gift of effectual expression, he could not help moving his Minister. He might not always turn his course, but he would always trouble his mind.'

The monarch's roles

The monarch is the head of state of the United Kingdom and whilst this role is heavily ceremonial, the monarch's assent is needed before legislation becomes law. The monarch chairs the Privy Council and exercises important prerogative powers. The monarch is also the head of the Commonwealth, which includes countries such as India and Canada. The monarch does not have any powers as the head of the Commonwealth, rather this role is ceremonial, but the monarch will use her position to conduct personal diplomacy with other heads of state. The monarch is the Supreme Governor of the Church of England. This role is inherited from Henry VIII breaking links with the Roman Catholic Church in the 1530s.

Should the United Kingdom become a republic?

Most countries are republics and there have been calls for the United Kingdom to become a republic and for the abolishment of the monarchy. If the United Kingdom became a republic then either the Prime Minister would become the head of state, or we might have an elected President who would take on many of the monarch's powers, as is the case in Germany or Italy. Polls suggest that the monarchy is still very popular, and it is telling that Alec Salmond, who is the First Minister of Scotland, would wish to keep the monarch as the head of state of an independent Scotland.

THE GOVERNMENT

The United Kingdom is governed by the executive. The government manages the country and is responsible for national matters such as transportation, health and defence. Many of these areas will be managed on a more local level by National Health Service Trusts and local authorities. However, it is the government that is ultimately responsible and takes key decisions.

The party that wins the most seats in the House of Commons at a General Election will have the right to form the next government. The leader of that political party will become the Prime Minister and he will be invited by the monarch to form her next government. The Prime Minister will then choose members of Parliament to serve as members of the government. The most senior positions in government entitle their holder to become a member of cabinet. The cabinet will control the most important areas of government policy. The House of Commons Disqualification Act 1975 limits the number of MPs that may become ministers. This is important as becoming a minister entitles the MP to a higher salary and other important benefits. Consequently, many MPs are loyal to their party because they are aiming to become a minister in the future. Senior ministers are known as Secretaries of State and will be responsible for running government departments. Junior ministers will help the Secretary of State to run the department. The actual government department will be run by the Civil Service which is independent of the political party in power and whose employees will remain in their jobs no matter what political party is in government.

We shall see that the political party with the next largest number of MPs will take on the role as the Official Opposition. Members of the opposition will be selected as shadow government ministers and are effectively a government in waiting (see Figure 7.2).

By convention all members of the government must be members of either the House of Commons or Lords. This means that in the United Kingdom there is a weak separation of powers between the executive and the legislature, as the same people will serve as a government ministers and as MPs. The situation in the United Kingdom can be contrasted with the United States of America, where the constitution expressly prohibits members of the legislature

> **Take note**
>
> The current government is a coalition government. The Conservative-Liberal Democrat government is the first peace-time coalition government since the 1930s.

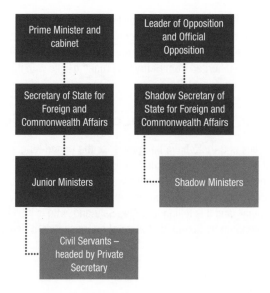

Figure 7.2 The government and the official opposition

from serving as members of the executive (see Figure 7.3). The government relies on whips, who are MPs, to encourage their fellow MPs from the governing party to vote in line with the government. The whips are accused of bullying MPs and threatening sanctions in the event that they do not vote to support government bills. MPs who are members of the governing party, but do not vote in accordance with the government's instructions, are known as rebels.

The cabinet

CORNERSTONE

Cabinet government

The cabinet takes the important decisions and it is chaired by the Prime Minister. The cabinet must take decisions collectively. The Prime Minister can determine the membership of cabinet.

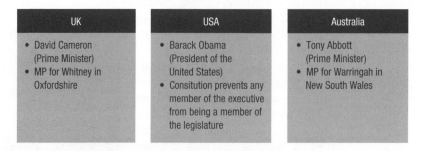

Figure 7.3 Contrasting the United Kingdom with the United States and Australia

The role of the cabinet is to direct government policy. Bagehot described it as 'a board of control chosen by the legislature, out of persons whom it trusts and knows, to rule the nation' (p. 67). The cabinet is comprised of the most senior members of the government and there will be between twenty-two and twenty-four members. The cabinet takes important decisions and the Prime Minister should consider the views of his colleagues.

Recently Prime Ministers have been accused of becoming presidential and ruling through an inner-circle of advisors and not involving the entire cabinet with making important decisions. Tony Blair (who was Prime Minister between 1997–2007) was accused of having a *kitchen cabinet*, which meant that the Prime Minister would rely on a small circle of advisers rather than his cabinet. Many of his decisions, including to invade Iraq in 2003, were discussed outside of cabinet which was informed once the decision had effectively been taken. This led some members of the cabinet to resign, complaining that they had not been properly consulted.

Cabinet government has developed from the days when the monarch would chair the meetings of his ministers, to a meeting chaired by the Prime Minister. The name Prime Minister became the term used to describe by the most important person in the cabinet.

The Prime Minister is responsible for deciding who to promote to a ministerial position and the monarch traditionally consents to the Prime Minister's request to use the prerogative to make the appointments. The 2010 Coalition Agreement states that the Prime Minister will not remove a Liberal Democrat minister without consulting the Deputy Prime Minister.

The convention of collective ministerial responsibility

In order for the cabinet to function its proceedings must be secret. A minister cannot speak freely if there is a risk that his opinions will be reported to the press by his colleagues. In order to avoid such publicity, the convention of **collective ministerial responsibility** operates to ensure that what is said during cabinet meetings is not revealed by those who attend. Ministers must not criticise decisions reached on a particular matter by the cabinet. It is essential that the cabinet speaks with one voice and there is no dissent. Occasionally, cabinet ministers will be allowed to take different public positions on policies which are controversial. This occurred during the referendum on whether the United Kingdom should continue its membership of the European Union in 1975, and the referendum on changing the voting system in 2011. Often there will be a leak, which is when a cabinet member will reveal what has been said to the press. In these circumstances the press will not reveal the name of their source. The decisions of the cabinet are binding on all ministers and if a minister cannot agree, then they ultimately must tender their resignation, as occurred when Michael Heseltine resigned in 1986 over the Westland affair. The 2010 Coalition Agreement explicitly states that the convention still applies unless exceptions are made.

CORNERSTONE

The convention of collective ministerial responsibility

Collective ministerial responsibility is important as this convention enables the cabinet to act as a whole and appear undivided when they make an important decision.

In *Attorney-General* v. *Jonathan Cape Ltd* [1976] QB 752 one of the issues to be determined was whether the convention of the collective ministerial had been breached. Richard Crossman had been a member of the Labour government and had served in the cabinet. Crossman had written a series of diaries known as the Crossman Diaries. Upon his death his estate and a publisher planned to publish his diaries and to serialise them in a national newspaper (*The Sunday Times*). The Attorney-General, who is a law officer of the Crown and a member of the government, sought to prevent publication and argued that the diaries revealed what had been discussed at cabinet meetings and that publication was not in the public interest. The court held that it was in the public interest that collective ministerial responsibility was protected; however they would only prevent publication for ten years after the events described. This meant that since the first volume of the diaries covered events that had occurred more than years previously the court was not willing to prevent publication.

CORNERSTONE

Attorney-General v. *Jonathan Cape Ltd* [1976] QB 752

In this case the court refused to hold that there was a legal obligation to comply with the convention of collective ministerial responsibility; rather the court had relied on the tort of confidentiality to prevent publication before ten years had expired. The importance of the convention would demonstrate that a duty of confidentiality existed, however the convention was not in itself legally enforceable. Lord Widgery CJ observed that the publisher had argued that a convention is 'an obligation founded in conscience only', and the judgment, whilst acknowledging the existence and importance of the convention, held that the cabinet discussions were only protected by the confidential character of the information discussed.

Lord Widgery CJ noted that the information would be unprotected once it lost its confidential character:

'It may, of course, be intensely difficult in a particular case, to say at what point the material loses its confidential character, on the ground that publication will no longer undermine the doctrine of joint Cabinet responsibility. It is this difficulty which prompts some to argue that Cabinet discussions should retain their confidential character for a longer and arbitrary period such as 30 years, or even for all time, but this seems to me to be excessively restrictive. The court should intervene only in the clearest of cases where the continuing confidentiality of the material can be demonstrated. In less clear cases – and this, in my view, is certainly one – reliance must be placed on the good sense and good taste of the Minister or ex-Minister concerned' (at 771).

It is clear that whilst not being legally binding the convention of collective ministerial responsibility was important to the court finding that the information had the necessary quality of confidentiality. Joseph Jaconelli (2005) considered the question of whether constitutional conventions bind:

'Was this additional element [the convention], which was decided in favour of the Attorney-General ("I find overwhelming evidence that the doctrine of joint responsibility is generally understood and practised and equally strong evidence that it is on occasion ignored") decisive in awarding him judgment on the general point? If the constitutional element were to be subtracted from the case – if the author of the diaries, say, was the director of a leading public company who had kept a record of discussions at board meetings which he now proposed to publish – would the result of the case have been the same? It is possible that the factor of collective responsibility had a critical impact on the result. What is clear is that the "enforcement" of the constitutional convention in such cases is parasitic on the ascription of rights and duties of hitherto uncertain extent. It is inconceivable that the breach of a constitutional convention could furnish a free-standing cause of action' ('Do constitutional conventions bind?' [2005] *Cambridge Law Journal* 149 at 16).

The Prime Minister

The Prime Minister's official residence is 10 Downing Street, which is a badly built and a rather small London townhouse, which once belonged to Sir Robert Walpole. Compared to the Kremlin and the White House, the official residence of the Prime Minister seems quite inappropriate to the importance of the office. However, the role of Prime Minister originates from the dominance of Robert Walpole during the reign of George I and George II.

> Walpole became the first minister of George I, the German-speaking king who ascended the British throne after the death of Queen Anne. Walpole oversaw cabinet meetings in the king's absence from 1721–42. Walpole is known as the first Prime Minister, although the term Prime Minister was not recognised as an official title until much later. It originally was used as a term of abuse, i.e. having too much power. There have been many Prime Ministers who have shaped the office and defined its importance: these include William Pitt the Younger, Benjamin Disraeli and the Marquess of Salisbury. During Disraeli's premiership the ability of the Prime Minister to dominate government was limited by the importance of cabinet ministers, who could develop their own policy. Salisbury attempted to combine the roles of Prime Minister with that of Foreign Secretary, and had to be forced to abandon the latter when he became older.

The Prime Minister is the public face of the government and many voters believe that at a General Election they are voting for who becomes the next Prime Minister (see Figure 7.4 for a timeline of UK Prime Ministers since 1976). This misconception is not helped by the first televised leadership debates in 2010 between the leaders of the three main political parties. However, as we have seen in Chapter 6, the electorate are actually voting for who will become their local MP and represent their constituency in the House of Commons.

The Prime Minister has considerable power and dominates the cabinet. The Prime Minister determines the choice of his cabinet (subject to party rules), and can dismiss cabinet ministers and

Figure 7.4 Prime Ministers since 1976 (NB David Cameron leads a coalition government)

reshuffle important posts. Very few ministers can successfully oppose the Prime Minister and keep their position inside the cabinet. One who did was Gordon Brown, who as the Chancellor, opposed many of Tony Blair's policies from 1997–2007. Gordon Brown was able to do this because he was supported by many Labour MPs and had a popular image as a very competent chancellor.

The Cabinet Office assists the Prime Minister and civil servants are based in 10 Downing Street. Recently, the Prime Minister has relied on special advisors who will advise on media issues, government policy and will act as spokesmen for the Prime Minister. There have been accusations that this reliance on political advisors will exclude the Civil Service and risks making the office presidential in nature.

Where do we find the law which created this office? In the United States of America the office of President was created by the constitution. However, in the United Kingdom the Prime Minister is a constitutional development, which has seen power shift from the monarch to the leader of the largest political party. The monarch has the prerogative power to choose the Prime Minister, but this choice is regulated by convention. The leader of the political party that can command the confidence of the House of Commons will become Prime Minister.

CORNERSTONE

The Prime Minister must be a member of the House of Commons

By convention the Prime Minister must be a parliamentarian and a member of the House of Commons. The last Prime Minister to be a member of the House of Lords was the Marquess of Salisbury in 1902. Since 1902 the monarch (before the day when leaders of political parties are chosen by their party) always chose an MP over a peer to become Prime Minister. The Prime Minister is the First Lord of the Treasury and is Minister for the Civil Service.

Each Prime Minister can determine their style of leadership; some may attempt to devolve responsibility to their cabinet colleagues and act as an equal, whilst others might wish to centralise the governing of the country from 10 Downing Street. In any event the allegation that a Prime Minister dominates his colleagues and exercises presidential powers is not a new one. Blick and Jones (2012) have written that:

'From Walpole's time onwards observers have frequently accused either individual Prime Ministers or the office itself of excessive dominance within government. In 1806 the incoming Prime Minister, Lord Grenville, described his immediate predecessor, William Pitt the Younger, as having led "a Cabinet of cyphers and a government of one man alone . . . [a] wretched system".

One critic of the Duke of Wellington as Prime Minister from 1828–30 called him a "Dictator". Sidney Low argued in 1904 that for "the greater part of the past half century . . . The office of premier has become more than ever like that of an elective President". David Lloyd George was described by Harold Laski in 1920 as "virtually the President of a State". In the 1960s John Mackintosh held that the "position and power of the Prime Minister has been the focal point of modern Cabinets"; and Richard Crossman that "the post war epoch has seen the final transformation of cabinet government into prime ministerial government".'

In any event the Prime Minister is held accountable to the media, the public, his own party and the House of Commons. A Prime Minister will be forced (or expected) to resign if:

- his government loses a vote of no confidence (Callaghan 1979 – technically did not resign but requested that Parliament was dissolved);
- she loses the leadership of her own political party (Thatcher 1990);
- his government does not obtain a majority of the seats in the House of Commons (Major 1997, Brown 2010) or cannot form a coalition (Brown 2010, Heath 1974);
- there is a major disaster such as a military/diplomatic crisis (Eden 1957);
- internal party politics necessitates his resignation (Blair 2007).

APPLICATION

What would happen if David Cameron was forced to stand down as leader of the Conservative Party, would he also have to stand down as Prime Minister? And if so, who would decide the person who would succeed Cameron as the next Prime Minister?

A government department

A government department such as the Ministry of Justice will employ thousands of civil servants and will be responsible for many important aspects of running the country. The Ministry of Justice has responsibilities for running the courts and the justice system. The department is headed by the Lord Chancellor who is the Secretary of State for Justice. To assist the Secretary of State there are a number of junior Ministers of State and Parliamentary Under Secretaries of State. They are all politicians and are members of either the House of Commons or the House of Lords. Alongside the politicians, the civil servants run the Ministry of Justice and will try and fulfil the ministerial objectives. The Civil Service is headed by the Permanent Secretary, who is not a politician and will remain in office despite a change in government. The Civil Service has an important role, as it is rare that a minister will be in charge of a department long enough to really understand how it works.

One example of a minister who moved from one department to another over a short period of time is John Reid MP, who from 1999–2007 was responsible for several government departments:

- Secretary of State for Scotland
- Secretary of State for Northern Ireland
- Leader of the House of Commons and Lord President of the Council
- Secretary of State for Health
- Secretary of State for Defence
- Secretary of State for the Home Department

CONTEXT

How qualified are ministers to run a government department? Jacqui Smith has admitted that when she was Home Secretary she lacked the experience to run such a large department. The Institute of Government has advised that ministers should receive training and that the Prime Minister should not appoint individuals to key positions without proper consideration. One cabinet minister was quoted as saying:

'The largest thing I'd run before this was my constituency office of four people – now I have a department of tens of thousands and a budget of billions.'

This means that the Civil Service will run a department and will attempt to give effect to the minister's agenda.

> The classic BBC comedy series *Yes Minister* explored the relationship between Jim Hacker, a minister, and his permanent private secretary, Sir Humphrey Appleby. The series parodied the Civil Service's relationship with ministers and in one famous scene, in the episode 'Economy Drive', Sir Humphrey explained that the civil service did not have to do everything that a minister demanded because of the fact that they were chosen by the electorate. The reasoning adopted by Sir Humphrey was that as there were some 300 MPs from the governing party and about 100 ministerial positions to fill, once those MPs who were not suitable were removed from the equation this left 100 MPs. This meant that a minister owed his office to the fact that everyone else was unsuitable. Further information about *Yes Minister* can be found at http://www.bbc.co.uk/comedy/yesminister/ and details about this episode at http://www.bbc.co.uk/programmes/b007jlbc.

REFLECTION

ACCOUNTABILITY

A minister will hold considerable power and will be responsible for a large government department. The Secretary of State for Defence will be responsible for the armed forces and the ongoing conduct of any oversees military action.

The minister will be responsible to his own political party, the Prime Minister, his colleagues in cabinet, Parliament, the public, his own constituents and the press. What exactly is the minister responsible for? The minister is responsible for his department, the policy and any failures for which his department is responsible. Finally, a minister is responsible for his own personal life, i.e. sexual affairs, financial irregularities and inappropriate friendships.

Professor Dawn Oliver (1999) looked at the parameters of ministerial accountability and identified the following areas of accountability:

- 'to the Prime Minister';
- to the House of Commons and the House of Lords;
- 'to the Parliamentary Commissioner for Administration and the Select Committee on the PCA';
- 'to the Comptroller and Auditor General, National Audit Office and Committee for Public Accounts';
- to the 'Parliamentary Party';
- to the 'National Party';
- to the 'General Public';
- to the press;
- to clients, who are those with whom the minister has links; and
- to the courts.

We will look at some important forms of ministerial accountability and consider their effectiveness.

The Ministerial Code

CORNERSTONE

The Ministerial Code

The Ministerial Code was first established in 1948 and sets out the standards expected of ministers. Ministers are obliged to follow the code, although it is not legally binding. The code was first made public in 1992.

Importantly, ministers must reveal all private interests to the Civil Service in order to avoid a conflict of interest between a minister's private interests and his role as a minister. If a minister breaches the code, then the available sanction is that minister's resignation or the risk of being dismissed by the Prime Minister. For example, the Secretary of State for Defence, Dr Liam Fox MP, breached the Ministerial Code in 2011 and was compelled (by the reaction of the press) to resign. The code promotes ministerial accountability and a duty not to mislead Parliament. Patricia Leopold (2009) notes that ministers upon leaving office are required not to lobby the government for two years (i.e. act on behalf of an interest group or business); if they do lobby within this time, there are no penalties which can be imposed.

Public accountability: freedom of information

CORNERSTONE

Freedom of Information Act 2000

The Freedom of Information Act 2000 imposes a legal obligation on public authorities to disclose information when requested by members of the public. A public authority must consider these requests and determine whether it is justified in withholding the material. The Act was intended to increase the transparency of government.

The executive exercises considerable power and it is important that we are able to have access to what happens. If the executive's actions were secret then how could we ensure that that the executive was truly accountable? Gavin Dewry (2011) wrote that, '[t]he biggest single obstacle to effective public accountability is lack of transparency. It is quite impossible for Parliament, the public and, for that matter, the media, to hold public authorities to account if their actions are shrouded in secrecy.' Therefore, freedom of information is extremely important to hold the government to account. Dewry notes that the Freedom of Information Act 2000 has proved controversial, because the executive can rely on loopholes and exemptions to prevent the revelation of certain information. *The Guardian* in February 2012 reported that the Ministry of Justice has revealed that the Freedom of Information Act 2000 has not improved accountably, nor has it improved governmental decision-making. There was a concern that the Act was being used by journalists who were fishing for a story. The Freedom of

Information Act 2000 covers 100,000 public authorities and imposes obligations for these authorities to consider and process requests made by members of the public. There are a considerable number of requests made each year, with some 200,000 requests being made in 2010. Rodney Austin (2007) criticised the Freedom of Information Act by calling it, 'a sheep in wolf's clothing . . . [as the Act] purports to provide a legally enforceable individual right to access governmental information subject only to specified and justifiable exemptions. It purports also to provide general publication duties in respect of governmental information. But in reality it does neither of these' (p. 397).

The convention of individual ministerial responsibility

CORNERSTONE

The convention of individual ministerial responsibility

The convention of **individual ministerial responsibility** is an important method of executive accountability. Ministers are expected as a matter of convention to act responsibly, and to ultimately resign in the event of failures in their departments or their own personal lives.

Ministers have the freedom to ignore this convention as a convention is not legally binding and cannot be enforced in a court; however, it must be stressed that a minister may be forced to resign depending on the amount of public, press and political support they receive. Ultimately, a minister who loses the confidence of the Prime Minister will be forced to resign or risk being dismissed. The Defence Select Committee which was investigating the Westland affair in the mid-1980s observed that ministerial responsibility was not as straightforward as a minister resigning, '[a] Minister does not discharge his accountability to Parliament merely by acknowledging a general responsibility and, if the circumstances warrant it, by resigning. Accountability involves accounting in detail for actions as a Minister' (HC 519, 1985–86 para 235).

Gay and Powell (House of Commons Research Paper 04/31, 2004) observe that the convention of ministerial responsibility requires that:

1. the minister informs and explains their actions to Parliament;
2. the minister apologises to Parliament;
3. the minister takes steps to remedy the problem; and
4. the minister, if necessary, tenders his resignation.

It is important to note that the person who determines whether a minister must resign is the Prime Minister. Even if a minister breaches the Ministerial Code and misleads Parliament, then it will be the Prime Minister who must decide whether to ask for and accept the minister's resignation. The Ministerial Code is explicit as to this:

'1.5) Ministers are personally responsible for deciding how to act and conduct themselves in the light of the Code and for justifying their actions and conduct to Parliament and the public. However, Ministers only remain in office for so long as they retain the confidence of the Prime Minister. He is the ultimate judge of the standards of behaviour expected of a Minister and the appropriate consequences of a breach of those standards.'

Departmental failures: when must a minister resign?

At the outset it is important to note that there have been calls to distinguish between a failure of policy and administrative failure. If it were a failure of a policy that was under the minister's control, then the minister should take responsibility and ultimately resign, whereas the Civil Service is responsible for administrative failings and civil servants should take responsibility where there have been failures. This distinction has modified the traditional approach to individual ministerial responsibility.

In looking at when ministers are expected to resign for failings in their departments, it is important to look at the Crichel Down affair and the guidance that emerged as a consequence of this scandal.

CORNERSTONE

The Crichel Down affair

The Crichel Down affair involved the sale of land which had been compulsorily purchased by the government in 1938. The family who owned the land had been promised in Parliament that they could repurchase the land at a later date. The promise was not kept and the family fought to be able to repurchase the land. The Crichel Down affair provided an opportunity for Parliament and the then government in 1954 to address ministerial responsibility. According to Griffiths (1955), '[c]onstitutionally, one of the most important questions raised was that of Ministerial responsibility'. The minister whose department was involved, Sir Thomas Dugdale, resigned – but he denied that a minister should take responsibility for all civil servant actions.

The Parliamentary debate in the aftermath of the Crichel Down affair looked at ministerial responsibility and whether the minister should protect the civil servants involved. During that debate, the most famous contribution was from Sir David Maxwell Fyfe who laid down four circumstances and looked at whether the minister should resign in each of these:

A minister *should* resign or defend the actions of the civil servant:

- where a minister orders a civil servant to act;
- where a civil servant who acts in accordance with a policy established by the minister;
- where a civil servant makes a mistake or causes a delay. If this is unimportant, the minister should take responsibility.

A minister *should not* resign or take responsibility:

- if the civil servant takes action without the approval of the minister, then the minister is not responsible and does not have to defend the civil servant.

> ### Take note
> A convention only exists if it is actually followed. We shall see that not all ministers feel obliged to resign in the event of a departmental failing.

Geoffrey Marshall observed that the resignation of Dugdale in 1954 and that of Lord Carrington in 1982 were 'precedents and with a dash of principle may be treated as evidence of a convention' (Marshall (eds) *Oxford Readings in Politics and Government – Ministerial Responsibility* (Oxford University Press: Oxford, 1989), p. 131).

Recently in 2013 Lord Carrington was interviewed by Jonathan Powell for the BBC (*'The Art of the Foreign Minister'* BBC Radio 4, broadcast on 19 May 2013). When asked about his resignation in 1982 over the Falklands War, Lord Carrington agreed that his decision was influenced by his experiences during the Crichel Down affair. Lord Carrington recalled that after Crichel Down he had attempted to tender his resignation to Sir Winston Churchill, the then Prime Minister, who had asked the junior minister if he really wanted to resign. Carrington's answer was no. It is clear from the interview that Carrington thought he should have resigned and that he had resigned over the Falkland in order to avoid an argument about who had been responsible for allowing the Argentineans to invade. It is a really interesting interview and can be found in full at http://www.bbc.co.uk/programmes/b01sdm13.

The fact that many other ministers do not offer to resign should not be taken as evidence that the convention of individual ministerial responsibility does not exist. Diana Woodhouse (1999) has observed that '[b]y the time the Conservative government left office in 1997, the convention of individual ministerial responsibility had been distorted to the point where evasion and half-truths had replaced any notion of giving an account and the acceptance of responsibility for political errors or misjudgements were seldom' (p. 127). The government had witnessed a number of scandals. Powell and Gay (2004) observed that the convention was fluid as it is unwritten and that '[i]n practice, few senior politicians are likely to base decisions affecting their political careers solely, or even mainly, on some uncertain constitutional convention, the exact details of which they may not be fully aware of.' Rhodes, Wanna and Weller observed that, '[the convention] is often said to be honoured only in breach. Ministers often seek to evade responsibilities and not "answer" for actions taken in their name. They rarely resign or stand aside unless the prime minister feels it expedient for them to depart than remain. Politics, not ethics, governs the convention. There may be a "smoking gun", it may be in the minister's hand, but that does not mean he or she will resign' (*Comparing Westminster* (OUP: Oxford, 2009), p. 37).

We will look at some key examples of when ministers have or have not resigned because of departmental failings.

Minister	Grounds	Resigned?
Lord Carrington and two ministerial colleagues	Failed to foresee the Argentinean invasion of the Falklands in 1982.	Yes
Sir Thomas Dugdale	Involved in the Crichel Down affair in 1954.	Yes
William Whitelaw	Home Secretary in 1982 when an intruder avoided the police and entered the Queen's bedroom. The Queen had to talk to the intruder until the police arrived.	No
Theresa May	Border checks not carried out in 2011. Claimed that it was not government policy but the initiative of civil servants. Refused responsibility and the civil servant at fault was dismissed.	No
George Brown	As Foreign Secretary refused to take the blame for a failure to properly handle compensation for former prisoners of war in the 1960s.	No

So when will a minister resign? Woodhouse noted that '[m]inisterial responsibility will always depend on the integrity of the ministers concerned', whilst Marshall stated that the existence of conventions required 'a dash of principle'.

Personal scandal: when must a minister resign?

The convention of individual ministerial responsibility also covers personal scandals. In the event of scandal a minister is often expected to resign, otherwise this will bring his position and department into disrepute. There are some key examples below of ministers who have refused or have resigned.

Minister	Grounds	Resigned?
Robin Cook	Had an affair and divorced his wife, whilst serving as Foreign Secretary (late 1990s/early 2000).	No
John Profumo	Minister of War, who had an affair with a prostitute, who was also the lover of a Russian spy (1963).	Yes
David Mellor	Had an affair (1992).	Yes
Earl of Caithness	Wife's suicide (1994).	Yes
Liam Fox	Allowed his friend to have access to the Ministry of Defence and to attend foreign trips and meetings (2011).	Yes
Ron Davies	Homosexual affair with stranger on Clapham common (1998).	Yes
Tim Smith	Accepted payments to ask questions in Parliament (1994).	Yes
Geoffrey Robinson	Failure to disclose all financial interests, as he was a discretionary beneficiary of an offshore trust, whilst looking into the law in this area (1998).	Yes

So why did Robin Cook refuse to resign? The answer is that Cook had the support of the Prime Minister and that there were no other circumstances which would have forced him to resign. Woodhouse notes that Mellor's and Profumo's resignations were because of other circumstances rather than just their adultery. Mellor's resignation is attributable to mishandling the press, whilst Profumo's mistress was sleeping with a Russian spy. Profumo never returned to politics and spent the rest of his life undertaking charitable work. Woodhouse notes that Cook's refusal to resign 'does not therefore indicate a change in the requirement of ministerial responsibility', just that there 'was neither a constitutional nor a political requirement for resignation' (pp. 111–112).

Does the convention of individual ministerial responsibility exist?

We have seen above that ministers cannot always be expected to resign for departmental failings or failures in their personal life. Academics have argued that the failure to resign should not negate the existence of the convention. Munro (2005) concluded that 'it seem preferable to say that there is a rule of some sort here, even if it cannot be stated with precision and is not invariably obeyed' (p. 86). We can see that Munro's conclusion is a valid one.

APPLICATION

A newspaper has uncovered that a minister has been having an affair. In which circumstances would you expect the minister to resign?

The minister has been spearheading a morality campaign [ ]

The minister's mistress had access to government information [ ]

The minister was having a homosexual affair and lied to the press [ ]

The minister has the support of the Prime Minister and is doing a good job [ ]

Parliamentary Resolution on Ministerial Accountability 1997

In 1997 the House of Commons and House of Lords passed a resolution that called for greater ministerial accountability to Parliament. The resolution was the result of the recommendations of the Public Service Select Committee. There was a concern that ministers and civil servants were not sufficiently accountable to Parliament. The Resolution on Ministerial Accountability (1997) established that the following principles should govern the conduct of Ministers of the Crown in relation to Parliament:

1. Ministers have a duty to Parliament to account and to be held to account, for the policies, decisions and actions of their departments and Next Steps Agencies.

2. It is of paramount importance that Ministers give accurate and truthful information to Parliament, correcting any inadvertent error at the earliest opportunity. Ministers who knowingly mislead Parliament will be expected to offer their resignation to the Prime Minister.

3. Ministers should be as open as possible with Parliament, refusing to provide information only when disclosure would not be in the public interest, which should be decided in accordance with relevant statute and the Government's Code of Practice on Access to Government Information.

4. Similarly, Ministers should require civil servants who give evidence before Parliamentary Committees on their behalf and under their directions to be as helpful as possible in providing accurate and truthful and full information in accordance with the duties and responsibilities of civil servants as set out in the Civil Service Code.

The rest of the resolution is clear that ministers are under an obligation to account to Parliament and to ensure that they and their civil servants give accurate information and sufficient help to parliamentary committees.

Executive accountability to Parliament

CORNERSTONE

Parliament must hold the executive to account

One of Parliament's most important functions is to hold the executive to account. The executive cannot act illegally and will rely on statutory powers from Parliament, in the form of delegated legislation. In addition to statutory powers, the executive can rely upon the prerogative powers.

The executive is accountable to Parliament and the House of Commons can bring down a government through a vote of no confidence. In the United Kingdom it is the executive that dominates Parliament, and a government will usually command the support of a majority of the House of Commons. If this is the case, then the ability of Parliament to hold the executive to account is significantly reduced and, importantly, the government enjoys the freedom to make whatever law it wishes. We have seen in Chapter 6 just how effective Parliament is in holding the executive to account. Importantly, we have noted the limited ability of Parliament to review the executive's use of the prerogative powers.

Executive accountability to the judiciary

The judiciary provides an important check and balance on the powers of the executive. The courts as we will see in Chapter 13 can judicially review executive decision-making using statutory and prerogative powers. Arguably, it is the courts rather than Parliament which controls executive use of the prerogative.

The courts are aware that it is the role of the executive to take important decisions which are needed to govern the country, and so are often unwilling to decide matters of policy. Recently, Lord Sumption has written extra-judicially about the limits of judicial review, arguing that the courts should avoid making policy decisions (FA Mann Lecture, 2011). We will look at the role of the courts in the constitution in Chapter 8.

The judiciary is independent of the executive and judges are no longer appointed by the Lord Chancellor, but instead through the independent Judicial Appointment Commission (see the Act of Settlement 1701 and the Constitutional Reform Act 2005). Ministers and civil servants who disregard court orders can be prosecuted for contempt of court (see for example *M* v. *Home Office* [1994] 1 AC 377 where the Home Secretary was threatened with contempt of court). This is unlike the Crown, which has immunity from being prosecuted for disobeying court orders.

The press and the electorate

Politicians need to be re-elected and so public opinion is important. The executive is held accountable by the public. A government that is seen as out of touch and unpopular will be voted out of office. Politicians have courted the press and the Prime Ministers have needed to have a close relationship with the owners of the leading newspapers. This close relationship between politicians and the press led in part to the Leveson Inquiry in 2012.

> **Take note**
>
> The courts can quash executive decisions, where for example a minister has acted *ultra vires*, which is when a minister acts outside of the powers conferred by Parliament in the form of delegated legislation. The courts can also question whether a minister has acted unreasonably, and can quash a decision that it deems to be unreasonable.

> Recently, this has proved embarrassing for politicians as the phone-hacking scandal has revealed just how close politicians and the press have been. An example of the influence the press have had in the United Kingdom is that John Major believed that he owed his victory in the 1992 General Election to *The Sun* endorsing the Conservative Party. The Leveson Inquiry revealed the close relationship between a senior journalist, Rebekah Brooks, and the former Prime Minister Gordon Brown (whose wife Sarah invited the journalist to a sleepover party) and the current Prime Minister, David Cameron (who went horse riding with her). Texts between Mr Cameron and Brooks, revealed her having to explain what 'lol' meant to the Prime Minister. Brooks and another former editor of the *News of the*

CONTEXT →

World, Andy Coulson, were prosecuted for their alleged involvement with phone hacking at the paper. After a lengthy trial Brooks was acquitted by a jury. Coulson, who had subsequently been the Prime Minister's director of communications, was found guilty of conspiracy to unlawfully intercept communications.

Official Loyal Opposition

The opposition in Parliament is known as Her Majesty's Most Loyal Opposition. The party which controls the second highest number of seats in the House of Commons is the official opposition. The leader of the opposition will ask the Prime Minister questions at Prime Minister's Question Time, and each government minister will be shadowed by a member of the opposition. The shadow cabinet is headed by the leader of the opposition. The opposition receives assistance from the Civil Service to help shadow ministers to prepare for government and to formulate alternative policies.

Delegated legislation and the prerogative powers

Ministers derive their power from delegated legislation and the prerogative powers. A minister's use of these powers can be judicially reviewed by the courts. A minister cannot act illegally.

THE CIVIL SERVICE

CORNERSTONE

The Civil Service

The Civil Service was traditionally not organised on a statutory basis and was instead organised under the prerogative. The Constitutional Reform and Governance Act 2010 finally placed the Civil Service on a statutory footing, long after it was first recommended in 1854.

Take note

Lobbying means that you advocate the views of a particular organisation and attempt to influence policy on its behalf. Organisations will employ lobbyists to work on their behalf. In 2010 several senior former ministers were caught offering to lobby on behalf of organisations and in 2013 journalists uncovered lobbying by MPs.

The head of the Civil Service is the Cabinet Secretary, and he is responsible for 500,000 civil servants. The Cabinet Secretary is a high-profile figure who will look to protect the interests of the civil servants and will at times disagree with the Prime Minister.

Civil servants work in the government departments and are not political appointees. The Liberal Prime Minister, William Gladstone, in 1853 sought to reform the Civil Service and asked Sir Stafford Northcote and Charles Trevelyan to make recommendations in their report. Their subsequent report recommended the creation of a professional and independent Civil Service. The reforms prevented the Civil Service from being used as political patronage, i.e. preventing posts in the Civil Service from being awarded to supporters of the government. The report called for promotion on merit and the requirement that anyone could apply to become a civil servant so long as they were able to pass an examination. In 1870 the Civil Service Commission (which was created in 1855) introduced examinations for junior members of the Civil Service and this ensured that the Civil Service was competent and professional (see Sir Ivor Jennings, *The Queen's Government* (Pelican: London, 1960), p. 106). This has meant that the key feature of the British Civil Service is neutrality and not loyalty to one particular political party. Nonetheless, it has become usual for governments to employ political advisors to give advice on policy issues.

There is a Civil Service Code and the civil servants are prevented from lobbying. Civil servants can take decisions using the discretionary powers delegated to a minister by Parliament under the *Carltona* principle (*Carltona Ltd* v. *Commissioners of Works* [1943] 2 All ER 560). There are restrictions on the decisions which civil servants may take using these delegated powers (see *R* v. *Secretary of State of the Home Department ex p. Doody* [1994] 1 AC 531). Where there has been unauthorised delegation to a civil servant, then the decision made by the civil servant can be judicially reviewed. Civil servants should be protected under the guidance laid down by Sir David Maxwell Fyfe following the Crichel Down affair. Despite this ministers have continued to blame civil servants for their department's failings.

LOCAL AUTHORITIES AND AGENCIES

Local authorities are responsible for running their communities. Local authorities are, amongst other things, responsible for waste management, schools and planning permission. The actions of a local authority can be judicially reviewed by the courts.

DEVOLVED POWERS

Powers have been devolved under the previous Labour government. In London there is an elected mayor, and in Scotland, Wales and Northern Ireland there are First Ministers who are responsible for their respective governments.

Mayor of London

The mayor of London is directly elected and is responsible for setting policies and a budget to govern the capital. The mayor governs more people than live in Scotland or Wales. The mayor is assisted by a large team of advisors.

Welsh Assembly

Post devolution the leader of the largest party in the National Assembly of Wales is the First Minister. The First Minister of Wales is responsible for chairing Welsh cabinet meetings and governing Wales using the powers devolved by the Westminster Parliament.

Scottish Government

The First Minister of Scotland is Alec Salmond. Mr Salmond is the leader of the ruling Scottish National Party and heads the Scottish government and chairs cabinet meetings. The Scottish National Party won an overwhelming majority in the 2011 Scottish parliamentary elections and now governs Scotland.

Northern Ireland

There is now power sharing in Northern Ireland and a Northern Ireland Assembly at Stormont. The Northern Ireland Assembly does not work on the Westminster model and all parties must share power, whereas at Westminster the largest party controls power.

KEY POINTS

- The position of Prime Minister has developed since the eighteenth century. Prime Ministers have been accused of becoming too presidential and relying on a small circle of advisers, as opposed to their cabinet colleagues.
- The convention of collective ministerial responsibility ensures the secrecy of cabinet deliberations.
- The convention of individual ministerial responsibility holds a minister accountable for their department's failings and their own personal affairs.
- The executive is held to account by the courts and Parliament.

CORE CASES AND STATUTES

Case	About	Importance
Attorney-General v. *Jonathan Cape Ltd* [1976]	It involved the publication of diaries that contained the contents of cabinet meetings. It was argued that this breached the convention of collective ministerial responsibility.	The decision is important as it explored the consequences of breaching the convention, and whether conventions are legally enforceable. The court held that they were not legally enforceable.

Statute	About	Importance
Freedom of Information Act 2000	This Act is concerned with making records accessible to the public.	The Act was intended to increase government accountability and provide freedom of information.

FURTHER READING

Austin, R. 'Freedom of Information Act 2000 – A sheep in wolf's clothing' in Jowell, J. and Oliver, D. (eds) *The Changing Constitution* 6th edn (Oxford University Press: Oxford, 2007)
This is an interesting and engaging look at whether the Freedom of Information Act 2000 has improved government accountability.

Bagehot, W. *The English Constitution* (Fontana: 1983)
The classic account of the constitution in the 1860s.

Blick, A. and Jones, G. *'The Institution of Prime Minister'* (2012) (available at http://www. number10.gov.uk/history-and-tour/the-institution-of-prime-minister/)

Bogdanor, V. *The Monarchy and the Constitution* (Oxford University Press: Oxford, 1995)
This is an authoritative account of the monarchy in the United Kingdom's constitution.

Bradley, A. and Ewing, K. *Constitutional and Administrative Law* 15th edn (Pearson: Harlow, 2011)
A detailed textbook which provides students with additional content to this book.

Dewry, G. 'The executive: Towards accountable government and effective governance?' in Jowell, J. and Oliver, D. (eds) *The Changing Constitution* 7th edn (Oxford University Press: Oxford, 2011)
An interesting chapter on executive accountability.

Griffith, J. 'The Crichel Down Affair' [1955] 18(6) *Modern Law Review* 556
A detailed overview of the Crichel Down affair.

Jaconelli, J. 'Do constitutional conventions bind?' [2005] *Cambridge Law Journal* 149
This article looks at whether conventions are binding and offers a chance to engage in a discussion of legal theory.

Leopold, P. 'Standards of public life' in Jowell, J. and Oliver, D. (eds) *The Changing Constitution* 7th edn (Oxford University Press: Oxford, 2011)
An interesting chapter that provides a modern viewpoint.

Maitland, F. *The Constitutional History of England* (Cambridge University Press; Cambridge, 1965)
A classic text on the history of the United Kingdom's constitution, which is written in a lively and accessible style.

Munro, C. *Studies in Constitutional Law* 2nd edn (Oxford University Press: Oxford, 2005)
This book is highly recommended as a way to further your understanding of the law.

Oliver, D. 'Ministerial accountability', in Butler, D. et al. *The Law, Politics and the Constitution: Essays in Honour of Geoffrey Marshall* (Oxford University Press: Oxford, 1999)
This chapter looks at ministerial accountability and provides an authoritative critique.

Wintour, P. *The Guardian*, 'Freedom of Information Act has not improved government, says MoJ', Monday 13 February 2012 (available at http://www.guardian.co.uk/politics/2012/feb/13/freedom-of-information-ministry-justice?INTCMP=SRCH)

Woodhouse, D. 'Individual Ministerial Responsibility and a "dash of principle"' in Butler, D. et al. *The Law, Politics and the Constitution: Essays in Honour of Geoffrey Marshall* (Oxford University Press: Oxford, 1999)
An interesting and detailed examination of this convention over the last thirty years.

CHAPTER 8

The courts and the judiciary

BLUEPRINT

The courts and the judiciary

LEGISLATION

- Constitutional Reform Act 2005

CONTEXT

- The importance of judicial independence since the Glorious Revolution.
- Judicial willingness to hold the executive to account.
- Reforms brought about by the Constitutional Reform Act 2005.

CONCEPTS

- The importance of judicial independence
- Judicial deference and judicial activism
- Section 5 CRA 2005 representations to Parliament
- The Ministry of Justice

- Do the courts effectively hold the executive to account?
- Is judicial activism inconsistent with the separation of powers?

- What is the function of the courts and judiciary?
- What is the relationship between the courts and the executive and the importance of separation of powers?
- Why do the courts defer to the executive when deciding whether to review certain types of decisions?

CASES

- *R v. Secretary of State for Social Security ex p. Joint Council for the Welfare of Immigrants* [1997]
- *Shaw v. DPP* [1962]
- *Rehman v. Secretary of State for the Home Department* [2001]
- *McGonnell v. United Kingdom* (28488/95) (2000)

SPECIAL CHARACTERISTICS

- The Supreme Court
- Who runs the Supreme Court?
- The Queen is the fount of justice
- A perception that judges are out of touch with members of the public
- The role of the Lord Chancellor prior to the Constitutional Reform Act 2005
- The courts must look at what Parliament intended

REFORM

- Will the courts ever have the ability to strike down Acts of Parliament? The US and Israeli courts gave themselves the power to do this.
- Is judicial deference to the executive a good or bad thing?
- In the future will there ever be a time where senior judges go through a political nomination procedure, as happens in the United States?

CRITICAL ISSUES

Setting the scene

The judiciary plays an important role in our constitutional system, as the courts are tasked with applying the law and interpreting Acts of Parliament. Members of the judiciary have traditionally observed the separation of powers and the doctrine of Parliamentary Sovereignty. But what does this actually mean? We will see how the courts by observing the separation of powers have shown deference to the executive and have avoided making decisions that should only be made by elected officials. We shall also see how the courts have acknowledged that Parliament is legally sovereign and consequently the courts cannot question or set aside an Act of Parliament. We will look at the function of the courts, how judges are appointed and whether they have adequate independence from the executive.

Chapter overview

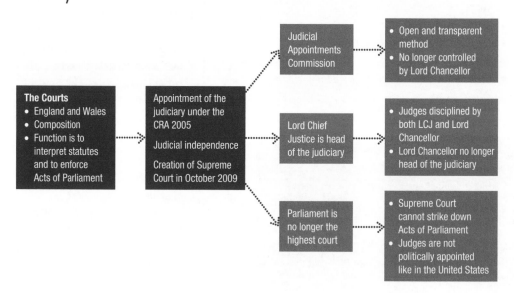

Before reading this chapter it is important to reflect on a number of key points:

- The separation of powers: in Chapter 3 we saw the importance of having the three branches of government distinguished from each other: making laws, using the law to govern the country and finally enforcing the law. It is important that the each branch of government is comprised of different people. The judiciary have traditionally supported the notion that the United Kingdom's constitution observes the separation of powers, whereas it has been academics that have dismissed the notion that the separation of powers is part of the United Kingdom's constitution. In this chapter we will look at whether the separation of powers exists with regards to the judiciary and the legal system. This will involve looking at the importance of judicial independence, as first stated in the Act of Settlement 1701 and then reiterated in the Constitutional Reform Act 2005. We will also look at judicial law-making and the role of senior members of the judiciary in overseeing governmental bodies and chairing public inquiries.

- Accountability of the executive: in Chapter 7 we looked at the executive and the considerable power which the government has. Since 1979, every government has enjoyed a majority in the House of Commons and this control of Parliament permits the government to introduce any legislation that it wishes.

- We will look at how the judiciary has held the executive to account by upholding the rule of law. The courts have held that the executive cannot act unless there is lawful authority for its actions (see *Entick* v. *Carrington* (1765) 19 State Tr 1029), or it is not illegal for it do so (see *Malone* v. *Metropolitan Police Commissioner (No.2)* [1979] 2 All ER 620). The courts have developed judicial review through a series of important common law decisions as an effective way of holding the executive to account. The importance of judicial review cannot be overstated; given the executive's dominance of Parliament it is the courts which have questioned the legality of detaining suspected terrorists indefinitely (*A* v. *Secretary of State for the Home Department* [2004] UKHL 56) and this led to the introduction of the Prevention of Terrorism Act 2005 and the use of control orders. The use of control orders and the use of closed material by the government (i.e. evidence not revealed to the person subject to the order) was considered by the House of Lords in *Secretary of State for the Home Department* v. *MB* [2007] UKHL 46.

- Judicial activism is controversial as according to the theory of the separation of powers it should be the executive and not the courts that make policy decisions. Equally, the courts should not intervene and question policy decisions if these are made lawfully using the powers given by Parliament to a local authority, health authority or indeed the government. However, the courts have been criticised for making policy decisions and for violating the separation of powers.

- Parliamentary Sovereignty is the key feature of the United Kingdom's constitution. The courts must give effect to an Act of Parliament. Under no circumstances can the courts refuse to give effect to an Act of Parliament, the only exception being where there is a conflict between an Act of Parliament and the law of the European Union (see the European Communities Act 1972). However, the courts cannot declare an Act of Parliament void, even where it violates human rights or the rule of law. The courts' role is to interpret an Act of Parliament; however, the courts have been accused of creative interpretation to avoid the effect of an Act of Parliament (*Anisminic Ltd* v. *Foreign Compensation Commission* [1969] 2 AC 147). This means that Parliament's intentions can in effect be ignored by the use of judicial interpretation.

THE COURTS AND JUDICIARY

CORNERSTONE

The Queen is the fount of justice

In the United Kingdom the Queen is the fount of justice and the courts carry out the administration of justice in her name.

We shall begin by exploring the Supreme Court and the impact of the Constitutional Reform Act 2005. See Figure 8.1 for a diagram of the court structure in England and Wales.

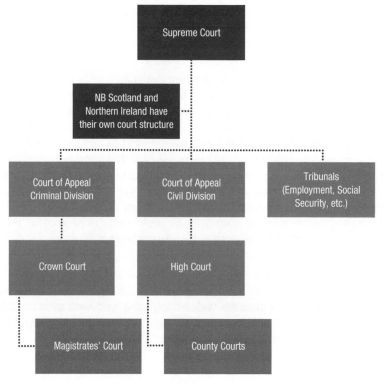

Figure 8.1 Basic court structure in England and Wales

THE UNITED KINGDOM'S SUPREME COURT

CORNERSTONE

Constitutional Reform Act 2005

The Constitutional Reform Act 2005 has had a significant impact on the judiciary. The Act changed the way judges were appointed, reformed the role of the Lord Chancellor and created a new Supreme Court.

The United Kingdom's Supreme Court came into existence on October 2009, having been created by the Constitutional Reform Act 2005. As we have seen in Chapter 3, the creation of the Supreme Court was intended to reinforce the perception that the judicial branch of the state was independent from both the government and the legislature. The theory of the separation of powers requires the three branches of government to each be separate in terms of function (i.e. their role) and personnel (i.e. membership).

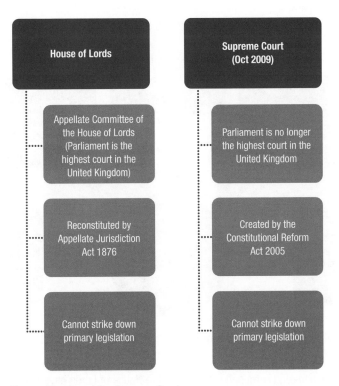

Figure 8.2 The House of Lords and the Supreme Court

Prior to the Constitutional Reform Act 2005, the position of the United Kingdom's highest court did not conform to the doctrine of the separation of powers (see Figure 8.2). As we shall see it was Parliament that was the highest court, and the judicial function of Parliament was carried out by specially appointed members of the House of Lords, known as Lords of Appeal in Ordinary (commonly referred to as the Law Lords). These Law Lords sat in the Parliament and could take part in parliamentary debates. Did this actually matter? In order to answer this it is necessary to consider the position prior to the Constitutional Reform Act 2005.

The position before the Constitutional Reform Act 2005

Parliament was the highest court

Historically Parliament was the highest court in the United Kingdom (see Figure 8.3). The judicial function of Parliament was carried out by specially appointed Lords, which as Lords of Appeal in Ordinary were members of the Appellate Committee of the House of Lords (see the Appellate Jurisdiction Act 1876). The court was known as the House of Lords, and its members the Law Lords, which caused confusion to many members of the public because the judges were members of the legislative chamber of the House of Lords.

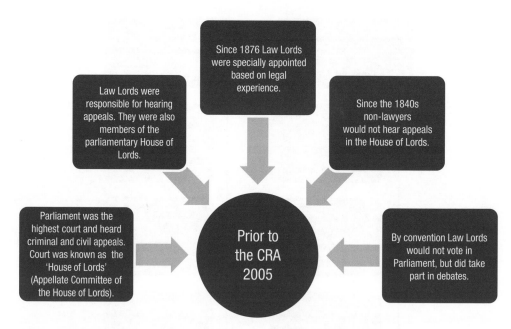

Figure 8.3 Position of the House of Lords before the Constitutional Reform Act 2005

Since the 1840s non-legally trained members of the House of Lords have not exercised its judicial function. Prior to this anyone who was a member of the parliamentary House of Lords, regardless of their legal training, was entitled to hear an appeal. As Lord Bingham observed, some cases were tried solely by non-lawyers, whilst on other occasions the non-lawyers would ignore directions on how to vote from the Lord Chancellor (see *Lives of the Law*, p. 159).

The Appellate Jurisdiction Act 1876 appointed lawyers to the House of Lords in order to carry out the judicial function of Parliament. However, even as late as 1883 a lay peer had attempted to vote on an appeal, and was refused permission to do so.

APPLICATION

The Duke of Thames (fictitious) is a non-lawyer member of the parliamentary House of Lords. Could he hear an appeal in 2008?

The Duke's great-great-great-great grandfather was a member of the parliamentary House of Lords. Could he hear an appeal in 1808?

The Law Lords as members of the parliamentary House of Lords

By convention the Law Lords did not vote, but took part in parliamentary debates in the legislative chamber of the House of Lords.

An example of judges taking part in parliamentary debates was Lord Browne-Wilkinson, who took part in the debate over the Human Rights Act 1998. His Lordship argued against making the jurisprudence (case law) of the European Court of Humans Rights binding on the House of Lords:

'Perhaps I may be heard briefly on this point because soon it will concern me intimately. I am not a great supporter of the amendment . . . the doctrine of precedent, whereby we manage to tie ourselves up in knots for ever bound by an earlier decision of an English court, does not find much favour north of the Border, finds no favour across the Channel and is an indigenous growth of dubious merit. It would be unhappy if in dealing with the convention law we enacted that an English court, unlike any other court subject to the convention, was bound to follow an earlier decision of the European Court at Strasbourg' (Hansard, HL, vol. 583, cols 490–527 (18 November 1997))

Lord Nicholls of Birkenhead took part in the parliamentary debate surrounding the Constitutional Reform Bill (later the CRA 2005) and observed that:

'I regret to have to say that the proposal, put forward with the best of intentions, is misguided. It is unnecessary and would do more harm than good. It is unnecessary because it would achieve nothing of real value. Under the present arrangements the Law Lords do not lack independence from government – no one suggests that they do. Nor do they lack independence from the legislature. By convention of this House, our Law Lords participate in its judicial business, as all your Lordships know. No one could suggest the Law Lords' membership in itself of your Lordships' House compromises our judicial independence in some way' (Hansard, HL, vol. 657, col 1228 (12 February 2004)).

The Law Lords would often deliver their judgments in the legislative chamber of the House of Lords, although they heard the appeal elsewhere in the Palace of Westminster. Lord Steyn noted that as the Law Lords delivered their judgments in the legislative chamber, this often led to confusion as it appeared to some members of the public that the non-lawyers in the House of Lords could vote ('The case for a Supreme Court' [2002] *Law Quarterly Review* 382). This overlap of function and personnel, with the Law Lords sitting in Parliament and exercising the judicial function of Parliament, led to the creation of an independent Supreme Court. Some interesting comments were made by a leading human rights lawyer, Baroness Kennedy QC, who was critical of the position prior to the creation of the Supreme Court:

'[The creation of a Supreme Court] will be a great moment in our transition to a modern constitutional state and would reinvigorate public confidence. The Law Lords, who by self-denying ordinance now rarely speak or vote in the House of Lords, should have their right to do so removed altogether. Just as it is inappropriate for a cabinet minister to sit as a judge, it is not acceptable for judges to sit in the legislature' (2005, p. 151).

Kennedy argued that the Law Lords should have no place in the legislative House of Lords, even though she noted that one Law Lord 'even claimed in a debate that being in the House kept him in touch with public concerns'.

The position after the Constitutional Reform Act 2005

CORNERSTONE

The United Kingdom Supreme Court

The Constitutional Reform Act 2005 created a new Supreme Court for the United Kingdom. The Supreme Court and the Judicial Committee of the Privy Council are based in the former Middlesex Guildhall. The Supreme Court is accessible to members of the public who can visit the court, browse the court's website and follow the court on twitter.

The reforms have reinforced public perception that the Supreme Court is independent from Parliament. Importantly, under section 137 of the Constitutional Reform Act 2005 its members are disqualified from sitting or voting in Parliament whilst they serve as Justices of the Supreme Court.

Control and membership of the Supreme Court

CORNERSTONE

Who runs the Supreme Court?

The Supreme Court is outside the control of the Lord Chief Justice, who, as a result of the Constitutional Reform Act 2005, is the head of the judiciary in England and Wales. The head of the Supreme Court is the President, who is assisted by a Deputy President.

Take note

Justices of the Supreme Court are not appointed because of their political views. Appointment to the Supreme Court should depend on merit and experience. This is important as the executive cannot control who will become a member of the Supreme Court, and subsequently ensures that the court will be deferential towards the current government.

In total there are twelve Justices of the Supreme Court. Presently there is only female member of the Supreme Court and that is Baroness Hale of Richmond. The Queen appoints Justices of the Supreme Court on the advice of the Prime Minister. A suitable candidate is presented to the Lord Chancellor by the Judicial Appointments Commission. The commission that recommends members of the Supreme Court will consist of President and Deputy President of the Supreme Court, and one member from the Judicial Appointment Commission and its counterparts from Scotland and Northern Ireland (Schedule 8).

Members of the Supreme Court will be appointed by a commission which will present its chosen candidate for approval. The Crime and Courts Act 2013 has amended the Constitutional Reform Act 2005 (s.27A) and will permit the Lord Chancellor and the President of the Supreme Court to make regulations concerning the commission and these could permit the Lord Chancellor to have the power to ask the commission to reconsider its selection or to reject the commission's selection.

A comparison with the United States Supreme Court

We will briefly compare the Supreme Courts of the United Kingdom and the United States.

Key facts	UK Supreme Court	US Supreme Court
Date of creation?	October 2009.	February 1790.
Created by?	Constitutional Reform Act 2005.	United States constitution and the Judiciary Act 1789.
How are justices appointed?	The Judicial Appointments Commission (JAC) appoints each new member. The JAC is independent from the executive.	Each new member is chosen by the President. However, the President's candidate must be approved during confirmation hearings in the Senate. The Senate could reject the President's choice.
Politically partisan?	The UK Supreme Court is not accused of being politically partisan. It is independent from the politics of whatever political party is in government.	The US Supreme Court is politically partisan, with justices being appointed because of their political views. There is a divide between justices who are Democratic and Republican appointments.
Power to veto primary legislation on the grounds that it is unconstitutional?	There is no power to do this. Although see the *obiter* comments in *R (Jackson)* v. *Attorney-General* [2005].	The Supreme Court in *Marbury* v. *Madison* [1803] gave itself the power to veto primary legislation. The US Supreme Court will challenge President Obama's Health Care legislation as to whether it is unconstitutional.

REFLECTION

The method of appointing members to the United Kingdom's Supreme Court is very different to the most famous Supreme Court in the world, the United States Supreme Court. The United States Supreme Court was established by the United States constitution and has played an important part in the constitutional development of the country. In the United States the Justices of the Supreme Court are political appointments by the President. The President's choice must be confirmed by Congress and his nominee is essentially a political appointment. This means that the US Supreme Court is often divided along party lines and thus very partisan as its members will vote according to their own partisan views. Controversially in 2000, the US Supreme Court effectively had to decide who would become the next President of the United States after there was a problem with counting votes in Florida. If more votes were permitted to be counted then there was a good chance that Al Gore would become President, whereas if no more counting was permitted, George W. Bush would become President. In *Bush* v. *Gore* 531 U.S. 98 (2000) the United States Supreme Court found in favour of Bush and he was declared President of the United States. The decision of the Supreme Court was controversial. According to Nicholson and Howard (2003):

> 'The fallout was immediate. Democrats accused the Court of engaging in partisan politics and handing the election to Republican presidential candidate George W. Bush. Republicans, on the other hand, spoke of the Court's courage in following the rule of law (and the Constitution) amidst great pressure . . . The [Supreme Court's] decision fell along ideological, and to some degree, partisan lines. The five most conservative justices formed the majority, while the four most liberal justices, including the two Democrats . . . dissented.'

In the United Kingdom it is important that the Supreme Court is not perceived as reaching a decision due to the judges' own political bias.

Judges do have to make some very difficult decisions and the Supreme Court will have the final say in all civil matters in the United Kingdom. Over the past decade the courts have had to decide some very controversial issues. Below are some important cases, involving issues that most people will have a view on (either one way or the other):

- The Court of Appeal in *Re A (Children) (Conjoined Twins: Medical Treatment) (No.2)* [2001] 1 FLR 267 had to decide whether a doctor could save one conjoined twin, if saving that twin would inevitably kill the other twin. The Court of Appeal held that the doctor could operate.

- In *R (Purdy)* v. *DPP* [2009] UKHL 45 the House of Lords had to decide whether the Director of Public Prosecutions was required to indicate what factors he would consider when deciding whether to prosecute anyone who assisted someone with a debilitating illness to travel abroad for the purpose of committing suicide. The House of Lords found in favour of Mrs Purdy's appeal and held that the DPP would need to issue offence-specific policy on the facts and circumstances which would be taken into account, when the DPP decided whether to prosecute.

- In *Airedale NHS Trust* v. *Bland* [1993] AC 789 the House of Lords had to decide whether withdrawing medical treatment from someone who was in a persistent vegetative state amounted to a violation of the sanctity of life. The House of Lords decided that since the patient could not consent, the task of deciding what was in the patient's best interest fell to the doctors. The court distinguished between taking active steps to end a life, which were not lawful, and withholding treatment which was lawful.

Do you think that if MPs had a say over who became a member of the Supreme Court, the candidates' views on divorce, religion, politics and abortion might influence their decision? Kenneth Clarke MP, the previous Lord Chancellor, when appearing before the House of Lords Constitutional Reform Committee was critical of introducing confirmation hearings for the appointment of members of the Supreme Court:

> 'I think there's a danger that they would become political . . . The US experience is just shocking. Some US confirmation hearings are just consumed by the social attitudes of the judge and his sexual history . . . Anything that got near that would be deplorable. Sooner or later you would have some stray MP asking what a judge's views are on this or that. A certain partisanship could creep in.'

REFLECTION

ROLE OF THE SUPREME COURT

The United Kingdom's Supreme Court is the court of final appeal for civil cases in the United Kingdom. It must be remembered that the United Kingdom is comprised of nation states which have their own independent legal systems:

- England and Wales
- Northern Ireland
- Scotland.

The Supreme Court is also the final court of appeal for criminal cases from the English and Welsh Court of Appeal, and the Northern Ireland Court of Appeal. Scotland's final court of criminal appeal is the High Court of Justiciary. However, the United Kingdom's Supreme Court can hear criminal appeals from Scotland only where there is a devolution issue involved.

When does the Supreme Court have jurisdiction to hear criminal appeals from Scotland?

Take note

The Scotland Act 1998 states that the United Kingdom Supreme Court does not have the jurisdiction to hear criminal appeals from Scotland unless there is a devolution issue for the court to resolve, which has been determined by two or more justices of the High Court of Justiciary.

In *Fraser (Nat Gordon)* v. *HM Advocate* [2011] UKSC 24 the Supreme Court held that it had jurisdiction to hear a criminal appeal from Scotland. The appellant had been convicted of arranging the murder of his wife. Subsequently, he had argued that there had been a miscarriage of justice. He appealed on the basis that the prosecution had failed to disclose relevant evidence during the trial. He also wished to include a devolution minute that would state that his case involved a human rights issue. The appellant had argued that the non-disclosure had violated the right to a fair trial, which was guaranteed by Article 6(1) of the European Convention on Human Rights. In *Fraser (Nat Gordon)* v. *HM Advocate* [2009] HCJAC 27 the High Court of Justiciary rejected both the appeal and the inclusion of the devolution minute. The court also refused the appellant's appeal to the Supreme Court. However, the Supreme Court held that under the Scotland Act 1998 it had the jurisdiction to hear the appeal. This was because the High Court of Justiciary had determined a devolution issue and it was arguable that the non-disclosure of evidence in the original trial had breached Article 6. The test used by the High Court of Justiciary to determine whether the evidence should have been disclosed was held to be incompatible with the appellant's human rights. A retrial was ordered and subsequently, the appellant was convicted by a jury in 2012. In 2013, Channel 4 televised the retrial and this was the first time that television cameras were allowed to film a criminal trial.

CORNERSTONE

How the Supreme Court works

Appeals are heard by between five and seven Justices of the Supreme Court. In exceptionally important cases there may be up to nine Justices of the Supreme Court hearing an appeal. Each judge hearing the appeal will give reasons for their decision and often the judges will reach the same decision, but based on different reasons. Occasionally a judge will disagree and will dissent from the majority.

Importance of the Supreme Court in the United Kingdom's constitutional system

The Supreme Court has already heard some important appeals. Many of these cases have been of constitutional significance (see Figure 8.4). These include *R* v. *Chaytor* [2010] UKSC 52 (see Chapter 6) and *Smith* v. *Ministry of Defence* [2013] UKSC 41 (see Chapter 10). The Supreme Court does not have the power to strike down an Act of Parliament. Its powers of reviewing the validity of an Act are limited to those conferred by Parliament by the European Communities Act 1972 and the Human Rights Act 1998. We have seen above that the United States Supreme Court gave itself the power to declare an Act of Congress to be unconstitutional. The United States Supreme Court can judicially review primary

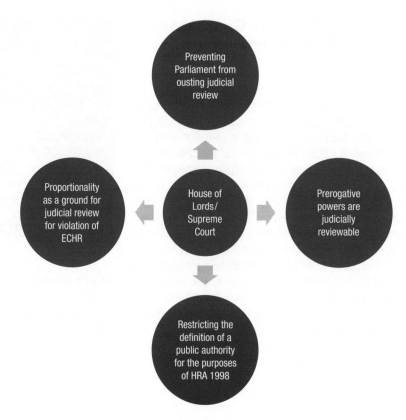

Figure 8.4 Importance of the House of Lords/Supreme Court

legislation. This is something that the United Kingdom's Supreme Court cannot do, as its powers under the European Communities Act 1972 and Human Rights Act 1998 are given by Parliament and could be revoked.

Could the United Kingdom's Supreme Court gain the power to judicially review primary legislation? In order to answer this we must appreciate that such a power conflicts with Parliamentary Sovereignty. It is worth considering the *obiter* in *R (Jackson)* v. *Attorney General* and the fact that both the United States and Israeli Supreme Courts gave themselves the power to judicially review primary legislation. We know from Chapter 1 that the United Kingdom along with New Zealand and Israel does not have a written constitution. In Israel the Supreme Court gave itself the power to review primary legislation. The Israeli cases of *Bergman* v. *Minister of Finance* (HCJ 98/69) [1969] IsrSC 23(1) 693 and *United Mizrahi Bank* v. *Migdal – Cooperative Village* (CA 6821/93) [1995] IsrSC 49(4) 221 have been described by Eli Salzberger 'as equivalents of the famous American case of *Marbury* v. *Madison*'. In *Mizrahi* the Supreme Court (in *obiter*) 'acknowledged the power of any court (not only the Supreme Court) to conduct judicial review of legislation against the two basic laws enacted by the Knesset in its capacity as a constituent assembly' (see 'Judicial Activism in Isreal' in Dickson 2007).

CONSTITUTIONAL REFORM ACT 2005: GUARANTEEING INDEPENDENCE OF THE JUDICIARY?

The Constitutional Reform Act 2005 did much to improve the separation of functions and personnel between the judicial and the executive and legislative branches of state (see Figure 8.5).

The Lord Chief Justice replaces the Lord Chancellor as the head of the judiciary of England and Wales

The Lord Chief Justice was made the head of the judiciary of England and Wales. In this capacity he replaces the Lord Chancellor. According to section 7(2) of the Constitutional Reform Act 2005 the Lord Chief Justice is tasked with representing the views of the judiciary to Parliament, the Lord Chancellor and the government. Lord Hailsham, who served as Lord Chancellor, had justified the many roles carried out by the Lord Chancellor, by arguing that the Lord Chancellor was in the best place to represent the view of judges to Parliament and the government. Section 7(2) gives the Lord Chief Justice the right to represent the views of judges. Section 5(1) permits the Lord Chief Justice to make representations to Parliament. The previous Lord Chief Justice has described section 5(1) as the 'nuclear option' (see Chapter 3).

INTERSECTION

See Chapter 3 for recent comments by Lord Judge CJ on the limitations of using section 5 CRA 2005 and the lack of dialogue between the judiciary and the other branches of the state.

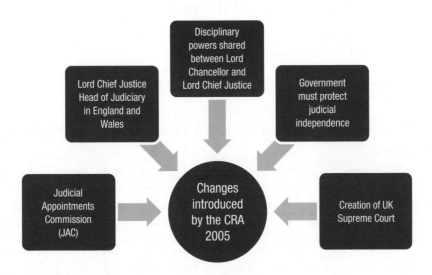

Figure 8.5 Changes introduced by the Constitutional Reform Act 2005

CORNERSTONE

Section 5 CRA 2005 representations to Parliament

'(1) The chief justice of any part of the United Kingdom may lay before Parliament written representations on matters that appear to him to be matters of importance relating to the judiciary, or otherwise to the administration of justice, in that part of the United Kingdom.'

The Lord Chief Justice is responsible for training, offering guidance and the deployment of the judiciary. The Lord Chief Justice has no responsibility towards the running of the Supreme Court.

The Judicial Appointments Commission

Section 61 creates the Judicial Appointments Commission. This was established in March 2006. Under section 64 the commission must have regard to encouraging diversity, and must select candidates based on merit and then only if they have good character. The commission consists of fourteen commissioners and a chairman, which consist of judges, practitioners and non-lawyers. In order to fill the posts of Lord Chief Justice and other senior members of the judiciary, the Lord Chancellor under section 69 may ask the commission to recommend a candidate. Under section 73 the Lord Chancellor can accept, reject or ask the commission to reconsider its recommendation. Similar provisions cover the appointment of Lord Justices of Appeal. If the Lord Chancellor rejects the commission's candidate or asks it to reconsider its selection, the Lord Chancellor is required to explain in his opinion why the person chosen was not a suitable candidate. This decision must be based on evidence and this helps to improve the transparency of judicial appointments. Sections 25 to 31 cover the appointment of judges to the Supreme Court. It is important to note that the Crime and Courts Act 2013 will transfer the Lord Chancellor's role in the appointment process for a large number of judges to the Lord Chief Justice (s.20).

Are judges representative of the population?

Many people often regard judges as being out of touch, and the average judge tends to be privately educated, middle-aged, white and male.

CORNERSTONE

A perception that judges are out of touch with members of the public

Penny Darbyshire has observed that in comedy sketches judges are portrayed as 'stern, old buffoons, ignorant of modern life . . . [w]hen judges are retired judges make radio comments, their accents and vocabulary betray their years at independent school and/or the Bar. They sound condescending . . . Famously, Harman J asked who "Gazza" was, when Paul Gascoigne played for England, and denied knowing who Kevin Keegan, or Bruce Springsteen, or Oasis were . . . Because journalists are vigilant for evidence of judges' ignorance, language can be misinterpreted . . . Judges commonly ask questions to which they know the answer, for the jury's sake' (Darbyshire 2011, p. 23). It is clear that this can do lasting damage to their reputation.

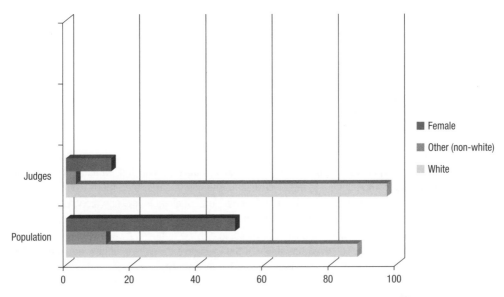

Figure 8.6 Composition of the judiciary – Ministry of Justice Consultation, reported in *The Guardian* (2012)

Figure 8.6 shows a statistical breakdown of the composition of the judiciary. We can see from Figure 8.6 that women and ethnic minorities are underrepresented in the judiciary. Baroness Hale is the first and only female member of the Supreme Court (and its predecessor, the House of Lords), and there have been no non-white members of either court. The Crime and Courts Act 2013 has inserted section 27(5A) into the CRA 2005. This allows the commission, when appointing a Justice to the Supreme Court, to favour one candidate over another, where both candidates are of equal merit, on the grounds that it will improve diversity.

> The problem is that the legal profession which the judges come from is predominately white and male. In January 2012, the Bar Council revealed that in 2010 only 34.8 per cent of barristers were female, and that 77.2 per cent of barristers were white, 10.2 per cent were from minority backgrounds and for 12.6 per cent of barristers there was no data. Barmes and Malleson have carried out research into the composition of the judiciary and have looked at potential reforms ('The Legal Profession as Gatekeeper to the Judiciary' (2011) 74(2) *Modern Law Review* 245). They have noted that whilst most lawyers are solicitors (85%), the Bar dominates when it comes to judicial appointment. This means that the composition of the Bar will reflect the composition of the judiciary. They note that 'any changes that occur are more likely to be driven by developments in the legal profession . . . than by calls for greater judicial diversity'.
>
> Do you think that where a male and female candidate are evenly matched for a judicial role, that the female candidate should be given the job? Could this be justified on the ground of attempting to make the judiciary more representative of the population?

REFLECTION

Discipline

Section 108 covers the disciplinary powers of the Lord Chancellor and the Lord Chief Justice. The Lord Chancellor ultimately has the power to remove a junior judge; however, there is a prescribed procedure in order to do this. The Lord Chief Justice's disciplinary powers can only be exercised in agreement with the Lord Chancellor, and include giving a judge a formal reprimand or suspending them from office. Importantly under section 110, a judge who has been disciplined can apply to the Ombudsman to review the exercise of the powers contained in section 108.

Judicial independence

CORNERSTONE

The importance of judicial independence

It is important that judges are independent of both the government and Parliament. If judges owed their positions and salaries to either of these branches of state, then there would be a real risk that the judiciary would cease to be truly independent. Judicial independence was enshrined in the Act of Settlement 1701, which stated that judicial office holders (High Court and above) held their offices subject to their good behaviour, and could only be removed by a resolution from both Houses of Parliament. This removed the ability of the executive to remove judges, and limited the ability of either House of Parliament to remove a judge for political reasons.

Why is judicial independence important? Prior to the Act of Settlement 1701 judges could be removed by the executive if a judge disagreed with the executive and found against them. In the early seventeenth century, Coke CJ defended the independence of the Bench against the Crown. In the *Case of Prohibitions* (1607) Twelfth Coke Reports, Coke advised the king that he could not intervene and determine cases, and in *Peacham's Case* (1615) State Trials, ii, 869–80, Coke refused to permit the king to force judges to deliberate individually rather than collectively. This was because Coke feared that this would undermine the judicial independence. Coke, according to J.R. Tanner, believed that the judges 'should be independent of the Crown and should act as arbiter of the Constitution to decide all disputed questions' (*Constitutional Documents in the Reign of James I 1603–1625* (Cambridge University Press: Cambridge, 1961), p. 176). Unsurprisingly, the king dismissed Coke for his attempts to limit the Crown's prerogative and views on the constitution.

> ### Take note
>
> Ann Lyon observed that '"Good behaviour" was a vague phrase and has yet to be judicially defined' and that only one judge has been removed by an address of both Houses of Parliament, that being the Irish judge, Sir Jonah Barrington in 1830. Judges who are not protected by this provision of the Act (circuit judges, etc.) can be disciplined by the Lord Chief Justice and Lord Chancellor.

Ann Lyon noted that James II (1685–88) had 'taken care to appoint judges who accepted his policies and was prepared to use his powers of dismissal against those who showed too great a degree of independence' (*Constitutional History of the United Kingdom*, (Cavendish: London, 2003), p. 243). In total James II had dismissed twelve judges and Charles II had likewise suspended judges. The Act of Settlement protects judges from being removed whilst they behave in office, i.e. subject to their good behaviour.

The effect of the Act of Settlement must be appreciated:

'The importance of these developments cannot be over-stated. For much of the 17th century, the judges had tended to interpret the law on the basis of what was good for the Crown. Very few were prepared to risk dismissal by incurring the king's wrath. From the early 18th century, the judiciary increasingly applied and developed the law without fear or favour' (Lyon 2003, p. 263).

Judicial independence has been reinforced by section 3 of the Constitutional Reform Act 2005, which places a duty on the executive to uphold judicial independence:

'(1) The Lord Chancellor, other Ministers of the Crown and all with responsibility for matters relating to the judiciary or otherwise to the administration of justice must uphold the continued independence of the judiciary.'

Lord Phillips, in a speech delivered to the UCL Constitution Unit in February 2011 ('Judicial Independence and Accountability: A View from the Supreme Court'), observed:

'If the rule of law is to be upheld it is essential that there should be an independent judiciary. The rule of law requires that the courts have jurisdiction to scrutinise the actions of government to ensure that they are lawful. In modern society the individual citizen is subject to controls imposed by the executive in respect of almost every aspect of life. The authority to impose most of those controls comes, directly or indirectly, from the legislature. The citizen must be able to challenge the legitimacy of executive action before an independent judiciary. Because it is the executive that exercises the power of the State and because it is the executive, in one form or another, that is the most frequent litigator in the courts, it is from executive pressure or influence that judges require particularly to be protected'.

Lord Phillips is quite clear that the courts must be able to protect citizens by providing a sufficient check on executive action. Without an independent judiciary, free from executive influence, the courts could not carry out this role effectively. An independent judiciary does not exist in countries such as China, where one political party controls the state, and this has an impact on the rule of law and preventing violations of human rights.

REFLECTION

Does the United Kingdom have judicial independence?

Munro has noted that 'Parliamentary motions (under the Act of Settlement 1701) for the removal of judges have been unsuccessful on a few occasions' (Munro 2005, p. 314). One example of this is Sir John Donaldson MR, who was faced with some 200 Labour MPs seeking his dismissal. Even if politicians cannot easily remove judges, the judiciary needs protection from being criticised in Parliament and by politicians in the press. The sub-judice rule prevents parliamentarians from commenting on current cases in Parliament, although they can criticise sentencing policy.

Did the role of the Lord Chancellor undermine judicial independence?

CORNERSTONE

The role of the Lord Chancellor prior to the Constitutional Reform Act 2005

Prior to the Constitutional Reform Act 2005 the Lord Chancellor was the head of the judiciary, which meant that he was responsible for appointing judges, for representing the views of the judiciary to the government, and for the discipline and training of judges. Additionally, the Lord Chancellor was able to sit as a judge in the House of Lords.

Lord Irvine QC

- Lord Chancellor 1997–2003
- Trained as a lawyer and served as a government minister
- Heard nine cases as a judge whilst Lord Chancellor
- Dismissed from office in 2003 by the Prime Minister

Figure 8.7 Lord Irvine, Lord Chancellor 1997–2003

The Constitutional Reform Act 2005 has significantly transformed the role of the Lord Chancellor and has notably transferred responsibility as head of the judiciary in England and Wales to the Lord Chief Justice, established a Judicial Appointment Commission and removed the right of the Lord Chancellor to sit as a judge (see Figure 8.7). Importantly, the Lord Chancellor is still a member of the executive, and his main title is now the Secretary of State for Justice and he is responsible for the Ministry of Justice.

CORNERSTONE

The Ministry of Justice

The Ministry of Justice is responsible for the running of the courts and the provision of legal aid. The recent reforms to legal aid have proved very controversial.

As we have seen above, the Lord Chancellor can still veto a judicial appointment and is jointly responsible for judicial discipline. However, there is now a degree of openness and, with regards to judicial appointments, the Lord Chancellor must give reasons and must be able to justify his decision.

Baroness Kennedy QC (2005) was critical that the Lord Chancellor (prior to the Constitutional Reform Act 2005) was able to sit as a judge, arguing that this served no purpose, as Lord Irvine, the last Lord Chancellor to sit as a judge, was only able to do this on a few occasions. Lord Bingham noted that until Lord Falconer announced in 2003 that he would no longer sit as a judge, the number of days that Lord Chancellors had sat in court had declined and that Lord Irvine as Lord Chancellor, had only sat as a judge in nine cases. Lord Bingham observed that the Lord Chancellor sitting as a judge in a court, which had to decide whether the government (of which he was a senior member) had acted illegally, raised questions of judicial impartiality:

> 'Lord Irvine himself accepted that he could not properly sit in cases of judicial review involving the government or its agencies, or devolution, or human rights, or any cases raising issues in which the government might reasonably be thought to have an interest. In the view of many, this would include crime' (Lord Bingham 2011, p. 84)

Diana Woodhouse (2002) has written that for most of the twentieth century Lord Chancellors had avoided sitting in cases where the government had a direct interest. However, Woodhouse observed that Lord Mackay had sat in *Pepper* v. *Hart* [1993] AC 593, which was a case that involved taxation. Lord Mackay according to Woodhouse, took the view 'that the government had no direct interest in Revenue cases [but this] . . . was disputed by, amongst others, Lords Lester and Goodhart, who believed that Lord Mackay was wrong to sit in the case' (p. 128).

REFLECTION

It was important that the Lord Chancellor should not sit as a judge where the government has either a direct or an indirect interest. The principles of natural justice require that no man can be a judge in his own court. Clearly in a wide number of areas there was a risk that the Lord Chancellor would have to determine an issue in which he and his ministerial colleagues had an interest. This arguably could give rise to accusations of judicial bias and a violation of Article 6 of the ECHR, which guarantees the right to a fair trial.

CORNERSTONE

McGonnell v. United Kingdom, No 28488/95 (2000) 30 EHRR 289

In *McGonnell* v. *United Kingdom* the European Court of Human Rights held that the situation in Guernsey, where the Bailiff of Guernsey was President of the Court of Appeal and also served in the legislature and the executive, violated Article 6 of the ECHR.

Lord Bingham had observed that the Lord Chancellor in his judicial capacity did not enjoy security of tenure and judicial independence as he could be removed from office by the Prime Minister. Thus the most senior judge in the country could be removed and therefore owed his position to the Prime Minister.

APPLICATION

The Home Secretary has been accused of acting illegally when using his statutory powers under the New Terrorism Act 1999 (fictitious), by ordering the detention of 200 suspected terrorists. The people arrested are British citizens. They are alleging that their detention violates Article 5 of the ECHR (the right to liberty).

Prior to the Constitutional Reform Act 2005 could the Lord Chancellor have heard their appeal in a judicial capacity?

If the government believed that the detained individuals posed a threat to national security, could it be presumed that the Lord Chancellor (as a member of government and privy to cabinet discussion) would be biased against the suspected terrorists?

We have seen that the role of the Lord Chancellor has been transformed by the Constitutional Reform Act 2005. However, in order to appreciate the significance of the changes you must be able to understand the position prior to the CRA 2005.

ROLE OF THE JUDICIARY

We have seen in Chapter 3 that the courts and the judiciary have a number of functions (see Figure 8.8). We shall briefly look at these.

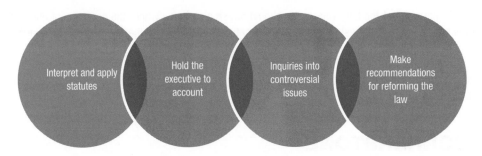

Figure 8.8 The role of the judiciary

Judges as law-makers

Do judges make law? Cases such as *Shaw* v. *DPP* [1962] AC 220 and *R* v. *R (Rape: Marital Exemption)* [1992] 1 AC 599 (HL) clearly demonstrate that the courts do in fact make law.

⊙ CORNERSTONE

Shaw v. *DPP* [1962] AC 220

In *Shaw* v. *DPP* the appellant had published a magazine containing advertisements by prostitutes. The court held that his conduct amounted to the common law offence of conspiracy to corrupt morals. In effect the court had made his conduct a criminal offence and therefore, in the absence of legislation criminalising his conduct, the appellant's conduct did not escape sanction. It had been argued by the appellant, that as Parliament had created legislation in this area, that the court could not use the common law to criminalise his actions. However, this argument was rejected as the court held that it still had a residual power to use the law to defend public morality. The court distinguished this from creating law, which only Parliament could do.

In *Shaw* v. *DPP* Viscount Simmonds held that the courts, in the absence of an applicable statute, would need to act in some circumstances to criminalise a novel form of obscenity, as otherwise the common law would be powerless to prevent the obscenity:

'In the sphere of criminal law I entertain no doubt that there remains in the courts of law a residual power to enforce the supreme and fundamental purpose of the law, to conserve not only the safety and order but also the moral welfare of the State, and that it is their duty to guard it against attacks which may be the more insidious because they are novel and unprepared for. That is the broad head (call it public policy if you wish) within which the present indictment falls . . .

'I now assert, that there is in that court a residual power, where no statute has yet intervened to supersede the common law, to superintend those offences which are prejudicial to the public welfare. Such occasions will be rare, for Parliament has not been slow to legislate when attention has been sufficiently aroused. But gaps remain and will always remain since no one can foresee every way in which the wickedness of man may disrupt the order of society.'

In fact vast amounts of the law of contract, tort and restitution have been created by the courts. According to the separation of powers it is Parliament and not the court which makes the law. However, the courts do make law and judicial decisions have transformed the law of negligence and the criminal law. Pannick (1987) has observed that, '[e]ager or not, qualified or not, the judge cannot avoid acting as legislator in exceptional cases at the appellate level' (p. 4).

Richard Buxton has observed with reference to cases such as *Hedley Byrne & Co Ltd v. Heller & Partners Ltd* [1964] AC 465, that the courts should be careful when using the common law to reform the law ('How the common law gets made: Hedley Byrne and other cautionary takes' [2009] *Law Quarterly Review* 60). Buxton notes that, '[t]he particular weaknesses of case law as an instrument of reform [include that] . . . The purpose of any case is to decide the issue between the parties, and not to reform the law'. For more detail on judges as law-makers please see Chapter 3.

REFLECTION

Interpret statutes

The courts interpret and give effect to Acts of Parliament. The courts use a number of rules to do this. Judges have been accused of interpreting statutes in such a way to ignore the intentions of Parliament. This is contrary to Parliamentary Sovereignty.

INTERSECTION ....

Refer to the controversial approach of Lord Steyn in *R* v. *A (Complainant's Sexual History)* [2001] UKHL 25 in Chapter 5 on Parliamentary Sovereignty.

According to Lord Hoffmann in *R* v. *Secretary of State for the Home Department ex p. Simms* [2000] 2 AC 115, when interpreting an Act of Parliament the courts in the absence of express words to the contrary should presume that Parliament had the best intentions and did not intend to violate fundamental rights: '[i]n the absence of express language or necessary implication to the contrary, the courts therefore presume that even the most general words were intended to be subject to the basic rights of the individual.' Lord Hoffmann had stated that the courts could not prevent Parliament from legislating contrary to an individual's fundamental rights.

In his 2011 F.A. Mann Lecture Lord Sumption, prior to joining the Supreme Court, noted that the courts have made unrealistic assessments of what Parliament intended. Sumption referred to the decision in *R* v. *Secretary of State for Social Security ex p. Joint Council for the Welfare of Immigrants* [1997] 1 WLR 275, where the Secretary of State had introduced regulations under powers given to him by the Social Security Contributions and Benefits Act 1992, which prevented asylum seekers who had not claimed benefits upon their arrival and also those whose application for asylum had been refused from claiming cash payments or seekers from claiming benefits. The majority of the Court of Appeal, aware of the consequences for the asylum seekers, had refused to believe that Parliament intended to give the executive such powers, and therefore held that the regulations were illegal (*ultra vires*).

CORNERSTONE

R v. *Secretary of State for Social Security ex p. Joint Council for the Welfare of Immigrants* [1997] 1 WLR 275 at 293

According to Simon Brown LJ:

'Parliament cannot have intended a significant number of genuine asylum seekers to be impaled on the horns of so intolerable a dilemma: the need either to abandon their claims to refugee status or alternatively to maintain them as best they can but in a state of utter destitution. Primary legislation alone could in my judgment achieve that sorry state of affairs.'

Sumption observed that judicial policy-making occurred where the courts took what are essentially political decisions; which are decisions that according to the separation powers, only to be made by the executive. This means that the court will look at how a minister has used the discretionary decision-making power which Parliament has given him, and when deciding whether the decision is illegal or not, might look at 'what it is thought right for Parliament to wish to do'. These are judgments which 'are by their nature political'. Referring to the decision in *Ex p. Joint Council for the Welfare of Immigrants*, Sumption commented that the courts' assessment as to what Parliament had intended, when giving the Secretary of State powers to make the regulations, was unrealistic. It is important to appreciate that the courts cannot review an Act of Parliament and they can only judicially review secondary or delegated legislation. The Social Security Contributions and Benefits Act 1992 had given the Secretary of State the power to make regulations (which were delegated legislation) and the courts could judicially review these. Depriving asylum seekers from financial assistance is a politically sensitive and controversial decision, and whether to restrict benefits is a political decision which ought to have been made by elected politicians.

APPLICATION

One of the ways that the courts can quash the regulation would be to find that the Secretary of State had acted illegally, i.e. that Parliament had not intended to give him powers to do X. Therefore the regulations enabling him to do X were illegal as the Secretary of State had no legal authority to do X.

Returning to Sumption's observations on the decision, the courts must have regard to what Parliament intended when enacting the legislation.

CORNERSTONE

The courts must look at what Parliament intended

In his 2011 F.A. Mann Lecture Jonathan Sumption QC considered the decision in *Ex p. Council for the Welfare of Immigrants* and observed that:

> '[The courts] therefore quashed regulations which had that effect. Parliament evidently did not agree. It immediately passed fresh legislation authorising such regulations in terms. Some might say that this was a vindication of the proper role of the Courts. They were not prepared to allow a harsh policy to be followed by the executive on such an issue until Parliament had authorised it in unmistakable terms. But another possible conclusion is that the Court of Appeal's view that Parliament could not have intended such a thing always was unrealistic. It ignored the political background to the legislation and underrated the level of Parliamentary concern about the effect of the UK's relatively generous level of social provision in drawing asylum-seekers across Europe to our shores'.

We have seen above that the House of Lords in *Anisminic* had interpreted a statutory attempt to exclude judicial review of an executive decision in such a way that ignored Parliament's intention. These are not isolated examples. However, Sumption's lecture was criticised by Sir Stephen Sedley LJ (2009), who disagreed with much of his argument. Sedley commented that 'there is a repeated insinuation that judicial interference in the political process regularly occurs: "The judicial resolution of inherently political issues is difficult to defend." It is not only difficult to defend; it does not happen'. Sedley rejected the view that judges 'routinely cross the boundary separating law from politics'.

Holding the executive to account

INTERSECTION

Chapter 7 explored the composition and functions of the executive and saw how the executive is held to account under the United Kingdom's constitution. We have seen that the executive is very powerful and governments have historically enjoyed a majority in Parliament. There is concern that Parliament does not effectively hold the executive to account and that this is detrimental to individual rights.

Take note

The judiciary serves as an important check on the power of the executive by ensuring that the government and public bodies are accountable. This accountability is crucial both at a national and local level as those affected by a decision of a local council or government department can ask the courts to review the validity of the decision.

The separation of powers requires that each branch of government is checked and balanced by the others. Given that the executive dominates Parliament, the role of the courts to hold the executive to account is very important.

Baroness Kennedy QC (2005) has observed that by reviewing the validity of the executive's actions the courts are upholding Parliamentary Sovereignty. Kennedy notes that judicial independence is important because if the executive controlled judicial appointments and tenure, there is a risk that the courts would be unable to carry out this role effectively:

'[I]t is not MPs who decide on whether a minister's actions are legal or illegal. Since 1688 our constitution has made it clear that the only way ministers can ultimately be rendered answerable to parliament is through judges in courts ensuring that they do not deploy powers that parliament has not given them. The judges are in fact asserting the supremacy of parliament rather than their own and they need to do so from a position of independence' (p. 127).

This statement is controversial as it ignores the role of Parliament in holding the executive to account. (Please refer to Chapter 6 to see how Parliament holds the executive to account.) However, it is arguable that the courts are often in a stronger position than Parliament to review and hold the executive to account.

Judicial review

Judicial review is an important way of holding the executive to account, whether at a national or local level. The decisions of a local authority often have an important impact on citizens' daily lives, such as a decision to grant or refuse planning permission and the decision to cut funding for local educational services.

INTERSECTION..

> Judicial review permits someone affected by the decision of a public body to have the decision reviewed by the court. We will look at this in more detail in Chapters 12 and 13.

A decision can be reviewed on the following grounds:

- The decision was unreasonable or irrational.
- The decision was illegal.
- The decision was not proportionate (where the decision violates the Convention rights).
- The decision lacked procedural fairness or the decision-maker was biased.
- The decision-maker has given a legitimate expectation and the decision would breach this.

Take note

It is important to note that the courts cannot judicially review an Act of Parliament. The courts can judicially review both delegated legislation and the prerogative (see the decision in *Council of Civil Service Unions v. Minister for the Civil Service* [1985] (*GCHQ*)).

There are limits on judicial review. Certain prerogative powers are considered to be non-justiciable and the courts are reluctant to question the decisions of the executive in areas such as foreign affairs and defence. The courts are aware that they lack the expertise and that it is the executive's role and not theirs to make these types of decisions. In *Rehman* v. *Secretary of State for the Home Department* [2001] UKHL 47 Lord Hoffmann had observed that:

'[T]he question of whether something is "in the interests" of national security is not a question of law. It is a matter of judgment and policy. Under the constitution of the United Kingdom and most other countries, decisions as to whether something is or is not in the interests of national security are not a matter for judicial decision. They are entrusted to the executive' (at [50]).

His Lordship's postscript to his judgment in *Rehman* is interesting, as it was delivered in the aftermath of the 9/11 terrorist attacks in the United States.

CORNERSTONE

Rehman v. *Secretary of State for the Home Department* [2001] UKHL 47

In *Rehman*, Lord Hoffmann stated in the postscript to his judgment that decisions of a national security nature should be taken by the executive and not usurped by the courts:

> 'It is not only that the executive has access to special information and expertise in these matters. It is also that such decisions, with serious potential results for the community, require a legitimacy which can be conferred only by entrusting them to persons responsible to the community through the democratic process. If the people are to accept the consequences of such decisions, they must be made by persons whom the people have elected and whom they can remove' (at [62]).

It not just decisions concerning national security which are considered non-justiciable. In Chapter 9 we will look at judicial review of the prerogative powers and how some subject-matter is considered inappropriate for the courts to review. Paul Daly has explored justiciability of certain types of decisions and has observed that whilst some decisions are considered non-reviewable, i.e. that they are primary non-justiciable, there are two different meanings. On the one hand the courts will not review a decision, whilst on the other the courts review the decision and have 'found judicial intervention to be inappropriate' ('Justiciability and the "Political Question" Doctrine' [2010] *Public Law* 160).

This means that the courts should avoid making policy decisions when carrying out judicial review. The court must review the decision under one of the judicial review grounds. As we shall see in Chapter 13 the courts when questioning whether a decision was unreasonable or disproportionate risk making a policy decision, which is a decision that according to the separation of powers must only be taken by the executive. This is because the courts are attempting to review whether the decision is a reasonable one, or whether it was proportionate and such decisions pose a risk that the court might attempt to substitute their own decision for that of the minister or local authority. It is worth considering the judgment of Lord Scarman in *R* v. *Secretary of State for the Environment ex p. Nottinghamshire CC* [1986] AC 240, where His Lordship stated that, 'Judicial review is a great weapon in the hands of the judges: but the judges must observe the constitutional limits set by our parliamentary system upon their exercise of this beneficent power' (at 250–51).

Dangers of judicial policy-making

Lord Sumption (2011) has warned that if the judiciary makes political decisions then it risks an introduction of 'democratic influence over their selection', i.e. a political nomination system. Sumption has warned that this would politicise the judiciary as has occurred in the United States:

> 'The attraction of judicial decision-making is that it is animated by a combination of abstract reasoning and moral value-judgment, and the decision imposed by the judiciary's plenitude of power to declare and enforce law. To some, this will seem more straightforward than the messy compromises required to build a political consensus. However, for those who

> ### Take note
> If judges use judicial review to make decisions as to the merits of a minister's or a local authority's actions, then there is a danger that the judges will cross the boundary between judicial review and making essentially political decisions.

are concerned with the proper functioning of our democratic institutions, the judicial resolution of inherently political issues is difficult to defend. It has no legitimate basis in public consent, because judges are quite rightly not accountable to the public for their decisions.'

It is the executive that must take political decisions, as they have democratic legitimacy and are accountable to the electorate in a way that judges are not. By deferring to the executive over inherently political decisions or ones that involve matters of defence, national security and foreign policy the courts uphold the theory of the separation of powers. That is not to say that the courts should not review executive action just because it is linked with defence or foreign affairs, as the courts have demonstrated that there are few areas of executive decision-making which the courts will refuse to review.

REFLECTION

We can see the changing judicial approach to non-justiciability of foreign policy decisions in *Marchiori* v. *Environment Agency* [2002] EU LR 225, where Laws LJ observed that, '[i]t seems to me, first, to be plain that the law of England will not contemplate what may be called a merits review of any honest decision of government upon matters of national defence policy.' However, His Lordship held that, '[d]emocracy itself requires that all public power be lawfully conferred and exercised, and of this the courts are the surety. No matter how grave the policy issues involved, the courts will be alert to see that no use of power exceeds its proper constitutional bounds' (at [38]). This is important as the courts will not refuse to review a decision where there has been a misuse of power.

Lord Sumption (2012) explored the judicial approach to foreign policy in a lecture at the LSE's Department of Government where he was of the opinion that, '[t]he last decade has witnessed the progressive retreat of the non-justiciability theory and the advance of the qualified division of powers theory, which as I have suggested is simply a rather grand way of emphasising the breadth of the government's discretion.' The courts will look at the actual decision in order to see whether it is amenable to review.

Lord Sumption viewed the judicial retreat from holding that foreign policy decisions were non-justiciable to be based on the 'growing emphasis on the protection of human rights and the barely concealed revulsion of English judges against the conduct of the United States'. His Lordship cited *Al Rawi* v. *Secretary of State for Foreign and Commonwealth Affairs* [2008] QB 289 and *Binyam Mohammed* v. *Secretary of State for Foreign and Commonwealth Affairs* [2011] QB 218 as examples of a changing judicial attitude. In *Al Rawi* the Court of Appeal reviewed the Foreign Secretary's decision not to intervene in Mr Al Rawi's detention in Guantanamo Bay. The decision was reviewed like any other public law decision would be, albeit the subject-matter warranting a wider margin of appreciation. In *Binyam Mohammed* the Court of Appeal allowed the publication of material which was embarrassing to the UK and US governments, and doubted the Foreign Secretary's assessment that publication would harm the United Kingdom's future cooperation with the United States.

INTERSECTION

For more examples of the courts' willingness to review previously non-justiciable areas of the prerogative please refer to Chapter 9.

Judicial activism

CORNERSTONE

Judicial deference and judicial activism

The role of the judiciary in holding the executive to account is of upmost importance in ensuring that the United Kingdom has executive accountability. Judges are often criticised for deferring to the executive on grounds such as relative institutional expertise or national security considerations, or on the other hand for being too active in terms of reviewing decisions made by the executive.

As we have seen, the judiciary must uphold Parliamentary Sovereignty and the separation of powers and as a consequence:

- The judiciary cannot review primary legislation and must give effect to Parliament's intention when interpreting an Act of Parliament.
- When judicially reviewing secondary legislation the courts must avoid making political decisions or decisions which are those that the executive is best placed to make.

Nonetheless judges have challenged the executive over policy decisions and have not always given effect to what Parliament intended. For more detail see Chapter 5 which looks at judicial use of section 3 of the HRA 1998.

Judicial deference

The courts have been accused of deferring to the executive on occasions and not adequately holding the executive to account. Allan (2006) criticised judicial deference to the executive where it meant that individual rights were not protected. Allan reviewed the consequences of judges deferring to the executive because of the presumed view that the executive had more expertise in that area. He argued that it is dangerous for judges to hold certain areas non-reviewable:

'A doctrine of justiciability seeks to insulate certain types of governmental action from judicial review without regard to their effect on the rights or interests of the persons involved. Invoking general notions of governmental expertise or superior democratic credentials, such a doctrine effectively places administrative discretion beyond the purview of the rule of law. The courts abandon their ordinary function of ensuring legality, within the relevant fields, leaving protection of the rights of those affected to the operations of the political process, which may or may not in time provide a remedy' (p. 671).

Allan does not support a doctrine of judicial deference to the executive and argues that deference can actually harm the separation of powers. Within the context of human rights, Allan notes that the 'surrender of judgment is inconsistent with the rigorous scrutiny of governmental action that the protection of human rights requires'. Looking at Allan's arguments it is clear that that if the courts defer to the executive and do not review the legality or reasonableness of an executive decision, then in that instance there is no accountability. The problem which has been identified is that some areas may appear to be far too sensitive politically, or diplomatically, for the courts to review executive action.

Aileen Kavanagh (2010) has written on judicial deference and has noted that in some circumstances it can be defended:

'However, a defence of the judicial duty to exercise a constitutionally appropriate degree of restraint when the context demands it, does not necessarily rest on a conservative view of the judicial role. The analysis provided here is compatible with an interventionist role for judges. It simply denies that judicial intervention is appropriate in every case and every context. Sometimes judges should recognise that they are not well-suited or well-placed to pass judgment on, or oppose, decisions of the elected branches of government. But when they are well-placed to do so, there is no justification for them to shy away from fulfilling their constitutional duty to the full. Giving deference when it is due is very different from kow-towing to the elected branches of government simply because they are elected' (p. 222).

We can see that the courts might be reluctant to review executive action where the decisions are deemed to be ill-suited for judicial review. A recent example of judicial deference is the Court of Appeal's decision in *R (Lord Carlile of Berriew & others)* v. *Secretary of State for the Home Department* [2013] EWCA Civ 199. Here the court held that the decision to prevent a prominent Iranian dissident from entering the United Kingdom in order to address parliamentarians was unsuitable for substantive review as to whether it was proportionate. The court was reluctant to be seen as usurping the executive's role in making decisions of this nature.

> The most striking recent example of judicial deference to the executive is the House of Lords' decision in *R (Bancoult)* v. *Secretary of State for the Foreign and Commonwealth Affairs (No.2)* [2008] UKHL 61. *Bancoult* is a controversial decision and illustrates the differing views as to the extent (or limitations) of judicial review. The case involved the Chagos Islands which are administered as the British Indian Ocean Territory. The islanders were removed from the islands in the 1970s after the United States requested the use of the largest island, Diego Garcia, as a military base. The treatment of the islanders was acknowledged as appalling. The islanders attempted to return to the unoccupied islands and after the Divisional Court finding in favour of Mr Bancoult (an islander), the then Foreign Secretary announced that the government would permit the islanders to return. However, in 2004 the government through an Order in Council (as the prerogative was used to legislate for British overseas territories) prevented the islanders from returning without the express permission of the government. The government had argued that Orders in Council could not be judicially reviewed. However, the House of Lords unanimously rejected this argument. Where their Lordships could not all agree was with the legality of exiling and preventing the return of the islanders.
>
> The majority held that there was prerogative power to do this and consequentially the executive had not acted illegally. This was disputed by Lords Bingham and Mance who rejected the view that such a prerogative power existed (the government could provide no precedent of its existence), and that despite the subject-matter of the decision (it involved foreign policy and national security) the courts could still question its legality and whether the executive had acted reasonably. Lord Hoffmann had observed that the rationality of the decision could not be reviewed by the courts as national security and diplomatic decisions are matters for the executive and not for the courts. Bridget Hadfield observed that the majority decision in *Bancoult* was 'a sad concluding note to the House of Lords' constitutional jurisprudence' (Hadfield, B. 'Constitutional Law' in Blom-Cooper, et al. 2009, p. 522). *Bancoult* is interesting because we have the majority deferring to the executive in a case which involved the forced expulsion of a people from their homeland. The minority argued that this was exile and was a violation of the islanders' basic rights.

REFLECTION

Judge-led inquiries

Judges are asked by the executive to chair **public inquiries** to review major events and to propose recommendations. The most famous recent example of a judge chairing an inquiry is Lord Justice

Leveson who looked at the culture, practice and ethics of the press. The inquiry has seen the Prime Minister David Cameron, and former Prime Ministers Tony Blair and Gordon Brown give evidence. The inquiry was prompted by allegations of illegal phone-hacking at a newspaper owned by News International (http://www.levesoninquiry.org.uk/). The publication of the Leveson report resulted in considerable political debate in the House of Commons. Eventually, the main political parties reached a consensus and they sought to introduce a royal charter to regulate the press. This cross-party royal charter had a rival proposal, which was supported by newspaper publishers who wished to prevent the government from preventing the charter to the monarch for her approval. In October 2013, the Press Standards Board of Finance Ltd attempted to get an injunction to prevent the cross-party royal charter from being approved. The court rejected their application for an injunction and judicial review (*R (Press Standards Board of Finance Ltd)* v. *The Secretary of State for Culture, Media and Sport* [2013] EWHC 3824 (Admin)). The monarch approved the royal charter. In May 2014, the Press Standards Board of Finance Ltd were unsuccessful in its attempt to judicially review the royal charter.

The Hutton Inquiry chaired by Lord Hutton was tasked with carrying out an investigation into the death of Dr David Kelly, who had been involved with the claims that Iraq had weapons of mass destruction in the build-up to the 2003 invasion (http://www.the-hutton-inquiry.org.uk/). The inquiry and the subsequent report were regarded by some commentators as flawed.

Law reform

The executive asks senior judges to review the law and to propose reform. Lord Roskill chaired the Roskill Committee which was tasked with proposing reforms for fraud trials.

> Lord Roskill's report in 1986 controversially proposed that serious fraud cases should be heard by specialist fraud tribunals consisting of a judge and two lay experts rather than a jury. The government ignored this recommendation. Lord Justice Auld carried out a review into criminal procedure and His Lordship's report contained many recommendations, many of which were enacted into law by the Criminal Justice Act 2003.

Baroness Kennedy QC (2005) criticised the use of judges by the government to carry out reviews of the law, because some areas of the report had constitutional significance and were extremely political. Kennedy QC was critical, observing that the government 'cherry-picked' the least expensive reforms and could point to judicial approval for their reforms (see pp. 151–152).

KEY POINTS

- The Constitutional Reform Act 2005 has had a significant impact on the judiciary and the office of Lord Chancellor.
- The Lord Chief Justice is now the head of the judiciary in England and Wales, and the Judicial Appointments Commission is responsible for judicial appointments.
- The Appellate Committee of the House of Lords was replaced with the United Kingdom Supreme Court.

→

- Judicial independence is very important and is secured through the Act of Settlement 1701 and the Constitutional Reform Act 2005.
- The judiciary serves an important role in holding the executive to account.
- Some decisions are considered unsuitable for merits-based judicial review. However, the types of decisions which are considered non-justiciable have been reduced, as the courts are more ready to review executive decisions.

CORE CASES AND STATUTES

Case	About	Importance
McGonnell v. *United Kingdom* (28488/95) (2000)	Whether the lack of the separation of powers in Guernsey in respect of the Bailiff of Guernsey breached Article 6 ECHR.	The European Court of Human Rights had held that the situation in Guernsey, where Bailiff of Guernsey was President of the Court of Appeal and also in the served in legislature and the executive, had violated Article 6 of the ECHR. This decision was relevant to the then position of the Lord Chancellor in the United Kingdom.
Shaw v. *DPP* [1962]	The appellant had published a magazine containing advertisements by prostitutes. The court held that his conduct amounted to the common law offence of conspiracy to corrupt morals.	The appellant argued that as Parliament had created legislation in this area that the court could not use the common law to criminalise his actions. This was rejected as the court still had a residual power to use the law to defend public morality. The court distinguished this from creating law, which only Parliament could do.
R v. *Secretary of State for Social Security ex p. Joint Council for the Welfare of Immigrants* [1997]	The issue to be determined was whether the minister had the statutory power to deprive certain asylum seekers of benefits.	It has been argued that there was questionable judicial interpretation of legislation in a manner that was inconsistent with Parliament's intention.
Rehman v. *Secretary of State for the Home Department* [2001]	The decision involved national security and the deportation of a Pakistani national. The House of Lords had held that someone could be a threat to national security even if his actions were directed against another country and not the United Kingdom.	This case is important as it contained a postcript from Lord Hoffmann which explored the relationship between the executive and the courts when a decision involved national security. The postscript was added to His Lordship's judgment after the terrorist attack on 11 September, 2001.

Statute	About	Importance
Constitutional Reform Act 2005	Introduced key constitutional reforms and helped to strengthen the separation of powers between the judiciary and the two other branches of government.	This Act created the Supreme Court and reformed the office of Lord Chancellor. The Lord Chief Justice is now the head of the judiciary in England and Wales. Introduced changes in the way judges are appointed.

FURTHER READING

Allan, T.R.S. 'Human rights and judicial review: a critique of "due deference"' [2006] 65(3) *Cambridge Law Journal* 671
Refer to this article for a critique of judicial deference.

Bingham, Lord *The Lives of the Law: Selected Essays and Speeches 2000–2010* (Oxford University Press: Oxford, 2011)
Parts of this book refers to the Constitutional Reform Act 2005 and the Lord Chancellor.

Blom-Cooper, L., Dickson, B. and Drewry, G. (eds) *The Judicial House of Lords 1876–2009* (Oxford University Press: Oxford, 2009)
This book is the authoritative account of the workings of the Appellate Committee of the House of Lords and the reasons for the creation of the Supreme Court.

Bradley, A.W. and Ewing, K.D. *Constitutional and Administrative Law* 15th edn (Pearson: Harlow, 2011)
An interesting and detailed textbook. Refer to this to develop your understanding of this topic.

Dickson, B. 'Judicial activism in the House of Lords 1995–2007' in Dickson, B. (eds) *Judicial Activism in Common Law Supreme Courts* (Oxford University Press: Oxford, 2007)
An interesting overview of the final years of the House of Lords.

Darbyshire, P. *Sitting in Judgment: The Working Lives of Judges* (Hart: Oxford, 2011)
A highly readable book based on the author's research into the judiciary, with first-hand accounts from judges on their role within the legal system.

Kavanagh, A. 'Defending deference in public law and constitutional theory' [2010] 126 *Law Quarterly Review* 222
Refer to this article for a defence of judicial deference.

Kennedy, Baroness *Just Law: The Changing Face of Justice and Why It Matters to Us All* (Vintage: London, 2005)
A very lively book which critiques the constitution and the role of the Lord Chancellor prior to the CRA 2005.

Malleson, K. 'Safeguarding judicial impartiality' [2002] 22(1) *Legal Studies* 53
Refer to this article for a detailed look at the rule against judicial bias.

Munro, C. *Studies in Constitutional Law* (Oxford University Press: Oxford, 2005)
Refer to this book for a series of interesting chapters on the constitution. Highly recommended.

→

Nicholson, S.P. and Howard, R.M. 'Framing support or the Supreme Court in the aftermath of "Bush v Gore" (2003) 65(3) *The Journal of Politics* 676
This article is recommended reading if you have an interest in the United States Supreme Court.

Pannick, D. *Judges* (Oxford University Press: Oxford, 1987)
A very brief overview of the judiciary prior to the Constitutional Reform Act 2005. This is very readable and covers judicial appointment, bias and provides general background reading.

Phillips, Lord 'Judicial independence and accountability: a view from the Supreme Court', lecture delivered to the UCL Constitution Unit, February 2011
An interesting lecture on the judiciary and the constitution.

Sedley, S. 'Judicial politics' (2012) 34(4) *London Review of Books* 15
An interesting critique of Lord Sumption's F.A. Mann Lecture 2011.

Sumption, Lord 'Judicial and political decision-making the uncertain boundary', The F.A. Mann Lecture 2011
This is an interesting lecture which provides a critique of judicial decision-making.

Sumption, Lord 'Foreign Affairs in the English Courts since 9/11', Lecture at the Department of Government, London School of Economics, 14 May 2012
An interesting lecture which explores the willingness of judges to review executive decision making in foreign affairs.

Woodhouse, D. 'The Office of Lord Chancellor – time to abandon the judicial role – the rest will follow' [2002] 22(1) *Legal Studies* 128
Refer to this article for a critique of the position of the Lord Chancellor prior to the CRA 2005.

CHAPTER 9
The prerogative

BLUEPRINT

The prerogative

LEGISLATION

- Constitutional Reform and Governance Act 2010

CONTEXT

- The transformation from absolute monarchy to constitutional monarchy.
- The clash between the monarch and Parliament, which led to the English Civil Wars and the Glorious Revolution.

CONCEPTS

- Blackstone's definition of the prerogative
- John Locke and the separation of powers
- The Privy Council
- Did Iraq, Libya and Syria create a convention?
- The Ponsonby Convention
- The Ram Doctrine
- The importance of judicial control over ministerial use of the prerogative
- The courts will apply an Act of Parliament
- The prerogative cannot be used in a manner which is unconstitutional

- How do we decide if a prerogative power exists?
- Which of the prerogative powers are still non-justiciable?

- What are the prerogative powers?
- Who uses the prerogative powers?
- Does Parliament effectively hold ministerial use of the prerogative powers to account?
- How do the courts hold ministerial use of the prerogative powers to account?

CASES

- *Attorney-General* v. *De Keyser's Royal Hotel Ltd* [1920]
- *Burmah Oil Company Ltd* v. *Lord Advocate* [1965]
- *Laker Airways Ltd* v. *Department of Trade* [1977]
- *Council of Civil Service Unions* v. *Minister for the Civil Service* [1985]
- *R* v. *Secretary of State for the Home Department ex p. Northumbria Police Authority* [1988]
- *R* v. *Foreign Secretary ex p. Everett* [1989]
- *R* v. *Secretary of State for the Home Department ex p. Fire Brigades Union and Others* [1995]
- *R (Abbasi)* v. *Secretary of State for Foreign and Commonwealth Affairs* [2002]

SPECIAL CHARACTERISTICS

- The historical role of the monarch
- The Privy Council – 'the cloak that covers'
- The Crown's legal prerogatives
- Use of the prerogative by ministers
- The circumstances in which Parliament can be dissolved before May 2015
- Prerogative powers permit ministers to act without parliamentary approval
- Weak parliamentary control over the use of prerogative powers

REFORM

- Should the prerogative be abolished and the powers placed on a statutory basis?
- How can parliamentary accountability of the prerogative be improved?

CRITICAL ISSUES

Setting the scene

The term 'prerogative' is confusing as it is often used but is seldom explained and therefore our aim is to define what is meant by the term prerogative, and then to see how the prerogative is used. It is important to appreciate that the prerogative is an important part of the constitution. Even in the twenty-first century the prerogative is an important source of executive power and is largely exercised by the government. The prerogative and the royal prerogative are same; the use of the word royal simply acknowledges that historically these powers were exercised by the monarch. The monarch still retains her personal prerogative powers, which include the dissolution of Parliament and royal assent to legislation. We will look at why the United Kingdom still has prerogative powers and how these powers are used in a manner that is unaccountable to Parliament. We shall then look at the role of the courts in providing a check and balance on the executive's use of the prerogative. Finally we will look at the proposed reforms and whether these will actually be implemented.

In this chapter we will:

- define the prerogative and see why it exists today and explore its origins;
- see how the prerogative is exercised by the government and the monarch today;
- consider whether parliamentary control of the prerogative is effective and what could be done to improve this;
- look at judicial control of the prerogative and how the courts have limited executive use of the prerogative powers.

Chapter overview

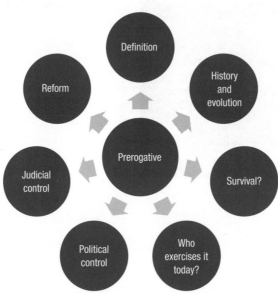

DEFINITION

The use of the prerogative by the monarch is largely a matter of constitutional convention. The prerogative is recognised by the common law and it permits the person exercising the prerogative powers considerable authority to take important decisions. These powers are outside of parliamentary control. This means that the power to make Orders in Council which affect the people of the United Kingdom is not conferred by an Act of Parliament, but is recognised by the common law, and is a relic from the time when England was ruled exclusively by the monarch. It is because of this royal connection that writers refer to the prerogative powers as the royal prerogative, although the majority of these powers are not exercised by the monarch personally, but rather by her ministers.

CORNERSTONE

Dicey's definition of the prerogative

In the late nineteenth century Dicey (1982) stated that the prerogative was 'the residue of discretionary power or arbitrary authority which at any one time is legally left in the hands of the crown' (p. 282). This meant that the prerogative was the remainder of the monarch's discretionary powers, i.e. these powers had not been conferred by Parliament.

We shall see what Dicey meant by what 'is legally left' in the hands of the monarch and her ministers.

CORNERSTONE

Blackstone's definition of the prerogative

Sir William Blackstone defined the prerogative as the powers that 'the King enjoys alone, in contradistinction to others, and not to those he enjoys in common with any of his subjects' (*Commentaries on the Laws of England 1765–69*).

According to Professor Blackburn (2004):

'The Crown "prerogative" is a concept well known to lawyers, though others often have difficulty grasping its nature and character. It is the term used to describe the network of inherent common law powers, privileges and immunities of the Crown which have existed since time immemorial and exist by virtue of past *de facto* judicial recognition' (p. 546).

The courts play an important role in limiting ministerial use of the prerogative by preventing the creation of new prerogative powers. The courts will not allow prerogative powers to be used where these are inconsistent with an Act of Parliament.

So what is the purpose of the prerogative? As we will explore below, the prerogative gives ministers considerable discretionary power to act without parliamentary approval. Unless an Act of

Take note

Parliament can ultimately control the prerogative by abolishing a particular power or by introducing statutory powers that overlap with the prerogative. An example of how this can occur is the decision of the House of Lords in *Attorney-General* v. *De Keyser's Royal Hotel Ltd* [1920] AC 508 which is explored below.

Parliament restricts its use, the minister can use the prerogative. Such powers do not sound democratic and offer little accountability, and as we shall see many academics, lawyers and politicians favour replacing the prerogative powers with an Act of Parliament.

> The decision to go to war is a prerogative power. The Prime Minister can legally declare war without the approval of Parliament. Tony Blair, the Labour Prime Minister in 2003, decided to allow the House of Commons to vote on whether to invade Iraq. Such a vote was not needed, as the decision could have been taken without Parliament's consent. Many observers believed that this vote established a constitutional convention which required that the deployment of British military forces would require a vote in Parliament. This argument has been strengthened by the decision in 2013 to allow Parliament a vote on whether to intervene in Syria. Parliament voted against military action and the Prime Minister stated that he would respect Parliament's decision.

CONTEXT

HISTORY AND EVOLUTION OF THE PREROGATIVE

CORNERSTONE

The historical role of the monarch

Before the development of cabinet government in the eighteenth century the monarch was responsible for running the country. The monarch would raise taxes, raise armies, dispense justice and oversee the administration of the kingdom. The monarch ruled through the Privy Council and was assisted by privy councillors who would act as advisors to the king or queen. The powers of the monarch were not granted by Parliament (as until the thirteenth century it did not exist); instead the monarch exercised the power that was necessary to govern the country.

The monarch was restricted from abusing his power by the nobility. The Baron's revolt against King John saw the monarch agreeing to have his power limited by the Magna Carta in 1215. The aristocracy could and did rebel against the monarch and so the fear of rebellion prevented the monarch from abusing his power.

Common law origin

The prerogative powers had a common law origin as a record of their existence was recorded in the case law and histories of the period. The power was recognised by the common law.

INTERSECTION

> The role of the monarch was gradually restricted by Parliament. For example, the ability to raise taxation was controlled by the need for parliamentary approval. However, as we shall see in Chapter 5, the idea of Parliamentary Sovereignty was not established until the start of the seventeenth century. This led to a conflict with the Stuart kings who believed that their prerogative power were absolute.

Sir Edward Coke CJ on the prerogative

Sir Edward Coke CJ was an important judge at the beginning of the seventeenth century. His judgments and extra-judicial writings show the development of the idea that the king was not above the law and that the courts would control the king's use of the prerogative. Coke demonstrates that the claim for royal absolutism (i.e. that the king was above the law and was not bound by the common law or an Act of Parliament) was rejected before the English Civil Wars.

The *Case of Proclamations* (1611) 12 Co. Rep 74 concerned a question by King James I to his judges concerning his use of proclamations. It must be appreciated that the House of Commons was concerned about the use of proclamations to impose new legal obligations, as according to J.R. Tanner, James I in the first years of his reign had issued proclamations more than Elizabeth I. Coke and the other judges held that:

1. Proclamations could not be used to create new offences.

2. Proclamations were not law.

According to Coke, 'it was resolved, that the king hath no prerogative but that which the law of the land allows him'. Tanner sums up the significance of this decision: '[t]he reply of the judges is one of the minor Charters of English liberty.' (*Constitutional Documents of the Reign of James I 1603–25* (Cambridge University Press: Cambridge, 1961), p. 174).

In the *Case of Fines* Coke, 3 Inst, 84, Coke stated, '[t]hat the Common Law hath so admeasured the Prerogatives of the King, that they should neither take away nor prejudice the inheritance of any.' This meant that that the prerogative could not be used to take away a common law right and so the prerogative was restricted by judicial decisions.

Coke upheld the supremacy of an Act of Parliament and would not allow the prerogative to take away fundamental common law rights. Guy Burgess (1996) summed up the changes in Coke's views on the prerogative:

'[Coke] always believed that the operation of the royal prerogative was bounded and restricted by the common law, but in his later writings and speeches the implications deduced from this proposition became more stringent. Not only did his later writings show no signs of a belief that certain royal powers were immune from legal limitation even with the king's consent in parliament, but on many specific points too he seems to have changed his mind. The general trend is towards binding ever more tightly the scope for royal discretion' (p. 200).

Royal proclamations

A royal proclamation cannot create new legal obligations and can only enforce existing legal obligations. Writing in 1820, Joseph Chitty observed that '[p]roclamations have been frequently made the tools of tyranny and oppression' and that Parliament gave Henry VIII the power under statute to make laws using royal proclamations and that this power was repealed after the king's death (*A Treaties on the Law of the Prerogatives of the Crown*).

Conflict between the monarch and Parliament (pre-Civil War)

The Stuart kings had an uneasy relationship with Parliament. In 1628, Parliament and Charles I agreed to restrict some of the most controversial prerogative powers of the king. Ann Lyon observed that, '[t]he Petition of Right required the king to endorse the proposition that he could not by the prerogative alone levy taxation, imprison with trial, billet troops or impose martial law . . . Though it has gone down as a key element of constitutional mythology, its immediate significance was small' (*Constitutional History of the United Kingdom*, (Cavendish: London, 2003), p. 208). Charles I ruled for eleven years (1629–40) without calling a Parliament. However, the king needed to raise money to finance his wars and to govern the country. Charles I used his prerogative powers to levy taxation. Taxation required parliamentary consent and in the *Case of Ship Money* (1637), the court ruled that the king could levy such a tax on his subjects in order to fund the navy. Eventually, Charles I was forced to recall Parliament in 1640.

This Parliament was known as the Long Parliament and it attempted to punish the king's key counsellors. Parliament forced the king to consent to the execution of Archbishop Laud and the Earl of Stafford. Soon afterwards the king declared war on Parliament and started the First English Civil War. By 1649 Parliament had defeated the king in two civil wars and the king was tried at Westminster Hall and executed.

Conflict between the monarch and Parliament (Post-Restoration 1660–88)

Eventually in 1660 the Stuart monarchy was restored and this period is known as the Restoration. James II (1685–88) clashed with Parliament and claimed that his prerogative permitted him to dispense with Acts of Parliament, as illustrated by the events surrounding *Godden* v. *Hales* (1686) 2 Shower KB 475.

In the case of *Godden* v. *Hales* (1686) 2 Shower KB 475 the king promoted a friend to the rank of colonel without the approval of Parliament, as was required by the Test Act. Herbert CJ gave judgment and upheld the use of the prerogative. The decision was not unanimous as some of the judges doubted the use of the prerogative powers. However, the majority held that king's use of the prerogative was not restricted by an Act of Parliament. The judgment was recorded that, 'the Kings of England were absolute Sovereigns; that the laws were the King's laws; that the King had a power to dispense with any of the laws of Government as he saw necessity for it; that he was sole judge of that necessity; that no Act of Parliament could take away that power.'

It is interesting to note the reasoning of Herbert CJ:

'To say the King cannot dispense with a law that is made *pro bono publico*, is to say, that he can dispense with no law at all; for all laws are supposed to be *pro bono publico*, when they are first made.

'To say that the dispensing with the law may be of dangerous consequence, is no argument at all, for that may be said of the exercise of the King's prerogative in many cases, supposing that he would abuse the exercise of it; none will deny but that the King hath power to proclaim war when he pleaseth, and yet it may be said that he may keep us always in war, and so ruin his subjects.'

Herbert CJ did not believe that there were *no* restrictions on the prerogative, but rather that an Act of Parliament was not one of them.

CONTEXT

What we can see is that the Stuart monarchs, most notably Charles I and James II, clashed with Parliament when they attempted to use their prerogative powers to govern in defiance of an Act of Parliament. According to Professor G.R. Elton, the Stuarts, unlike the Tudors, who avoided controversy in their use of the prerogative as a flexible source of non-statutory powers, spoilt the prerogative by treating it as a source of absolutism (*The Tudor Constitution: Documents and Commentary*, 2nd edn, Cambridge University Press: Cambridge, 1982). This is interesting as this was the last attempt by the monarch to usurp the supremacy of Parliament.

The Glorious Revolution, the Bill of Rights and the survival of the prerogative (1688–)

As discussed in Chapter 7, Parliament invited William of Orange and his wife Mary to become joint monarchs in 1688. This is known as the Glorious Revolution as James II fled to France and Parliament now asserted its supremacy.

The new Parliament abolished some of the prerogative powers and replaced others with Acts of Parliament. The monarchy was preserved because the rule of Parliament and the Lord Protector (exercising both the legislature and executive functions during the Commonwealth) had been unpopular. There were many who favoured the return of a monarch as head of the executive, who would have responsibility for diplomacy and war. One such supporter of this separation of powers was John Locke.

CORNERSTONE

John Locke and the separation of powers

'Where the legislative and executive power are in distinct hands (as they are in all moderated monarchies and well-framed governments) there the good of the society requires that several things should be left to the discretion of him that has the executive power' John Locke, *The Second Treaties on Civil Government* (Basil Blackwell: Oxford, 1946), p. 80.

Locke defended the use of discretionary powers by noting that the legislature could not predict what laws would be needed in the future for the good of the population. This discretionary power to act 'for the public good' was defined by Locke as the prerogative.

The survival of the prerogative

As the prerogative powers are used at the discretion of the executive without parliamentary approval and accountability, why did Parliament simply not abolish all the prerogative powers? The answer is that the executive needed discretionary powers to act, and that soon parliamentarians would form part of the executive. This was because the monarchs soon stopped making day-to-day decisions concerning the running of the country and surrendered their day-to-day powers to the cabinet.

Take note

The cabinet was comprised of parliamentarians that would form the government and continues to this day to govern the country on behalf of the monarch. Today the monarch has no real choice over the composition of her government. The leader of the government is the Prime Minister. The Prime Minister is the leader of the political party which has the most number of seats in the House of Commons. The party which has a majority of seats in the House of Commons forms the government.

This means that the government had little to gain from surrendering the prerogative powers and Parliament little choice (given the dominance of the legislative branch by the executive) in legislating to abolish them. According to Professor Munro (2005), '[i]t is not surprising that modern governments have found it useful to retain such broad discretionary powers to act, which enable action to be taken without the necessity of prior parliamentary approval' (p. 271).

The prerogative ceased to become contentious as the remaining prerogative powers of the monarch were controlled by convention, and the majority of the powers were exercised by the government.

THE PREROGATIVE TODAY

We will now look at how the prerogative is exercised today. This will involve looking at the composition and function of the Privy Council. We will then look at who exercises the prerogative and the different categories of prerogative powers.

The Queen in Council

CORNERSTONE

The Privy Council

The Privy Council was the mechanism that was used by the monarch to govern the country. Today, whilst the Privy Council still exists, it is the government that runs the country and the bulk of government business is done outside of the Privy Council (i.e. in government departments).

Today membership of the Privy Council includes senior politicians from the government and the opposition and members of the Royal Family. The Privy Council still serves an important role. First, the Privy Council has a judicial function and, secondly, Orders in Council can be made during meetings of the Privy Council.

Judicial function

Some members of the Commonwealth still use the Judicial Committee of the Privy Council as their highest appeal court. In these countries the Privy Council will be the highest court and its decision will be legally binding. The role of the Privy Council has diminished over time as many Commonwealth countries now have their own appeal courts. Recently, Jamaica has announced that it is considering no longer sending cases to the Privy Council. The Judicial Committee hearing a Jamaican case would often have to decide whether to permit an execution.

CONTEXT

As result of the Constitutional Reform Act 2005 the Privy Council is now based in the new Supreme Court building. The cases that are appealed to the Privy Council are heard by the Justices of the Supreme Court.

Orders in Council

CORNERSTONE

The Privy Council – 'the cloak that covers'

In evidence to the Public Administration Select Committee in 2004, the Privy Council was described by William Hague MP as 'the cloak that covers' a number of important activities (p. 12). Hague argued that the prerogative powers exercised through the Privy Council ought to be made subject to parliamentary control.

Orders can be made during meetings of the Privy Council. The Lord President, who will be a senior government minister, will oversee the meeting of the Privy Council. Ministers can use the prerogative (or statutory powers) to make Orders in Council. Such orders do not require parliamentary sanction, as Orders in Council require the assent of the monarch. Recent Orders in Council include the monarch consenting to the appointment of ministers, proclamations regarding the minting of coinage to mark key events and changes to a university's charter. As we shall see below, Orders in Council have been used by the government to legislate for British Overseas Territories.

During Privy Council meetings everyone including the Queen will stand. This practice originated during the reign of Queen Victoria (1837–1901).

We will look now at the types of prerogative power exercised today:

- Exercise of the prerogative by the government in the Queen's name.
- Exercise of the prerogative by the monarch and where the monarch has actual choice.
- Exercise of the prerogative by the monarch where the monarch has very little choice, as the use of the prerogative is regulated by constitutional convention.

CORNERSTONE

The Crown's legal prerogatives

The Queen is the fount of justice and is responsible for the administration of law and justice in the United Kingdom. The monarch has prerogative powers to create courts and appoint judges and this power was exercised on behalf of the monarch by the Lord Chancellor (prior to the Constitutional Reform Act 2005). The Crown no longer has immunity from being sued in contract and tort (Crown Proceedings Act 1947), although the monarch is personally immune from prosecution.

Exercise of the prerogative by the government in the Queen's name

CORNERSTONE

Use of the prerogative by ministers

Due to the United Kingdom's system of cabinet government most prerogative powers are now exercised by ministers. A minister will have at her disposal powers which are conferred by an Act of Power, which are statutory powers, and the prerogative, which is a non-statutory power (see Figure 9.1). Powers conferred by Parliament may give a minister the power to create secondary legislation that is known as delegated legislation. A minister can create legislation or use the power provided under the Act to do certain things. The prerogative powers are not conferred by Parliament and the existence and extent of the precise prerogative powers will be found by looking back at the common law.

According to Dicey, the retention of the prerogative powers by each successive government, 'leaves in the hands of the Premier and his colleagues, large powers which can be exercised, and constantly are exercised, free from Parliamentary control'. This is a major criticism of the prerogative. Academics, lawyers and politicians have called for reform and we shall look at this below.

We will now look at the main prerogative powers which are exercised by the government. As we explore these below, it might be worthwhile to think about the impact that these prerogative powers have on our daily lives.

1. The deployment and use of the armed forces overseas

The deployment of British armed forces overseas and the declaration of war is a prerogative power. Although war has not been formally declared since 1939, British forces have been involved in military action in Egypt, Korea, the Falklands, Afghanistan, Iraq and Libya. The government does not need parliamentary approval for military action, although the funding of military operations will need to be supported by additional funds through an Act of Parliament.

Figure 9.1 Statutory and non-statutory ministerial power

CORNERSTONE

Did Iraq, Libya and Syria create a convention?

The most controversial use of the prerogative to deploy UK armed forces was the 2003 invasion of Iraq. The then Prime Minister, Tony Blair, gave the House of Commons a vote on whether to support military action. The vote took place whilst British troops were preparing to invade Iraq. The House of Commons voted in favour of military action. There was no legal requirement for the vote, and at the time some observers believed that the vote might have created a new convention. This meant that in the future the government would be obliged to seek the support of the House of Commons before declaring war. In 2011, David Cameron permitted the House of Commons to vote on the decision to deploy British forces to Libya. In 2013, the House of Commons was given the opportunity to vote on whether to support military involvement in Syria and voted against this. David Cameron announced that he respected the decision. This vote had international implications and triggered President Obama to announce that he wished to involve Congress in the decision as to whether to commit American forces. The decision to permit the House of Commons to vote in 2013 reinforces the view that there is now a clearly established convention requiring the House of Commons to vote before committing British forces to military action. For an interesting discussion on this see G. Phillipson, 'Historic Commons' Syria vote: the constitutional significance (Part I)' UK Const. L. Blog (19 September 2013) (available at http://ukconstitutionallaw.org).

The government's ability to respond to global events without the approval of the House of Commons is an important reason for keeping this power as part of the prerogative. Although in the case of Afghanistan, Iraq and arguably Libya (from a defence, if not a humanitarian perspective), there was no immediate need to act and therefore there was sufficient time to hold such a vote.

> In the United States of America it is Congress and not the President which has the power to declare war. The President has extensive power to deploy US armed forces around the world and engage in hostilities. This allows the President to deploy forces without Congress having first declared war. The War Powers Act 1973 delegates the power to declare war to the President. The President has sixty days to seek Congress' authorisation.
>
> CONTEXT

In 2004 the House of Commons Public Administration Select Committee issued a report, *Taming the Prerogative: strengthening ministerial accountability to Parliament*, which called for the prerogative powers to be laid out on a statutory footing. The proposed statute was the Ministers of the Crown (Executive Powers) Bill. Clause 5 and 6 of the bill would restrict the use of British forces in armed conflict and the declaration of war with a resolution from both Houses of Parliament. However, no resolution was needed if the deployment of armed force was in self-defence. Giving evidence to the committee in 2004, William Hague MP stated:

> 'I think that actually should be laid down in an Act of Parliament or in the Standing Orders of the House . . . the power to commit troops to action needs codifying, so that parliamentary approval is required before it takes place or as soon as possible thereafter if the circumstances do not permit such a vote to be taken beforehand.'

2. Making and ratifying treaties

Because of the UK's dualist legal system once a treaty has been ratified by the executive, it must then be enacted into English law by an Act of Parliament. An example is the Hague-Visby Rules 1968 which were enacted into domestic law by the Carriage of Goods by Sea Act 1971.

Foreign policy and the making and ratifying of treaties are the functions of the executive (see Locke's *Second Treatise on Government*), and the government uses the prerogative to undertake these.

CORNERSTONE

The Ponsonby Convention and the Constitutional Reform and Governance Act 2010

The Ponsonby Convention, or rule, requires that the government lay a new treaty before Parliament. This gives Parliament twenty-one days to debate the treaty. This, according to the Ponsonby Convention, must happen before the treaty can be ratified. There is now a legal requirement to do this under the Constitutional Reform and Governance Act 2010. This has limited the use of the prerogative (see Barrett 2011).

3. The power to issue, refuse, impound and revoke passports

The government has the prerogative power to issue, refuse, impound and revoke passports. This is an important power as it restricts travel from the United Kingdom. A citizen can be effectively prevented from ever leaving the United Kingdom. The use of the prerogative to issue passports has been controversial. One example is the refusal to grant the Egyptian national Mr Mohammed Al Fayed a British passport, which resulted in allegations of MPs being paid cash to ask questions in Parliament about this. According to Lord Lester, in his evidence to the 2004 Public Administration Select Committee, 'it seems to me entirely anomalous that the right to freedom of movement, which is a fundamental right, should be subject, at least in theory, entirely to the prerogative, unregulated by Parliament'.

4. Acquiring and ceding territory

The government can use the prerogative to acquire and cede British territory. An example of this is the Heligoland islands which are just off the north-eastern coast of Germany. These islands were part of the British Empire until 1890 when the government under the Heligoland–Zanzibar Treaty exchanged the islands for the German territory of Zanzibar. The decision to exchange these territories was unpopular with the monarch. The decision was made for strategic reasons.

5. The conduct of diplomacy

The government has the prerogative power to conduct foreign policy and can send and receive ambassadors. Foreign policy is the responsibility of the Secretary of State for the Foreign and Commonwealth Affairs, although the Prime Minister will dominate foreign policy by his dealings with foreign leaders (e.g. Tony Blair and Presidents Bill Clinton and George W. Bush, or Margaret Thatcher and President Ronald Reagan).

6. The organisation of the Civil Service

The Civil Service has now been placed on a statutory basis (Constitutional Reform and Governance Act 2010) and is no longer organised under the prerogative powers. Previously this meant that the creation of government departments such as the Ministry of Justice (2007) did not require parliamentary approval. In the United States and Canada the approval of the legislature is required before the creation of government departments.

Prerogative powers exercised by the government through ministers' recommendations to the monarch

The monarch has in reality surrendered certain prerogative powers to the government. The government will make recommendations to the monarch and the monarch will agree to these. These powers have been gradually relinquished by the monarch.

1. The granting of honours or decorations

The honour system in the United Kingdom has been controversial as the choice of which individuals would receive honours was made by the government. The honour system is contentious as it was seen as a way to reward political allies. Recently, there has been an attempt to open up the honour system by allowing individuals to recommend local people who have served their community. The Honours and Appointments Secretariat was established in 2008 and it recommends the granting of honours to the Prime Minister, who will then make a recommendation to the monarch. Some honours are at the personal gift of the monarch and are not granted on the advice of ministers; these include the Order of the Garter.

2. The prerogative of mercy

The prerogative of mercy is used to grant pardons to those who have been convicted of criminal offences. In December 2013, Alan Turing, an important mathematician during the 1940s and '50s who is most famously credited with breaking the Enigma code in the Second World War, was pardoned for a criminal conviction in the 1950s. The conviction related to homosexual activity and the offence is now obsolete.

3. The granting of peerages

The granting of peerages is distinct from the honours system. A hereditary peerage, prior to the House of Lords Act 1999, would entitle an individual to sit in the legislative chamber of the House of Lords. Today a life peerage entitles the recipient to become a member of the House of Lords. There have been accusations that peerages have been granted in return for donations to political parties. In 2006 the then Prime Minister was interviewed by the police over allegations that large sums had been given to the Labour Party in exchange for peerages. The House of Lords Appointments Commission will vet the nominations for peerages and ultimately a recommendation will be made to the monarch. Nonetheless, the granting of peerages is very political as a newly elected government will wish to create enough peers to ensure that their legislation is not defeated in the House of Lords.

4. The appointment of ministers

In the United Kingdom the Prime Minister has developed from being the first among equals to exercising virtual control over the cabinet. The Prime Minister will make decisions as to the appointment of ministers. The monarch will authorise the appointments made by the Prime Minister. Since the late nineteenth century the monarch can no longer attempt to block ministerial appointments.

Take note

The monarch still exercises some important prerogative powers. It is important to note that these prerogative powers are regulated by conventions and so the monarch's freedom to act as she wishes is restricted by a non-legal rule.

Take note

The limitations on the monarch's use of the prerogative were discussed by Professor Blackburn in 'Monarchy and the personal prerogatives' [2004] *Public Law 546*. Refer to this article for details on these limitations.

Take note

This means that the monarch could choose anyone to form the government and run the United Kingdom. This seems at odds with the actual system that operates today, but it must be remembered that the monarch traditionally took an active part in the governance of the country and it was only 300 years ago that Sir Robert Walpole became the first Prime Minister, and this only occurred over the monarch's disinterest with government.

Personal prerogatives of the monarch that are regulated by constitutional conventions

Legally if not constitutionally, the monarch still has considerable powers at her disposal. The ability of the monarch to use these powers is now restricted by the political changes which have occurred over the last two centuries: the most important of these being universal male and female suffrage. The survival of the British monarchy is based on the constitutional restrictions which have been placed upon the prerogative. It is important that the monarch must remain neutral and not be seen to endorse or disagree with the policies of a particular political party and that she must use her prerogative powers in a manner that avoids controversy. For example, Queen Victoria's close friendship with Viscount Melbourne and subsequent disagreements with her other Prime Ministers was at the time controversial, as it risked the neutrality of the monarchy.

1. The choice of government and Prime Minister

It is Her Majesty's government that exercises many of the key executive powers in the United Kingdom. Under the prerogative the monarch technically has the power to choose her own government.

Often when people vote they take the view that they are voting for the person who becomes Prime Minister. Thus, there is a strong degree of personality politics, as we might vote for a political party based upon the personality and attributes of the party leader. In the 2010 General Election, the party leaders agreed to take part in televised debates and thus reinforced this misconception. In reality at the General Election we vote for who will become our local MP. The MP will most likely belong to a political party. The political party which has the most seats will dominate the House of Commons and the legislative agenda of that Parliament. According to convention, it is the leader of that political party who will be asked to form the next government. In the 1997, 2001 and 2005 General Elections the Labour Party enjoyed a majority in the House of Commons. In 2010 the Conservatives won more seats than the other parties but did not enjoy an overall majority. Consequentially the Conservatives formed a coalition government with the Liberal Democrats.

In 1997 the monarch could have asked John Major to form a government, even though his Conservative Party had significantly fewer MPs than Labour. Legally, there is no requirement that Tony Blair would become Prime Minister in 1997. Had this occurred, the Conservatives would have been unable to govern the United Kingdom, as they could not command a majority in the House of Commons. The government would have been unable to pass any laws, it would have been accused of being undemocratic, it would have been viewed as unpopular in the press and with the electorate, and finally it would have risked being destroyed by a vote of no confidence that would trigger a fresh General Election. The monarch would have faced considerable controversy and risked becoming very unpopular (indeed this might have prompted calls for a republic).

The last monarch to seriously challenge the House of Commons over his right to choose his own government was George III in 1783. George III eventually backed down and allowed the parliamentary grouping that enjoyed a majority to form a government. The king was forced to do this as no one else would form a government. Even then there was a risk of unrest caused by the monarch's unconstitutional use of his prerogative powers. (See Cannon, J. *The Fox-North Coalition: Crisis of the Constitution 1782–1784*, Cambridge University Press: Cambridge, 1969.)

The role of convention

The monarch's prerogative powers are regulated by convention. The Prime Minister must be from the House of Commons. Additionally, the Prime Minister must command the support of the House of Commons. This means that in practice it is the political party which enjoys a majority in the House of Commons, which will form the next government.

Traditionally, the monarch had to choose between leader figures in a party that had a majority in the House of Commons. This happened in 1963 when the Prime Minister Harold Macmillan resigned due to ill health. The monarch had to make a choice between two senior Conservative politicians. Such a choice was controversial. The need to make this choice has been largely removed by internal party rules. The Labour Party had always had internal leadership rules, but in 1965 the Conservative Party introduced leadership rules. As a consequence the monarch has not had to make a choice since 1963.

In our system there is a risk that the monarch could still be involved in political controversy where there is a hung Parliament (that is, when no one party enjoys a majority in the House of Commons). The monarch might be forced to make a choice between different political parties. In 1931 as result of the Great Depression, George V responded to the collapse of the Labour government by asking the other parties to form a national government. This was very controversial and the king was criticised by the Labour Party. There were concerns that the 2010 General Election would result in a hung Parliament and that the monarch might have to make a choice between Labour and the Conservatives. In 2010, as no political party secured a majority and after the Prime Minister failed to form a coalition government, the monarch asked the leader of the opposition who had entered into a coalition to form a government.

Can the monarch dismiss the Prime Minister?

Once appointed, the monarch has the prerogative power to dismiss the Prime Minister. The last Prime Minister to be dismissed was Lord Melbourne in 1834 by William IV. Even then the dismissal proved ineffective, as Lord Melbourne commanded the majority of the House of Commons and was quickly reinstated (Heffer, S. *Power and Place: The Political Consequences of King Edward VIII* (Phoenix: London, 1999), pp. 296–297).

2. The Dissolution of Parliament (or calling a fresh General Election)

The Prime Minister could request the monarch to dissolve Parliament. This would trigger a General Election. The right to dissolve parliament is one of the monarch's prerogative powers and the monarch could refuse such a request. Once again, convention regulates the monarch's ability to refuse such a request. The monarch would by convention grant the Prime Minister his request to dissolve Parliament.

The monarch's actual dissolution is regarded as a formality. For example Edward VII in 1905 was shocked that the Prime Minister, Arthur Balfour, had informed the House of Commons that Parliament would be dissolved because the Cabinet had decided to do this (Heffer, S. *Power and Place: The Political Consequences of King Edward VIII* (Phoenix: London, 1999) pp. 113–114).

Take note

This has been changed by the Fixed-term Parliaments Act 2011 which stipulates that the Parliament of 2010 is to last until 2015. This removes the prerogative power to dissolve Parliament before 2015 and consequently this restricts the ability of the Prime Minister to call an early General Election.

Prior to 2011 the lifetime of each Parliament was a maximum of five years (Parliament Act 1911). After this, the Prime Minister would have to ask the monarch to dissolve Parliament and this would trigger a General Election. At any time during these five years the Prime Minister could ask the monarch to dissolve Parliament. This enabled the Prime Minister to call a General Election at a time favourable to his party. Equally, a Prime Minister who did not enjoy a majority in the House of Commons might risk another General Election in order to gain a majority.

CORNERSTONE

The circumstances in which Parliament can be dissolved before May 2015

Section 2 of the Fixed-term Parliaments Act states that Parliament can only be dissolved before 2015 if firstly, there is a successful vote of no confidence in the government. The last successful vote was in 1979. In 1979 the government of James Callaghan lost such a vote and Callaghan immediately asked the monarch to dissolve Parliament and this triggered a General Election. The Act preserves the convention that a government must resign after losing a vote of no confidence. Secondly, Parliament can be dissolved if more than two-thirds of the House of Commons vote in favour of an early General Election.

3. Royal assent

In Chapter 5 we saw that an Act of Parliament is legally sovereign. However, before a bill becomes law the monarch must give royal assent. Unless this is given the bill is not law and the courts will not enforce it. The monarch has the prerogative power to give or refuse her assent.

In the United States the President can also refuse his assent to bills passed by Congress. Whilst Congress can override the President's refusal where a two-thirds majority in both Houses of Congress votes to do this, there is no legal device available to do this in the United Kingdom. The President is elected every four years by the American people and as an elected official he has the legitimacy to exercise his veto. The monarch is not elected and for many it would not be legitimate for the monarch to use her prerogative powers to veto legislation.

The last monarch to refuse royal assent was Queen Anne in 1708. Previously monarchs including William III had refused their assent to bills. The bill in question was the Scottish Militia Bill 1707. It was intended to regulate the militia across the newly created United Kingdom by including Scotland in these arrangements. The Queen acting upon the advice of her ministers refused her assent. This is the last time that a monarch has refused their assent to a bill. This has given rise to a convention that royal assent should not be refused. Despite the existence of the convention, the monarch has the prerogative power to refuse royal assent. This convention has survived the conflicts between monarch and the House of Commons since 1708.

It is interesting to consider whether a monarch would ever refuse royal assent and if so in what circumstances this would be, and what the resulting consequences would be. The monarch legally could refuse her assent despite the existence of the convention. Equally, an Act of Parliament could not abolish the requirement that the monarch must give assent, unless the monarch gave her assent to a bill abolishing this prerogative power. Writing in the mid-nineteenth century, Walter Bagehot regarded the monarch as lacking the ability to veto legislation and he observed that if Parliament presented her with a bill for her own death warrant, then the monarch must sign it (see *The English Constitution*).

A striking example of the convention binding a monarch's prerogative power was the controversial Fox's India Bill in 1783. George III detested his government and the bill, but nonetheless accepted that his power to veto legislation had gone into abeyance and was forced to rely on his supporters to defeat the controversial bill in the House of Lords. However, as recently as 1913, George V believed that he could refuse royal assent to the Irish Home Rule Bill. Whether George V would have vetoed the bill is now redundant, as the outbreak of the First World War and the Easter Rising in 1916 made Irish independence inevitable.

Professor Blackburn (2004) questioned what would happen where the monarch faced an ethical dilemma over proposed legislation:

> 'What if, after the future accession of Charles III, the new King is given a Bill to sign by the government that he finds fundamentally at odds with his own personal conscience and core beliefs? Such a situation arose in Belgium in 1990, where King Baudouin did believe there was a personal element in the Royal Assent, which as a result caused him to refuse to sign a Bill legalising abortion, on the grounds that he was a devout Catholic . . . it is not difficult to imagine the philosophically inquiring and soul-searching personality of Prince Charles having similar difficulties in reconciling his private beliefs with his public duties if and when he were ever confronted by such a dilemma as monarch' (p. 546).

REFLECTION

PARLIAMENTARY CONTROL OF THE PREROGATIVE

As we have seen above, the prerogative is largely exercised by the government. The government will have at their disposal a considerable amount of power which has not been conferred on them by Parliament. When statutory powers are conferred on a minister there is a debate as to whether these powers are needed, the extent of the powers and clear limitations are imposed. It is possible to find the statutory power and see if the minister has exceeded his power. This is not the case with prerogative powers. These powers are outside the control of Parliament. These powers are not consolidated and written down, but exist through precedents from case law and history.

CORNERSTONE

Prerogative powers permit ministers to act without parliamentary approval

'These powers are among the most significant that governments possess, yet Ministers regularly use them without any parliamentary approval or scrutiny . . . We recognise that Parliament is not powerless in the face of these weighty prerogatives. In the past, it has limited or abolished individual prerogative powers, and has also put some prerogatives on a statutory footing . . . But these restrictions on Ministers' prerogative powers are inevitably limited. Ministers still have very wide scope to act without Parliamentary approval. Perhaps more surprisingly in an era of increasing freedom of information, Parliament does not even have the right to know what these powers are. Ministers have repeatedly answered parliamentary questions about Ministers' prerogative powers by saying that records are not kept of the individual occasions on which those powers are used, and that it would not be practicable to do so. Ministers have also said that it would be impossible to produce a precise list of these powers, and have asserted that, as Rt Hon John Major put it when he was Prime Minister "It is for individual Ministers to decide on a particular occasion whether and how to report to Parliament on the exercise of prerogative powers".' The House of Commons Public Administration Select Committee's fourth report, *Taming the Prerogative: Strengthening Ministerial Accountability to Parliament* (2004).

The flexibility that the prerogative gives a minister is the reason why the request for a complete list was rejected. However, this means that ministerial use of the prerogative is uncertain. It could be argued that all ministers are accountable to Parliament, but as the government is likely to enjoy a majority in the House of Commons there is little that will be done to hold a minister to account. Parliament could abolish or restrict the use of the prerogative. This is problematic as the government has no incentive to see its own powers reduced.

The Ram Doctrine

CORNERSTONE

The Ram Doctrine

Ministerial use of the Ram Doctrine is also problematic, as the doctrine states that a minister can do anything so long as he is not prevented from doing so by the law. The use of the Ram Doctrine has been criticised as unconstitutional as it permits arbitrary use of discretionary powers.

Lester and Weait ('The use of ministerial powers within parliamentary authority: the Ram doctrine' [2003] *Public Law* 415) state that:

'The notion that a minister or government department can do anything that a natural person can do, provided it is not forbidden from doing so, fails to have regard not only to the United Kingdom's obligations under the European Convention but also to the modern constitutional position of public authorities, including ministers and their departments. Public authorities have legal obligations by virtue of the public nature of their functions as servants of the public. So much is clear from the principles of public law, including the principle of legality, and from the constitutional scheme contained in the Human Rights Act 1998, and the devolution legislation. These principles preclude arbitrary action by the executive or any other public authority. It is therefore disappointing to find civil servants within the Cabinet Office propounding what is now a constitutional and legal heresy.'

Weak parliamentary control

CONERSTONE

Weak parliamentary control over the use of the prerogative powers

Parliament's control of the executive is an important check and balance and the absence of effective accountability over the use of the prerogative is a problem. According to Munro (2005) 'the exercise of prerogative powers is imperfectly subject to parliamentary control, and in many – perhaps most – instances removed from the purview of the Parliamentary Ombudsman' (p. 278).

The ultimate parliamentary control is legislation to abolish the prerogative; however, this would not happen unless initiated by the government. Select committees do provide a review of ministerial use of the prerogative, but this can be ineffective as ministers do not have to provide a complete list of their powers. In *R (Bancoult)* v. *Secretary of State for Foreign and Commonwealth Affairs (No.2)* [2008] UKHL 61 the issue concerned colonial legislation made under the prerogative. The Foreign Affairs Committee should have reviewed the colonial legislation before it came into effect. But the committee was bypassed on grounds of secrecy and the colonial legislation was brought into force without any parliamentary scrutiny.

JUDICIAL CONTROL OF THE PREROGATIVE

CORNERSTONE

The importance of judicial control over ministerial use of the prerogative

It is because political control is ineffective that judicial control is extremely important. The courts have limited the extent of the prerogative since the *Case of Proclamations*. Effective judicial control of the prerogative ensures that the executive is held to account. This accountability is crucial to ensure that powers are not abused.

In Chapter 13 we shall see that the courts, through judicial review, can prevent the executive from abusing its statutory powers. Traditionally, the prerogative could not be judicially reviewed, but as we shall see the courts are now able to judicially review the prerogative. Judicial control is an important check and balance on executive accountability (see Figure 9.2).

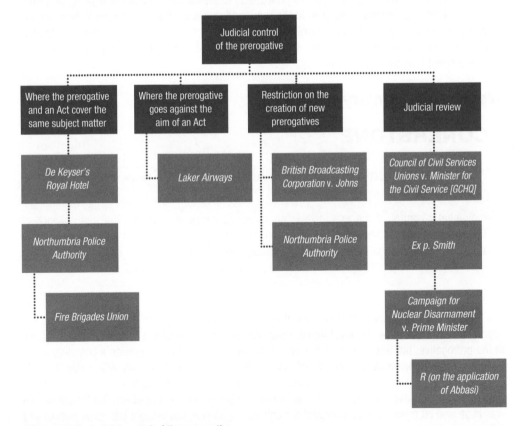

Figure 9.2 Judicial control of the prerogative

The courts have held the executive's use of the prerogative to account. This has been achieved in a number of ways:

- First, the courts have upheld the supremacy of Parliament by preventing the prerogative from being used in a way that was either expressly contrary or went against the intention of an Act of Parliament.
- Secondly, the courts have restricted the creation of new prerogative powers and have prevented any prerogative powers that no longer exist from being used.
- Finally, the courts can judicially review ministerial use of the prerogative.

1. Inconsistency with an Act of Parliament

CORNERSTONE

The courts will apply an Act of Parliament

Where an Act of Parliament is inconsistent with a prerogative power, then the prerogative goes into abeyance. Whilst the Act remains on the statute book the prerogative cannot be used.

The courts will not allow a minister to use his prerogative power where an Act of Parliament covers the same subject-matter. The courts are giving effect to Parliamentary Sovereignty. Parliament is the highest law-maker and since the seventeenth century the prerogative can no longer be used to disregard a statute (see Figure 9.3).

CORNERSTONE

Attorney-General v. *De Keyser's Royal Hotel Ltd* [1920] AC 508

In this case the government requisitioned a hotel to house the headquarters of the newly formed Royal Flying Corps. This occurred during the First World War. The government sought to rely on the prerogative to take possession of land and buildings for the defence of the realm. The hotel owner argued that they were entitled to compensation under the Defence Act 1842. The Defence of the Realm Consolidation Act 1914 did not affect the ability to recover compensation. The House of Lords held that compensation was payable. The government could not seek to rely on the prerogative where an Act of Parliament existed covering the same subject-matter. The prerogative power would go into abeyance, which meant that it could not be used unless the inconsistent Act was amended or repealed. This judgment gave effect to Parliamentary Sovereignty.

Figure 9.3 Where an Act of Parliament is inconsistent with the prerogative

The opinion of Lord Atkinson addressed a number of issues. First, His Lordship raised the fact that the Act imposes restrictions on the executive and that the court must not allow the prerogative to be used to avoid these. Secondly, if the prerogative and an Act covered the same subject-matter the prerogative did not disappear altogether, rather it went into abeyance. This means that the executive must use its statutory power rather than its prerogative power. Lord Atkinson in *De Keyser's Royal Hotel Ltd* (at 539) stated that:

> 'It is quite obvious that it would be useless and meaningless for the Legislature to impose restrictions and limitations upon, and to attach conditions to, the exercise by the Crown of the powers conferred by a statute, if the Crown were free at its pleasure to disregard these provisions, and by virtue of its prerogative do the very thing the statutes empowered it to do. One cannot in the construction of a statute attribute to the Legislature (in the absence of compelling words) an intention so absurd. It was suggested that when a statute is passed empowering the Crown to do a certain thing which it might theretofore have done by virtue of its prerogative, the prerogative is merged in the statute. I confess I do not think the word "merged" is happily chosen. I should prefer to say that when such a statute, expressing the will and intention of the King and of the three estates of the realm, is passed, it abridges the Royal Prerogative while it is in force to this extent: that the Crown can only do the particular thing under and in accordance with the statutory provisions, and that its prerogative power to do that thing is in abeyance. Whichever mode of expression be used, the result intended to be indicated is, I think, the same – namely, that after the statute has been passed, and while it is in force, the thing it empowers the Crown to do can thenceforth only be done by and under the statute, and subject to all the limitations, restrictions and conditions by it imposed, however unrestricted the Royal Prerogative may theretofore have been.'

Lord Parmoor stated that the court could challenge the executive's assertion as to the extent of their prerogative powers. Lord Parmoor rejected the view that the prerogative could be used to take possession of or occupy land and buildings without paying compensation. As we shall see below, the court's task is one of conducting a historical enquiry to see whether there exists such a prerogative power and how it can be used. Lord Parmoor observed that,

> 'If no precedents can be found prior to the year 1688 of a claim to use and occupy the land of the subject for an indefinite time without the payment of compensation, it would be improbable that such precedents would be found at a later date' (at 573).

Lord Parmoor identified the important role the courts played in protecting citizens from the executive's use of the prerogative. His Lordship stated,

> 'The growth of constitutional liberties has largely consisted in the reduction of the discretionary power of the executive, and in the extension of Parliamentary protection in favour of the subject, under a series of statutory enactments. The result is that, whereas at one time the Royal Prerogative gave legal sanction to a large majority of the executive functions of the Government, it is now restricted within comparatively narrow limits' (at 568).

This process is important in order for the rule of law to operate as by relying on statute as opposed to the prerogative, there is a consistency of application. Lord Parmoor's argument supports the view that an unrestrained approach to the prerogative will harm civil liberties.

It is not just where the prerogative is inconsistent with an Act of Parliament that the court will restrict its use. If Parliament has intended to achieve X by passing an Act and the government's use of the prerogative would undermine X, then the courts may restrain the use of the prerogative. This occurred in *Laker Airways Ltd* v. *Department of Trade* [1977] QB 643 (see Figure 9.4).

Figure 9.4 The issue in *Laker Airways*

CORNERSTONE

Laker Airways Ltd v. *Department of Trade* [1977] QB 643

In *Laker Airways* Mr Laker had set up an airline and wished to challenge British Airways by running a transatlantic service between London and the United States. Laker Airways would require a licence from both the United States and United Kingdom's aviation authorities. The UK Civil Aviation Authority (CAA) granted a licence which was then revoked by the UK government.

The government wished to protect the monopoly of the state-owned British Airways. Air travel between the US and UK was governed by the Bermuda Treaty which stated that each state would appoint designated carriers to carry passengers on each route. The decision to make Laker Airways a designated carrier (and to grant a licence) was made by the CAA subject to the Civil Aviation Act 1971. Section 3(1) of the Act set out four objectives that had to be satisfied when granting licences, the second of these was to prevent British Airways having a monopoly. Laker Airways was approved as a designated carrier. The government then announced that there would only be one designated carrier for each route and this would prevent Laker Airways from running a transatlantic service. This governmental guidance on the issuing of licences was regarded as unlawful by Laker Airways. It was argued by the government that the power to withdraw a designation was a prerogative power and that the court could not investigate how it was used.

The Court of Appeal in *Laker Airways* had to consider whether the prerogative could be used to withdraw the designation. Lord Denning MR acknowledged that that Secretary of State could have used his statutory powers under section 4 of the CAA 1971 to withdraw the designation. Therefore, the Secretary of State could not use the prerogative here and had exceeded his discretionary powers, which meant that the guidance given to the CAA was illegal and could not override the statutory criteria that the CAA should follow.

Roskill LJ considered the question of whether the government could use the prerogative to revoke the designation. The government had argued that there were no restrictions on using the prerogative, as designations were made under the Treaty of Bermuda. Roskill LJ referred to *De Keyser's Royal Hotel Ltd* and looked at whether the CAA 1971 had fettered the prerogative from being used. His Lordship took the view that the CAA 1971 imposed a restriction on the prerogative. This was because Parliament must have intended the process of granting licences to have restricted the ability of the prerogative to revoke them outside of the statutory framework. Roskill LJ in *Laker Airways* stated that:

'The two powers are inextricably interwoven. Where a right to fly is granted by the Authority under the statute by the grant of an air transport licence which has not been lawfully revoked and cannot be lawfully revoked in the manner thus far contemplated by the Secretary of State,

I do not see why we should hold that Parliament in 1971 must be taken to have intended that a prerogative power to achieve what is in effect the same result as lawful revocation would achieve, should have survived the passing of the statute unfettered so as to enable the Crown to achieve by what I have called the back door that which cannot lawfully be achieved by entry through the front. I think Parliament must be taken to have intended to fetter the prerogative of the Crown in this relevant respect. I would therefore dismiss this appeal.'

Lawton LJ observed that the prerogative if unfettered could be used to go against the statutory framework: 'the Attorney-General was submitting that a licence to operate a scheduled route, which had been granted under statute and after full inquiry by the Authority and which had been made effective internationally by designation, could be rendered useless by a decision of the Secretary of State made without the holder being given any opportunity of being heard or appealing to the courts.' It is clear that the prerogative could be restricted by implication if it was inconsistent with the intention of Parliament. Put simply, the statute was pro-competition whereas the prerogative was used to create a monopoly.

CORNERSTONE

R v. Secretary of State for the Home Department ex p. Fire Brigades Union and Others [1995] 2 WLR 464

In this case the executive's use of the prerogative power was held to conflict with an Act of Parliament. What was interesting here was that the prerogative was found to be incompatible with a yet to be introduced statutory provision. The issue concerned criminal injuries compensation. The statutory scheme under the Appropriation Act 1994 would be more favourable to those injured than the prerogative scheme. The Secretary of State had declared that the statutory provisions would not be brought into force.

The House of Lords ruled that the Secretary of State could not validly refuse ever to introduce the statutory provisions, just to ensure that the prerogative scheme remained valid. Lord Browne-Wilkinson's judgment discussed the approach of the courts where an Act of Parliament and the prerogative are inconsistent. His Lordship stated:

'My Lords, it would be most surprising if, at the present day, prerogative powers could be validly exercised by the executive so as to frustrate the will of Parliament expressed in a statute and, to an extent, to pre-empt the decision of Parliament whether or not to continue with the statutory scheme even though the old scheme has been abandoned.'

His Lordship acknowledged that following *De Keyser's Royal Hotel* there would only be inconsistency once the provisions were introduced, as only then would rights be conferred on the victims of crime. What was different here was that the decision of the Secretary of State to not introduce the provisions, which the House of Lords held to be invalid. This was because the Secretary of State had illegally used his powers as conferred by Parliament.

2. Restrict the abuse of discretionary powers

The prerogative is a discretionary power and traditionally could not be judicially reviewed (this changed in the House of Lord's decision in *Council of Civil Service Unions* v. *Minister for the Civil*

Service [1985] AC 374). According to Blackstone the prerogative could exist where there were no conflicting laws, but it could not be exercised in a manner that was unconstitutional.

CORNERSTONE

The prerogative cannot be used in a manner which is unconstitutional

Sir William Blackstone (*Commentaries*, vol. I, p. 252) stated that:

> 'For prerogative consisting . . . in the discretionary power of acting for the public good, where the positive laws are silent, if that discretionary power be abused to the public detriment, such prerogative is exerted in an unconstitutional manner.'

In *Laker Airways* Lord Denning MR had stated that:

> 'It is a serious matter for the courts to declare that a minister of the Crown has exceeded his powers. So serious that we think hard before doing it. But there comes a point when it has to be done. These courts have the authority – and I would add, the duty – in a proper case, when called upon to inquire into the exercise of a discretionary power by a minister or his department. If it is found that the power has been exercised improperly or mistakenly so as to impinge unjustly on the legitimate rights or interests of the subject, then these courts must so declare.'

Today it would be possible to judicially review the Secretary of State's use of the prerogative in these circumstances, and to apply the same grounds which are used when reviewing the use of statutory powers (see Chapters 12 and 13).

3. Decide upon the existence and impose limitations on the extent and use of the prerogative

In *Entick* v. *Carrington* (1765) 19 St Tr 1030 Lord Camden denied that there existed a power for the Secretary of State to search the premises of a radical pamphleteer. His Lordship famously stated that he could find no precedent of such a power existing. The role of the court is very important in deciding the limitations on executive discretionary power. In *De Keyser's Royal Hotel* the House of Lords accepted that there existed a prerogative to requisition property and goods in times of war, but rejected the argument put forward by the government that there was no obligation to pay compensation. Lord Aitkens stated that,

> '[I]t does not appear that the Crown has ever taken for these purposes the land of the subject without paying for it, and that there is no trace of the Crown having, even in the times of the Stuarts, exercised or asserted the power or right to do so by virtue of the Royal Prerogative' (at 539).

Take note

The prerogative, unlike a statute, cannot be found easily by reference to Westlaw or LexisNexis. The court when looking at, first, whether a prerogative power exists and, secondly, whether it can be used in the way argued by the government, must embark on a search for legal and historical precedents.

CORNERSTONE

Burmah Oil Company Ltd **v.** *Lord Advocate* **[1965] AC 75**

In this case the House of Lords had to decide whether the prerogative could be used to destroy property during war, without the requirement that compensation would be paid. During the Second World War the British Commander in Burma ordered that the company's oil wells were to be destroyed to prevent them falling into the hands of the Japanese. The House of Lords held that there existed a prerogative power to order the destruction of private property in times of war, but as a general rule there was no right to deny compensation. The court drew a distinction between military operations (where compensation was not payable) and preventative measures (where it was payable). This was an important limitation on the use of the prerogative, as the House of Lords held that it could not be used to deny compensation. The government responded to the decision by introducing a bill to Parliament, which as the War Damages Act 1965 retrospectively reversed the House of Lords' decision.

Lord Reid in *Burmah Oil* considered the approach that the court should adopt. His Lordship stated:

> 'The prerogative is really a relic of a past age, not lost by disuse, but only available for a case not covered by statute. So I would think the proper approach is a historical one: how was it used in former times and how has it been used in modern times?'

The approach of Lord Reid in *Burmah Oil* was to view the judge as a historian. This is critical. The prerogative is the remnants of the monarch's discretionary powers and must be restricted to how it is actually used. If the court permitted the prerogative powers to be extended by novel uses unsupported by precedent, then the executive could be seen as creating new prerogative powers or resurrecting long since abandoned powers.

CORNERSTONE

R **v.** *Secretary of State for the Home Department ex p. Northumbria Police Authority* **[1988] 2 WLR 590**

Controversially, the Court of Appeal in *Ex p. Northumbria Police Authority* permitted the prerogative to be used despite the existence of an Act of Parliament that covered the same subject-matter.

In *Ex p. Northumbria Police Authority* the prerogative in question was that of maintaining the peace (see Figure 9.5). The Secretary of State wished to supply riot equipment to chief constables without the permission of the local police authority. This was contested by the Northumbria Police Authority. They argued that they had a monopoly under the Police Act 1964 to supply their police force and that section 41 did not give the Secretary of State the power to do this. Section 4 of the Act established the role of the police authority to equip the police force in their area. They also argued that there was no prerogative power to do this. It would appear that Parliament intended for the police authority to supply and equip the police under the Act. However, the Secretary of State argued that he had pre-rogative power to do this, and the use of the prerogative power was not inconsistent with the Act.

Figure 9.5 The issue in *Ex p. Northumbria Police Authority*

In delivering his opinion Crome-Johnson LJ dismissed the argument that section 41 of the Police Act did not give the Secretary of State the authority to supply the police with riot equipment. His Lordship then proceeded to discuss whether in the absence of such a power in section 41, the Secretary of State could use the prerogative to do this. Counsel for the police authority had argued that there was no prerogative power enabling the Secretary of State to equip the police. His Lordship dismissed this argument and stated that such a prerogative did exist.

Crome-Johnson LJ continued to discuss the argument that the prerogative, if it existed, would be incompatible with the Police Act. His Lordship found that there would be no inconsistency as 'section 4 does not expressly grant a monopoly, and that granted the possibility of an authority which declines to provide equipment required by the chief constable there is every reason not to imply a Parliamentary intent to create one'. Therefore the prerogative power to equip the police would not go into abeyance, as there was no parliamentary intention that the Act would confer the only method to equip the police. The prerogative was not attempting to deprive someone of their statutory rights (*De Keyser's* the right to compensation, and *Ex p. Fire Brigades Union* the right to higher compensation); rather it provided an additional method to supply the police. However, there was clearly a statute to govern the equipping of the police and surely it is arguable that any such prerogative power ought to go into abeyance. Crome-Johnson LJ readily accepted the existence of the prerogative without evidence of a clear precedent.

Interestingly, Nourse LJ rejected the need for a complete list of the prerogative powers and argued that the absence of a precedent should not be fatal. Nourse LJ seemingly rejected a restrictive approach to the prerogative and instead accepted that such a prerogative ought to have existed, despite the lack of evidence as to its existence. His Lordship's assumption that it does exist is supported by Lord Campbell CJ in *Harrison* v. *Bush* (1855) 5 E&B 344 and Hood Phillips in his textbook. Nourse LJ observed:

'References in reported cases and authoritative texts to a prerogative of keeping the peace within the realm are admittedly scarce. The police authority relied especially on Chitty's silence as to that matter in his Prerogatives of the Crown (1820). I do not think that the scarcity is of any real significance. It has not at any stage in our history been practicable to identify all the prerogative powers of the Crown. It is only by a process of piecemeal decision over a period of centuries that particular powers are seen to exist or not to exist, as the case may be. From time to time a need for more exact definition arises. The present need arises from a difference of view between the Secretary of State and a police authority over what is necessary to maintain public order, a phenomenon which has been observed only in recent times. There has probably never been a comparable occasion for investigating a prerogative of keeping the peace within the realm.

'I have already expressed the view that the scarcity of references in the books to the prerogative of keeping the peace within the realm does not disprove that it exists. Rather it may point to an unspoken assumption that it does. That assumption is, I think, made in the judgment of Lord Campbell C.J. in *Harrison* v. *Bush* (1855) 5 E. & B. 344, 353. Professor Hood Phillips has taken it for granted in Constitutional and Administrative Law, pp. 272–281, and so may other learned authors whose works do not specifically refer to it.

'For these reasons I am of the opinion that a prerogative of keeping the peace within the realm existed in mediaeval times, probably since the Conquest and, particular statutory provision apart, that it has not been surrendered by the Crown in the process of giving its express or implied assent to the modern system of keeping the peace through the agency of independent police forces.'

REFLECTION

The assumption that such a prerogative power must exist is controversial. Given that the prerogative is used by the executive without the need to be accountable to Parliament, it is only the courts that can constitutionally hold ministerial use of the prerogative to account. Tomkins (2005) referred to *Ex p. Northumbria Police Authority* and stated that 'ministers do from time to time claim new prerogative powers for themselves and when they do the courts have not demonstrated great eagerness to stop them' (p. 133).

Recently the majority of the House of Lords in *R (Bancoult)* v. *Secretary of State for Foreign and Commonwealth Affairs (No.2)* [2008] UKHL 61 accepted that the prerogative power to legislate for British colonies could extend to exiling the entire population of the British Indian Ocean Territory (BIOT).

The prerogative in question was the power to create laws for the peace, order and good government of British colonies. The islanders had been expelled in the 1970s and wished to return. It was argued that there was no prerogative power to exile the islanders. This argument was rejected by the majority. In 2001 the Divisional Court had held the decision to expel the islanders to be invalid (*R (Bancoult)* v. *Secretary of State for Foreign and Commonwealth Affairs (No.1)* [2001] QB 1067). Laws LJ had noted that the prerogative power to legislate for the BIOT was not unrestrained and there was a limit to the extent of the prerogative power claimed, as 'the colonial legislature's authority is not wholly unrestrained. Peace, order and good government may be a very large tapestry, but every tapestry has a border'.

In the House of Lords, Lord Bingham and Lord Mance in powerful dissenting arguments had held that there was no precedent of such a power existing. Lord Bingham stated that in the absence of evidence that such a prerogative existed, then 'authority negates the existence of such a power'. His Lordship referred to Sir William Holdsworth who had written that '[t]he Crown has never had a prerogative power to prevent its subjects from entering the kingdom, or to expel them from it' (Holdsworth, W. *A History of English Law*, vol. X 7th edn (Sweet & Maxwell: London, 1938), p. 393). Lord Mance noted that it 'would be surprising if any precedent could be found for such a provision, and none has been shown'. It would appear the absence of a precedent will not be fatal to ministerial use of the prerogative, however important the rights that are deprived by its use.

CONTEXT

The Chagos Islands are located to the south of the Maldives. The largest island Diego Garcia is home to an American airbase. There have been accusations that the airbase has been used for the secret rendition of suspected terrorists. The islanders had been removed (in an underhanded manner, often arranging on false pretences visits to Mauritius) in order for the United States to build an airbase.

4. Prevent the creation of new prerogative powers

The courts will not allow the executive to create new prerogative powers. In *British Broadcasting Corporation* v. *Johns* [1964] WLR 1071 Diplock LJ stated that:

> '[I]t is 350 years and a civil war too late for the Queen's courts to broaden the prerogative. The limits within which the executive government may impose obligations or restraints upon citizens of the United Kingdom without any statutory authority are now well settled and incapable of extension.'

This is an important check on the executive's use of the prerogative. The prevention on the creation of new prerogatives has been undermined by judicial assumptions about the existence of prerogatives. In 2009 the Ministry of Justice observed in its report *The Governance of Britain, Review of the Executive Royal Prerogative Powers: Final Report*: 'the ban on creating new prerogatives can be undermined by courts recognising prerogatives which were previously of doubtful provenance, or adapting old prerogatives to modern circumstances'.

5. Judicial review of the prerogative

Traditionally it was thought that the prerogative was immune from judicial review. This meant that the courts could not review whether the use of the prerogative was procedurally unfair or unreasonable. The prerogative was held to be judicially reviewable by the House of Lords in *Council of Civil Service Unions* v. *Minister for the Civil Service* [1985] AC 374. The Government Communications Headquarters (GCHQ) is the intelligence hub of British security and is responsible for intelligence gathering and intercepting information. The case is known in shorthand as *GCHQ*.

CORNERSTONE

Council of Civil Service Unions v. *Minister for the Civil Service* [1985] AC 374

The staff at GCHQ had been allowed to join trade unions since 1947. The management had always consulted with the trade union officials when the terms of employment were to be varied. The Civil Service was not regulated by statute, but by the prerogative and the Prime Minister is minister responsible for the Civil Service. The Prime Minister wished to prevent employees at GCHQ from belonging to trade unions. Rather than consult with the trade union officials as had happened previously, the Prime Minister in 1982 unilaterally varied the contracts of employment through an Order in Council. In response the trade unions attempted to judicially review the decision, arguing that the unilateral variation was unfair as there was a legitimate expectation that the employees and officials would have been consulted. Counsel for the government argued that whilst the courts could enquire as to the existence and extent of the prerogative, it could not review the exercise of valid prerogative powers. This argument drew a distinction between statutory powers conferred on a minister by Parliament whose exercise could be reviewed, and non-statutory prerogative powers that could not be reviewed.

The House of Lords rejected the argument that there was a distinction between statutory and non-statutory powers for the purpose of judicial review. The ministerial use of the prerogative could be reviewed to see whether its exercise was unfair. On the facts the House of Lords held that breach of the legitimate expectation of the employees at GCHQ could be justified because of national security considerations. Lord Diplock acknowledged that the prerogative powers could be quite mundane and yet so important as 'they extend to matters so vital to the survival and welfare of the nation as the conduct of relations with foreign states and – what lies at the heart of the present case – the defence of the realm against potential enemies'. His Lordship stated that he could 'see no reason why simply because a decision-making power is derived from a common law and not a statutory source, it should *for that reason only* be immune from judicial review'. Lord Fraser stated that there should be no difference between whether the powers had been conferred under statute or by the prerogative: 'I am unable to see why the words conferring the same powers should be construed differently merely because their source was an Order in Council made under the prerogative.' See Figure 9.6 for a summary of the judicial approach taken following *GCHQ*.

Take note

The important thing to note about *GCHQ* is that whilst the prerogative was held to be reviewable, certain prerogative powers were considered by Lord Roskill to be non-justiciable (i.e. non-reviewable). The reason is that the courts did regard themselves as being able to review decisions such as national security. These decisions were best taken by the executive and not the courts. This meant that the decision in *GCHQ* still demonstrated that the judges were deferential to the executive.

Those parts of the prerogative which are non-justiciable

Lord Roskill held certain prerogative powers to be non-justiciable. These included defence, foreign policy, ministerial appointments and the dissolution of Parliament. Lord Roskill had stated:

'I do not think that that right of challenge can be unqualified. It must, I think, depend upon the subject matter of the prerogative power which is exercised. Many examples were given during the argument of prerogative powers which as at present advised I do not think could properly be made the subject of judicial review. Prerogative powers such as those relating to the making of treaties, the defence of the realm, the prerogative of mercy, the grant of honours, the dissolution of Parliament and the appointment of ministers as well as others are not, I think, susceptible to judicial review because their nature and subject matter are such as not to be amenable to the judicial process. The courts are not the place wherein to determine whether a treaty should be concluded or the armed forces disposed in a particular manner or Parliament dissolved on one date rather than another.'

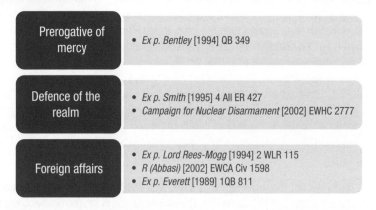

Figure 9.6 The judicial approach following *GCHQ*

This self-imposed restriction demonstrates that Lord Roskill was aware that the courts lacked the expertise and the constitutional position to review whether Mrs X was a suitable choice of minister. The monarch when acting on the Prime Minister's recommendation is best placed to decide this sort of decision. The decision to enter into a treaty with country Y is also arguably best decided by the Foreign Secretary and not by the courts. The decision to go to war or deploy forces abroad would be difficult for the courts to review. The theory of the separation of powers is based on the executive taking such decisions and not the judiciary. Commenting on the decision Clive Walker (1987) observed:

> 'Thus, on the one hand, their Lordships readily concluded that the exercise of prerogative powers is now subject to review, but, on the other hand, their judgments went to equal pains to cordon off from review many of the important and frequent usages of those powers. The most explicit champion of the cause of judicial self-abnegation was Lord Roskill' (p. 62).

Post *GCHQ*

Whilst *GCHQ* is an important case in terms of making the executive accountable, judicial decisions since then have encroached upon Lord Roskill's reserved list of non-justiciable prerogative powers.

Prerogative of mercy

In *GCHQ* the prerogative of mercy was held to be non-justiciable. In *R* v. *Secretary of State for the Home Department ex p. Bentley* [1994] QB 349 the Divisional Court held that the prerogative of mercy was **justiciable** (i.e. reviewable). This case concerned the refusal of the Secretary of State to grant a posthumous pardon to the Mr Bentley, who had been executed after being convicted of murdering a police officer in 1952. Watkins LJ held that the prerogative of mercy could be reviewed as Lord Roskill's list of non-justiciable prerogatives was only *obiter*.

Defence of the realm

In *R* v. *Ministry of Defence ex p. Smith* [1995] 4 All ER 427 the Ministry of Defence dismissed members of the armed forces because they were homosexual. This dismissal had occurred under a policy made under the prerogative. The Ministry of Defence had argued that the policy was non-justiciable because it was connected to the defence of the realm. This argument was rejected by the Divisional Court which reviewed the policy. Simon Brown LJ held that 'only cases involving national security properly so called and where in addition the courts really do lack the expertise or material to form a judgment on the point at issue' would be non-justiciable.

> **Take note**
>
> The decision in *Ex p. Smith* demonstrates that only genuine national security decisions will be non-justiciable and this is because the courts are not best placed to review the decision.

The decision to invade Iraq in 2003 was challenged by the Campaign for Nuclear Disarmament, who sought judicial review as to whether the UN Resolution 1441 permitted military invasion. In *Campaign for Nuclear Disarmament* v. *Prime Minister of the United Kingdom* [2002] EWHC 2777 the court held that foreign affairs and the deployment of British forces were non-justiciable. The court stated that these were forbidden areas (although whether they were justiciable was based on the subject-matter) and the government had the expertise in taking the decision to deploy British forces.

Foreign affairs

The decision to ratify the Treaty on European Union (Maastricht) 1992 was held to be non-justiciable in *R* v. *Secretary of State for Foreign and Commonwealth Affairs ex p. Lord Rees-Mogg* [1994] 2 WLR 115. William Rees-Mogg had attempted to review the legality of transferring increased powers to the new European Union.

In *Bancoult (No.2)* the government had argued that colonial legislation made through an Order in Council was not reviewable as it had equivalence to primary legislation. The House of Lords dismissed the government's argument and held that it could be reviewed by the courts; however, the court was not best placed to decide the issue, due to national security and foreign policy considerations.

The Foreign and Commonwealth Office is responsible for relations with foreign states. The diplomatic dealings with other countries concerning British nationals were held to be non-justiciable in *GCHQ*. This was reiterated in *R* v. *Secretary of State for Foreign and Commonwealth Affairs ex p. Ferhut Butt* (1999) 116 ILR 607 where Lightman J had stated that:

> 'The general rule is well established that the courts should not interfere in the conduct of foreign relations by the Executive, most particularly where such interference is likely to have foreign policy repercussions . . . This extends to decisions whether or not to seek to persuade a foreign government of any international obligation (e.g. to respect human rights) which it has assumed.'

Lightman J was of the opinion that the courts had no role to play concerning that representations which were made to a foreign power on behalf of a British national. Henry LJ had stated that it was non-justiciable because the executive has local knowledge and were best place to make these decisions.

In *R (Abbasi)* v. *Secretary of State for Foreign and Commonwealth Affairs* [2002] EWCA Civ 1598 the court refused to judicially review the decision of the Foreign Office's refusal to make representations to the United States regarding the internment of a British National in Guantanamo Bay. Mr Abbasi was detained indefinitely without trial after being captured in Afghanistan. The Secretary of State had argued that the decisions of the executive in its dealings with other countries, which concerned the treatment of British nationals was non-justiciable.

CORNERSTONE

R (Abbasi) v. Secretary of State for Foreign and Commonwealth Affairs [2002] EWCA Civ 1598

In *Abbasi* the court rejected the argument that there could never be scope for judicial review of the executive's refusal to offer diplomatic assistance to a British national in Mr Abbasi's circumstances. A British national would have a legitimate expectation that the Secretary of State would consider making representations. This meant that so long as the Secretary of State had considered whether to make representations to the United States government concerning Mr Abbasi, then the actual decision of whether to make a representation and the actual diplomacy deployed was non-justiciable.

Lord Phillips MR gave the judgment of the court and held that had the Secretary of State refused outright to consider making a representation, then his decision would have been reviewable. This was regarded as an extreme case and unlikely to occur. What was clear is that the court refused to allow the Secretary of State to invoke foreign affairs to prevent any review. Whether the courts could review the prerogative power of foreign affairs would depend on the subject matter. Lord Phillips MR stated:

'Whether to make any representations in a particular case, and if so in what form, is left entirely to the discretion of the Secretary of State. That gives free play to the "balance" to which Lord Diplock referred in GCHQ. The Secretary of State must be free to give full weight to foreign policy considerations, which are not justiciable. However, that does not mean the whole process is immune from judicial scrutiny. The citizen's legitimate expectation is that his request will be "considered", and that in that consideration all relevant factors will be thrown into the balance . . .'

'It is not an answer to a claim for judicial review to say that the source of the power of the Foreign Office is the prerogative. It is the subject matter that is determinative.'

CORNERSTONE

R v. Foreign Secretary ex p. Everett [1989] 1 QB 811

The granting of passports was found to be justiciable in *Everett* after the government introduced a policy which stated that new passports would not be issued for British subjects who had a warrant outstanding for their arrest. Mr Everett lived in Spain and was refused a passport. He sought to judicially review the decision. Taylor LJ contrasted the non-justiciable matters of high policy, such as the making of treaties, and those prerogative powers which were essentially administrative and were therefore justiciable, namely the decision to grant a passport.

REFORMING THE PREROGATIVE

The prerogative powers have been restricted by the growth of legislation. However, the remaining powers are imprecise and unaccountable to Parliament. It is arguable that the courts provide the only effective review of ministerial use of the prerogative. The problem as identified above is that the government finds the prerogative useful and however keen politicians are to reform the prerogative, this enthusiasm does not extend to their time in government.

An example is the Labour Party before winning the 1997 General Election which was concerned about the prerogative power to go to war. Jack Straw ('Abolish the Royal Prerogative' in A. Barnett (ed.) *Power and the Throne: The Monarchy Debate* (Vintage: London, 1994), pp. 125 and 129) had argued that, '[t]he royal prerogative has no place in a modern western democracy . . . [The prerogative] has been used as a smoke-screen by Ministers to obfuscate the use of power for which they are insufficiently accountable.'

CONTEXT

In 2004 the House of Commons Public Administration Select Committee report identified the need for reform (see *Taming the Prerogative: Strengthening Ministerial Accountability to Parliament*). The chief problem identified with ministerial use of the prerogative was the lack of accountability to Parliament. Professor Brazier proposed the solution that was supported by the Select Committee.

Professor Rodney Brazier recommended the passing of legislation that would require the government to compile a complete list of all their prerogatives within six months. These prerogative powers would then be restricted by legislation and this would increase the accountability of ministers to Parliament. The enhanced accountability would mean that Parliament would have a right to know about ministerial action before the minister acted, as opposed to the current situation where Parliament would be informed afterwards. Some key prerogative powers could only be used with the consent of Parliament, such as the decision to deploy the armed forces and enter into treaties. The power to dissolve Parliament would be made under statutory rules and this would restrict the use of the prerogative. The draft bill that was annexed to the 2004 report presents a major restriction on ministerial non-statutory powers. The government did not adopt the draft bill.

The government responded in 2007 by launching *The Governance of Britain* Green Paper to look into reforming the prerogative powers. This was followed by the *Governance of Britain* White Paper in 2008. In *The Governance of Britain Review of the Executive Prerogative Powers: Final Report* (2009) the Ministry of Justice outlined the steps being taken to review ministerial use of the prerogative. The report rejected the introduction of a statutory footing for all of these powers and stated that there was sufficient parliamentary control of the prerogative. The report noted that many of the prerogative powers have been replaced with statutory powers and that they offered much needed flexibility. In this final report it was stated (p. 24) that:

'Parliament already exerts considerable oversight in the areas covered by these powers, for example through the Foreign Affairs Committee, the Intelligence and Security Committee and through calling Ministers to account. Change could only be contemplated after a lengthy and thorough review, which the Government does not believe to be an effective use of resources at present, given the extensive oversight of these powers already in place.'

Professor Tomkins (2005) argues that the reforms proposed do not go far enough and that the government cannot be relied upon to reform the prerogative. Tomkins criticised the report by the select committee as ineffective and argues that Parliament needs to act, rather than rely on the government of the day to reform the prerogative. It can be observed that independent Parliamentary action is very unlikely to happen:

'No government can realistically be expected to volunteer to surrender (their prerogative) powers: this is not the way politics works. The Stuart kings . . . did not volunteer to surrender power. They were forced into it . . . If the prerogative is going to be wrested away from the government it is going to be as a result of parliamentary insistence, not government self-sacrifice' (p. 134).

KEY POINTS

- The prerogative has been defined by academics such as Dicey and Blackstone.
- Despite being known as the 'royal' prerogative, most prerogative powers are exercised by the government.

- The monarch still has personal prerogative powers that are regulated by constitutional conventions.
- The lack of accountability of ministerial use of the prerogative to Parliament is countered by increased judicial overview of how the prerogative powers are exercised.
- The *GCHQ* decision permits the courts to judicially review the exercise of prerogative powers, although certain powers are still considered by the courts to be non-justiciable.
- There have been calls for the prerogative powers to be replaced by statutory powers.

CORE CASES

Case	About	Importance
Attorney-General v. *De Keyser's Royal Hotel Ltd* [1920]	The government had relied on the prerogative to take possession of land and buildings for the defence of the realm. The issue was as to the level of compensation payable to the owners.	The House of Lords held that where an Act of Parliament existed covering the same subject-matter as the prerogative, that the prerogative power would go into abeyance.
Laker Airways Ltd v. *Department of Trade* [1977]	The use of the prerogative to restrict competition in the transatlantic airline industry.	The Court of Appeal held that the prerogative was being used in a way that conflicted with statutory framework of the Civil Aviation Act 1971.
R v. *Secretary of State for the Home Department ex p. Fire Brigades Union and Others* [1995]	The executive's use of the prerogative power was found to conflict with an Act of Parliament.	The prerogative was found to be incompatible with a yet to be introduced statutory provision.
Burmah Oil Company Ltd v. *Lord Advocate* [1965]	During the Second World War the British Commander in Burma had ordered that the company's oil wells were to be destroyed to prevent them from falling into the hands of the Japanese.	The House of Lords held that compensation had to be paid where the prerogative power was used to destroy property compensation.
R v. *Secretary of State for the Home Department ex p. Northumbria Police Authority* [1988]	This case was about supplying the police with riot equipment.	The court permitted the prerogative to be used despite the existence of an Act of Parliament that covered the same subject-matter.
Council of Civil Service Unions v. *Minister for the Civil Service* [1985]	The banning of trade union membership at GCHQ.	The House of Lords held that there was no distinction between statutory and non-statutory powers for the purposes of judicial review. The court held that it could review ministerial use of the prerogative.

→

Case	About	Importance
R (Abbasi) v. *Secretary of State for Foreign and Commonwealth Affairs* [2002]	A British national was held by the United States at Guantanamo Bay in Cuba. The Foreign and Commonwealth Office had refused to make representations on Mr Abbasi's behalf to the United States.	The court rejected the argument that there could never be scope for judicial review of the executive's refusal to offer diplomatic assistance to a British national.
R v. *Foreign Secretary ex p. Everett* [1989]	The use of the prerogative power to refuse to issue a passport to a British citizen.	The Court of Appeal held that the decision to grant passports was reviewable by the courts.

FURTHER READING

Allott, P. 'The courts and the executive: four House of Lords decisions' [1977] *Cambridge Law Journal* 255
An interesting article on the relationship between the courts and the executive.

Barrett, J. 'The United Kingdom and Parliamentary scrutiny of treaties: recent reforms' [2011] *International and Comparative Law Quarterly* 225
This article looks at recent developments.

Blackburn, R. 'Monarchy and the personal prerogatives' [2004] *Public Law* 546
An interesting article on the personal prerogatives of the monarch.

Blake, R. 'Constitutional monarchy: the prerogative powers' in Butler, D. et al. *The Law Politics and the Constitution: Essays in Honour of Geoffrey Marshall* (Oxford University Press: Oxford, 1999)
A short chapter on the monarch's prerogative powers.

Bradley, A.W. and Ewing, K. *Constitutional and Administrative Law* 15th edn (Pearson: Harlow, 2011)
This book provides additional detail to help you develop your understanding of this topic.

Burgess, G. *Absolute Monarchy and the Stuart Constitution* (Yale: New Haven, 1996)
An extremely interesting book, which is very detailed as it puts the events of the seventeenth century into context.

Cohn, M. 'Medieval chains, invisible inks: on non-statutory powers of the executive' [2005] *Oxford Journal of Legal Studies* 97
An interesting article on the prerogative.

Dicey, A.V. *Introduction to the Study of the Law of the Constitution*, (Liberty Fund: Minneapolis, 1982)
The classic account of the constitution and is very readable.

House of Commons Public Administration Select Committee's fourth report *Taming the Prerogative: Strengthening Ministerial Accountability to Parliament* (2004)
The proposed reforms and the draft bill to reform the prerogative. It is recommended that you refer to this report.

Ministry of Justice *The Governance of Britain Review of the Executive Prerogative Powers: Final Report* (2009)
An overview of the prerogative in the twenty-first century.

Monaghan, C. 'Show me the precedent! Prerogative powers and the protection of the fundamental right not to be exiled: Lord Mance in *R (Bancoult)* v. *Secretary of State for Foreign and Commonwealth Affairs (No.2)* [2007] UKHL 61' in Geach, N. and Monaghan, C. (eds) *Dissenting Judgments in the Law* (Wildy, Simmonds & Hill: London, 2012)
A detailed look at the decision in *Bancoult*.

Munro, C. *Studies in Constitutional Law* 2nd edn (Oxford University Press: Oxford, 2005)
A very useful book which provides an interesting look at the constitution.

Tomkins, A. *Our Republican Constitution* (Hart Publishing: Oxford, 2005)
This book looks at the constitution, its origins and current problems.

Walker, C. 'Review of the prerogative: the remaining issues' [1987] *Public Law* 62
This article looks at the prerogative since the *GCHQ* case.

PART 3
Human rights

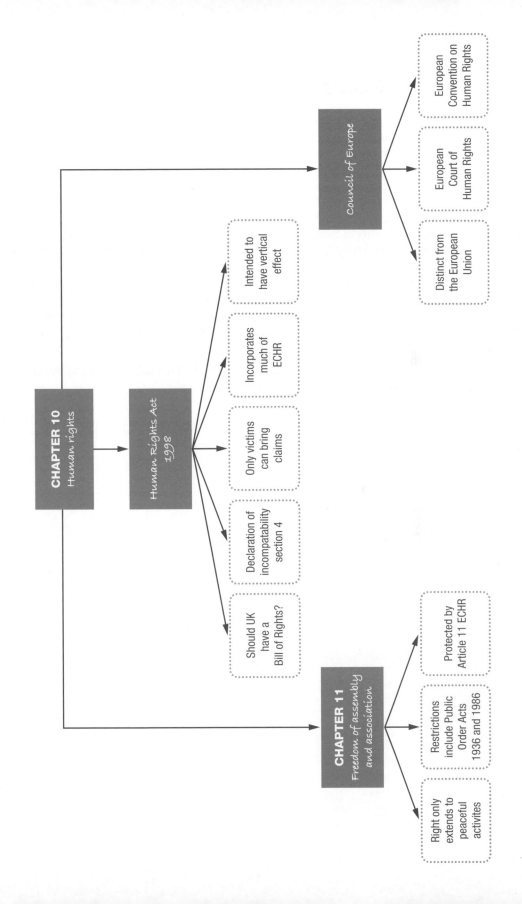

PART 3 INTRODUCTION

Part 3 of Blueprints *Constitutional and Administrative Law* is concerned with human rights and the importance of the European Convention on Human Rights (ECHR). The ECHR was established after the Second World War, in response to the brutality which had occurred, such as the Holocaust and the murder of prisoners of war. Chapter 10 looks at the meaning of human rights, the different protection afforded to important rights in domestic law. We shall also look at France and the United States of America. We will then look at the ECHR and many of the important Convention rights. The role of the European Court of Human Rights (ECtHR) will be explored and why the United Kingdom's recent governments have had a difficult relationship with the court. The Human Rights Act 1998, its main provisions, the way Convention rights are enforced, and attempts to reform the Act will be discussed in detail.

Finally, Chapter 11 looks at Article 11 ECHR and the Public Order Acts. Article 11 protects the right to freedom of peaceful assembly and association. However, Article 11 is a qualified right and can be restricted. Parliament has created legislation which restricts our rights to unfettered freedom of assembly and association. There are requirements needed to be satisfied for anyone who wishes to organise a protest or to hold a rally.

It must be remembered that any restriction of a qualified right must be in accordance with the law, or prescribed by law, and must also be proportionate.

CHAPTER 10
Human rights

BLUEPRINT

Human rights

KEY QUESTIONS

LEGISLATION

- Human Rights Act 1998
- Article 34 of the European Convention on Human Rights (ECHR)
- Derogations under Article 15 ECHR

CONTEXT

- The common law protected many important rights.
- The UK ratified the ECHR but did not incorporate it into domestic law until the Human Rights Act 1998.

CONCEPTS

- Proportionality
- Margin of appreciation
- Habeas corpus
- The United States Declaration of Independence
- Declaration of the Rights of Man 1789
- Interpretation of legislation to ensure ECHR compliance
- Vertical and horizontal effect of the HRA 1998
- What is a public authority under the HRA 1998?

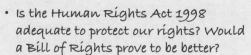

- Is the Human Rights Act 1998 adequate to protect our rights? Would a Bill of Rights prove to be better?
- Why is the Human Rights Act 1998 so controversial with some sections of society?

- What are human rights?
- What are the Council of Europe and the ECHR?
- How does the ECtHR operate?
- What is the effect of the Human Rights Act 1998?

CASES

- *Aston Cantlow and Wilmcote with Billesley Parochial Church Council* v. *Wallbank* [2003]
- *YL* v. *Birmingham City Council* [2007]
- *Smith* v. *Ministry of Defence* [2013]
- *Eweida* v. *United Kingdom* (2013)

REFORM

- Will the United Kingdom introduce a Bill of Rights which will replace the Human Rights Act?
- Which rights would be protected by a British Bill of Rights?
- Should the Human Rights Act 1998 be protected from repeal?

SPECIAL CHARACTERISTICS

- European Court of Human Rights
- Council of Europe
- Commission on a Bill of Rights
- Why according to Dicey did the United Kingdom not need a Bill of Rights
- The long road to Strasbourg
- Ability of a court to make a declaration of incompatibility
- Why Lord Steyn preferred using section 3 rather than section 4 HRA 1998
- What will amount to 'torture'?

CRITICAL ISSUES

Setting the scene

Human rights, the European Court of Human Rights, the Human Rights Act 1998 and a British Bill of Rights have been written about by national newspapers for the past decade, often quite negatively. The concept that we all have human rights, from the person protected from being discriminated against because of their gender or sexuality, to the newspaper columnist who enjoys freedom of expression, is not controversial. What, however, is controversial is the protection afforded under the European Convention on Human Rights to people who are deemed by some elements of the media to be 'undeserving' of having their human rights protected. Human rights can be the subject of an entire module on the LLB and so here we will only look briefly at the individual Convention rights. We will look at what is meant by human rights, the European Convention on Human Rights, the European Court of Human Rights and the Human Rights Act 1998.

We have used the term 'human rights', but what exactly is meant by human rights? According to Griffin, human rights 'is a right that a person has, not in virtue of any special status or relation to others, but simply in virtue of being human' ('First steps in an account of human rights' (2001) *European Journal of Philosophy* 306). This definition sees rights afforded to all humans and there is no distinction as to who they apply to. Many people will disagree as to what will and will not amount to a human right. We shall see that the proponents of a UK Bill of Rights want to broaden the rights which are already given a special status.

Chapter overview

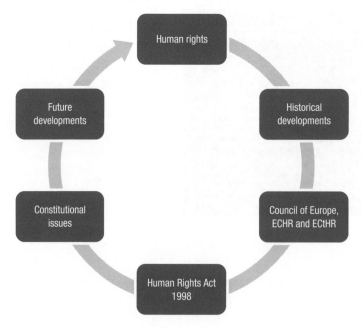

WHAT ARE HUMAN RIGHTS?

The rights that are classified as fundamental human rights will often depend on who is drafting a statement of rights. The drafters of the United States Bill of Rights and the French Declaration of the Rights of Man had incorporated rights such as the freedom of expression and personal liberty. We shall see the development of fundamental rights, which cumulated in the Universal Declaration of Human Rights and the European Convention on Human Rights (ECHR).

Before you read the rest of this chapter, can you think of the rights which you would protect? Could there be any restriction on these rights? If there was to be a restriction, why and in which circumstances could a right be restricted? The chances are that your list of protected rights would be broadly similar to the ECHR. What would be interesting is the relative importance that you might choose to give each right. Would rights be absolute and thus impossible for a state to restrict, or would they be qualified, meaning that a state could justify restricting a right? It might be worth considering freedom of expression and whether the press should be subject to any degree of state control?

REFLECTION

PROTECTION OF LIBERTY

Until the Human Rights Act 1998 there was nothing on the statute book resembling a modern Bill of Rights in the United Kingdom. That is not to say that fundamental liberties such as a fair trial and freedom from arbitrary government action have not been considered important.

The United Kingdom is not unique. Australia's federal constitution does not have any legislative bill of rights, because the drafters of its constitution could not see 'any particular connection between rights protection and federation' (Saunders, C. *The Constitution of Australia* (Hart Publishing: Oxford, 2011), pp. 16–17). Some Australian states such as Victoria have, however, introduced a bill of rights at a state level (pp. 285–286).

CONTEXT

CORNERSTONE

Why according to Dicey did the United Kingdom not need a Bill of Rights

A.V. Dicey was a leading academic and writer on the constitution. He took the view that the United Kingdom did not require a fundamental bill of rights, as citizens' rights were protected by the common law. Dicey argued that the common law was more effective than a statement of fundamental rights.

Figure 10.1 Key developments in the protection of civil liberties and fundamental rights

Lustgarten and Leigh (1999) observed that:

> 'Dicey's hostility to the idea of fundamental rights, as embodied in the French Declaration of the Rights of Man of 1789, was as much empirical as philosophical: he doubted their effective worth. Hence his famous assertion that "the Habeas Corpus Acts declare no principle and define no rights, but they are for practical purposes worth a hundred constitutional articles guaranteeing individual liberty."'

This was a view shared by the Conservative Prime Minister, John Major, who rejected the need for a British Bill of Rights, arguing that civil liberties were adequately protected by the law. We will have a look at the major developments in the protection of liberties and 'rights' in the United Kingdom and the rest of the world (see Figure 10.1).

Magna Carta 1215

The English monarchs had their power to rule challenged by the nobility. King John was forced to sign the Magna Carta in 1215. The barons were attempting to check the king's arbitrary power and were intending to protect their own interests against the Crown. The original charter was annulled by Pope Innocent III shortly afterwards, but it was reissued by Edward I and the most important provision, Chapter 29, states that:

> 'No Freeman shall be taken or imprisoned, or be disseised of his Freehold, or Liberties, or free Customs, or be outlawed, or exiled, or any other wise destroyed; nor will We not pass upon him, nor [condemn him] but by lawful judgment of his Peers, or by the Law of the Land. We will sell to no man, we will not deny or defer to any man either Justice or Right.'

Chapter 29 is still in force today. It was concerned with safeguarding the liberty of the Crown's subjects from arbitrary punishment without first having been tried by a jury of their peers. In English legal tradition trial by jury has been strongly regarded as an important right, and any attempt to restrict trial by jury has been met with hostility (see the Auld Report, Mode of Trial Bills 1999 and 2000, and sections 43–44 of the Criminal Justice Act 2003).

Dr Bonham's Case (1609) 8 Coke Reports 113b

Sir Edward Coke CJ regarded the common law as safeguarding the important rights and liberties of the Crown's subjects. Coke famously stated that, 'the common law will controul Acts of Parliament, and sometimes adjudge them to be utterly void: for when an Act of Parliament is against common right and reason, or repugnant, or impossible to be performed, the common law will controul it, and adjudge such Act to be void' (Dr Bonham's Case (1609) 8 Coke Reports 113b at 118a). Coke CJ observed that the common law would not let Parliament legislate against important rights that were protected by the common law. Dicey (1982) dismissed the idea that the courts would have the ability to declare Acts of Parliament void because they are immoral was dismissed: 'A modern judge would never listen to a barrister who argued that an Act of Parliament was invalid because it was immoral.'

Petition of Right 1628

The Petition of Right 1628 restricted the power of King Charles I to use his prerogative powers to undermine the rights of his subjects. Sir Edward Coke played an important role in drafting the petition and it stated that only Parliament could authorise taxes and that people could only be imprisoned in accordance with English law. Charles I was forced to accept the petition.

Habeas corpus

CORNERSTONE

Habeas corpus

Habeas corpus is a prerogative writ and gives you the right to prevent yourself from being unlawfully detained. If you are detained you have the right to be brought before a court or magistrate to determine whether there is evidence to detain you.

The first Act to reinforce the prerogative writ was the Habeas Corpus Act 1679 which stated that it was, '[a]n act for the better securing the liberty of the subject, and for prevention of imprisonments beyond the seas'. Habeas corpus cannot be used to appeal a decision of the court, and is primarily intended to challenge the validity of executive action in areas such as immigration and the criminal law. Habeas corpus was suspended by Parliament during the 1790s on the initiative of the Prime Minister, William Pitt the Younger, because of the fear of civil disorder during the French Revolution. Parliament has allowed for indefinite detention without trial, see the Anti-Terrorism, Crime and Security Act 2001 which permitted the Home Secretary to order the detention of suspected foreign terrorists.

Bill of Rights 1689

The Bill of Rights was enacted after the Glorious Revolution and protected parliamentary freedoms and limited the power of the executive. It included the freedom not to suffer cruel and unusual punishment, and not to be set excessive bail.

INTERSECTION ....

Please refer to Chapters 2 and 6 for more detail on the Bill of Rights and the protections that were afforded to parliamentarians and citizens.

Edmund Burke on the constitution

Edmund Burke was a famous politician and philosopher and was dismissive of the formal protection offered by the French Declaration of the Rights of Man (see below).

Edmund Burke in *Reflections on the Revolution in France* observed that the English constitution protected the liberties of Englishmen:

'You will observe, that from the Magna Charta to the Declaration of Rights, it has been the uniform policy of our constitution to claim and assert our liberties, as an entailed inheritance derived to us from our forefathers . . . without any reference whatever to any other more general or prior right' (p. 119).

Burke was critical of the French revolution and the rights conferred by the new constitution. We can see that Burke believed that the rights were enjoyed without the need to be conferred by the state (Pelican Classics: Harmondsworth, 1978).

United States Declaration of Independence and Bill of Rights

In 1776, the thirteen British North American colonies declared their independence from Great Britain and with this rejected being ruled from Westminster. American colonists accused Britain of violating their rights, such as Parliament imposing taxation on the colonies without the assent of the colonial assemblies.

CORNERSTONE

The United States Declaration of Independence

Continental Congress, Declaration of Independence 4 July 1776:

'We hold these truths to be self-evident, that all men are created equal, that they are endowed by their Creator with certain unalienable Rights, that among these are Life, Liberty, and the pursuit of Happiness. That to secure these rights, Governments are instituted among Men, deriving their just powers from the consent of the governed. That whenever any Form of Government becomes destructive of these ends, it is the Right of the People to alter or to abolish it, and to institute new Government, laying its foundation on such principles and organizing its powers in such form, as to them shall seem most likely to effect their Safety and Happiness.'

What did the American colonists mean? The Declaration of Independence held that all men are born equal and that people automatically have certain rights. These rights do not have to be given by the state in order to exist. However, at the time that the Declaration of Independence was written, slavery existed in the American colonies and it would continue for almost another ninety years. Therefore, these rights did not extend to African American slaves or Native Americans.

The United States constitution has a special legal status and is protected from repeal by the legislature or the executive. To amend the constitution it is necessary to go through a lengthy and complex procedure. The constitution was amended (the first amendment) to incorporate a Bill of Rights which was ratified in 1791. The rights protected included freedom of speech, press freedom and freedom of assembly. The state was not allowed in peacetime to force citizens to house soldiers and the power of the state to search private premises was restricted. Trial by jury in civil cases was protected, as was the right of citizens to carry arms. The constitution and the Bill of Rights are protected by the Supreme Court which has the power to strike down any statute which it considers to be unconstitutional.

> **Take note**
>
> The United States Bill of Rights increased the protection afforded to citizens under the English Bill of Rights 1689.

Declaration of the Rights of Man 1789

The French Revolution occurred in 1789 and would eventually see the monarchy abolished and the king executed in 1793. In 1789 the National Assembly of France issued the Declaration of the Rights of Man. This was intended to protect individual rights from intrusion by the legislature or the executive. However, the revolution would result in the reign of terror and mass executions, before Napoleon reintroduced a monarchy in 1804.

CORNERSTONE

Declaration of the Rights of Man 1789

The following are some of the most important provisions:

Article 1: 'Men are born and remain free and equal in rights. Social distinctions may be founded only upon the general good.'

Article 4: 'Liberty consists in the freedom to do everything which injures no one else; hence the exercise of the natural rights of each man has no limits except those which assure to the other members of the society the enjoyment of the same rights. These limits can only be determined by law.'

It is clear that the exercise of rights in France in 1789 would only be limited where they would injure others. The only restrictions would be legal restrictions. Freedom of expression and religion would be permitted, subject to the condition that it did not disturb the public good or break the law. Property rights would be protected and property would only be confiscated by the state in circumstances proscribed by law.

The Universal Declaration of Human Rights 1948

The United Nations was established by the allied powers during the Second World War and it adopted the Universal Declaration of Human Rights in 1948. Article 1 states that, 'All human beings are born free and equal in dignity and rights. They are endowed with reason and conscience and should act towards one another in a spirit of brotherhood'. Article 2 is clear that human beings enjoy these rights regardless of race, religion or sexuality.

COUNCIL OF EUROPE

CORNERSTONE

The Council of Europe

The Council of Europe was established in 1949 after the Second World War. It is based in Strasbourg and was established to prevent future human rights abuses.

Take note

It is important not to confuse the Council of Europe with the European Union and its institutions (see Figure 10.2). Both were established for different reasons and in consequence of the Second World War. Membership of the Council of Europe is wider than the European Union, with 47 member states, opposed to the European Union's 28. For example, Turkey is applying to become a member of the European Union, but is already a member of the Council of Europe. The Treaty of Lisbon saw the accession of the European Union to the European Convention on Human Rights and it has the legal obligations that arise from this.

The Second World War had been preceded by fascist governments in Germany and Italy (amongst others), where human rights had been violated. The Second World War saw the Holocaust and wholesale murder of Jews, homosexuals, gypsies, political opponents of the Nazi party and many other groups. One of the powerful advocates for setting up the Council of Europe was the former British Prime Minister, Sir Winston Churchill. Churchill, who had been an opponent of appeasing Hitler in the 1930s, stated in Strasbourg on 12 August 1949 that:

'The dangers threatening us are great but great too is our strength, and there is no reason why we should not succeed in achieving our aims and establishing the structure of this united Europe whose moral concepts will be able to win the respect and recognition of mankind, and whose physical strength will be such that no one will dare to hold up its peaceful journey towards the future.'

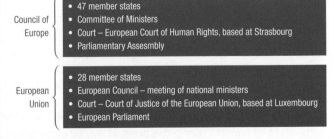

Council of Europe
- 47 member states
- Committee of Ministers
- Court – European Court of Human Rights, based at Strasbourg
- Parliamentary Assesmbly

European Union
- 28 member states
- European Council – meeting of national ministers
- Court – Court of Justice of the European Union, based at Luxembourg
- European Parliament

Figure 10.2 The European Union and the Council of Europe

The Council of Europe promotes human rights, democracy and the rule of law. It actively pursues these and it should be remembered that the Council of Europe is far more than just the European Convention on Human Rights.

Institutions of the Council of Europe

We will now look at the institutions of the Council of Europe.

Parliamentary Assembly

The Parliamentary Assembly has 318 representatives from each of its member states' national parliaments. They meet four times a year and propose initiatives. The Parliamentary Assembly elects the judges of the European Court of Human Rights and the Commissioner for Human Rights. The Parliamentary Assembly has the power to suspend a member state's membership of the Council of Europe, if that state has repeatedly breached its obligations.

Commissioner for Human Rights

The Commissioner for Human Rights is tasked with promoting respect for human rights within the forty-seven member states.

European Court of Human Rights

CORNERSTONE

The European Court of Human Rights (ECtHR)

The ECtHR is based in Strasbourg and it hears petitions from individuals and states concerning alleged violations of human rights.

The first case heard by the ECtHR was *Lawless* v. *Ireland* (1961) (Application No. 332/57). The ECtHR can fine states which have violated Convention rights. The ECtHR recognises that each member state is different, in terms of culture, politics, society and legal system, and therefore applies the **margin of appreciation**.

Decisions are delivered by a Chamber Judgment, although the parties can request a referral to the Grand Chamber, where seventeen judges will hear the case. The ECtHR was reformed in 1998 and now sits as a full-time court. In 2012 a conference in Brighton (which was arranged through the Committee of Ministers) considered ways to reform the ECtHR.

Take note

The margin of appreciation means that '[The ECtHR] case law lays down a minimum "floor" of human rights protection, not an optional "ceiling"' (Wadham, J., Mountfield, H. and Edmundosn, A. *Blackstone's Guide to the Human Rights Act 1998* 3rd edn (Oxford University Press: Oxford, 2003), p. 44). Therefore, the court acknowledges that contracting states such as Russia, Turkey, Switzerland and Spain are not the same and a uniform approach in terms of the precise protection of human rights is not helpful.

In the United Kingdom the ECtHR has received controversial press coverage. The United Kingdom does not allow prisoners to vote and this blanket ban (i.e. no permitted exceptions) was successfully challenged in *Hirst* v. *United Kingdom (No.2)* (Application 74025/01). Prisoner voting is a contentious issue and the role of the ECtHR has proved controversial as many people regard Parliament as the body that should decide this issue (see Chapter 6 for more details).

Another controversial issue has been the inability of the United Kingdom to deport the radical Muslim cleric, Abu Qatada, to Jordan, because of the risk that the Jordanian authorities would use evidence obtained by torture against him, which would violate Article 6 (*Othman* v. *United Kingdom* (2012) 55 EHRR 1). The consequence of the decision was that there was talk of the United Kingdom temporarily leaving the European Convention in order to deport him. The United Kingdom then sought assurances from Jordan that evidence obtained by torture would not be used against him. Having received this assurance the Home Secretary decided to resume the deportation. The Home Secretary's decision was successfully challenged by Abu Qatada (see *Othman* v. *Secretary of State for the Home Department* [2013] EWCA Civ 277). This decision led the United Kingdom to have to enter into a treaty with Jordan to guarantee that such evidence would not be used against Abu Qatada. Some elements of the press have been highly critical of the protection afforded to Abu Qatada. For example, see 'Qatada "to be booted out by Sunday": At last! Britain deals with hate preacher as farcical bid to deport him finally nears its conclusion', *The Daily Mail*, 2 July 2013.

European Convention on Human Rights

The European Convention on Human Rights (ECHR or the Convention) is central to the Council of Europe. The members who have signed the treaty have agreed to respect fundamental freedoms and rights. It was adopted in 1950 and ratified in 1951 by member states. In 1953 the ECHR came into force. Given the key role of British lawyers in drafting the ECHR, it is somewhat ironic that it the United Kingdom has been extremely slow in incorporating the ECHR into domestic law.

UNITED KINGDOM AND THE ECHR

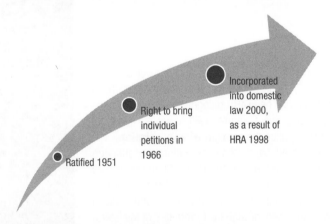

Figure 10.3 The United Kingdom's relationship with the ECHR and ECtHR

CORNERSTONE

The long road to Strasbourg

Despite the prominent role of British lawyers it was not until 1966 that Harold Wilson's Labour government allowed individuals to bring petitions to the ECtHR at Strasbourg. This permitted individuals to sue the United Kingdom's government for alleged violations of Convention rights. British citizens were faced with having to bring their cases to Strasbourg, which became known as the 'long road to Strasbourg'. Bringing a case to the ECtHR proved expensive and was a lengthy process. This meant that Convention rights could not be protected by domestic courts, and only a very small fraction of those whose rights were violated would be able get redress for this.

The Labour government wished to incorporate the Convention rights into domestic law (see Figure 10.3). The intention of the new government was clear in 1997 (Rights Brought Home: The Human Rights Bill 1997 [1.14]):

'It takes on average five years to get an action into the European Court of Human Rights once all domestic remedies have been exhausted; and it costs an average of £30,000. Bringing these rights home will mean that the British people will be able to argue for their rights in the British courts – without this inordinate delay and cost.'

Findings against the United Kingdom did sometimes lead to changes in the law. For example, the decision in *Malone* v. *United Kingdom* (1985) 7 EHRR 14 resulted in the Interception of Communications Act 1985.

REFLECTION

An example of the differences between the protection of individuals' rights before a domestic court and the ECtHR was demonstrated in *R* v. *Secretary of State for Defence ex p. Smith* [1996] QB 517. In *Ex p. Smith* the United Kingdom had dismissed homosexual military personnel. The Court of Appeal held that this did not violate administrative law, as it was not unreasonable to dismiss the personnel. We shall see in Chapter 13 that the decision was challenged as being unreasonable. The ECtHR in *Smith* v. *United Kingdom* (2000) 29 EHRR 493 held that the decision violated Article 8 of the ECHR as dismissing the personnel was not proportionate. Because English judges were not able to rely on the jurisprudence of the ECtHR and the ECHR in protecting the rights of citizens, it is hardly surprising that many people were forced to bring their cases to Strasbourg.

Judges could not apply the ECHR domestically – did the existing common law adequately protect human rights?

Sir Leslie Scarman (1974) took the view that the common law did not adequately protect human rights. His Lordship favoured limiting the ability of Parliament to legislate contrary to fundamental rights. His Lordship noted Coke CJ's classic quote from *Dr Bonham's* case, which stated that the common law would not apply an Act of Parliament that violated an important common law right. Scarman observed:

'There are many who believe that the response of the common law to pressure for the incorporation of a declaration of human rights into English law should be, quite simply, that it is unnecessary. The point is a fair one and deserves to be taken seriously. When times are normal and fear is not stalking the land, English law sturdily protects the freedom of the individual and respects human personality. But when times are abnormally alive with fear and prejudice, the common law is at a disadvantage: it cannot resist the will, however frightened and prejudiced it may be, of Parliament' [pp. 16–17].

Sir Leslie Scarman warned that the courts are powerless against an Act of Parliament and stated that:

'It is the helplessness of the law in face of the legislative sovereignty of Parliament which makes it difficult for the legal system to accommodate the concept of fundamental and inviolable human rights. Means therefore have to be found whereby (1) there is incorporated into English law a declaration of such rights, (2) these rights are protected against all encroachment, including the power of the state, even when that power is exerted by a representative legislative institution such as Parliament' [pp. 14–15].

It is clear that Parliamentary Sovereignty prevents the courts from challenging an Act of Parliament. However, many lawyers argued that the common law did adequately protect fundamental rights.

Of course many important rights had been developed in English law, and these included:

- Habeas corpus
- The Magna Carta
- Petition of Right
- Bill of Rights
- Natural justice and procedural fairness.

Lustgarten and Leigh (1999) refer to the opinion of Simon Brown LJ in *Ex p. Smith* [1995] 4 All ER 427, who stated that the courts could be less deferential to the executive:

'[I]f the Convention . . . were part of our law and we were accordingly entitled to ask whether the policy answers a pressing social need and whether the restriction on human rights involved can be shown to be proportionate to its benefits, then clearly the primary judgment (subject only to a limited "margin of appreciation") would be for us and not others: the constitutional balance would shift' (p. 509).

Prior to 2000, judges could not develop English law in conformity with the jurisprudence of the ECtHR, neither could they give effect to the ECHR. Simon Brown LJ's comments are indicative of the gulf between what the court was able to do before and after the enactment of the HRA 1998.

New Labour: bringing rights home

The Labour Party was determined to incorporate the ECHR into domestic law. This would allow individuals the right to enforce the Convention rights in domestic courts against the state, without having the delay and the expense of going to Strasbourg. As part of the Labour manifesto, Jack Straw and Paul Boateng wrote 'Bringing Rights Home' in 1996, which led to Rights Brought Home: The Human Rights Bill 1997.

HUMAN RIGHTS ACT 1998

CORNERSTONE

The Human Rights Act 1998

In October 2000, the Human Rights Act 1998 [HRA 1998] came into force and has proven to be a very controversial statute. It has significant constitutional importance, as for the first time everyone has been given rights by Parliament that could be enforced in a domestic court. The impact of the HRA 1998 is not just confined to constitutional and administrative law, but also extends to every other area of law.

The Human Rights Act 1998 is an important constitutional statute

The HRA 1998, in the absence of a British Bill of Rights, confers freestanding rights that can be enforced in a domestic court. These rights are constitutionally significant, as no one would deny that the rights to a fair trial or freedom of assembly and association are important in a twenty-first-century democracy.

> ### Take note
>
> The HRA 1998 is an ordinary statute and can be both expressly and impliedly repealed by another Act of Parliament. In *Thoburn v. Sunderland City Council* [2002] EWHC 195 (Admin) Laws LJ suggested in *obiter* that there was a special status of constitutional statutes which included the HRA 1998, and that these could not be impliedly repealed. This is only *obiter* and the HRA 1998 could be both expressly or impliedly repealed.

REFLECTION

The Human Rights Act 1998 is a controversial statute. In September 2014, the Prime Minister, David Cameron, announced that a future Conservative government would repeal the Human Rights Act 1998 and replace it with a British Bill of Rights. The Coalition government established a Commission on a Bill of Rights to look at whether a British Bill of Rights was needed. The commission's final report was not unanimous, but overall it generally supported the introduction of a Bill of Rights (see below).

The Conservative Party has criticised Strasbourg and the perceived interferences of that court into issues such as prisoner voting rights. The Conservative Party has often been portrayed as wishing to abolish the HRA 1998:

> 'Two years ago David Cameron, said he would abolish the Act after it emerged that the killer of London headmaster Philip Lawrence could not be extradited because of human rights considerations.
>
> Last night, the Conservatives reasserted their policy. Dominic Grieve, the Shadow justice secretary, said: "The Human Rights Act is not the only way to implement human rights in Britain."
>
> David Davies, the Welsh Conservative MP, a member of the Home Affairs select committee, said: "We should tear up the Human Rights Act and replace it with something that protects law abiding citizens from violent criminals . . . The Human Rights Act has given drug addicts in jail the right to sue for the inconvenience of not having heroin."'
> 'Keir Starmer under attack after human rights broadside', *The Times*, 22 October 2009

We can see that if the HRA 1998 was repealed by a future Conservative government then it would be replaced by a British Bill of Rights which would continue to incorporate the ECHR into domestic law. We can also see that the current government and previous governments have encountered problems with the judiciary which has restricted government action using the powers afforded by the HRA 1998. The Conservatives are seeking to change Britain's relationship with the ECtHR.

Section 1 HRA incorporates the European Convention on Human Rights

The HRA 1998 has incorporated much of the ECHR into domestic law. Section 1 incorporates the following rights and fundamental freedoms:

- Articles 2 to 12 and 14 of the ECHR
- Articles 1 to 3 of the First Protocol
- Article 1 of the Thirteenth Protocol.

The relationship between the domestic courts and the European Court of Human Rights

Section 2 of the HRA 1998 deals with the court's interpretation of the Convention rights. Subsection (1) instructs the court that:

'A court or tribunal determining a question which has arisen in connection with a Convention right must take into account any –

(a) judgment, decision, declaration or advisory opinion of the European Court of Human Rights,

(b) opinion of the Commission given in a report adopted under Article 31 of the Convention,

(c) decision of the Commission in connection with Article 26 or 27(2) of the Convention, or

(d) decision of the Committee of Ministers taken under Article 46 of the Convention,

whenever made or given, so far as, in the opinion of the court or tribunal, it is relevant to the proceedings in which that question has arisen.'

Importantly section 2(1) does not make the jurisprudence of the ECtHR binding on English courts. Instead the court must take the decisions of the ECtHR into account. As we have seen earlier in Chapter 3, Lord Browne-Wilkinson, during parliamentary debate, opposed the attempt to make the decisions binding.

The relationship between Strasbourg and domestic courts has given rise to the **mirror principle**, where British courts will develop domestic law in line with Strasbourg's jurisprudence. The domestic court will only depart from the jurisprudence of Strasbourg in exceptional circumstances.

In *R (Ullah)* v. *Special Adjudicator* [2004] UKHL 26, Lord Bingham observed:

> 'While such case law is not strictly binding, it has been held that courts should, in the absence of some special circumstances, follow any clear and constant jurisprudence of the Strasbourg court . . . This reflects the fact that the Convention is an international instrument, the correct interpretation of which can be authoritatively expounded only by the Strasbourg court. From this it follows that a national court subject to a duty such as that imposed by section 2 should not without strong reason dilute or weaken the effect of the Strasbourg case law. It is indeed unlawful under section 6 of the 1998 Act for a public authority, including a court, to act in a way which is incompatible with a Convention right. It is of course open to member states to provide for rights more generous than those guaranteed by the Convention, but such provision should not be the product of interpretation of the Convention by national courts, since the meaning of the Convention should be uniform throughout the states party to it. The duty of national courts is to keep pace with the Strasbourg jurisprudence as it evolves over time: no more, but certainly no less' (at [20]).

We can see that Lord Bingham emphasised the importance of the uniformity of interpretation of the ECHR. The final say as to how the ECHR was given to Strasbourg. The domestic court should avoid adopting a more generous interpretation of the ECHR. An exception to applying the principles established by Strasbourg was held to apply in *R* v. *Horncastle* [2009] UKSC 14, where the Supreme Court refused to apply the jurisprudence of the ECtHR because the fine balance contained in domestic law was not sufficiently accommodated by Strasbourg. The Supreme Court believed that the rules contained under the Police and Criminal Evidence Act 1984 still permitted the defendant to have a fair trial.

In *Secretary of State for the Home Department* v. *AF (No.3)* [2009] UKHL 28 Lord Rodger commented that, '[e]ven though we are dealing with rights under a United Kingdom statute, in reality, we have no choice: Argentoratum locutum, iudicium finitum – Strasbourg has spoken, the case is closed.' In an article in 2012 Lord Irvine, the former Lord Chancellor, disagreed that the domestic courts did not have a choice:

> 'I beg to differ. Section 2 of the HRA means that the domestic court *always has a choice*. Further, not only is the domestic court *entitled* to make the choice, its statutory duty under s.2 *obliges* it to confront the question whether or not the relevant decision of the ECHR is sound in principle and should be given effect domestically. Simply put, the domestic court must decide the case for itself' (Lord Irvine 2012, p. 237).

Lord Irvine believed that the domestic courts are under a constitutional duty to say when Strasbourg has made a mistake. When this occurs, the courts should not apply Strasbourg's jurisprudence. Sir Philip Sales QC responded to Lord Irvine's article, which had called for domestic courts to develop their own interpretation of the Convention rights ('Strasbourg jurisprudence and the Human Rights Act: a response to Lord Irvine' [2012] *Public Law* 253). Sales argued that the domestic courts in mirroring Strasbourg's jurisprudence were adopting the preferred approach and is justified by the reason for passing the Human Rights Act 1998.

The mirror principle means that the Supreme Court takes into account the interpretation given by Strasbourg of the Convention rights. Baroness Hale (2012) has observed extra-judicially, '[i]f you come and listen to a human rights case being argued in the Supreme Court, you will be struck by the amount of time counsel spend referring to and discussing

REFLECTION

the Strasbourg case law. They treat it as if it were the case law of our domestic courts. This is odd, because the Strasbourg case law is not like ours. It is not binding upon anyone, even upon them' (p. 65). Baroness Hale commented that many people had criticised the court for not developing domestic human rights jurisprudence independently of Strasbourg, and argued that that there were cases 'where we have definitely gone further than Strasbourg had gone at the time and probably further than Strasbourg would still go'.

However, Lord Justice Laws in his 2013 Hamlyn Lecture disagreed with Lord Bingham's approach to section 2 and held that the domestic should develop and interpret the ECHR without feeling obliged to follow Strasbourg:

> 'Essentially (1) s.2 of the 1998 Act enjoins no subservience to the Strasbourg jurisprudence: it is to be "[taken] into account". (2) Lord Bingham's reference to "the correct interpretation" of the Convention, and his statement that it is in the hands of the Strasbourg court implies that there is such a thing: a single correct interpretation, a universal jurisprudence, across the boundaries of the signatory States. I think that is a mistake. (3) So close an adherence to Strasbourg gravely undermines the autonomous development of human rights law by the common law courts.' ('Lecture III: The Common Law and Europe' at [25]).

Lord Judge CJ takes a similar view:

> 'Personally, I have never doubted, and have spoken publicly to the effect that the words mean what they say. To take account of the decisions of the European Court does not mean that you are required to apply or follow them. If that was the statutory intention, that would be the language used in the statute . . .
>
> 'In my view, the Strasbourg Court is not superior to our Supreme Court.' ('Constitutional Change: Unfinished Business' 4 December 2013 at [41]–[42]).

The interpretation of Acts of Parliament

We shall see that section 6(1) makes it unlawful for a **public authority** to act in a manner which is incompatible with Convention rights (see Figure 10.4). However, it is not unlawful under section 6(2) for a public authority to apply the provisions of an Act of Parliament which is incompatible with Convention rights. This is hugely significant for the person who has been directly affected by the public authorities' actions.

Public authority acted in accordance with an Act of Parliament which violated the ECHR.

- No violation of ECHR unless section 3 can be used
- If section 3 cannot be used, then the court will issue a DOI (section 4) and is unlikely to award damages

Public authority did not act in accordance with an Act of Parliament, when it violated ECHR.

- Clear violation of ECHR
- Court can award remedies

Figure 10.4 Did the public authority act in accordance with the law?

Section 3: Interpretation of legislation

CORNERSTONE

Interpretation of legislation to ensure ECHR compliance

Section 3(1) instructs the courts (High Court and above) to interpret primary and secondary legislation to make them compatible with the Convention rights: 'So far as it is possible to do so, primary legislation and subordinate legislation must be read and given effect in a way which is compatible with the Convention rights.'

Note that the courts can only interpret legislation so far as it is possible to do so, which means that the courts cannot ignore Parliament's intention. This means that if an Act of Parliament is incompatible with Convention rights that the courts can read down words in the Act to make the Act compatible – however, they cannot do this, if doing so, would ignore Parliament's intention (see Figure 10.5). Importantly, section 3(2)(c) states that if the courts are unable to interpret the legislation to give effect to Convention rights, then it 'does not affect the validity, continuing operation or enforcement of any incompatible subordinate legislation'.

INTERSECTION

For more detailed coverage on how the courts use section 3 HRA 1998 please refer to Chapter 5 where we look at the impact of section 3 on Parliamentary Sovereignty.

Section 3 gives the court an important power to interpret an Act of Parliament to prevent it from being incompatible with the ECHR. We must remember that the court cannot ignore Parliament's intention, as this would offend Parliamentary Sovereignty. Nonetheless, the courts have considerable freedom to interpret legislation to protect Convention rights. Controversially in *R* v. *A (No.2)* [2002] 1 AC 45 Lord Steyn relied on section 3 to permit a rape victim's previous sexual history to be adduced as evidence by the defence, whereas Parliament had expressly legislated to prevent this.

Where primary legislation can be interpreted to give effect to the Convention rights, the **victim** is entitled to a remedy under section 8 of the HRA 1998. This is because in retrospect the public authority (although acting legally at the time) has now violated the victim's Convention rights and the violation is now no longer in accordance with the law. Section 8(1) permits the court to 'grant such relief or remedy, or make such order, within its powers as it considers just and appropriate'. Crucially, the public authority must be acting illegally (see Figure 10.6).

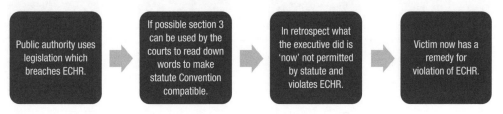

Figure 10.5 The use of section 3 HRA 1998

Take note
If the public authority acted without legal authority to detain someone for an invalid reason, then as there was no Act of Parliament which authorised the pubic authority's action, there would no need to consider the use of section 3 as the public authority's actions were illegal and the court could award a remedy under section 8.

Figure 10.6 Public authority acts without lawful authority

The House of Lords in *R* v. *Lambert* [2002] 2 AC 545 used section 3 to protect the defendant's right to a fair trial under Article 6 ECHR. This case involved the burden of proof being placed on a defendant accused of being in possession of illegal drugs under section 28 of the Misuse of Drugs Act 1971.

Declaration of incompatibility

CORNERSTONE

Ability of a court to make a declaration of incompatibility

Section 4 of the HRA 1998 permits the High Court or any more senior court to make a declaration of incompatibility. Under section 4(2) the declaration of incompatibility can be made where 'the court is satisfied that the provision is incompatible with a Convention right, it may make a declaration of that incompatibility'. Section 4 is used where the court is unable using section 3 to interpret the legislation to give effect to the Convention rights.

What must be remembered is that section 4 does not give the court the power to strike down offending Acts of Parliament or secondary legislation made in accordance with the powers delegated by Parliament (see Figure 10.7). Subsection (6) is clear that the making of a declaration of incompatibility, (a) 'does not affect the validity, continuing operation or enforcement of the provision in respect of which it is given; and (b) 'is not binding on the parties to the proceedings in which it is made'.

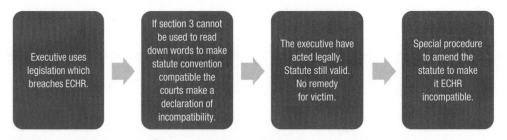

Figure 10.7 The use of section 4 HRA 1998 to issue a declaration of incompatibility

Section 4 of the HRA 1998 does not permit the courts to strike down an Act of Parliament (even if it did then this would be incompatible with Parliamentary Sovereignty). Instead the courts can make a declaration of incompatibility, which does not affect the validity of legislation. Conor Gearty (2006) is in favour of the position in the United Kingdom where the courts are unable to strike down legislation, as this system, unlike the United States does not remove the ability of Parliament to legislate contrary to human rights. Gearty observed that:

> 'There is something inherently distasteful about elected representatives waiting to see whether their judgments about the public interest, made on a bona fide basis with the interests of the community genuinely at heart, meet with the approval of a bench of unelected and unaccountable lawyers' (p. 92).

Gearty was of the opinion that 'declarations of incompatibility are courteous requests for a conversation, not pronouncements of truth from high' (p. 96). In the United States, legislation which affects human rights is often challenged in the Supreme Court and recent examples include the US Defence of Marriage Act which had a key provision struck down, as it discriminated against same-sex couples who did not qualify for the benefits afforded to married heterosexual couples.

REFLECTION

The consequence of the courts issuing a declaration of incompatibility, rather than interpreting the statute under section 3 to give effect to Convention rights, is that the victim is unable to enforce their Convention rights.

Lord Steyn has argued in favour of judicial use of section 3 as opposed to section 4. His Lordship explained his reasons for this in *Ghaidan* v. *Godin-Mendoza* [2004] UKHL 30.

> **Take note**
>
> The effect of a declaration of incompatibility does not affect the validity of the Act of Parliament, which through the judicial observance of Parliamentary Sovereignty remains good law and the public authority is not prevented from breaching the victim's Convention rights.

CORNERSTONE

Why Lord Steyn preferred using section 3 rather than section 4 HRA 1998

The case concerned a same-sex relationship and whether the surviving partner could be protected under the Rent Act 1977. His Lordship stated that, '[t]he linch-pin of the legislative scheme to achieve (bringing rights home) . . . was section 3(1). Rights could only be effectively brought home if section 3(1) was the prime remedial measure, and section 4 a measure of last resort' (at [46]). Lord Steyn observed that, '[w]hat is necessary, however, is to emphasise that interpretation under section 3(1) is the prime remedial remedy and that resort to section 4 must always be an exceptional course. In practical effect there is a strong rebuttable presumption in favour of an interpretation consistent with Convention rights'. His Lordship is stating that section 3 ought to be the preferred remedy, and section 4 only should be used where the court cannot rely upon section 3 (at [50]). →

Lord Nicholls of Birkenhead stated that section 3 cannot be used to permit the court to interpret the statute to have 'a meaning which departs substantially from a fundamental feature of an Act of Parliament (and therefore the court) . . . is likely to have crossed the boundary between interpretation and amendment' (*Re S (Children) (Care Order: Implementation of Care Plan), Re W (Children) (Care Order: Adequacy of Care Plan)* [2002] UKHL 10 at [40]). Lord Nicholls was adamant that the courts must not be tempted to use section 3 as a way to amend legislation (to change the meaning), rather that is the job for Parliament and the court's role was to interpret the statute before it (at [39]).

An example of where the court has used section 4 rather than section 3 is the decision in *R (Anderson)* v. *Secretary of State for the Home Department* [2002] UKHL 46. The Home Secretary's power to fix sentencing tariffs (a minimum sentence) was found to be incompatible with Article 6, which guarantees the right to a fair trial. This was because the sentence was a judicial matter and it should not be made by the executive. The House of Lords refused to use section 3 to interpret section 29 of the Crime (Sentences) Act 1997 in a way that protected the victim's right under Article 6 ECHR, but instead issued a declaration of incompatibility. Lord Bingham in his judgment observed that Parliament gave the Home Secretary discretionary powers to fix tariffs, therefore to use section 3 to restrict his discretion would go against Parliament's intention:

'Since, therefore, the section leaves it to the Home Secretary to decide whether or when to refer a case to the board, and he is free to ignore its recommendation if it is favourable to the prisoner, the decision on how long the convicted murderer should remain in prison for punitive purposes is his alone. It cannot be doubted that Parliament intended this result when enacting section 29 and its predecessor sections . . . To read section 29 as precluding participation by the Home Secretary, if it were possible to do so, would not be judicial interpretation but judicial vandalism: it would give the section an effect quite different from that which Parliament intended and would go well beyond any interpretative process sanctioned by section 3 of the 1998 Act' (at [31]).

Lord Steyn agreed with Lord Bingham:

'Counsel for the appellant invited the House to use the interpretative obligation under section 3 to read into section 29 alleged Convention rights, viz to provide that the tariff set by the Home Secretary may not exceed the judicial recommendation. It is impossible to follow this course. It would not be interpretation but interpolation inconsistent with the plain legislative intent to entrust the decision to the Home Secretary, who was intended to be free to follow or reject judicial advice. Section 3(1) is not available where the suggested interpretation is contrary to express statutory words or is by implication necessarily contradicted by the statute. It is therefore impossible to imply the suggested words into the statute or to secure the same result by a process of construction' (at [59]).

Remedial action

Section 10 permits the government to amend legislation which violates the ECHR. Schedule 2 establishes the procedure for ministers to use remedial orders to amend offending legislation. The procedure states that the draft order must be approved by a resolution of both Houses of Parliament, unless the matter is considered urgent. Constitutionally there is no requirement that the government takes remedial action; however, the effect of a declaration of incompatibility most often will compel remedial action to be taken. Returning to *R (Anderson)*, the government responded by repealing the offending legislation by introducing the provisions in the Criminal Justice Act 2003. In *A* v. *Secretary of State for the Home Department* [2004] UKHL 56 the House of Lords held that the Home Secretary's decision to detain suspected foreign terrorist suspects indefinitely without trial amounted to a violation of Articles 5 and 14 ECHR.

> **Take note**
>
> Article 5 guarantees a right to liberty and Article 14 prohibits discrimination.

The House of Lords made a declaration of incompatibility and the government responded by eventually replacing indefinite detention with control orders. Control orders place restrictions on when an individual can leave their house.

Section 19 HRA 1998

Section 19 of the HRA 1998 has imposed an obligation on the minister in charge of a bill to inform Parliament upon introducing the bill, whether the bill is compatible with Convention rights. This is important as compatibility with the Convention rights will be an important consideration during the drafting and parliamentary debates on the bill.

> **Take note**
>
> Section 19 does not prevent incompatibility, rather it imposes a duty to expressly state whether there will be incompatibility with the ECHR.

What is a public authority?

CORNERSTONE

Vertical and horizontal effect of the HRA 1998

The Human Rights Act 1998 was only intended to have a **vertical effect**. That is Convention rights were only intended to be enforced against public authorities which have breached a Convention right. The Act was not intended to have a horizontal effect, which means that the Convention rights were not meant to be enforceable against private parties, such as individuals and companies.

CORNERSTONE

Section 6 – what is a public authority under the HRA 1998?

So what then is a public authority for the purposes of the HRA 1998? Section 6(1) makes it 'unlawful for a public authority to act in a way which is incompatible with a Convention right'. Subsection (3) states that ' "public authority" includes – (a) a court or tribunal, and (b) any person certain of whose functions are functions of a public nature, but does not include either House of Parliament or a person exercising functions in connection with proceedings in Parliament'.

In reality the Convention rights can have a horizontal effect, which means that an individual can enforce their right to respect for a private and family life under Article 8 ECHR against a private party,

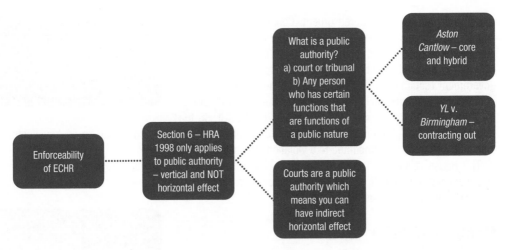

Figure 10.8 What is a public authority for the purposes of the HRA 1998?

such as a tabloid newspaper. This is due to the court's status as a public authority under section 6(3) (see Figure 10.8). The courts must act in a way that is not incompatible with the ECHR and this means that the court must give effect to the Convention rights.

APPLICATION

How can the Convention rights have a horizontal effect? Imagine that Victor, a famous politician, has been photographed leaving his mistress's house, and wishes to prevent publication of the pictures in a national newspaper. Because the HRA 1998 does not permit the Convention rights to be enforced horizontally against private parties, Victor would need to bring an action against the newspaper in private law. The particulars of claim would be for breach of the tort of confidence. Once in court Victor could then argue that his right under Article 8, which protects his right to respect for his private and family life, has been breached. The court, as a public authority, must give effect to the ECHR and this is known as indirect horizontal effect. The court will read the jurisprudence of Strasbourg into the domestic tort of confidence and in the absence of a domestic tort of privacy it could prevent the publication of the photographs.

'[A]ny person certain of whose functions are functions of a public nature'

In *Aston Cantlow and Wilmcote with Billesley Parochial Church Council* v. *Wallbank* [2003] UKHL 37 the question was whether a parochial church council was a public authority within the meaning of section 6(3) HRA 1998. The case involved the Wallbank's obligation to pay towards the upkeep of the church or more precisely, to contribute towards the upkeep of the church's chancel.

Liability towards the repair of a church is a risk for those people buying property in villages, and surprisingly in towns and cities as well. When buying a property it is advisable to carry out a chancel repair search to ensure that you are not going to end up paying for the upkeep of a local church.

CONTEXT

The House of Lords distinguished between two types of public authorities, a core public authority and a hybrid public authority. The House of Lords held that the parochial church council was neither a core nor hybrid public authority and that the enforcement of the defendant's contribution towards the upkeep of the church was a private law matter.

Lord Nicholls' judgment in *Aston Cantlow* is very important. His Lordship noted that the HRA 1998 does not define what is meant by a public authority. His Lordship stated that examples of what is a public authority include 'government departments, local authorities, the police and the armed forces' (at [7]). However, '[I]n the interests of efficiency and economy, and for other reasons, functions of a governmental nature are frequently discharged by non-governmental bodies. Sometimes this will be a consequence of privatisation, sometimes not' (at [9]). Lord Nicholls emphasised that it was important was whether the functions carried out where of a public nature. It did not mean that the functions had to be of a governmental nature (at [10]). These private enterprises carrying out these functions could be a public authority, where the act is a public function rather than a private act. A hybrid public authority will carry out 'both public and non-public functions'.

> ### Take note
> Core public authority – a body whose functions are effectively governmental and all of which are of a pubic nature.
>
> Hybrid public authority – a body which carries out functions, some of which are of a public nature.

CORNERSTONE

Aston Cantlow and Wilmcote with Billesley Parochial Church Council v. Wallbank [2003] UKHL 37

The decision in *Wallbank* considered whether a parochial church council was a public authority for the purposes of section 6 HRA 1998. Lord Nicholls questioned when a function carried out by a body is a public function for the purposes of section 6 HRA 1998. His Lordship stated at [12]:

> 'What, then, is the touchstone to be used in deciding whether a function is public for this purpose? Clearly there is no single test of universal application. There cannot be, given the diverse nature of governmental functions and the variety of means by which these functions are discharged today. Factors to be taken into account include the extent to which in carrying out the relevant function the body is publicly funded, or is exercising statutory powers, or is taking the place of central government or local authorities, or is providing a public service.'

His Lordship did not regard the parochial church council as a core public authority, since the Church of England promoted its own interests and '[t]his is far removed from the type of body whose acts engage the responsibility of the state under the European Convention' (at [14]). Lord Nicholls then considered whether it was a hybrid public authority and stated that 'it is not necessary to analyse each of the functions of a parochial church council and see if any of them is a public function. What matters is whether the particular act done by the plaintiff council of which complaint is made is a private act as contrasted with the discharge of a public function' (at [16]).

> ### Take note
> We can see that:
> - A private company could be a public authority if it is carrying out public functions.
> - To determine whether a body is a core public authority it is necessary to look at its funding, statutory powers and whether it is acting in the place of national or local government.

Contracting out

CORNERSTONE

YL v. Birmingham City Council [2007] UKHL 27

In this case the House of Lords held that a private care home that provided care and accommodation was not exercising functions of a public nature. The majority held that the relationship between the residents and the care home was of a private law nature and was on a commercial basis.

Lord Scott held that the care home was not a public authority because it:

'[I]s a company carrying on a socially useful business for profit. It is neither a charity nor a philanthropist. It enters into private law contracts with the residents in its care homes and with the local authorities with whom it does business. It receives no public funding, enjoys no special statutory powers, and is at liberty to accept or reject residents as it chooses . . . and to charge whatever fees in its commercial judgment it thinks suitable. It is operating in a commercial market with commercial competitors.'

Lord Scott warned that if every time a local authority contracted out a function to a private company, it made that company a hybrid public authority, then 'where does this end? Is a contractor engaged by a local authority to provide lifeguard personnel at the municipal swimming pool a section 6 (3)(b) public authority? If so, would a local authority employee engaged by the local authority as a lifeguard at the pool become a public authority?' (at [30]). Furthermore, His Lordship likened a care home to a private school or hospital and dismissed the argument that residents required special protection. Lords Neuberger and Mance concurred with Lord Scott and rejected the view that a company carrying out a function for a local authority would be a hybrid public authority. Parliament reversed the effect of decision by introducing section 145 of the Health and Social Care Act 2008. For a critique of the decision see Costigan (2012).

Only a victim can bring proceedings under the HRA 1998

It is important to note that only a **victim** can bring proceedings under the HRA 1998. Section 7(3) states that, '[i]f the proceedings are brought on an application for judicial review, the applicant is to be taken to have a sufficient interest in relation to the unlawful act only if he is, or would be, a victim of that act.' Subsection (7) makes reference to Article 34 ECHR, stating that 'a person is a victim of an unlawful act only if he would be a victim for the purposes of Article 34 of the Convention'.

CORNERSTONE

Article 34 of the European Convention on Human Rights – Individual applications

'The Court may receive applications from any person, non-governmental organisation or group of individuals claiming to be the victim of a violation by one of the High Contracting Parties of the rights set forth in the Convention or the Protocols thereto. The High Contracting Parties undertake not to hinder in any way the effective exercise of this right.'

Time Limit

Section 7(5) states that proceedings against a public authority under the HRA 1998 must be brought 'before the end of – (a) the period of one year beginning with the date on which the act complained of took place; or (b) such longer period as the court or tribunal considers equitable having regard to all the circumstances'.

Violating convention rights is not a criminal offence

Section 7(8) states that '[n]othing in this Act creates a criminal offence. This is important as a violation of Convention rights is not a criminal matter.

Jurisdictional issues – when and where do the Convention rights apply?

The Convention rights will only apply where a violation falls within the jurisdiction of a contracting state. This means that if there is an allegation there has been a violation of a Convention right in Bordeaux, the domestic French courts and ultimately Strasbourg will have jurisdiction to decide whether there has been a breach. For the purposes of the HRA 1998 domestic courts will not be able to give effect to the ECHR unless:

- The court has jurisdiction under Article 1, which states that '[t]he High Contracting Parties shall secure to everyone within their jurisdiction the rights and freedoms defined in Section I of this Convention'; or

- The court has jurisdiction under Article 56, where the contracting state has extended the application of the ECHR to a colonial territory under its control.

Article 1

The Grand Chamber in *Al-Skeini* v. *United Kingdom* (2011) 53 EHRR 18 held that the court had jurisdiction to hold that there had been a breach of Article 2, where Iraqi nationals had died whilst being detained by the British Army in Basra. The court held that there was a jurisdictional link between the United Kingdom and the deaths, because whilst the general rule was that jurisdiction was territorial and did not extend beyond a contracting states own territory, where a contracting state exercised effective control there could be a jurisdictional link. Prior to *Al-Skeini*, the Grand Chamber's decision in *Bankovic* v. *Belguim* (Admissibility) (52207/99) had held that jurisdiction was territorial and was concerned with whether the breach occurred in the contracting state's territory, rather than whether the breach occurred whilst the state had control.

CORNERSTONE

Smith v. *Ministry of Defence* [2013] UKSC 41

The Supreme Court in *Smith* v. *Ministry of Defence* held that the United Kingdom's jurisdiction under Article 1 covered military personnel who were killed on active service outside of military bases in Iraq. The government had previously accepted that soldiers on military bases were within the United Kingdom's jurisdiction. Therefore the soldiers enjoyed the right to life under Article 2.

This overruled the earlier decision in *R (Smith)* v. *Oxfordshire Assistant Deputy Coroner* [2010] UKSC 29, which held that the soldiers on active duty were not within the United Kingdom's jurisdiction for the purposes of Article 1. The decision in *Smith* v. *Ministry of Defence* has been criticised by retired military leaders, such as Lord West, for interfering in military operations. Giving judgment Lord Hope had warned that the courts should proceed carefully and should draw a distinction between battlefield decisions and decisions taken off the battlefield (such as the supply of military equipment and the amount of training given to soldiers).

Article 56

Article 56 gives the contracting state the decision of whether to extend the Convention rights to its overseas territories.

This opt-in under Article 56 reflects the time that the Convention was drafted, when the signatories had colonial empires and did not wish to automatically extend the rights beyond their own metropolitan territories. In *Chagos Islanders* v. *United Kingdom* (App. No. 35622/04) (2013) 56 EHRR SE15 the ECtHR rejected an application by the Chagossians, as it was held that the alleged violations did not fall within the jurisdiction of the United Kingdom. This was because the United Kingdom had not extended its jurisdiction under Article 56, nor did the alleged violations fall within the United Kingdom's jurisdiction for the purposes of Article 1. It was argued that the court should have jurisdiction because the decision to remove the islanders and prevent their return was taken in the United Kingdom and the United Kingdom exercised complete control of the territory. This decision followed the court's earlier decision in *Quark Fishing Ltd* v. *United Kingdom* (2007) 44 EHRR SE4. For more detail see Monaghan, C. 'The Chagossians go to Strasbourg: Convention Rights and the Chagos Islands' [2013] *European Human Rights Law Review* 309.

CONTEXT

Take note

Section 1 of the HRA 1998 incorporates the European Convention on Human Rights. It only incorporates:

a. Articles 2 to 12 and 14 of the Convention

b. Articles 1 to 3 of the First Protocol

c. Article 1 of the Thirteenth Protocol.

THE CONVENTION RIGHTS

The Convention rights can be divided between those rights which are absolute, limited and qualified (see Figure 10.9). Articles 2 (apart from lawful acts of war), 3, 4 and 7 are absolute rights and member states are not permitted to derogate from these. This means that the member state cannot justify violating any of these rights, whereas member states are permitted in certain circumstances to derogate from limited rights (Articles 5, 6, 12 and 14). Articles 8, 9, 10 and 11 are qualified rights and restrictions on these rights can be justified by the member state.

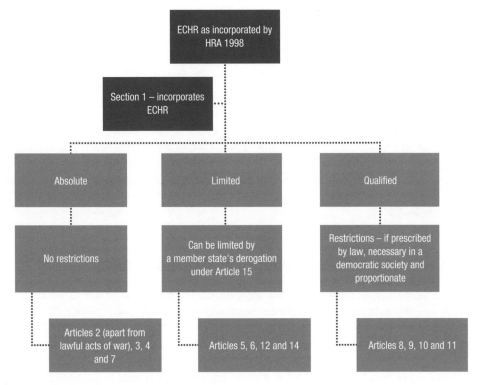

Figure 10.9 Overview of the Convention rights

The Convention rights are set out in schedule 1. The core Convention rights are:

Article 2: Right to life

Article 2(1) states that, '[e]veryone's right to life shall be protected by law. No one shall be deprived of his life intentionally save in the execution of a sentence of a court following his conviction of a crime for which this penalty is provided by law.' The state is permitted to take life where it uses force 'which is no more than absolutely necessary' to defend others, to arrest a suspect or prevent escape, or to quell a riot or insurrection.

Article 3: Prohibition of torture

Article 3 states that, '[n]o one shall be subjected to torture or to inhuman or degrading treatment or punishment.' Article 3 can be breached where there has either been (i) torture, or (ii) inhuman or (iii) degrading treatment. Even severe interrogation techniques by the security services will not necessarily amount to torture, unless they are considered to have reached the required level of intensity of suffering.

CORNERSTONE

What will amount to 'torture'?

In *Ireland* v. *United Kingdom* (1979–80) 2 EHRR 25 the security service had used five techniques during interrogations of suspects in Northern Ireland and whilst Strasbourg considered there to 'exist . . . violence which is to be condemned both on moral grounds and also in most cases under the domestic law of the Contracting States', there needed to be a 'distinction between "torture" and "inhuman or degrading treatment", should by the first of these terms attach a special stigma to deliberate inhuman treatment causing very serious and cruel suffering.' We can see that for torture to exist the suffering must be very serious and cruel. In *Maslova* v. *Russia* (2009) 48 EHRR 37 the repeated rape of a suspect by two police officers amounted to torture, as it was an especially cruel act.

Article 4: Prohibition of slavery and forced labour

Article 4 prevents slavery, servitude or compulsory labour. The member state will not be in breach where the labour is a condition of the sentence (community service), it is military service, it is imposed on individuals during a calamity or an emergency, or it is part of normal civic obligations. Some European countries still require military service and so this would not amount to a breach of Article 4.

Recently, a jobseeker who was forced to undergo unpaid work in a shop in order to keep her entitlement to benefits took the government to court. In *R (Reilly)* v. *Secretary of State for Work and Pensions* [2012] EWHC 2292 (Admin) the court rejected the argument that this amounted to a breach of Article 4. Although the regulations requiring unpaid work were quashed on appeal as they did not comply with the section 17A of the Jobseekers Act 1995, the Court of Appeal held that there had not been a breach of Article 4 (*R (Reilly)* v. *Secretary of State for Work and Pensions* [2013] EWCA Civ 66). Upon appeal the Supreme Court held that this did not amount to a breach (*R (Reilly)* v. *Secretary of State for Work and Pensions* [2013] UKSC 68).

CONTEXT

Article 5: Right to liberty and security

Article 5 states that, '[e]veryone has the right to liberty and security of person.' The member state cannot deprive anyone of their liberty unless the reason for the detention falls within the circumstances in paragraph (1)(a)–(f), and it is in accordance with a procedure prescribed by law. These circumstances include 'the lawful arrest or detention of a person effected for the purpose of bringing him before the competent legal authority on reasonable suspicion of having committed an offence or when it is reasonably considered necessary to prevent his committing an offence or fleeing after having done so'. Paragraphs [2]–[4] outline the requirements which must be met when a person is deprived of their liberty.

Article 6: Right to a fair trial

Article 6 establishes the right to a fair trial. This applies to both criminal and civil proceedings. Paragraph 2 establishes the presumption of innocence and paragraph (3) sets down the minimum rights of a person accused of committing a criminal offence. Article 6(3) states that everyone charged with a criminal offence must have access to legal assistance and the deprivation of legal advice has been found to amount to a breach (*Magee* v. *United Kingdom* (2000) (28135/95) (2001) 31 EHRR 35).

Article 7: No punishment without law

Article 7 prevents retrospective criminalisation of any act or omission which was not a criminal offence at the time it originally took place. It also prevents a higher penalty from being imposed than the penalty that existed when the criminal offence took place. This is why those who are accused of committing a criminal offence before the law has been reformed will be charged and prosecuted under the old rather than the new law.

Article 8: Right to respect for private and family life

The right to respect for private and family life has been protected by the courts. Article 8 extends to protecting:

- The right for asylum seekers to remain in the United Kingdom.
- Rights in the workplace. In *Halford* v. *United Kingdom* (20605/92) (1997) 24 EHRR 523 the ECtHR held that intercepting the phone calls of a senior police officer at home and work, where there had been no prior warning, would amount to a breach of Article 8. This was because the employee had a reasonable expectation of privacy.
- Article 8 has had an impact on housing law and planning law. In *Buckley* v. *United Kingdom* (20348) (1997) 23 EHRR 101 the ECtHR ruled that the refusal of planning permission did not breach Article 8. Whilst Article 8 covered the right to respect the landowner's right to live on the land, the infringement of refusing planning permission was in accordance with the law, it was necessary and proportionate. The decision in *Buckley* was applied in *Harrow LBC* v. *Quazi* [2003] UKHL 43, where the right to evict a tenant who had no legal or equitable rights to remain was found not to infringe Article 8. The decision in *Quazi* was doubted in *Manchester City Council* v. *Pinnock* [2010] UKSC 45, where Article 8 was held to protect anyone who was going to be disposed from their home by a local authority. In all situations, the court would have to apply the test of proportionality to assess whether the infringement was lawful.
- Taking blood samples from a child without the parents' consent amounted to a breach of Article 8 in *MAK* v. *United Kingdom* (45901/05) (2010) 51 EHRR.

A right to privacy?

In *Kaye* v. *Roberston* [1991] FSR 62 Glidewell LJ stated that in English law there was no tort of privacy and that there could be no action for breach of privacy. The only action was in the existing common law torts. Glidewell LJ observed:

> 'It is well-known that in English law there is no right to privacy, and accordingly there is no right of action for breach of a person's privacy. The facts of the present case are a graphic illustration of the desirability of Parliament considering whether and in what circumstances statutory provision can be made to protect the privacy of individuals.'

However, in *Douglas* v. *Hello! Ltd (No.1)* [2001] QB 967 the Court of Appeal held that there had been a breach of the tort of confidence and this could protect the claimants Convention rights through this common law tort.

Sedley LJ considered whether there was a right to privacy in English law: 'we have reached a point at which it can be said with confidence that the law recognises and will appropriately protect a right of personal privacy.' Sedley LJ held that the reasons for the court recognising this right of privacy was the Human Rights Act which 'requires the courts of this country to give appropriate effect to the right to respect for private and family life set out in article 8 of the European Convention for the Protection of Human Rights and Fundamental Freedoms'.

Sedley LJ observed that the law no longer needed to focus on constructing an artificial duty of confidentiality:

'What a concept of privacy does, however, is accord recognition to the fact that the law has to protect not only those people whose trust has been abused but those who simply find themselves subjected to an unwanted intrusion into their personal lives. The law no longer needs to construct an artificial relationship of confidentiality between intruder and victim: it can recognise privacy itself as a legal principle drawn from the fundamental value of personal autonomy.'

Sedley LJ held that Article 8 should have horizontal effect and that the courts should give effect to Article 8 in a dispute between two private parties. This was because the courts are instructed to act in a manner compatible with the ECHR. As a consequence of the claimant's private law claim for breach of confidence, Douglas had a right to privacy under Article 8. Sedley LJ considered that as both Article 8 and 10 were qualified rights and not absolute, any interference with these rights must be proportionate.

The House of Lords in *Campbell* v. *MGN Ltd* [2004] UKHL 22 extended breach of confidence to include taking a picture of a celebrity in public, where that celebrity has a reasonable expectation of privacy. Naomi Campbell is a famous model and had publically stated that she did not take drugs. She was photographed leaving Narcotics Anonymous and sued for breach of confidence. The House of Lords discussed in detail the weighing up of the competing demands of Articles 8 and 10. It is important to note that both are qualified rights and can be restricted.

The ECtHR has held that individuals have a right to a private life where there is a reasonable expectation of privacy and this was reiterated in *Von Hannover* v. *Germany* (2005) 40 EHRR 1 and *Von Hannover* v. *Germany* (40660/08 and 60641/08) [2012] EMLR 16.

> **Take note**
>
> The rights under Article 8 have been given indirect horizontal effect by the courts. This is because there is no right to privacy in domestic law.

Article 9: Freedom of thought, conscience and religion

Article 9 protects the freedom of thought, conscience and religion of those living in a member state. This is an important Article as the twentieth century saw mass killings of Jews during the Second World War and Muslims during the Balkans War. People are permitted to have and to change religious beliefs and to manifest these in public.

CORNERSTONE

Eweida v. United Kingdom (2013) 57 EHRR 8

The United Kingdom was taken to the ECtHR by a number of parties who have been prevented from manifesting their religious belief (*Eweida* v. *United Kingdom* (2013) 57 EHRR 8). It was alleged that there was a violation of the four applicants' rights under Articles 9 and 14. We will look at the decision of the court in relation to two of the applicants:

- Eweida was a former British Airways employee who was prevented from wearing a cross at work. Eweida was successful at the ECtHR, which held that the domestic courts had not struck the correct balance between permitting Eweida to manifest her religious belief at work and British Airways' desire to maintain a corporate image. The United Kingdom had breached the positive obligation under Article 9, which required that the domestic law protected individuals' rights under Article 9.

- Ladele worked as a registrar for a local authority and because of her Christian faith refused to be designated as a registrar for same-sex civil partnerships. This resulted in her losing her job. The court held that there had not been a breach as the balance struck by the domestic authorities fell within the United Kingdom's margin of appreciation.

Article 10: Freedom of expression

This is an important right as free speech is essential in a democracy and permits different political views to be represented. There needs to be a free press which is not censured by the state and can hold the executive to account. Freedom of expression is important for the spoken word, traditional print media and the internet. The use of social media proved important in the Arab Spring that toppled dictators, and Twitter allows issues to trend within this country and raise debate. Article 10 is a qualified right and can be restricted under Article 10(2). However, any restrictions must be prescribed by law and necessary in a democratic society. Furthermore, any restrictions must be proportionate.

CONTEXT

The British press has exposed many important scandals such as the abuse of parliamentary expenses, which has led to the prosecution of many parliamentarians. However, the press has been accused of many negative practices such as phone-hacking and making false accusations about individuals. A public inquiry was chaired by Lord Justice Leveson and investigated the culture, practice and ethics of the press. The report called for press regulation that would be underpinned by statute.

The recommendation in the Leveson Report for press regulation has proved controversial. The report's recommendations have been challenged by some politicians and elements of the press. They argue that regulation would restrict the freedom of expression by the press and harm free speech. The three main political parties agreed that the press would be regulated by a royal charter, rather than by statute. However, the press have submitted to the Privy Council their own proposals for an alternative royal charter. The rival proposals differed from the one put forward by the three main political parties, as future regulation would have to be agreed by the bodies including trade bodies. Former editors would be allowed to sit on the panel regulating the press, and the readers of the publication would have a say over how the press was regulated. In October 2013, the Press Standards Board of Finance Ltd applied to the court to get an injunction to prevent the government from presenting the cross-party royal charter to the Queen. However, in *R (Press Standards Board of Finance Ltd)* v. *The Secretary of State for Culture, Media and Sport* [2013] EWHC 3824 (Admin) the court rejected the application for an injunction and to judicially review the proposed royal charter. The Press Standards Board of Finance Ltd were unsuccessful in their appeal to the Court Appeal in May 2014.

Article 11: Freedom of assembly and association

Article 11 states that, '[e]veryone has the right to freedom of peaceful assembly and to freedom of association with others, including the right to form and to join trade unions for the protection of his interests.' This is important as peaceful assembly and the right to associate with others is important in a democracy. Trade union membership is vital to protect workers' rights and was only decriminalised in the nineteenth century. We will look at this in more detail in Chapter 11.

Article 12: Right to marry

The right to marry and to establish a family is an important right. A man and a woman in the United Kingdom may marry upon reaching the age of sixteen. There are limitations on this right, which include the criminalisation of bigamy and incest. In *B* v. *United Kingdom* (2006) 42 EHRR 11 the ECtHR held that there had been a breach of Article 12, where a father-in-law and daughter-in-law were prevented from marrying whilst their respective spouses were still alive.

Take note

There is no definition of when the state can interfere and restrict these rights. Where the right is limited it may only be restricted where the member state derogates under Article 15. In order to derogate from the ECHR any restriction on the Convention rights will need to be proportionate.

Article 14: Prohibition of discrimination

Article 14 prevents people from being denied the Convention rights by reasons including race, religion, sexuality and colour.

Restricting the Convention rights

In *A* v. *Secretary of State for the Home Department* [2004] UKHL 56 the circumstances for a derogation to be used was accepted by the majority of the House of Lords (with only Lord Hoffmann dissenting as to whether there was an emergency threatening the life of the nation). However, the House of Lords found the Home Secretary's decision to be disproportionate and discriminatory and violated Article 14. This was because it was discriminatory in permitting the detention solely on the grounds of nationality or immigration status.

CORNERSTONE

Derogations under Article 15 ECHR

1. 'In time of war or other public emergency threatening the life of the nation any High Contracting Party may take measures derogating from its obligations under this Convention to the extent strictly required by the exigencies of the situation, provided that such measures are not inconsistent with its other obligations under international law.

2. 'No derogation from Article 2, except in respect of deaths resulting from lawful acts of war, or from Articles 3, 4 (paragraph 1) and 7 shall be made under this provision.

3. 'Any High Contracting Party availing itself of this right of derogation shall keep the Secretary-General of the Council of Europe fully informed of the measures which it has taken and the reasons therefor. It shall also inform the Secretary-General of the Council of Europe when such measures have ceased to operate and the provisions of the Convention are again being fully executed.'

Where the right is qualified the member state may restrict it, but must do so in circumstances where the restriction is prescribed by law and proportionate. In *A* Lord Bingham stated that, 'Article 15 requires that any measures taken by a member state in derogation of its obligations under the Convention should not go beyond what is "strictly required by the exigencies of the situation". Thus the Convention imposes a test of strict necessity or, in Convention terminology, proportionality' (at [30]).

Proportionality

CORNERSTONE

Proportionality

If there is a violation of a Convention right then the court must adopt the test of **proportionality** (see Figure 10.10). The court must ask whether the public authority's actions were proportionate to the violation.

In no circumstances can a public authority restrict a Convention right without lawful authority. If the public authority is not pursuing a legislative objective, then it is acting illegally. The qualified rights, e.g. Articles 8, 10 and 11 can be restricted where the restriction is either:

- in accordance with the law or prescribed by law;
- necessary in a democratic society. It is here that the question of proportionality would be key.

INTERSECTION

We will look in more detail at proportionality as a ground for judicial review in Chapter 13. Since the decision in *R (Daly)* v. *Secretary of State for the Home Department* [2001] 2 AC 532 the domestic courts can ask whether the decision was proportionate, rather than whether it was unreasonable. This will necessarily involve a higher standard of review. We will see that the classic limb test for proportionality was formulated by Lord Clyde in *De Freitas* v. *Permanent Secretary of Ministry of Agriculture, Fisheries, Land and Housing* [1999] 1 AC 69. However, Lord Reed's judgment in *Bank Mellat* v. *Her Majesty's Treasury (No.2)* [2013] UKSC 39 endorsed the use of a fourth limb.

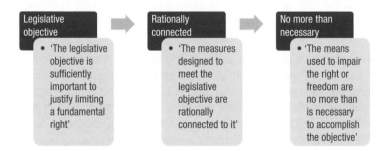

Figure 10.10 The test for proportionality

It is important to note, as Lord Reed reiterated in *Bank Mellat* that, '[a]n assessment of proportionality inevitably involves a value judgment at the stage at which a balance has to be struck between the importance of the objective pursued and the value of the right intruded upon. The principle does not however entitle the courts simply to substitute their own assessment for that of the decision-maker' [71].

Margin of appreciation

CORNERSTONE

Margin of appreciation

Because of the large number of political and cultural differences between the member states, the ECtHR has developed a margin of appreciation, which essentially gives each state discretionary scope and avoids setting uniform standards for strict observance of each Article.

Helen Fenwick (1999) has argued that the margin of appreciation was not suitable for domestic courts when applying the ECHR:

'The doctrine of the margin of appreciation is a distinctively international law doctrine, based on the need to respect the decision-making of nation states within defined limits. Therefore it would not appear to have any application in national law. As Sir John Laws puts it: "The margin of appreciation doctrine as it has been developed at Strasbourg will necessarily be inapt to the administration of the Convention in the domestic courts for the very reason that they are domestic; they will not be subject to an objective inhibition generated by any cultural distance between themselves and the state organs whose decisions are impleaded before them." However, under section 2 of the Human Rights Act the domestic judiciary "must take into account" any relevant Strasbourg jurisprudence, although they are not bound by it' (p. 63).

Lord Hope in *A* v. *Secretary of State for the Home Department* was clear that the large margin of appreciation given by the ECtHR on derogations 'cannot be taken as the last word on the matter so far as the domestic courts are concerned. That is especially so in this case, as section 30 of the 2001 Act itself recognises that the derogation may be reviewed by the judiciary' (at [131]). This is a clear statement that the domestic courts should not follow the approach of the ECtHR. Lord Bingham in *A* v. *Secretary of State for the Home Department* drew an analogy between the margin of appreciation and judicial deference to the executive on political matters:

'These were matters of a political character calling for an exercise of political and not judicial judgment. Just as the European court allowed a generous margin of appreciation to member states, recognising that they were better placed to understand and address local problems, so should national courts recognise, for the same reason, that matters of the kind in issue here fall within the discretionary area of judgment properly belonging to the democratic organs of the state. It was not for the courts to usurp authority properly belonging elsewhere' (at [37]).

Lord Reed reiterated this in *Bank Mellat (No.2)*, where His Lordship noted that the test for proportionality as applied by Strasbourg afforded contracting states a margin of appreciation, and thus 'the approach adopted to proportionality at the national level cannot simply mirror that of the Strasbourg court' [71].

UNITED KINGDOM BILL OF RIGHTS

CORNERSTONE

Commission on a Bill of Rights

The Coalition government established a Commission on a Bill of Rights in March 2011. It has been tasked with investigating ways to create a UK Bill of Rights to replace the HRA 1998, by incorporating the Convention rights. Its term of reference states that the Commission 'will examine the operation and implementation of these obligations, and consider ways to promote a better understanding of the true scope of these obligations and liberties' (http://www.justice.gov.uk/about/cbr).

This is quite telling, as the Conservative Party has been critical of judicial use of the Convention rights. The commission's second consultation paper was published in July 2012 (http://www.justice.gov.uk/downloads/about/cbr/second-consultation/cbr-second-consultation.pdf) detailing the responses to its first consultation paper. Interesting points to note include:

- Opponents of a Bill of Rights point out that the HRA 1998 is effective.
- Supporters argue that the word UK would distance the association with Europe, allow other rights to be given the same status as the Convention rights, and perhaps become entrenched (cannot be repealed by Parliament) as part of a UK written constitution. Such new rights could include a right to equality and extend the private law protection in the Equality Act 2010.
- Some of the respondents called for the right to trial by jury to be included, and for a greater level of protection for criminal and civil justice than what currently exists under Article 5–7.
- Some of the respondents called for guidance to be given to courts on how to balance the competing qualified rights of Article 8 and 10 (see Chapter 11).
- The definition of public authority (or lack of it) under the HRA 1998 has been criticised and better guidance is needed.

The Commission published its final report in December 2012, 'A UK Bill of Rights? The Choice Before Us'. The report concluded that there was a strong argument in favour of a Bill of Rights, but said that this was a matter for Parliament. The report's conclusion was far from unanimous as it was supported by only seven out of the nine commissioners. The two dissenters, Baroness Kennedy QC and Philippe Sands QC, were critical of the commission's findings.

Read the Commission on a Bill of Rights' second consultation paper and the ideas discussed. Then read the commission's final report 'A UK Bill of Rights? The Choice Before Us'. What are your thoughts on these? Perhaps you and your colleagues could arrange a discussion on this and debate the ideas.

Mark Elliot (2013) was critical of the commission's report and observed that, '[t]he bizarre collection of individually and co-authored papers appended to the main Report demonstrates that the majority itself is united by an agreement so formal as to be largely meaningless' (p. 137). Elliot notes that the commission did not provide a definitive list of the rights which should be included, and that there is no clear conscious of whether the right to trial by jury would be included. Elliot observed that:

'If the Report is tentative about *what* rights should be upheld by a domestic Bill of Rights, it is even more circumspect when it comes to *how* those rights should be protected. The mechanisms for protecting rights "should be broadly similar" to those found in the HRA, according to the Report, there is particular – but not uniform – enthusiasm for retaining declarations of incompatibility. However, no clear position is adopted on whether – and, if so, to what extent – the interpretative and obligation under section 3 of the HRA should survive.'

Elliot was critical that the majority's position 'is inspired by little more than gut feelings generated by anecdotal evidence' and seemed to think that a British Bill of Rights which was broadly similar to the HRA 1998 would avoid the perceived unpopularity of the HRA 1998. Elliot referred to the high level of support for the ECHR's incorporated in domestic law in the consultations and stated that, 'it is quite extraordinary that the findings of the Commission's own consultations appear to have played such a marginal role in informing the majority's conclusions.'

According to Klug and Williams (2013):

'The quest to rebrand the existing human rights framework to make it more popular is clearly at variance with the objective of substantively changing it [and the Commission] fails to identify a reliable evidence base for its claimed "ownership" problem. Having dismissed polling as "notoriously unreliable" (para. 80), the majority Commissioners virtually discount the 96 per cent of responses to the Commission's consultation exercises expressing support for retaining the HRA' (p. 460).

This is critical, as the commission proceeded on a basis that the HRA 1998 was unpopular and in need of a makeover. The report was criticised as not indicating in which direction the majority wished to go. The main utility of the report according to Klug and Williams, 'is to illuminate the contours of the "British" Bill of Rights debate and the likely direction of travel if there is a Conservative Government following the next general election'.

KEY POINTS

- The European Convention on Human Rights was incorporated into domestic law by the Human Rights Act 1998.

- The European Court of Human Rights is based in Strasbourg and oversees the interpretation of the ECHR. The domestic courts will mirror the principles established in Strasbourg's jurisprudence.

- The Conservative Party supports the creation of a British Bill of Rights which will replace the HRA 1998.

- The HRA 1998 was not intended to restrict Parliamentary Sovereignty. However, section 3 permits the court considerable interpretive powers and section 4 allows the court to make a declaration of incapability.

- The HRA 1998 was intended to have vertical effect and can be enforced against public authorities. However, Convention rights can be enforced against private parties via indirect horizontal effect.

CORE CASES AND STATUTES

Case	About	Importance
Aston Cantlow and Wilmcote with Billesley Parochial Church Council v. Wallbank [2003]	This decision concerned a chancel repair obligation. One of the questions to be determined was whether a parochial church council could be a public authority for the purposes of the Human Rights Act 1998.	Lord Nicholls identified two types of public authority. The first was a core public authority – a body whose functions are effectively government and all of a public nature, and the second was a hybrid public authority – a body which carries out functions, some of which are of a public nature
YL v. Birmingham City Council [2007]	The question to be determined was whether a care home, which had contracted with a public authority to provide care services, was a public authority. If it was a public authority then the Human Rights Act 1998 applied.	The majority of the House of Lords ruled that it was not a public authority.
Smith v. Ministry of Defence [2013]	The case involved British soldiers who had been killed on active service in Iraq.	The Supreme Court held that the United Kingdom's jurisdiction under Article 1 ECHR covered military personnel who were killed on active service outside of military bases in Iraq.
Eweida v. United Kingdom (2013)	Eweida was a former British Airways employee who was prevented from wearing a cross at work.	Eweida was successful at the ECtHR, which held that the domestic courts had not struck the correct balance between permitting Eweida to manifest her religious belief at work and British Airways' desire to maintain a corporate image.

→

Statute	About	Importance
Human Rights Act 1998	Incorporates the majority of the ECHR into domestic law.	Key statute that permits Convention rights to be enforced domestically against public authorities. It is illegal for a public authority to act contrary to Convention rights.
Article 34 of the European Convention on Human Rights (ECHR)	It states that the ECtHR may 'receive applications from any person, non-governmental organisation or group of individuals claiming to be the victim'. The violation must be by one of the contracting parties to the ECHR.	Section 7(7) of the Human Rights Act 1998 states that in order to be a victim for the Act you have to be a victim for the purposes of Article 34.
Derogations under Article 15 ECHR	Certain of the Convention rights can be derogated (that is suspended) under Article 15.	In order to derogate from a Convention right the requirements in Article 15 must be met.

FURTHER READING

Bennett, T. 'The relevance and importance of third party interests in privacy cases' (2011) 127 *Law Quarterly Review* 531
This article looks at recent developments in the domestic courts' approach to privacy.

Costigan, C. 'Contracting out of the Human Rights Act 1998' in Geach, N. and Monaghan, C. (eds) *Dissenting Judgments in Law* (Wildy, Simmonds & Hill: London, 2012)
An interesting critique of the majority's judgment in *YL* v. *Birmingham*.

Dicey, A.V. *Introduction to the Study of the Law of the Constitution* (Liberty Fund: Minneapolis, 1982)

Elliot, M. 'A damp squid in the long grass: the report of the Commission on a Bill of Rights' [2013] *European Human Rights Law Review* 137
A critique of the report on a British Bill of Rights.

Fenwick, H. 'The Right to Protest, the Human Rights Act and the Margin of Appreciation' [1999] 62(4) *Modern Law Review* 491
This article addresses some important issues concerning the Human Rights Act 1998.

Gearty, C. *Can Human Rights Survive – Hamlyn Lectures 2005* (Cambridge University Press: Cambridge, 2006)
A thought-provoking series of lectures on human rights and the challenges faced in the twenty-first century.

Hale, Baroness '*Argentoratum locutum*: Is Strasbourg or the Supreme Court supreme?' (2012) 12(1) *Human Rights Law Review* 65
This article offers a judicial perspective on the relationship between Strasbourg and the domestic courts.

Irvine, Lord 'A British interpretation of Convention rights' [2012] *Public Law* **237**
The former Lord Chancellor argues in favour of domestic courts developing a distinctive British human rights jurisprudence.

Klug, F. and Williams, A. 'The choice before us? The report of the Commission on a Bill of Rights' [2013] *Public Law* **460**
A critique and analysis of the report on a British Bill of Rights.

Lustgarten L. and Leigh I. 'Making rights real: the courts, remedies, and the Human Rights Act' [1999] *Cambridge Law Journal* **509**
An interesting article on the HRA 1998.

Marshall, G. 'Two kinds of compatibility: more about section 3 of the Human Rights Act 1998' [1999] *Public Law* **377**
An interesting article on the effect of section 3 HRA 1998.

Oliver, D. 'The frontiers of the state: public authorities and public functions under the Human Rights Act' [2000] *Public Law* **476**
This article looks at the meaning of public authorities under section 6 HRA 1998.

Scarman, Sir Leslie *English Law – The New Dimension*, **The Hamlyn Lectures (Stevens & Sons: London, 1974) pp. 14–15**
This book addresses the problems regarding the protection of human rights in the UK consitution.

Wadham, et al. *Blackstone's Guide to the Human Rights Act 1998* **6th edn (Oxford University Press: Oxford, 2011)**
A useful guide to the workings of the Human Rights Act 1998.

Useful websites:

Council of Europe website: http://hub.coe.int/

The Universal Declaration of Human Rights: http://www.un.org/en/documents/udhr/index.shtml

Declaration of the Rights of Man: http://avalon.law.yale.edu/18th_century/rightsof.asp

United States Bill of Rights: http://www.archives.gov/exhibits/charters/declaration.html/

European Convention on Human Rights: http://www.echr.coe.int/NR/rdonlyres/D5CC24A7-DC13–4318-B457–5C9014916D7A/0/CONVENTION_ENG_WEB.pdf

Responses to judicial use of sections 3 and 4 HRA 1998: http://www.justice.gov.uk/downloads/publications/moj/2010/responding-human-rights-judgements-2009–2010.pdf

Commission on a Bill of Rights: http://www.justice.gov.uk/about/cbr, second consultation paper: http://www.justice.gov.uk/downloads/about/cbr/second-consultation/cbr-second-consultation.pdf

CHAPTER 11

Freedom of assembly and association

BLUEPRINT

*Freedom of assembly
and association*

LEGISLATION

- Public Order Act 1936, Public Order Act 1986
  and the Criminal Justice and Public Order Act
  1994
- Article 11 ECHR

CONTEXT

- In the 1980s the
  government clashed
  with trade unions.
  There were violent battles
  between the police and
  trade union members,
  such as the miners.
- The 1930s saw the rise
  of extreme political
  parties whose members
  used violence and wore
  military uniforms.

CONCEPTS

- Kettling
- The meaning of procession
- Breach of the peace

- Should kettling be prohibited or is it a
  necessary method of controlling large crowds?
- Do the Public Order Acts unnecessarily
  prevent peaceful protest? Should we have
  to notify the police in advance of peaceful
  demonstrations?

- Do we have freedom of assembly and association in the United Kingdom?
- What limitations are imposed on Article 11 ECHR by the Public Order Acts?

CASES

- *R (R)* v. *DPP* [2006], *Harvey* v. *DPP* [2011] and *Southard* v. *DPP* [2006]
- *Austin* v. *Commissioner of the Police of the Metropolis* [2009]
- *R (Laporte)* v. *Chief Constable of Gloucestershire* [2006]
- *R (R)* v. *DPP* [2006]

SPECIAL CHARACTERISTICS

- How is a riot defined?

REFORM

- Increasing the ability to protest without giving prior notification to the police.
- Will the development of Article 10 and 11 case law restrict the existing statutory requirements?
- Will a future Conservative government reform the right to strike by introducing a requirement that a certain percentage of all eligible voters must have voted to support the industrial action?

CRITICAL ISSUES

Setting the scene

Imagine that you are planning a protest against the government's decision to raise tuition fees. You decide that you will march through London and protest outside the Houses of Parliament. There will be over 50,000 protestors and you have no intention of being violent or disruptive, as all you wish to do is to protest. Are you permitted to protest without informing the police, will the police be able to prevent your protest from proceeding and could you be guilty of a criminal offence if you refuse to follow any conditions imposed by the police? We shall see that although Article 11 of the European Convention on Human Rights states that we have the right to freedom of assembly and association, the authorities can impose restrictions on this right. However, these restrictions must be necessary in a democratic society.

Chapter overview

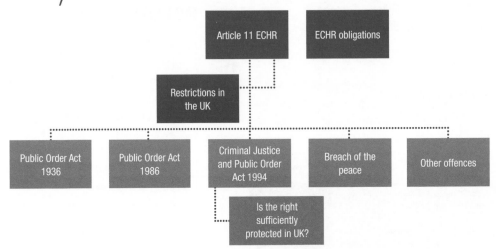

PUBLIC ORDER AND HUMAN RIGHTS

CORNERSTONE

Public Order Act 1936, Public Order Act 1986, and the Criminal Justice and Public Order Act 1994

The key legislation in this area are the:

- Public Order Acts 1936 and 1986
- Criminal Justice and Public Order Act 1994.

These Acts of Parliament restrict the right to freedom of assembly and association. They are import-ant in understanding how the police can control and regulate public protests, travellers and protect groups in society from the views and unwanted attention of others.

This chapter is concerned with the freedom of assembly and association. This means the right to associate with the people that you choose to and to assemble freely in public places. The right to do these is protected by Article 11 ECHR. However, we shall see that Parliament has restricted this freedom in the interest of public order and security. We shall focus on the Public Order Acts 1936 and 1986, as well as the Criminal Justice and Public Order Act 1994.

INTERSECTION

Article 10 ECHR states that we have the right to freedom of expression and this right is relevant to any discussion on the freedom to have peaceful assemblies and associations. This is because the freedom of expression protects the wearing of slogans, the use of placards and signs, and above all free speech. These are elements of any protest and a restriction which limits Article 11 may also limit Article 10.

Article 11: Freedom of assembly and association

Article 11 of the ECHR protects the right to freedom of peaceful assembly and association. This is a qualified rather than an absolute right, meaning that restrictions can be imposed which restrict this right.

Article 11(1) states that:

Everyone has the right to freedom of peaceful assembly and to freedom of association with others, including the right to form and to join trade unions for the protection of his interests.

The right is for peaceful activity and does not protect activities which are violent. Article 11 specifically refers to trade union membership. Trade union membership is important as it enables workers to organise themselves to protect their rights and negotiate better working conditions.

Until the 1870s trade union membership was illegal as it amounted to conspiracy in criminal law. The Trade Union and Labour Relations (Consolidation) Act 1992 (TULR(C)A 1992) protects the rights of trade union members not to suffer detriment in the recruitment process and at work, as well as giving trade unions and their members the right to strike. The RMT trade union has recently brought a case to the European Court of Human Rights (ECtHR) arguing that English law restricts the ability of trade unions to take industrial action. In *R.M.T.* v. *United Kingdom* [2014] ECHR 31045/10, the ECtHR held that there had been violation of Article 11. The statutory protection under the TULR(C)A 1992 is narrow and contains a number of procedural requirements which make it difficult to take industrial action (see *British Airways Plc* v. *Unite the Union* [2010] EWCA Civ 669). The law has placed restrictions on picketing, which means that workers taking industrial action are restricted in their ability to demonstrate outside their own and associated workplaces. Trade unions have protection in law to prevent them from being sued by employers in the event of trade union members taking part in industrial action. An example of the limited protection afforded to trade unions is *Express Newspapers Ltd* v. *McShane* [1979] 1 WLR 390, where the Court of Appeal held that industrial action by the National Union of Journalists did not fall within the statutory protection and therefore the employers were able to obtain an injunction to prevent the industrial action. Lord Denning favoured a narrow interpretation of the statutory immunity and stated that, 'I would also draw attention to the fact that, when Parliament granted immunities to the leaders of trade unions, it did not give them any *rights*. It did not give them a *right* to break the law or to do wrong by inducing people to break contracts. It only gave them immunity if they did' (at 395). The Court of Appeal's decision was reversed by the House of Lords in *Express Newspapers Ltd* v. *McShane* [1980] AC 672.

CONTEXT

No restriction can be placed on the rights under Article 11 unless the restriction is:

- prescribed by law; and
- is necessary in a democratic society. Examples of when a restriction would be necessary include:
  - in the interests of national security or public safety, or
  - for the prevention of disorder or crime, or
  - for the protection of health or morals, or
  - for the protection of the rights and freedoms of others.

What does prescribed by law mean? It was defined by the ECtHR in *The Sunday Times* v. *The United Kingdom* (1979–80) 2 EHRR 245. The court identified two requirements which must be met:

'First, the law must be adequately accessible: the citizen must be able to have an indication that is adequate in the circumstances of the legal rules applicable to a given case. Secondly, a norm cannot be regarded as a "law" unless it is formulated with sufficient precision to enable the citizen to regulate his conduct: he must be able – if need be with appropriate advice – to foresee, to a degree that is reasonable in the circumstances, the consequences which a given action may entail' (at [40]).

There is no requirement that everyone must know the intricacies of the legal system, but rather that we should be capable, should we wish, of finding out what the law is and obtain advice to determine the legality of our actions.

The aim of the restriction must be necessary in a democratic society and the measure must be proportionate, i.e. it must go no further than what is necessary to achieving the legitimate aim which is being pursued.

INTERSECTION

The test to determine whether a restriction is proportionate is outlined in Chapter 13. You should refer to the requirements which must be satisfied before a decision will be held to be proportionate.

Crucially, Article 11(2) states that, '[t]his Article shall not prevent the imposition of lawful restrictions on the exercise of these rights by members of the armed forces, of the police or of the administration of the State.'

In our daily lives we choose to associate with others whether they are friends, family or others who share the same political or religious views as ourselves.

In *Redfearn* v. *United Kingdom* (47335/06) [2013] IRLR 51 the ECtHR ruled that there had been a violation of Article 11 after an employee was dismissed for being a member of, and a political candidate for, the British National Party. The ECtHR held that there was insufficient protection in domestic law for an employee's political associations. The ECtHR observed that it was possible for employers to impose restrictions on employees' rights to safeguard the rights of others. However the right to have the freedom to join political parties was a key requirement of a democracy and that 'the Court considers that in the absence of judicial safeguards a legal system which allows dismissal from employment solely on account of the employee's membership of a political party carries with it the potential for abuse' (at [55]). The lack of protection for employees dismissed by reason of their political beliefs amounted to a violation of Article 11.

CONTEXT

THE PUBLIC ORDER ACT 1936

It is an offence under section 1(1) of the Public Order Act 1936 (POA 1936) to wear a uniform 'signifying his association with any political organisation or with the promotion of any political object' in a public place or at a public meeting. The purpose of section 1 was to prevent the political organisations in the United Kingdom from taking on quasi-military characteristics.

> In Germany during the 1920s and 30s the Nazi party had a quasi-military branch known as the Brownshirts or SA, and in Italy Mussolini's fascists had a quasi-military branch known as the Blackshirts. In the 1930s, the former Labour minister, Sir Oswald Mosley, was the leader of the British Union of Fascists in the 1930s. His political supporters wore black shirts to signify their association to the party. Mosley's supporters clashed with rival communists in London's East End at the battle of Cable Street in 1936 and eventually Mosley was arrested at the start of the Second World War. The POA 1936 was designed to prevent the use of political uniforms.

CONTEXT

Section 2 of the POA 1936 prevents the training and organisation of quasi-military organisations. The Act is designed to prevent the recruitment of political forces which could be used to usurp the functions of the state, such as the police. The Act also prohibits the wearing of uniform by supporters, which is to be used as 'signifying his association with any political organisation or with the promotion of any political object'. This is important as during the 1930s political quasi-military units were being used as a way of intimidating political opponents and undermining the state. A good example of this is how Hitler was invited to become Chancellor of Weimar Germany in 1933, because the authorities felt that they needed the support of his quasi-military SA (Brownshirts). Sections 1 and 2 of the POA 1936 have been used to outlaw paramilitary organisations in Northern Ireland, such as the Irish Republican Army (IRA).

APPLICATION

Imagine that Go Green, a (fictitious) political party, decides that it needs to raise its public profile. The party decides to ask a famous fashion designer to create a uniform for party members to wear. Go Green plan to have all its 20,000 members wear this uniform at its conference in Swindon. The members will then proceed to an environmental rally in London. Go Green has been contacted by a party member who is concerned that if they do this, that they might be guilty of committing an offence under section 1 of the POA 1936. This is because the uniform signifies the members' association with Go Green.

THE PUBLIC ORDER ACT 1986

The Public Order Act 1986 (POA 1986) covers offences such as riot and affray, as well as the requirements for those organising public processions and assemblies. Finally, the POA 1986 covers the prohibition of racial hatred. We shall look at these in turn and see how the Act operates in practice.

Figure 11.1 Public Order Act 1986 key offences

REFLECTION

Peter Thornton QC has described the POA 1986 as 'an Act that strikes at the very heart of legitimate protest, particularly spontaneous protest. It extends existing police controls over processions and marches, it creates for the first time in the history of our law statutory controls over open-air meetings and picketing . . . (and) Above all it gives the police . . . an almost unchallengeable discretion, described by the Prime Minister . . . as a "blank cheque"' (*Decade of Decline: Civil Liberties in the Thatcher Years* (National Council for Civil Liberties: London, 1989), pp. 35–36). We shall see that the POA 1986 severely restricts legitimate protest by restricting the ability to exercise our democratic rights. An example of spontaneous protest was in 2010 when members of the public gathered at the Liberal Democrats head office and protested against their decision to enter into a coalition government with the Conservatives. Stone and Bonner (1987) commented that the changes introduced by the Act 'constitute steps down a route that is potentially damaging to police–community relations and to the expression of free speech by way of procession and assembly'. Therefore we can see that there is a delicate balance between safeguarding public order and the right to freedom of expression and the right to freedom of assembly and association.

The POA 1986 creates several important offences (see Figure 11.1).

Riot

CORNERSTONE

How is a riot defined?

Section 1 of the POA 1986 creates the offence of riot. Riot requires that '12 or more persons who are present together use or threaten unlawful violence for a common purpose and the conduct of them (taken together) is such as would cause a person of reasonable firmness present at the scene to fear for his personal safety'.

The common purpose for why the people are present together can be inferred from their conduct. Any of the twelve or more persons present 'using unlawful violence for the common purpose is guilty of riot'. Therefore, anyone present but who does not use unlawful violence would not be guilty under section 1. Riot carries a maximum custodial sentence of ten years. In order for an offence to be committed a person of reasonable fitness must fear for their personal safety; however, such a person need not be present and so this is a hypothetical test.

Elements for section 1 Riot	Satisfied?
Do we have twelve or more persons present together?	Yes or no?
Do we have the use or threatening of unlawful violence?	Yes or no?
Is it for a common purpose?	Yes or no?
Would the conduct of them (taken together) cause a (hypothetical) person of reasonable firmness present at the scene to fear for his personal safety?	Yes or no?
Did the defendant accused of rioting actually use unlawful violence?	Yes or no?
Offence committed?	If YES to all the above

Violent disorder

Section 2 of the POA 1986 concerns the offence of violent disorder. The crucial difference between riot and violent disorder is that whereas riot requires twelve persons to be present and an offence to be committed by a person actually using unlawful violence, violent disorder requires three persons to be present and a person can be guilty if they either threaten or use unlawful violence. If tried on indictment at the Crown Court, a person guilty of violent disorder could receive a maximum five-year custodial sentence.

Elements for section 2 Violent Disorder	Satisfied?
Do we have three or more persons present together?	Yes or no?
Do we have the use or threatening of unlawful violence?	Yes or no?
Would the conduct of them (taken together) cause a (hypothetical) person of reasonable firmness present at the scene to fear for his personal safety?	Yes or no?
Did the defendant accused of violent disorder actually use or threaten unlawful violence?	Yes or no?
Offence committed?	If YES to all the above

APPLICATION

Imagine that during the London riots in 2011 Hilda and her friends decided to target Enfield Town Centre. They use their phones to arrange to meet up. Having met up they start to swear and scream abuse at nearby shoppers and Hilda has a large cricket bat in her hands which she is waving at the shoppers. The police arrest Hilda and her friends. The police are unsure what offence to charge them with. PC Smith counts eleven people present and so realises that no offence under section 1 has been committed. However, there are sufficient people present for an offence under section 2 to have been committed. Based upon the circumstances Hilda could be guilty of the offence of violent disorder, as she is threatening unlawful violence and the conduct of her and her friends would cause a (hypothetical) person of reasonable firmness present at the scene to fear for his personal safety. Finally, Hilda herself is threatening unlawful violence.

Affray

Section 3 of the POA 1986 outlines the offence of affray. There needs to be only one person who has used or threatened unlawful violence towards another person. However, the threat cannot be by the use of words alone.

Elements for section 3 Affray	Satisfied?
Do we have one or more person?	Yes or no?
Do we have the use or threatening of unlawful violence towards another? (Note – threat cannot be by the use of words alone)	Yes or no?
Would the conduct of them (taken together) cause a (hypothetical) person of reasonable firmness present at the scene to fear for his personal safety?	Yes or no?
Offence committed?	If YES to all the above

Fear or provocation of violence

There are two ways to the commit the offence of fear or provocation of violence under section 4 of the POA 1986 (the *actus reus* of the offence):

1. section 4(1)(a) – using towards another person threatening, abusive or insulting words or behaviour; or

2. section 4(1)(b) – distributes or displays to another person any writing, sign or other visible representation which is threatening, abusive or insulting.

A person commits offences if he intends 'to cause that person to believe that immediate unlawful violence will be used against him or another by any person, or to provoke the immediate use of unlawful violence by that person or another, or whereby that person is likely to believe that such violence will be used or it is likely that such violence will be provoked'. This is the *mens rea* of the offence.

There only needs to be one person involved for an offence to be committed. The threatening, abusive or insulting words or behaviour must be used towards another person. This means that the words are used 'in the presence of' and 'in the direction of another person directly' (*Atkin* v. *DPP* (1989) 89 Cr App R 199). Whether the words used will qualify depends on their ordinary meaning. In *Brutus* v. *Cozens* [1972] 2 All ER 1297 it was stated that 'an ordinary sensible man knows an insult when he sees or hears it'. Section 4(2) states that the offence can be committed in a public or private place, but that no offence will be committed if the victim was inside a private dwelling.

> **Take note**
> Although an offence under section 4 cannot be committed where the victim is in the private dwelling, an offence can be committed where the defendant shouts at the victim out of a window. It is important to note this distinction.

Intentional harassment, alarm or distress

The offence of intentional harassment, alarm or distress contrary to section 4A POA 1986 was introduced by the Criminal Justice and Public Order Act 1994.

The offence can be committed in two ways:

1. section 4A(1)(a) – where the defendant uses threatening, abusive or insulting words or behaviour, or disorderly behaviour; or

2. section 4A(1)(b) – where the defendant displays any writing, sign or other visible representation which is threatening, abusive or insulting, which causes that person or another person harassment, alarm or distress.

Section 4A is wider than section 4 because of the lower threshold of disorderly behaviour, which means that football hooligans or people who are drunk could fall within this provision. The behaviour must have the intention to cause the victim harassment, alarm or distress. Once again this is a lower threshold than section 4.

CORNERSTONE

R (R) v. *DPP* [2006] EWHC 1375 (Admin), *Harvey* v. *DPP* [2011] EWHC 3992 (Admin) and *Southard* v. *DPP* [2006] EWHC 3449

Should a police officer be harassed or distressed by rude words whilst in the line of duty? In *R (R)* v. *DPP* [2006] EWHC 1375 (Admin) the Divisional Court considered what was meant by 'distressed' for the purposes of section 4A. The defendant had been convicted by a youth court for calling a police officer a 'wanker' and making masturbatory gestures at the officer. At the time the incident had taken place the defendant was twelve years old and was less than five feet tall. The police officer was over six feet tall and weighed over seventeen stone. The police officer claimed that he was distressed by the defendant's behaviour. The question for the court was whether the police officer had actually been distressed. The court stated: 'the word "distress" in this context requires emotional disturbance or upset. It does not have to be grave but nor should the requirement be trivialised. There has to be something which amounts to real emotional disturbance or upset'. The conviction was overturned. →

Within the context of section 5 POA 1986 (see below) the court in *Harvey* v. *DPP* [2011] EWHC 3992 (Admin) commented that, '[a] number of cases establish that expletives such as "fuck" or "fucking" are potentially abusive words, whether the addressee is a police officer or a member of the public. But Parliament has not made it an offence to swear in public as such' (at [6]). However, it is clear that a rude word on its own does not constitute an offence, as the actual requirements of the offence must actually be satisfied. With this in mind it is worth considering the meaning of 'harassment', which was considered in *Southard* v. *DPP* [2006] EWHC 3449 (Admin), where the defendant had told a police officer to 'fuck off'. The police officers had been carrying out a stop and search. The court stated that:

'Harassment, alarm and distress do not have the same meaning. One can be harassed, even seriously harassed, without experiencing emotional disturbance or upset at all. However, although the harassment does not have to be grave, it should not be trivial. The court has to find that the words or behaviour were likely to cause some real, as opposed to trivial, harassment.'

We need to remember that the defendant must intend to cause harassment, alarm or distress.

Harassment, alarm or distress

The offence of harassment, alarm or distress under section 5 POA 1986 can be committed in two ways:

1. section 5(1)(a) – using threatening, abusive or insulting words or behaviour, or disorderly behaviour; or

2. section 5(1)(b) – displays any writing, sign or other visible representation which is threatening, abusive or insulting, within the hearing or sight of a person likely to be caused harassment, alarm or distress thereby.

The meaning of harassment and distress is the same for section 5 as it is for section 4A. Subsection (3) outlines the defences, which are that the defendant did not believe that there was someone likely to be caused harassment, alarm or distress within hearing, or that the words or behaviour were used in a dwelling and there was no reason to believe that it would be heard or seen by someone outside, or that the defendant's conduct was reasonable. The crucial difference between section 5 and section 4A is that under the former there is no need for the defendant to intend to cause harassment, alarm or distress.

Racial hatred and hatred on the grounds of religion or sexual orientation

The POA 1986 criminalises the use of words or behaviour that is likely to stir up racial, religious or sexual hatred. This prohibits the performances of plays and the publication of material. There are defences available.

The freedom to hold a procession or an assembly

We have already considered public order offences such as riot and affray, and now we will explore the freedom to hold a procession or an assembly (see Figure 11.2). This will entail looking at the right to protest, to march, gather and join together for a common cause. This is a fundamental requirement for a modern democratic state.

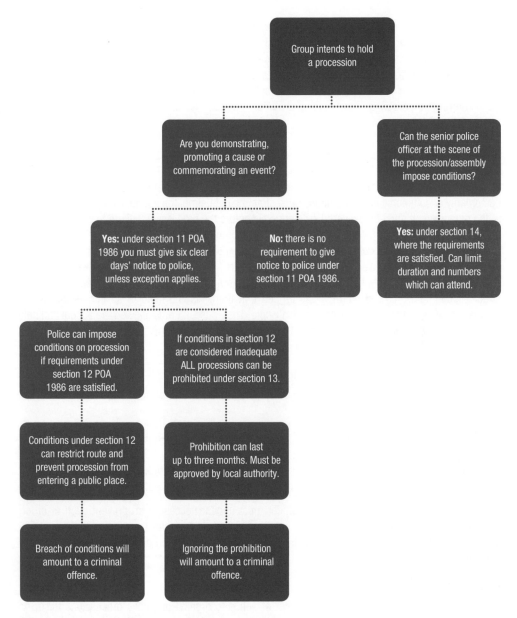

Figure 11.2 The requirements for holding a procession or an assembly

Advance notice of public processions

CORNERSTONE

The meaning of procession

The meaning of procession was defined by Lord Goddard CJ in *Flockhart* v. *Robinson* [1950] 2 KB 498 at 502.

'A procession is not a mere body of persons: it is a body of persons moving along a route. Therefore the person who organises the route is the person who organises the procession . . . [A person will be] organising the procession because, although he did not organise the body of people, he organised the route. There is no other way of organising a procession, because a procession is something which proceeds. By indicating or planning the route a person is in my opinion organising a procession.'

Section 11 POA 1986 states that if you intend to hold a public procession to demonstrate, publicise a cause or to commemorate an event, then you need to give written notice to the police, unless it is not reasonably practicable to do so. This requirement does not apply to funerals or processions which are customarily or commonly held. The notice must state the date, time, the intended route and the names of the organisers. It must be delivered six clear days before the procession. Failure to comply with the notice requirements under section 11 will amount to a criminal offence.

In *R (Kay)* v. *Commissioner of Police of the Metropolis* [2008] UKHL 69 an organised cycle ride had taken place each month over the period of twelve years. The cyclists followed no fixed route. The police informed the cyclists that they would need to inform them within six days of each cycle ride under section 11 POA 1986. The cyclists argued that there was no need to do this as this was a procession which was customarily or commonly held. The House of Lords allowed the appeal and held that no notice was required under section 11 because the procession could amount to one which was commonly or customarily held, despite having no fixed route.

Imposing conditions on public processions

Section 12 POA 1986 gives a senior police officer the power to impose conditions on a procession, where he reasonably believes:

- it may result in serious public disorder, serious damage to property or serious disruption to the life of the community; or
- the purpose of the persons organising it is the intimidation of others with a view to compelling them not to do an act they have a right to do, or to do an act they have a right not to do.

The directions given by the senior police officer must appear necessary to 'prevent such disorder, damage, disruption or intimidation' and the conditions imposed can alter the route of the procession or prohibit it from entering a public place. Failure to comply with the order will amount to a criminal offence.

Prohibiting public processions

Section 13 POA 1986 permits the chief officer of police to prohibit all public processions for up to three months. Such a power will only exist where he 'reasonably believes that, because of particular circumstances existing in any district or part of a district, the powers under section 12 will not be sufficient to prevent the holding of public processions in that district or part from resulting in serious public disorder'. Therefore, the statute requires a reasonable belief that the powers under section 12 will prove insufficient to prevent serious public order. The application is made to the local authority.

Imposing conditions on public assemblies

Section 16 POA 1986 defines a public assembly as an assembly of two or more persons in a public place (somewhere the public has a right of access, i.e. the local town centre) which is wholly or partly open to the air. The senior police officer at a public assembly may under section 14 POA 1986 impose conditions, where he reasonably believes that:

- it may result in serious public disorder, serious damage to property or serious disruption to the life of the community; or
- the purpose of the persons organising it is the intimidation of others with a view to compelling them not to do an act they have a right to do, or to do an act they have a right not to do.

If either of the above are satisfied, then the conditions that the senior officer can impose can:

- limit its duration;
- limit the numbers of people who can attend.

So long as it appears necessary to impose these conditions in order 'to prevent such disorder, damage, disruption or intimidation'. Failure to comply with the conditions imposed will amount to a criminal offence.

> ### Take note
> According to section 14(2), the senior police officer for the purposes of section 14 means the most senior police officer present or at the assembly, or if the conditions are imposed before the assembly will take place the chief officer of police for that area.

Furthermore, section 14A gives police the powers to prohibit trespassory assemblies. This applies to assemblies which will be held on land that the public has no right or a limited right to access. The police under section 14C have the power to stop people from proceeding to trespassory assemblies.

....**APPLICATION**

Action for Animals [AFA] (fictitious) is an anti-vivisection charity that plans to hold a procession to protest against animal testing. The organisers give notice to the police authority where the procession will take place, a full six days before the planned march. The route will go past Testing Incorporation's headquarters, which is an organisation that carries out animal testing. There will be 1,000 people at the protest and the police are concerned that some of the protestors will be violent. The police can impose conditions on the public procession under section 12 POA 1986, or ban it under section 13 POA 1986, but only if certain requirements are met.

CRIMINAL JUSTICE AND PUBLIC ORDER ACT 1994

The Criminal Justice and Public Order Act 1994 (CJPOA 1994) covers illegal raves and trespassers and gives the police powers to remove trespassers. It also covers travellers who are encamped on land without permission from the relevant authority. The Act is aimed at those exercising an alternative lifestyle such as New Age travellers and those who attend raves. Allen and Cooper (1995) were critical of the creation of ever more board public order offences under the CJPOA 1994, and noted that the affect of the Act is that: '[p]ublic order is valued more than freedom of expression; the pressure to conform is greater than respect for non-conformity; the values of the majority justify the suppression of the values and lifestyles of minorities such as gypsies and other travellers' (p. 364).

Highways Act 1980

Section 137 of the Highways Act 1980 makes it an offence to 'wilfully obstruct the free passage along a highway' without lawful authority or excuse.

BREACH OF THE PEACE

CORNERSTONE

Breach of the peace

The Court of Appeal in *R* v. *Howell (Errol)* [1982] QB 416 defined the circumstances when a breach of the peace would arise:

> 'there is a breach of the peace whenever harm is actually done or is likely to be done to a person or in his presence to his property or a person is in fear of being so harmed through an assault, an affray, a riot, unlawful assembly or other disturbance.'

In English Law a breach of the peace is not a criminal offence but is based on an application to bind over, i.e. an obligation not to breach the peace.

In *R (Laporte)* v. *Chief Constable of Gloucestershire* [2006] UKHL 55 the House of Lords held the following at common law:

- Police officers and members of the public have the power to take measures short of arrest, or to carry out an arrest, in order to prevent a breach of breach from occurring, or where they reasonably believed that a breach of the peace was to occur.

- However, if no breach of the peace had occurred there needed to be a reasonable apprehension of an imminent breach before action could be taken. According to Lord Mance, the question of when a breach of the peace would be imminent 'has to be judged in the context under consideration'.

CORNERSTONE

R (Laporte) v. Chief Constable of Gloucestershire [2006] UKHL 55

In R (Laporte) the police had prevented three coaches from proceeding to Gloucestershire, where a protest was taking place. The police had taken action short of arrest because they believed that a breach of the peace would occur. The House of Lords held that there had been a violation of Article 11 because the interference with the right to peaceful assembly and association had not been prescribed by law, and even if it had been, the police's action had been a disproportionate restriction on the protestors' rights.

The use of kettling by the police at demonstrations

CORNERSTONE

Kettling and Austin v. Commissioner of the Police of the Metropolis [2009] UKHL 5

Kettling is a tactic used by the police to control crowds during protests. The police will cordon protestors and will prevent the crowd from leaving until the risk of violence or damage to property has been reduced.

The case of Austin v. Commissioner of the Police of the Metropolis [2009] UKHL 5 concerned a protest in London and a very large group of protestors, some of whom were disorderly, who reached Oxford Circus and were placed in a cordon by the police. This tactic is known as kettling. People could not leave unless with the permission of the police. They were denied access to toilet facilities, food and drink. Austin had not been involved in the protest and asked permission to leave the police cordon and this was refused. Upon appeal the House of Lords held that the police had acted legally at common law as they had acted to prevent an imminent breach of the peace. The claimant had argued that their Article 5 ECHR right to liberty had been violated. The House of Lords held that Article 5 was a qualified right and could be restricted. The court held that the right balance had been struck by the police and therefore the restriction on the claimant's liberty was proportionate (see Figure 11.3 for Article 5 restrictions).

The ECtHR ruled that the use of kettling did not violate Article 5 because the police had isolated the protestors to avoid a likely risk of damage and injury, and therefore the police action was necessary and proportionate (Austin v. United Kingdom (39692/09)(2012) 55 EHRR 14).

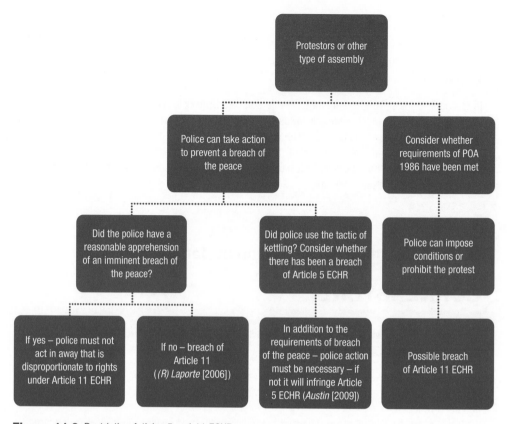

Figure 11.3 Restricting Articles 5 and 11 ECHR

KEY POINTS

- Article 11 protects the right to freedom of assembly and association.
- The police can impose conditions and prohibit processions under the Public Order Act 1986.
- Political uniforms and paramilitary training are illegal under the Public Order Act 1936.
- Each public order offence requires slightly different elements in order to be committed.

CORE CASES AND STATUTES

Case	About	Importance
R (R) v. *DPP* [2006]	A child was arrested for harassing a police officer, after calling him a 'wanker' and making masturbatory signs.	This case considers what amounted to harassment under section 4A POA 1986.
Harvey v. *DPP* [2011]	The court considered whether the use of a swear word such as 'fuck' or 'fucking' amounted to a criminal offence when directed at a police officer or another member of the public.	These words on their own did not amount to a criminal offence. For an offence to arise the other requirements under the POA 1986 needed to be satisfied.
Southard v. *DPP* [2006]	The police had carried out a stop and search and had been told to 'fuck off'.	The court considered the meaning of harassment for the purposes of section 5 of the POA 1986.
R (Laporte) v. *Chief Constable of Gloucestershire* [2006]	Police prevent three coaches from proceeding to a demonstration.	The House of Lords considered what the requirements were for a breach of the peace. They held that the police had acted illegally in violating the protestors' rights under Article 11 ECHR.
Austin v. *Commissioner of the Police of the Metropolis* [2009]	The use of kettling by the police at a demonstration in London.	The House of Lords ruled that kettling did not violate Article 5 ECHR as the police could take action to prevent a breach of the peace.

Statute	About	Importance
Article 11 ECHR	The right of freedom of peaceful assembly and association.	Any restrictions need to be prescribed by law and necessary in a democratic society.
Public Order Act 1936	Makes the wearing of uniforms by political parties a criminal offence.	Prevented the use of paramilitary forces by political parties, as had occurred in Germany during the 1920s and 30s.
Public Order Act 1986	Restrictions on public protests and assemblies, as well as creating public order offences.	Any protest or assembly will need to consider whether they must give advanced notice to the police. The police can impose conditions and ultimately prohibit the event.
Criminal Justice and Public Order Act 1994	This Act created additional public order offences.	The offences were largely aimed at travellers and illegal raves.

FURTHER READING

Allen, M. and Cooper, S. 'Howard's Way: a farewell to freedom?' [1995] *Modern Law Review* **364**
This article explores the Criminal Justice and Public Order Act 1994. It provides a useful critique of the legislation.

Bradley, A.W. and Ewing, K.D. *Constitutional and Administrative Law* **15th edn (Pearson: Harlow, 2011)**
See chapter 24 for a detailed discussion on public order and Article 11 ECHR. Refer to this chapter for a useful overview of the law.

Ewing, K.D. *Bonfire of the Liberties: New Labour, Human Rights, and the Rule of Law* **(Oxford University Press: Oxford, 2010)**
A highly critical and knowledgeable critique of legal developments over the past decade. Refer to this for academic discussion.

Reid, K. 'Letting down the drawbridge: restoring the right to protest at Parliament' [2013] 3(1) *Law Crime and History* **16**
This article explores the restriction on the right of protest at the Houses of Parliament.

Stone, R. and Bonner, D. 'The Public Order Act 1986: steps in the wrong direction?' [1987] *Public Law* **202**
This article critiques the Public Order Act 1986. Refer to this to understand the significance of the developments.

PART 4
Administrative law

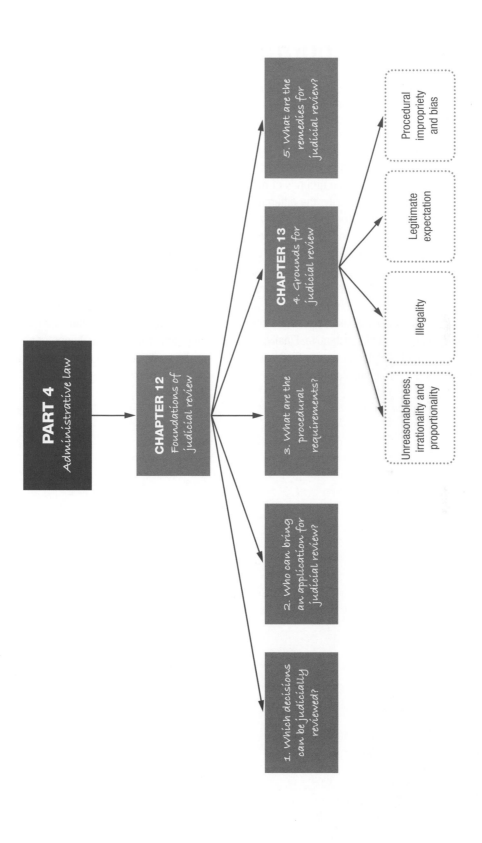

PART 4 INTRODUCTION

Part 4 of Blueprints *Constitutional and Administrative Law* focuses on administrative law and in particular, judicial review. The importance of judicial review in holding the executive to account and preventing abuse of power is outlined in Chapter 12. In addition to an introduction to the theory behind judicial review, there is coverage of the requirements needed to bring an application. We will explore what exactly is meant by the term public body, just who can have standing, whether a private company can bring an application for judicial review and the remedies that are available.

Chapter 13 will explore the grounds of review. We will look at when a decision can be challenged on the basis of illegality, the different sub-categories of illegality, such as using powers for an improper purpose, considering irrelevant considerations and unauthorised delegation. We will also consider the test for when a decision will be unreasonable and irrational. These as we shall see are used to challenge a decision where there has not been a breach of a Convention right, whereas, where a Convention right has been restricted, the courts will ask whether the restriction was proportionate. Many academics prefer proportionality as a test, as it has a lower threshold of review; and consequentially, it has been argued that proportionality should replace the traditional unreasonableness test. We shall also consider legitimate expectation, which can be both procedural and substantive. Finally, the chapter will consider procedural impropriety and the requirements needed to ensure that a decision is fair. This will include looking at the right to be heard and the rule against bias.

CHAPTER 12

Foundations of judicial review

BLUEPRINT

*Foundations of
judicial review*

LEGISLATION

- Part 54 of the Civil Procedure Rules
- Section 31 of the Senior Courts Act 1981

CONTEXT

- Judicial review is an important check on government and local authorities.
- Judicial review has developed throughout the twentieth century.
- The House of Lords in GCHQ held that prerogative powers were judicially reviewable.

CONCEPTS

- Ouster clauses
- The High Court
- What is meant by procedural exclusivity?
- A claimant must have sufficient interest to bring judicial review
- An individual's standing
- Interest groups

- Should the courts be able to judicially review primary legislation?
- Should the time limit for judicial review be increased?

- What is judicial review?
- What decisions are reviewable?
- Who can seek to have a decision judicially reviewed?

CASES

- R v. *Disciplinary Committee of the Jockey Club ex p. Aga Khan* [1993]
- R v. *Panel on Takeovers and Mergers ex p. Datafin Plc* [1987]
- R v. *Secretary of State for Foreign and Commonwealth Affairs ex p. World Development Movement Ltd* [1995]

SPECIAL CHARACTERISTICS

- Judicial review is not an appeal
- Historical role of the courts in reviewing executive action
- Both statutory powers and the prerogative can be judicially reviewed
- Only a public body can be judicially reviewed

REFORM

- Will the proposed Coalition government reforms make it more difficult for individuals to make an application for judicial review? (https://consult. justice.gov.uk/digital-communications/ judicial-review-reform)
- As is currently proposed by the government, should the time limit for judicial review for certain types of issues be reduced from three months?

CRITICAL ISSUES

Setting the scene

The purpose of judicial review is to hold the executive at both a national and local level to account, which includes governmental agencies and anyone else who is responsible for making decisions of a public law nature. The courts play an important part in protecting the citizen's rights against the state. Examples of how judicial review can be used might include challenging the refusal of planning permission and elderly residents who have been told that they will move to another care home, despite being promised that they will not be moved. It has been noted in Chapters 6 and 7 that the parliamentary scrutiny of the executive is no longer always effective as a means to hold the executive to account. A government has not lost a vote of no confidence in the House of Commons since 1979, and even the current Coalition government enjoys a comfortable majority in the House of Commons. Lord Steyn's comments at the beginning of his judgment in *R (Jackson)* v. *Attorney-General* [2005] UKHL 56 are apt as His Lordship warned that every government since 1979 had enjoyed a majority and as a consequence it could dominate the House of Commons. Arguably, this means that the ability of Parliament to hold the government to account is limited. Therefore, the ability of the courts to review central government, local authorities and executive agencies is crucial to ensuring accountable government.

Judicial review is a check on the executive's discretionary decision-making powers and prevents the government from acting outside of their powers, either statutory or prerogative. We have seen in Chapter 4 the importance of the rule of law in English law. Neither the executive nor its agencies can act outside the powers given to it by Parliament, or the residual prerogative powers which are exercised by ministers.

Ministers are given the power to take decisions and make delegated legislation under statute. The courts must be able to prevent a minister, or indeed the local authority, from misusing this power; whether it is using this power for a purpose that Parliament did not intend or acting in a way that the court considers to be unreasonable. It is important to note that judicial review is not concerned with the validity of an Act of Parliament, nor whether the statute is unconstitutional.

In this chapter we will look at:

- what is meant by judicial review and what purpose does it serve;
- when can a decision be judicially reviewed;
- who can bring an application for judicial review; and
- what are the remedies that are available.

In Chapter 13 we shall look at the grounds under which a decision of a **public body** may be reviewed by the courts.

Chapter overview

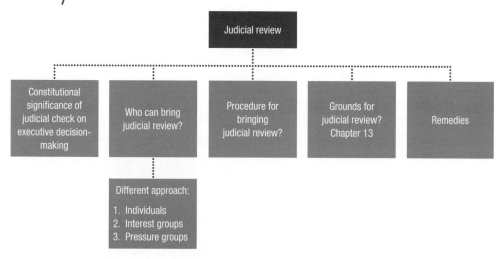

OVERVIEW OF ADMINISTRATIVE LAW

Administrative justice is important in the twenty-first century. The government, ministerial departments, executive agencies and local authorities play an important role in our lives and, consequently, they exercise considerable power over us. How are they held to account? How can you, a citizen, challenge the action of a government department or seek redress for poor service, poor decision-making or rudeness? It is important to appreciate that administrative law could be taught as a distinct module and whilst this book covers judicial review, you may learn about tribunals and the Parliamentary and Health Service Ombudsman (PHSO) as a form of administrative remedy.

- **Tribunals** developed in response to the growth of the state and were established to allow individuals to challenge administrative decisions. The modern Tribunal Service was created by the Tribunals, Courts and Enforcement Act 2007 as a result of the Leggatt Review of Tribunals in 2000.

- The PHSO combines the roles of the Parliamentary **Ombudsman** and the Health Service Ombudsman. These roles were created by the Parliamentary Commissioner Act 1967 and the Health Service Commissioners Act 1993. The PHSO is independent from government and is an important form of administrative redress. The PHSO will only investigate if there is evidence of maladministration or service failure, which has caused injustice or hardship. There is no right of direct access to the Parliamentary Ombudsman and the complaint must be brought by an MP.

- Public inquiries are administrative in nature, rather than judicial. No judicial sanction will flow from an inquiry; rather the inquiry will make recommendations which may indirectly lead to legal sanction. The Inquiries Act 2005 allows the government to create a public inquiry and establishes the procedure to be used.

- The Crown Proceedings Act 1947 (CPA 1947) was intended to reform the liability of the Crown. The CPA 1947 applies to both the Crown (government departments, etc.) and to local authorities. However, under section 40(1) the monarch still retains a personal immunity from being sued in her personal capacity. It is no longer necessary to obtain the permission of the Attorney-General. Section 1 of the CPA 1947 permits individuals to sue the Crown as a matter of right.

EXTENT OF JUDICIAL REVIEW

Only secondary legislation and prerogative powers exercised by ministers can be reviewed by the courts. The courts cannot review primary legislation. This is unlike the United States, where the United States Supreme Court can review primary legislation and if the legislation is held to be unconstitutional, the court can strike it down.

The importance of judicial review

CORNERSTONE

Judicial review is not an appeal

It is important to note that judicial review is not an appeal. The court is not deciding whether it thinks that the actual decision was correct, rather the court is reviewing the decision and seeing if the decision is invalid because it is unreasonable, irrational, illegal, procedurally unfair, or whether there has been a breach of legitimate expectation. Even if the court quashes the original decision and orders that the decision-maker remakes the decision, this does not mean that the applicant will get the outcome they want. Judicial review is concerned with how the decision was made and not the actual decision itself. However, it should be noted that the courts will look at whether a decision was unreasonable or irrational, a process which will look at the merits of the actual decision.

So why does this matter? Imagine that you have applied for a funding from your local council because you are looking after a disabled dependant. The funding is refused, but no reason is given for this. Understandably, you will be upset about this and would expect to have been told the reasons for this. Initially, you had been told to apply by the council and had been assured that you were eligible for funding. Someone else you know, whose circumstances are similar, has received funding and you cannot see why your application was refused. What can you do about this? The answer is that you can apply to judicially review the council's decision.

> Judicial review has been used to challenge the decision to cancel the refurbishment of schools by the Coalition government in 2010, the positioning of missile batteries on top of flats during the 2012 London Olympics, preventing an anti-war protestors from staying overnight in Parliament Square and a Conservative council from selling off council houses in order to gain votes.

CONTEXT

Constitutional significance

In Chapter 1 we saw that the United Kingdom does not have a codified constitution. The incorporation of the European Convention on Human Rights (ECHR) into domestic law by the Human Rights Act 1998 (HRA 1998), prevents a public authority (section 6(1) HRA 1998) from violating Convention rights. However, given the executive's dominance of Parliament, judicial review provides a method to scrutinise the use and interpretation of the statutory powers afforded to the executive. It must be emphasised that the validity of legislation cannot be reviewed, only the use of the legislation by the executive.

INTERSECTION

Executive accountability is an important aspect of any constitutional and administrative law module and it is vital that you place judicial review within the broader context of how the government of the day is held to account. The executive's use of prerogative powers is inadequately subjected to Parliamentary scrutiny, as the powers are not derived from Parliament and therefore, there is little that Parliament can realistically do, short of abolishing or replacing it with legislation, to restrict the way a minister uses a certain prerogative power. We have seen this in Chapters 6, 7 and 9 when we explored the role of Parliament, the executive and the extent of the prerogative powers.

Judicial review is important as it enables the courts to hold the executive to account, as ministerial use of both statutory and prerogative powers can be reviewed by the courts. However, judicial review raises some important constitutional problems. According to the theory of the separation of powers, it is the executive that is responsible for governing the country and developing policies, the powers needed to govern are given by Parliament or are the prerogative powers which Parliament has not abolished. There is a danger that if the courts subject the executive's decision-making process to too rigorous a scrutiny, then the courts might attempt to supplement their own decision for that of the executive. Therefore, judicial review must balance protecting citizens' rights with the need to avoid making policy decisions, when these decisions should only be made by the executive.

REFLECTION

The importance of judicial review cannot be underestimated as a means to safeguard the rights of individuals and businesses. An example of this is Virgin Trains, which in 2012 judicially reviewed the decision to award the West Coast rail franchise to a rival company. Virgin Trains had argued that there were major flaws with the franchise bidding process. Recently, Camden Council was unsuccessful in judicially reviewing the decision to go-ahead with High Speed Rail 2.

Professor H.W.R. Wade argued that the judicial review of the executive powers to prevent abuse had made an impact on everyone's lives, by preventing the government from creating a monopoly over air travel to the United States (*Laker Airways Ltd* v. *Department of Trade* [1977] QB 643) and by preventing the government from cancelling 'our television licences if we do something quite lawful but of which he disapproves' (*Congreve* v. *Home Office* [1976] QB 629) (see Wade 1980).

Historical development

CORNERSTONE

Historical role of the courts in reviewing executive action

The English courts have historically challenged the executive's misuse of power. In a famous example, Sir Edward Coke CJ prevented King James I from claiming more prerogative powers that what the law allowed the king to have (*Case of Proclamations* (1611) 12 Co. Rep 74). The courts had restricted the monarch's powers to those recognised in law and prevented the monarch from claiming new powers. Decisions such as *Entick* v. *Carrington* [1765] 19 State Tr 1029 demonstrates judicial willingness to prevent the government from acting illegally.

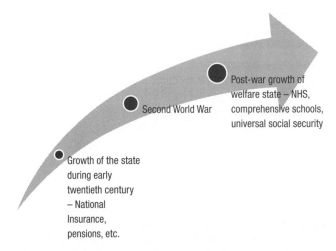

Second World War

Post-war growth of
welfare state – NHS,
comprehensive schools,
universal social security

Growth of the state
during early
twentieth century
– National
Insurance,
pensions, etc.

Figure 12.1 Key developments in the growth of the modern state

Historically the courts imposed limits on the power of the executive, namely that the government could not act outside the law (see Figure 12.1). This is essential for the rule of law. The case of *R* v. *Cambridge University ex p. Bentley* (1724) 93 ER 698 demonstrated the importance of natural justice as a fundamental concept in English law. In *Ex p. Bentley* Eyre J observed that it was important that a person is able to defend themselves, 'I remember to have heard it observed by a very learned man upon such an occasion, that even God himself did not pass sentence upon Adam, before he was called upon to make his defence' (at p. 704). The willingness of the courts to review executive action was considerably lower in *Local Government Board* v. *Arlidge* [1915] AC 120. In *Arlidge* the House of Lords held that a person affected by an administrative decision did not have a right to see the inspector's report which had led to the decision, neither did he have a right to make oral representations to the decision-maker. This case is viewed by many lawyers as undermining the concept of natural justice. The growing power of the modern state was met with increased judicial deference, which continued throughout the Second World War and 1950s post war Britain. The House of Lords' decision in *Liversidge* v. *Anderson* [1942] AC 206 is an extreme example of judicial deference to the executive. The case involved the detention of foreign nationals during the Second World War. A majority of the House of Lords held that the Home Secretary had the power to detain and the courts could not question the Home Secretary's decision. Lord Atkin dissented from the majority and observed:

> 'The appellant's right to particulars, however, is based on a much broader ground, a principle which again is one of the pillars of liberty in that in English law every imprisonment is prima facie unlawful and that it is for a person directing imprisonment to justify his act.'

This meant that the Home Secretary had to show that he was using his powers lawfully, by establishing that the conditions for imprisonment without charge were satisfied.

In the 1960s, the judiciary once again regained their constitutional role and started to effectively hold the executive to account. The House of Lords in *Ridge* v. *Baldwin* [1964] AC 40 HL held that the requirements of natural justice applied to all administrative decisions. However, modern decisions such as *R (Bancoult)* v. *Secretary of State for the Foreign and Commonwealth Office (No.2)* [2008]

UKHL 61 demonstrate the continuing reluctance of the judiciary to review some areas of the executive's decision-making powers. More recently, Lord Sumption, writing extra-judicially, has called for judicial restraint in reviewing government policy.

Proposed reforms to judicial review

In 2012, the Coalition government proposed key reforms to judicial review. These proposed reforms are aimed at reducing the number of applications for judicial review. The Ministry of Justice is intending to reduce the cost of judicial review and is of the view that unmeritorious claims are abusing the system. The reforms to judicial review are extremely controversial and have been criticised by senior members of the judiciary, practitioners and academics.

The Secretary of State for Justice was critical of judicial review being used to challenge government policy, writing in *The Telegraph* (20 April 2014) that many decisions have 'been the subject of legal action, so-called judicial reviews, instigated by pressure groups, designed to force the Government to change its mind over properly taken decisions by democratically elected politicians. This includes using the legal system as a weapon to try to stop the difficult decisions we are taking to secure a better future for our country as part of our long-term economic plan'. The reforms to judicial review are linked to the reforms to legal aid.

Considering the fact that the applicant only has three months at present in which to submit his application, any reduction to the time limit could prove to be problematic. The time limit to judicially review a planning decision has now been changed and is six weeks. This change was introduced by the Civil Procedure (Amendments No.4) Rules 2013, which modifies Part 54.5 of the Civil Procedure Rules 1998. You should note that this only applies to planning decisions.

Further reforms are currently being considered by Parliament. Clause 64 of the Criminal Justice and Courts Bill 2014 is currently in the House of Lords and will amend section 31 of the Senior Courts Act 1981 (SCA 1981). Subclause (2) will insert subsection (3B) into the SCA 1981. It informs the court that:

> **'When considering whether to grant leave to make an application for judicial review, the High Court – (a) may of its own motion consider whether the outcome for the applicant would have been substantially different if the conduct complained of had not occurred, and (b) must consider that question of the defendant asks it to do so.'**

Subclause (3C) directs the High Court on this matter: '[i]f, on considering that question, it appears to the High Court to be highly likely that the outcome for the applicant would have been substantially different, the court must refuse to grant leave'.

Clause 64 of the Criminal Justice and Courts Bill 2014 will reform the ability of the court to grant relief. Subclause (1) of the bill inserts a new subsection (2A) into the SCA 1981, which states that:

> **'The High Court – (a) must refuse to grant relief on an application for judicial review, and (b) may not make an award under subsection (4) on such an application, if it appears to the court to be highly likely that the outcome for the applicant would not have been substantially different if the conduct complained of had not occurred.'**

These reforms are designed to prevent unmeritorious claims from proceeding and have proved to be extremely controversial.

The Criminal Justice and Courts Bill 2014 will restrict the award of protective costs orders which currently protect the applicant from excesses costs in the event that they are unsuccessful. It is important to note that a bill is not law and will not become law until it has received royal assent.

No distinction between statutory and non-statutory powers

CORNERSTONE

Both statutory powers and the prerogative can be judicially reviewed

The House of Lords in *Council for Civil Service Unions* v. *Minister of the Civil Service* [1985] AC 374 (*GCHQ*) held that there was no distinction between judicial review of prerogative and statutory powers. This is important given the considerable prerogative powers that the government has at its disposal. It should be remembered that Lord Roskill held that some areas of the prerogative were non-justiciable. This meant that they were not considered suitable for review by the courts. Recently, Prerogative Orders in Council were held by the House of Lords in *Bancoult (No.2)* to be judicially reviewable.

Ousting judicial review

CORNERSTONE

Ouster clauses

An **ouster clause** is an attempt by Parliament to restrict the courts from reviewing how a minister or local authority exercises their statutory power. It will prevent individuals from challenging a decision by seeking judicial review. According to the doctrine of Parliamentary Sovereignty the courts should follow Parliament's intention. However, the courts have interpreted such clauses in a way which permits judicial review. The most famous example is the decision in *Anisminic Ltd* v. *Foreign Compensation Commission* [1969] 2 AC 147.

Anisminic Ltd v. *Foreign Compensation Commission*

Is it possible for Parliament to prevent the courts from reviewing how a minister or local authority uses the powers which have been conferred on them by statute (ousting judicial review)? Section 4(4) of the Foreign Compensation Act 1950 stated that any determination of the Foreign Compensation Commission could not be questioned in court. Read literally this would have excluded the court from reviewing the decision. Such a clause in a statute is known as an ouster clause. The House of Lords in *Anisminic Ltd* v. *Foreign Compensation Commission* [1969] 2 AC 147 were asked to review the decision that prevented Anisminic from recovering compensation for property it had lost in Egypt in 1956. The House of Lords held that judicial review was not ousted by the use of an ouster clause in section 4(4) of the Foreign Compensation Act 1950, as the Foreign Compensation Commission had made a mistake as to their powers and therefore the decision was only a purported determination. Therefore it was not a valid decision and was not protected by section 4(4).

Judicial review can be excluded by implication. An example of this is *R* v. *Secretary of State for the Environment ex p. Upton Brickworks* [1992] JPL 1044, where the court held that judicial review was excluded because the statute had stated that where an order was issued then only a statutory remedy could be applied for. However, the court stated that had there been an abuse of process in issuing the order, then judicial review would have been available. In *R (A)* v. *Director of Establishments of the Security Service* [2009] UKSC 12 the Supreme Court held that judicial review could not be brought by a former member of the UK security services. The reason why the Administrative Court did not have the jurisdiction to hear the application was because section 65(2)(a) of the Regulation of Investigatory Powers Act 2000 stated that the Investigatory Powers Tribunal was to have exclusive jurisdiction. The Supreme Court distinguished this case from *Anisminic*, as their Lordships held that section 65(2)(a) was not attempting to oust judicial review, rather it outlined the source of judicial scrutiny. The difference in these two cases was that Parliament in the Foreign Compensation Act 1950 had intended to remove *all* judicial scrutiny.

BRINGING AN APPLICATION FOR JUDICIAL REVIEW

The remainder of this chapter will focus on bringing an application for judicial review. In order to bring an application a number of criteria must be satisfied:

1. The decision is amenable to judicial review:
   (a) if it was made by a public body and it is a public law decision;
   (b) if the body was not established by statute or prerogative, then it can be amenable if its functions are of a public law nature;
2. The correct procedure has been used:
   (a) it must be a public law rather than private law issue;
   (b) the application must be brought within the three-month time limit;
3. The applicant has a sufficient interest in the decision:
   (a) individual applicants;
   (b) interest groups bringing the application on behalf of its members;
   (c) pressure groups campaigning against a decision.

We shall look at each of these in turn. When approaching a question on judicial review the structure of your answer is very important, as your lecturer will expect you to deal with each issue in turn.

Which court?

CORNERSTONE

The High Court

An application for judicial review must be made to the Queen's Bench Division of the High Court. This has been the case since 1977 as there is no longer a need to use different courts depending on the remedy which you are seeking. In England and Wales, unlike in many other European jurisdictions, there is no separate administrative court in England and Wales. This means that the High Court will hear both private law and public law claims. The Administrative Division of the High Court which will hear the application.

Is the decision amenable to judicial review?

CORNERSTONE

Only a public body can be judicially reviewed

The decision being reviewed must have been made by a public body. It must be emphasised that judicial review concerns public law and not private law issues; therefore, judicial review cannot be brought against private parties. There are some exceptions to this, and we shall see below that a private party such as a business, can be judicially reviewed, where they are carrying out functions of a public nature.

In *R* v. *Panel on Takeovers and Mergers ex p. Datafin Plc* [1987] QB 815 the court held that the decision of the panel was amenable to judicial review. This was because although the panel was not created either by statute or the prerogative, the functions it exercised in reviewing and regulating takeovers in the City of London were of a public law nature. The panel had liaised with the Treasury and therefore exercised quasi-governmental powers (see Figure 12.2).

CORNERSTONE

Is the body amenable to judicial review – the test from *R* v. *Panel on Takeovers and Mergers ex p. Datafin Plc* [1987] QB 815

The key test to determine whether a decision is amenable to judicial review is to ask whether the body exercises public law functions and not to rely solely on the source of its powers. The test was established in *Ex p. Datafin Plc*. This test requires the court to look at the functions carried out by the body and to ask whether these functions are of a public law nature.

Sir John Donaldson MR had outlined the circumstances in which a body would be amenable to judicial review. Donaldson MR (at p. 847) had stated that:

'I do not agree that the source of the power is the sole test whether a body is subject to judicial review . . . Of course the source of the power will often, perhaps usually, be decisive. If the source of power is a statute, or subordinate legislation under a statute, then clearly the body in question will be subject to judicial review. If, at the other end of the scale, the source of power is contractual, as in the case of private arbitration, then clearly the arbitrator is not subject to judicial review . . .

But in between these extremes there is an area in which it is helpful to look not just at the source of the power but at the nature of the power. If the body in question is exercising public law functions, or if the exercise of its functions have public law consequences, then that may . . . be sufficient to bring the body within the reach of judicial review.'

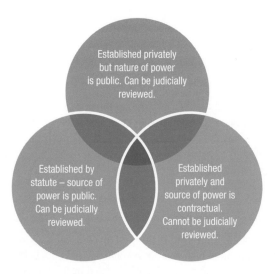

Figure 12.2 Nature and the source of the body's power

.... **APPLICATION**

Bouncer & Parking Ltd (BPL) supplies security and event staff to nightclubs, festivals and pubs. BPL have acquired the right to run HMP Doverbury, which houses high-risk prisoners. Whilst BPL may be a private company for the purposes of running the prison, BPL would be considered a public body. This is because BPL is carrying out functions of a public nature. BPL could be judicially reviewed by the prisoners.

The Jockey Club and religious faiths

If there is a dispute, can the aggrieved party judicially review the decision of the organisation, or are they limited to private law remedies? One argument which has been used to argue that the decision is amenable to judicial review is the 'but for test'. The premise behind the 'but for test' can be best explained in *R* v. *Chief Rabbi of the United Hebrew Congregations of Great Britain and the Commonwealth, ex p. Wachman* [1993] 2 All ER 249, where Simon Brown J had stated the test as, '[w]ere there no self-regulatory body in existence, Parliament would almost inevitably intervene to control the activity in question.'

Does it always mean that where the government would have to intervene to create a regulating body, then such a body would be classed as a public body carrying out functions of a public law nature? The answer is no. The question is whether the functions carried out are governmental.

> **Take note**
>
> Many professions and sports have formed organisations to govern their affairs and anyone wishing to operate in a profession or take part in a sport professionally must agree to the terms of that organisation's membership rules. This means that there often will be a contract between the members and the organisation which will mean that any dispute over that organisation's decision is likely to be a private law matter.

CORNERSTONE

R v. *Disciplinary Committee of the Jockey Club, ex p. Aga Khan* [1993] 1 WLR 909

In this case the Aga Khan sought to judicially review the decision of the Jockey Club. The Court of Appeal held that the decision was not amenable to judicial review because it was not a public law decision. Although the Jockey Club had been established by the prerogative its functions were not governmental and it existed to regulate horse racing. The relationship between the Jockey Club and members such as the Aga Khan was contractual. Therefore, this was a private law matter.

Sir Thomas Bingham had stated that even if the Jockey Club did not exist and Parliament had to legislate to create a new body, then that new body would still not be a public body as it did not exercise any public functions. It is clear that if the body is created by the prerogative or statute, but exists only to regulate the dealings of a certain sport and membership of the body is contractual, then that body's decision will not be amenable to judicial review (see Figure 12.3).

In *Ex p. Wachman* the court refused to judicially review the decision of the Chief Rabbi, who had decided that a Rabbi was unfit to hold office. The court held that religious rules and the regulation of the requirements to hold office were not governmental and was of no concern to the government.

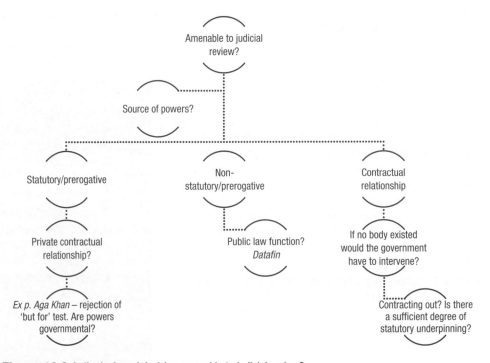

Figure 12.3 Is the body and decision amenable to judicial review?

The Football League sought to judicially review the Football Association's decision to create the Premier League in *R* v. *Football Association ex p. Football League* [1993] 2 All ER 833. Permission was refused because the Football Association was not considered to be a public body. The reason was that the Football Association was a governing body whose powers came from private law. This was because its membership and governance were based on a contractual relationship between it and the clubs. The Football Association had not been set up by the state, indeed it was created by football teams to govern the sport and had it not existed, then the state would not have created it. Rather like other sports, private individuals and clubs would intervene and create such a body.

The decision in *Ex p. Football League* was followed in *R* v. *Panel of the Federation of Communication Services Ltd ex p. Kubis* (1999) 11 Admin LR 43. This case involved a trade association whose members had agreed contractually to be bound by its rules. When the association revoked a member's licence for breach of the rules, he sought to judicially review its decision. The court refused his application as the decision-making body was not created by statute and the relationship between the parties was contractual.

Contracting out by the local authority to a private care provider

In *R* v. *Servite Houses ex p. Goldsmith* (2001) 33 HLR 35 the local authority had a statutory duty to provide care for those groups in society who were in need of care and attention under the National Assistance Act 1948 (s.21(1)(a)). The local authority was permitted to contract with other bodies to provide this service. This is known as contracting out.

> Today it is common for local authorities to contract out services to private bodies. This might include the provision of care for the elderly and the provision of social housing. Contracting out of services is encouraged as a way to save money. The problem is that the party responsible for carrying out this service is a private body and therefore the question is whether it is amenable to judicial review.

CONTEXT!

The decision in *Ex p. Goldsmith* concerned an action for judicial review which had been brought by residents of a care home run by Servite Houses. Servite Houses was a private body which provided services for the local authority. Servite Houses decided to close the care home. The question was whether the decision was amenable to judicial review. Moses J (at [56]) stated:

> 'The court is concerned to decide where a case lies in the spectrum between, at one end, a body whose source of power is statutory and, at the other end, a body whose source of power is contractual. Thus, both ends of the spectrum require the courts to determine the issue of amenability by reference to the source of power, statutory on the one hand and contractual on the other. Between those two extremes lie many cases where the source of power test no longer provides an answer to the question of amenability.'

Reference was made to *Ex p. Datafin* where the amenability to judicial law was based on the public law nature of its function. However, if the powers are contractual then the body would not be amenable to judicial review (*Ex p. Aga Khan*). The fact that government might have had to intervene and create such a body if none existed was irrelevant, because the body's powers would be based on the contract between it and its members. Therefore, such a body would have no special statutory powers. However, the court would have to draw a distinction between private bodies which had a statutory underpinning and were subject to government regulation. The court required more than just statutory regulation as to how the services were to be provided, as it 'must be able to identify sufficient statutory penetration which goes beyond the statutory regulation of the manner in which the service is provided' [76].

The court held that the National Assistance Act did not create sufficient statutory underpinning as section 26, which permitted outsourcing, was silent as to how the accommodation was to be provided. The statutory duty was discharged by the local authority arranging accommodation. Moses J held (at [77]):

> 'In my judgment that is a crucial distinction. It is the distinction between legislation which adds a public function to the private functions of a private body and legislation which permits a public law duty to be discharged by entry into private law arrangements. It does not seem to me that the applicants can successfully contend that because legislation permits a public authority to enter into arrangements with a private body, the functions of the private body are, by dint of that legislation, to be regarded as public functions.'

It would appear that, where services have been contracted out to a private company, judicial review could still be brought where there was a sufficient degree of statutory underpinning. So when will there be a sufficient degree of statutory underpinning? The decision in *Ex p. Goldsmith* can be contrasted with the decisions in *R* v. *Cobham Hall School ex p. G* [1998] ELR 389, *R (A)* v. *Partnerships in Care Ltd* [2002] EWHC 529 (Admin) and *R* v. *Advertising Standards Authority ex p. Insurance Services* (1990) 2 Admin LR 77, where there was a sufficient degree of statutory underpinning to make the decision in both cases amenable to judicial review. In *Ex p. G* an independent school was participating in a scheme to provide assisted places which was regulated by the Education Act 1996. Therefore, the school was carrying out a public function and the decision to remove a child on the scheme was amenable to judicial review. In *Ex p. Insurance Services* the decision of a private regulator was amenable to judicial review because had it not existed, then a governmental body would have to carry out its functions. The functions it carried out were held to be of a public law nature. In *Partnerships in Care Ltd* it was held that the treatment of mentally ill patients was a public law function and there was sufficient statutory underpinning which meant that the hospital had to follow statutory guidelines on treating patients.

The decision in *Ex p. Goldsmith* was followed *in R (Heather)* v. *Leonard Cheshire Foundation* [2001] EWHC Admin 429. The charity managed care homes and the local authority provided funding by paying to house those in need of care. It was argued that the charity was a public body for the purposes of judicial review and a public authority under the Human Rights Act 1998. Both these arguments were unsuccessful. Based on the public body argument the court held that there was insufficient statutory underpinning for the charity to be carrying out functions of a public law nature. A similar decision was reached in *YL* v. *Birmingham City Council* [2007] UKHL 27 where a care home was held not to be a public authority for the purposes of the HRA 1998.

REFLECTION

BRINGING A CLAIM

Bringing judicial review involves two stages. The first is where the court determines whether to allow the application to proceed and the second is the full substantive hearing which will involve the actual grounds for judicial review. This chapter is concerned with the first stage.

It must be remembered that the court will only grant an application for judicial review where there is a *prima facie* case to answer. Therefore the claimant must adduce evidence to demonstrate that one of the grounds for judicial review exists.

Correct procedure

CORNERSTONE

Part 54 of the Civil Procedure Rules and section 31 of the Senior Courts Act 1981

In order to make an application for judicial review, section 31 of the Senior Courts Act 1981 requires that the correct rules have been followed. The rules governing judicial review can be found in Part 54 of the Civil Procedure Rules.

Part 54.5 states that the deadline for submitting a claim form is three months after the events which gave rise to the claim occurred. The time limit is strict as not even the parties themselves are able to agree to extend the time limit.

Part 54.3 states the judicial review procedure applies where the claimant is seeking a declaration or an injunction. Part 54.2 states that judicial review must be used where the claimant is seeking a mandatory order, a prohibiting order or a quashing order. We shall look at the available remedies below.

Procedural exclusivity

CORNERSTONE

What is meant by procedural exclusivity?

The House of Lords in *O'Reilly* v. *Mackman* [1983] 2 AC 237 held that where a person's public law rights had been breached, that person could only bring an application for judicial review. This was because judicial review was the exclusive procedure to be used in these circumstances. Therefore you must determine whether the claim is a public law or a private law matter.

In *O'Reilly* v. *Mackman* several prisoners had alleged that the Board of Visitors, when deciding to discipline them by forfeiting a remission of sentence, had breached their public law rights. However, as they were out of time for bringing judicial review, they sought a private law remedy. The House of Lords refused to permit this as judicial review would have provided a remedy. Lord Diplock held that because:

> '[A]ll remedies for infringements of rights protected by public law can be obtained upon an application for judicial review, as can also remedies for infringement of rights under private law if such infringements should also be involved [so to permit a person to sue a public body in private where there was protection afforded in public law would be] contrary to public policy and as such an abuse of process of the court' (at p. 10).

In *Roy* v. *Kensington and Chelsea and Westminster Family Practitioner Committee* [1992] 1 AC 624 the House of Lords allowed a general practitioner to bring an action against the Family Practitioner Committee in private law, despite the action involving a public law decision. The decision in *O'Reilly* was doubted in *Clark* v. *University of Lincolnshire and Humberside* [2000] 1 WLR 1988 where the Court of Appeal permitted a private law action for breach of contract, despite the case concerning both private law and public law issues. The case concerned a student whose work was marked at zero after she was accused of plagiarism. The student alleged that the university had breached their regulations. Therefore, it would appear that judicial review does not have procedural exclusivity where an action involves public law issues and private law issues. Given the strict three-month time limit for submitting an application for judicial review, this liberalisation of the approach of procedural exclusivity has meant that the longer time limit for bringing claims in private law is still available as an alternative remedy.

STANDING

CORNERSTONE

A claimant must have sufficient interest to bring judicial review

In order to bring an applicant for judicial review the claimant must have **standing**, that is *locus standi*. Section 31(3) of the Senior Courts Act 1981 states that 'the court shall not grant leave to make such an application unless it considers that the applicant has a sufficient interest in the matter to which the application relates'. This means that unless a person (or a group) has sufficient interest, then they are unable to bring an application for judicial review.

The issue of sufficient interest was addressed in *R* v. *Inland Revenue Commissioners ex p. National Federation of Self Employed and Small Businesses Ltd* [1982] AC 617. The case concerned an application brought by the National Federation who sought to challenge the decision of the Inland Revenue to grant casual workers in Fleet Street a tax amnesty. The House of Lords were critical of treating standing as always a preliminary issue as the factual and legal context, which would be explored at the hearing, should be discussed alongside the question of whether the applicant had sufficient interest. The issue of standing should be linked to the merits of the claim. The House of Lords ruled that the National Federation did not have sufficient interest in the matter. It was clear that none of the members of the National Federation were affected by the decision and the interests of one taxpayer should not concern another.

The law draws a distinction between individuals bringing an application for judicial review and groups (see Figure 12.4). The courts are far more willing to grant judicial review for an individual than a group. However, we can see that an individual whose claim was frivolous or vexatious will not have standing. This is because the merits of the application are important.

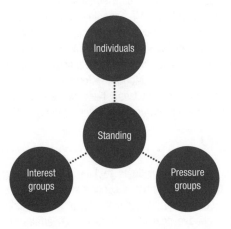

Figure 12.4 Standing

Individuals

⊕ **CORNERSTONE**

An individual's standing

An individual who has sufficient interest in the matter will have standing to bring an application for judicial review. If the decision prejudicially affects your interests then you are deemed to have standing. Indeed, the absence of personal interest will not be an impediment for standing. In *R (Kides)* v. *South Cambridgeshire DC* [2002] EWCA Civ 1370, Jonathan Parker LJ stated that,

> 'I cannot see how it can be just to debar a litigant who has a real and genuine interest in obtaining the relief which he seeks from relying, in support of his claim for that relief, on grounds (which may be good grounds) in which he has no personal interest. It seems to me that a litigant who has a real and genuine interest in challenging an administrative decision must be entitled to present his challenge on all available grounds' [133–134].

This is narrower than the test for victim under section 7 HRA 1998, where the applicant must be directly affected.

In *R* v. *Secretary of State for the Home Department ex p. Venables* [1998] AC 407 the killers of Jamie Bulger were able to judicially review the Home Secretary's sentencing decision, which involved fixing a tariff period of fifteen years. This was because the decision had prejudicially affected their interests.

Challenging government policy

Individuals are able to challenge government policy and will be regarded as having sufficient interest. In *R* v. *HM Treasury ex p. Smedley* [1985] QB 657 a UK taxpayer was able to judicially review the government's undertaking to make payments to the European Community's Consolidated Fund. The court regarded standing and the seriousness of the issue as interlinked. Slade LJ stated that if the matter would have been 'of a frivolous nature' then the application could have been disposed of. The application was granted because '[i]t raises a serious question'. Regarding standing, Slade LJ stated that, 'I do not feel much doubt that Mr. Smedley, if only in his capacity as a taxpayer, has sufficient *locus standi* to raise this question by way of an application for judicial review.' In *R (Wheeler)* v. *Office of the Prime Minister* [2008] EWHC 1409 (Admin) the claimant had standing to review the application of the Labour government's decision not to hold as promised a referendum on the ratification of the Lisbon Treaty. Finally, Lord Rees-Mogg, the former editor of *The Times*, was able to judicially review the ratification of the Maastricht Treaty because he was a UK citizen (see *R* v. *Secretary of State for Foreign and Commonwealth Affairs ex p. Rees-Mogg* [1994] 2 WLR 115.

INTERSECTION

Although the courts have held that individuals seeking to challenge government policy could have standing, it is clear that where the policy concerns foreign affairs (i.e. membership of the European Union) then the courts will hold that the issue is non-justiciable. We have seen in Chapter 9 that certain prerogative powers such as foreign affairs are considered to be non-justiciable. This was held to be the case in *Wheeler* and *Rees Mogg*.

Interest groups

⊕ CORNERSTONE

Interest Groups

An interest group will represent members and will often make representations to the government about their members' needs and, if necessary, will judicially review any decision which adversely affects their members. If an interest group, or an association, represents members who are prejudicially affected by a decision then they will be able to bring an application for judicial review on behalf of their members.

In *R* v. *Liverpool Corporation ex p. Liverpool Taxi Fleet Operators Association* [1972] 2 QB 299 the taxi owner's association was considered in order to have standing in order to bring judicial review. Lord Denning MR stated that the ability to bring judicial review 'does not include a mere busybody who is interfering in things which do not concern him; but it includes any person who has a genuine grievance because something has been done or may be done which affects him'. Therefore, as Liverpool council's decision to go back on its word regarding the issuing of new taxi licenses had prejudicially affected its members, the association had a sufficient interest. Similarly in *Covent Garden Community Association* v. *Greater London Council* [1981] JPL 183 an association was formed to protect the interests of residents and was deemed to have standing to bring judicial review. The case concerned an application to quash a decision of the council's planning committee.

Busybodies or concerned citizens

In *R* v. *Secretary of State for the Environment ex p. Rose Theatre Trust Co (No.2)* [1990] 1 QB 504 members of the public, who wished to challenge a decision not to schedule the remains of a theatre as a monument, were held not to have sufficient interest in bringing judicial review. The court in *Ex p. Rose Theatre Trust Co (No.2)* was of the view that simply contacting the secretary of state about a decision was not enough to give concerned citizens sufficient interest. The court took the view that Parliament under section 31 of the Senior Courts Act 1981 only intended those with 'a sufficient interest in the matter to which the application relates' to bring a claim. Schiemann J stated '[m]erely to assert that one has an interest does not give one an interest . . . The fact that some thousands of people join together and assert that they have an interest does not create an interest if the individuals did not have an interest.' However, this decision has not been applied rigidly in subsequent cases.

The courts have adopted a more liberal approach to standing for pressure groups, such as where none of the group members have a direct interest, but there is no one else who can realistically bring an application for judicial review.

⊕ CORNERSTONE

R v. *Secretary of State for Foreign and Commonwealth Affairs ex p. World Development Movement Ltd* [1995] 1 WLR 386

In this case a pressure group was held to have sufficient interest to challenge a decision of the Secretary of State to fund the construction of a hydro-electric power station in Malaysia. The pressure group had argued that the decision to finance the project was illegal. The court held that the pressure group had sufficient interest.

Why was the World Development Movement held to have standing? Rose LJ in *Ex p. World Development Movement Ltd* stated that:

- The courts have now taken a more liberal approach to standing.

- Standing should be addressed along with the far more important question of the substantial merits of the application. This means that the courts should not refuse an application based solely on whether an applicant has sufficient interest.

- Factors which were important in granting standing here were: 'the importance of vindicating the rule of law . . . the importance of the issue raised . . . the likely absence of any other responsible challenger . . . the nature of the breach of duty against which relief is sought . . . and the prominent role of these applicants in giving advice, guidance and assistance with regard to aid.' These factors meant that the pressure group had sufficient interest.

- Rose LJ drew a comparison with the lenient approach to standing where the individual had a genuine interest in the matter, and stated: 'it seems to me that the present applicants, with the national and international expertise and interest in promoting and protecting aid to underdeveloped nations, should have standing in the present application.'

The seriousness of the matter, and the fact that there were no other responsible challengers, permitted the Child Action Poverty Group to bring an application to judicially review delays in processing benefits (*R v. Secretary of State for Social Services ex p. Child Poverty Action Group* [1990] 2 QB 540). Greenpeace sought to challenge permission which permitted radioactive waste to be discharged from a power station (*R v. Inspectorate of Pollution ex p. Greenpeace Ltd (No.2)* [1994] 4 All ER 329). Greenpeace was held to have sufficient interest because of its expertise in the area, its international reputation and the fact that it represented members who lived near the power plant, who otherwise would not have brought the application.

The liberal approach can also be seen in *R v. Somerset CC ex p. Dixon* [1998] Env LR 111. The case involved an application for judicial review which sought to challenge the decision to allow a quarry to be extended. The county had argued that the applicant should not have standing, as they were not prejudicially affected by the decision. Sedley J stated that it was possible for concerned members of the public, who were neither busybodies, nor troublemakers, to alert the court to illegality:

> 'Public law is not at base about rights, even though abuses of power may and often do invade private rights; it is about wrongs – that is to say misuses of public power; and the courts have always been alive to the fact that a person or organisation with no particular stake in the issue or the outcome may, without in any sense being a mere meddler, wish and be well placed to call the attention of the court to an apparent misuse of public power. If an arguable case of such misuse can be made out on an application for leave, the court's only concern is to ensure that it is not being done for an ill motive . . .
>
> Mr Dixon is plainly neither a busybody nor a mere troublemaker, even if the implications of his application are troublesome for the intended respondents. He is, on the evidence before me, perfectly entitled as a citizen to be concerned about, and to draw the attention of the court to, what he contends is an illegality in the grant of a planning consent which is bound to have an impact on our natural environment.'

Having read Sedley J's comments above, it can be observed that a person who does not have sufficient interest in the traditional sense could still bring an application for judicial review.

APPLICATION

Consider the two examples below. In what circumstances will a pressure group be held to have sufficient interest in a matter?

Example 1: The North London Football Supporters Guild (NFLSG) would like to challenge the decision of the Secretary of State to contribute £23,000,000 towards converting the Big Sports Stadium into a new football stadium, which will be used by East Ender United FC. The question here is whether NFLSG would have a sufficient interest in the decision. They appear to be a supporters' association and could represent their members. However, are the interests of their members affected by the decision of the Secretary of State? Or are they just interfering in a matter which they have no interest in? We would need to consider the decision in *Ex p. National Federation of Self Employed and Small Businesses Ltd*. NFLSG would be unlikely to have a sufficient interest and would be unable to judicially review the decision. This could be contrasted with a situation where a football club is denied funding from the Secretary of State, whereas another club receives funding.

Example 2: The Asylum Seekers Support Group (ASSG) is a charity that has been set up to look after the interests of asylum seekers in the United Kingdom. ASSG wishes to challenge the decision of the Secretary of State to reduce benefit payments to those asylum seekers whose application to remain in the United Kingdom has been rejected. We can presume that ASSG does not have members who are directly affected by the decision. However, as a charity they could have sufficient interest to bring judicial review, as shown by cases such as *Ex p. Child Poverty Action Group* and *Ex p. Greenpeace Ltd (No.2)*. We would need to consider ASSG's expertise, reputation and whether anyone else would realistically be able to bring an application for judicial review.

REMEDIES

The application may be awarded one or more of the following remedies (see Figure 12.5). It is important to note which remedy the applicant in any given circumstance will be seeking. We shall divide the remedies between non-prerogative and prerogative remedies.

Figure 12.5 Remedies available for judicial review

Non-prerogative remedies

Since the Judicature Acts 1873–75 any court can award the equitable remedy of an injunction. An injunction will prevent a party from acting in a certain way or force a party to act in a certain way. Breach of an injunction will result in contempt of court. The House of Lords in *M* v. *Home Office* [1994] 1 AC 377 held that injunctions were available against ministers and government departments. Therefore, Crown immunity has been restricted with regards to liability for breach of an injunction. In *M* v. *Home Office* the Home Secretary had ordered the removal of a political asylum seeker to Zaire. The court ordered the Home Secretary to return the asylum seeker to the United Kingdom, but the Home Secretary refused to comply with the injunction. The House of Lords held that injunctions could be used against officers of the Crown and they did not enjoy immunity.

The court can by way of a declaratory judgment state the parties' respective rights and, importantly for the purposes of judicial review, the applicant can ask the court to state whether the public body will be permitted by statute or the prerogative to act in a certain way. For example, an applicant may ask whether a planning committee can legally refuse to have a public hearing, and a declaratory judgment will merely state whether refusing to have a public hearing will be legal. It is also possible to recover damages where they would be available in private law.

Prerogative remedies

The court can award a number of prerogative remedies. A prohibitory order will stop a public body from acting in a certain way, a mandatory order will compel a public body to use its powers properly and to act in a certain way, whilst a quashing order, will nullify the decision and the decision-maker will have to remake the decision. It must be noted that even if the original decision is quashed, the applicant may still not necessarily get the decision they want when the public body makes a new decision.

CONTEXT

When the Coalition government came into power in 2010, Michael Gove, the Secretary of State for Education, decided to change the previous government's policy of rebuilding and refurbishing schools. It was decided that many schools would no longer be included in the list of those to be refurbished or rebuilt. However, the communication of this decision was rushed and many schools were informed that they were still included, when in fact a decision had been taken to remove them from the list. The decision was challenged by many local authorities. In *R (Luton BC)* v. *Secretary of State for Education* [2011] EWHC 217 (Admin) the Secretary of State for Education was ordered to reconsider his decision and have regard to the equality impact of the decision. This case is interesting as it illustrates the limits of judicial review. Consider the judgment of Holman J, who stated:

'[T]he Secretary of State must, I stress must, reconsider the position of each of the claimants with an open mind and paying due regard to whatever representations they may respectively make. But provided he discharges that duty and his equality duties, the final decision on any given school or project still rests with him. He may save all, some, a few, or none. No one should gain false hope from this decision.' [126]

This was a clear warning that a quashing order would always lead to the new decision leading to the applicant's preferred outcome.

KEY POINTS

- Judicial review serves as an important check on the executive. It prevents the executive from abusing its powers.
- Judicial review is not an appeal of the substantive decision.
- Only the decisions of a public body are amenable to judicial review.
- You must have sufficient interest to bring an application for judicial review. It is possible for both individuals and groups to bring an application for judicial review.
- There is currently a three-month time limit for bringing an application for judicial review.
- There are a number of remedies available for judicial review, including a quashing order.

CORE CASES AND STATUTES

Case	About	Importance
R v. *Panel on Takeovers and Mergers ex p. Datafin Plc* [1987]	There was an attempt to judicially review a body that oversaw mergers and acquisitions in the City of London.	Despite not being established by statute or the prerogative, the body was held to be exercising public law functions and therefore it could be reviewed.
R v. *Disciplinary Committee of the Jockey Club ex p. Aga Khan* [1993]	The Aga Khan sought to judicially review a decision which had been made by the Jockey Club.	The Court of Appeal held that the Jockey Club's decision was not amenable to judicial review, because its functions were not of a public law nature and there was a private law (i.e. contractual) relationship between the Jockey Club and the Aga Khan.
R v. *Secretary of State for Foreign and Commonwealth Affairs ex p. World Development Movement Ltd* [1995]	The decision of the Foreign Secretary to pay towards the construction of a dam in Malaysia was judicially reviewed.	The applicants were a pressure group, World Development Movement. The court held that the applicants had standing.

→

Statute	About	Importance
Part 54 of the Civil Procedure Rules	Establishes the produce for judicial review.	Refer to Part 54 for the procedure which will be used to make an application for judicial review.
Section 31 of the Senior Courts Act 1981	Section 31 concerns the court's jurisdiction to judicially review decisions made by public bodies.	Refer to section 31 for detail about the court's jurisdiction, remedies available, etc.

FURTHER READING

Bradley, A.W. and Ewing, K.D. *Constitutional and Administrative Law* **15th edn (Pearson: Harlow, 2011)**
Refer to this textbook for more detailed coverage of judicial review.

Carroll, A. *Constitutional and Administrative Law* **7th edn (Pearson: Harlow, 2013)**
A useful book which provides some additional information on judicial review.

Ligere, E. 'Locus standi and the public interest: a hotchpotch of legal principles' [2005] *Journal of Planning and Environmental Law* **292**
Provides a useful overview of the development of standing for judicial review and the differences with a 'victim' for the purposes of the HRA 1998.

Wade, H.W.R. *Constitutional Fundamentals*, **The Hamlyn Lectures, 1980 (Stevens, 1980)**
A very interesting and authoritative exploration of administrative law.

Wade, H.W.R and Forsyth, C.F. *Administrative Law* **10th edn (Oxford University Press: Oxford, 2009)**
A very detailed and thorough account of judicial review and coverage of all of the key cases. This book is extremely useful reading in addition to any set text.

CHAPTER 13

Grounds for judicial review

BLUEPRINT
Grounds for judicial review

CONTEXT

- The incorporation of the ECHR into domestic law and the use of proportionality as a ground for judicial review (*Daly*).
- The development of *Wednesbury* unreasonableness.
- The historical role of the courts in protecting natural justice.
- The end of the distinction between judicial and administrative decisions for fairness (*Ridge* v. *Baldwin*).

LEGISLATION

- Human Rights Act 1998

CONCEPTS

- Unreasonableness
- Irrationality
- Proportionality
- Illegality
- Legitimate expectation
- Procedural impropriety
- Fettering of discretion
- Keeping the door ajar
- Natural justice

- What are the constitutional risks of judges reviewing governmental policy?

- What are the grounds for judicial review?
- How rigorously do the courts review a decision made by a public body?

CASES

- *Associated Provincial Picture Houses Ltd* v. *Wednesbury Corporation* [1948]
- *Council for Civil Service Unions* v. *Minister of the Civil Service* [1985]
- *R* v. *Secretary of State for the Home Department ex p. Doody* [1994]
- *R* v. *North and East Devon Heath Authority ex p. Coughlan* [2001]
- *Ridge* v. *Baldwin* [1964]
- *Dimes* v. *Grand Junction Canal Proprietors* (1854)
- *R* v. *Bow Street Metropolitan Stipendiary Magistrate ex p. Pinochet Ugarte (No.2)* [2000]
- *Porter* v. *Magill* [2001]

SPECIAL CHARACTERISTICS

- The courts must avoid misusing judicial review

REFORM

- Should (as Sir Jeffrey Jewel and Professor Craig have argued) proportionality replace unreasonableness as a ground for judicial review?
- Is there still a place for unreasonableness (as argued by Sir Philip Sales)?
- Could primary legislation ever be judicially reviewed?

CRITICAL ISSUES

Setting the scene

We have seen the procedure for bringing judicial review and now we will look at the grounds for bringing an application for judicial review. It is important to understand how these grounds arise and how they can be used to challenge the executive's decision. You should note that it is possible for more than one ground to be argued in an application for judicial review and so it is not possible to look at these grounds in isolation when considering the validity of a decision. The cases mentioned below involved challenges to decisions as diverse as banning hunting, selling off council homes and cancelling funding for a private education. These decisions impact on the rights of citizens and therefore judicial review serves an important role in preventing abuse of power and protecting the rights of individuals.

Lord Diplock in *Council of Civil Service Unions and Others* v. *Minister for the Civil Service* [1985] AC 374 [*GCHQ*] identified the grounds which were available for judicial review: 'one can conveniently classify under three heads the grounds upon which administrative action is subject to control by judicial review. The first ground I would call "illegality," the second "irrationality" and the third "procedural impropriety." That is not to say that further development on a case by case basis may not in course of time add further ground.' Although, Lord Diplock did suggest that in the future proportionality could become a ground for judicial review. We shall look at these grounds in detail below and see how they can arise.

The grounds on which an application for judicial review can be made are:

- Unreasonableness or irrationality
- Proportionality
- Illegality
- Legitimate expectation
- Procedural impropriety and bias.

Where the court finds that a ground for judicial review has been established, the court can award the claimant one or more of the remedies discussed previously in Chapter 12. These grounds are used to challenge the decision-maker's decision, thus in effect it permits the court to prevent the executive from abusing its powers.

Chapter overview

UNREASONABLENESS OR IRRATIONALITY AS A GROUND FOR JUDICIAL REVIEW

CORNERSTONE

Unreasonableness

A decision can be challenged where the court is of the opinion that the decision-maker has acted unreasonably. This requires the court to assess whether the decision is one which no other reasonable decision-maker would make.

It is important to appreciate that the decision-maker is not being challenged on the basis that he has exceeded his powers (acting illegally), but rather it is the substance of his actual decision that is being challenged (see Figure 13.1). This raises important constitutional questions, as the courts are asking whether the decision is so unreasonable that no other decision-maker would reach the same decision.

CORNERSTONE

Associated Provincial Picture Houses Ltd v. *Wednesbury Corporation* [1948] 1 KB 223

The decision in this case established the unreasonableness test. It involved the decision to ban children from going to the cinema on a Sunday. Lord Greene MR considered what was meant by ➔ unreasonableness and held that:

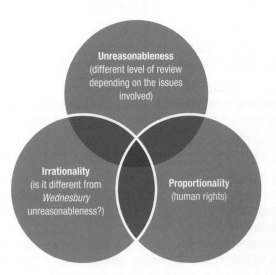

Figure 13.1 Unreasonableness, irrationality and proportionality

> 'It is true to say that, if a decision on a competent matter is so unreasonable that no reasonable authority could ever have come to it, then the courts can interfere. That, I think, is quite right; but to prove a case of that kind would require something overwhelming, and, in this case, the facts do not come anywhere near anything of that kind.'
>
> The decision in the present case was not held to be unreasonable. The case gave rise to the test known as ***Wednesbury* unreasonableness**.

An example of when a decision would be unreasonable was given by Warrington LJ in *Short* v. *Poole Corporation* [1926] Ch 66, if a teacher was dismissed 'because she had red hair, or for some equally frivolous and foolish reason, the Court would declare the attempted dismissal to be void'.

CORNERSTONE

Council of Civil Service Unions and Others v. *Minister for the Civil Service* [1985] AC 374 [*GCHQ*] and the test for 'irrationality'

In the *GCHQ* case Lord Diplock offered a new formulation of the *Wednesbury* test, which asked whether the decision-maker has acted irrationally. His Lordship stated that a decision would be irrational if the decision was one 'which is so outrageous in its defiance of logic or of accepted moral standards that no sensible person who had applied his mind to the question to be decided could have arrived at it'. Lord Diplock held that judges would be able to distinguish between a rational and irrational decision. Indeed, His Lordship stated that, '"Irrationality" by now can stand upon its own feet as an accepted ground on which a decision may be attacked by judicial review.'

Is there a difference between unreasonableness and irrationality? In *A* v. *North Somerset Council* [2009] EWHC 3060 (Admin) at [36] Mr Justice Jarman QC stated that:

- 'Unreasonableness is an objective concept which operates across a spectrum dependent upon the importance of the issues at stake. The test is high . . . but a claimant does not have to demonstrate a decision that is so bizarre that the author must be regarded as temporarily unhinged.'

- 'What the term "irrationality" generally means in this area of the law is a decision which does not add up, in which in other words there is an error of reasoning which robs the decision of its logic.'

In *A* v. *North Somerset Council* the court held that whilst unreasonableness was 'an objective concept' and that '[t]he test is high' for establishing that a decision was unreasonable, 'a claimant does not have to demonstrate that 'a decision that is so bizarre that the author must be regarded as temporarily unhinged.' This narrows the potential interpretation of Lord Diplock's formulation of irrationality, where an irrational decision was one which is 'so outrageous in its defiance of logic or of accepted moral standards' meaning that no sensible decision-maker would reach such a decision.

Constitutional problems

CORNERSTONE

The courts must avoid misusing judicial review

As discussed in Chapter 12, the courts must be aware of the important constitutional principle of the separation of powers and thus must avoid restricting the discretionary powers of a minister or local authority, unless the decision is truly one which is unreasonable.

As Lord Scarman stated in *R* v. *Secretary of State for the Environment ex p. Nottinghamshire County Council* [1986] AC 240 at 251, 'Judicial review is a great weapon in the hands of the judges: but the judges must observe the constitutional limits set by our parliamentary system upon their exercise of this beneficent power.' Therefore, if Parliament has given discretionary power to a minister, then the courts can review the validity of the decision only where there has been an abuse of power and the decision exceeds the powers conferred by Parliament.

However, the courts have recognised that where important rights are concerned then the court can exercise a heightened review. Conversely, the courts will be reluctant to review decisions which are of a political nature. In *Ex p. Nottinghamshire County Council* the House of Lords was asked to review a financial decision by the Secretary of State. This according to Lord Scarman involved the exercise of discretion which 'inevitably requires a political judgment on his part'. Lord Scarman, because of the political nature of the decision, was of the opinion that:

> '[T]he courts below were absolutely right to decline the invitation to intervene . . . But I cannot accept that it is constitutionally appropriate, save in very exceptional circumstances, for the courts to intervene on the ground of "unreasonableness" to quash guidance framed by the Secretary of State and by necessary implication approved by the House of Commons, the guidance being concerned with the limits of public expenditure by local authorities and the incidence of the tax burden as between taxpayers and ratepayers. Unless and until a statute provides otherwise, or it is established that the Secretary of State has abused his power, these are matters of political judgment for him and for the House of Commons. They are not for the judges or your Lordships' House in its judicial capacity.'

Lord Templeman agreed with Lord Scarman's approach and held that whilst '[t]he courts will not be slow to exercise the powers of judicial review in order to strike down illegality or abuse of power', on the facts, however, the Secretary of State's action was lawful. It is apparent that where a political decision is being made by a minister, that the courts will not hold the decision to be unreasonable, unless there is evidence of abuse of power.

The courts' power to review administrative decisions was considered by Lord Bridge in *R* v. *Secretary of State for the Home Department ex p. Bugdaycay* [1987] AC 514. The case concerned an application for asylum. The Home Secretary had refused the application and the asylum seeker brought an application for judicial review. The House of Lords held that the decision whether to grant asylum was one for the executive and therefore was valid, although the court held that the decision to remove one of the immigrants could be quashed. This was because the decision as to whether there was a danger in returning the applicant to his home country needed to be taken after considering the evidence provided. On the facts the evidence had not been considered. Giving judgment, Lord Bridge noted that, although the courts had limited powers of review, the courts are:

'[E]ntitled to subject an administrative decision to the more rigorous examination, to ensure that it is in no way flawed, according to the gravity of the issue which the decision determines. The most fundamental of all human rights is the individual's right to life and when an administrative decision under challenge is said to be one which may put the applicant's life at risk, the basis of the decision must surely call for the most anxious scrutiny.'

We can see that depending on the type of decision, the courts will adopt a different level of review.

Would a ban on homosexual military personnel be considered reasonable? This was a question which was addressed by the English courts in the 1990s. In *R* v. *Ministry of Defence ex p. Smith* [1996] QB 517 military personnel sought to challenge the decision of the Ministry of Defence, which had dismissed them from the armed forces. This occurred before the passing of the Human Rights Act 1998 and therefore, the domestic courts could not consider whether there had been a violation of Articles 8 and 14. The court had to ask whether the decision was reasonable. Sir Thomas Bingham MR stated that the court should adopt a heightened review where there has been a substantial interference with human rights. This case is important as it demonstrates that the courts will adopt a sliding scale of review depending on the type of decision that they are reviewing. However, we should note that the heightened review may not be adequate to protect individual's rights. Sir Thomas Bingham MR had stated:

REFLECTION

'The court may not interfere with the exercise of an administrative discretion on substantive grounds save where the court is satisfied that the decision is unreasonable in the sense that it is beyond the range of responses open to a reasonable decision-maker. But in judging whether the decision-maker has exceeded this margin of appreciation the human rights context is important. The more substantial the interference with human rights, the more the court will require by way of justification before it is satisfied that the decision is reasonable in the sense outlined above' (at 554).

Therefore if a decision involves interference with human rights then the courts will more actively review the decision. It is important to note that the heightened review under the *Wednesbury* unreasonableness test was found to be inadequate to protect the military personnel's rights. The Court of Appeal found that the Ministry of Defence's decision to dismiss the homosexual military personnel was not unreasonable. This was despite applying the heightened standard of review. Importantly, it could not be said that a reasonable decision-maker would not have reached this decision.

> **Take note**
>
> It is important to consider the different standards of review under the traditional unreasonableness test, the test for irrationality and that of proportionality.

The appellants in *Ex p. Smith* subsequently brought their case to the European Court of Human Rights (ECtHR). The ECtHR ruled that the military personnel's Convention rights had been violated, and that the violation could not be justified as it was not proportionate (*Smith* v. *United Kingdom* (33985/96) (2000) 29 EHRR 493). The ECtHR acknowledged that the Court of Appeal was aware that there had been a violation of Article 8 ECHR and that the decision may not be proportionate, however, as the ECHR had yet to be incorporated into domestic law the domestic court had been unable to consider this.

PROPORTIONALITY AS A GROUND FOR JUDICIAL REVIEW

We shall now consider the development of proportionality as a ground for judicial review and look at whether it should replace unreasonableness (see Figure 13.2).

Figure 13.2 The development of proportionality

Before the Human Rights Act 1998 the test for proportionality could not be used in domestic law

The House of Lords in *R* v. *Secretary of State for the Home Department ex p. Brind* [1991] 1 AC 696 held that the decision by the Home Secretary to ban direct speech from a proscribed terrorist organisation was not illegal, as the decision was not unreasonable. The House of Lords considered the approach of the ECtHR when reviewing infringements of Convention rights. The ECtHR would ask whether the infringement was proportionate. The use of proportionality as a ground for review in domestic law was rejected, as Lord Ackner stated, '[u]nless and until Parliament incorporates the Convention into domestic law . . . there appears to me to be at present no basis upon which the proportionality doctrine applied by the European Court can be followed by the courts of this country.'

> Senior members of Sinn Fein during the 'Troubles' in Northern Ireland were banned from being able to directly broadcast in the United Kingdom. This meant that whenever Gerry Adams, the then leader of Sinn Fein, would deliver a speech, organisations like the BBC would have to dub his voice with that of an actor. This ban has since been lifted.

CONTEXT

The impact of the Human Rights Act 1998

The Human Rights Act 1998 incorporated the ECHR into domestic law. This meant that Convention rights could be directly enforceable in domestic courts where there had been an infringement by a public authority.

INTERSECTION

It is important to understand the effect of the Human Rights Act 1998 and the requirement under section 6(1) that '[i]t is unlawful for a public authority to act in a way which is incompatible with a Convention right'. We shall see that the HRA 1998 has provided for domestic enforcement of the European Convention on Human Rights. Chapter 10 outlines how the HRA 1998 works in practice and the meaning of public authority.

In *R (on the application of Alconbury Developments Ltd)* v. *Secretary of State for the Environment, Transport and the Regions* [2001] UKHL 23 Lord Slynn thought the time had come to use proportionality where there were infringements of Convention rights. His Lordship observed that, '[t]rying to keep the Wednesbury principle and proportionality in separate compartments seems to me to be unnecessary and confusing.' However, proportionality must not be used to 'provide for a complete rehearing on the merits of the decision. Judicial control does not need to go so far.' This is important as a merits-based review would risk violating the separation of powers.

The House of Lords in *R (Daly)* v. *Secretary of State for the Home Department* [2001] UKHL 26 considered the power of the prison authorities to search a prisoner's cell, without the prisoner being present, and read to his legal correspondence. According to Lord Bingham the decision was successfully challenged 'on an orthodox application of common law principles . . . and an orthodox domestic approach to judicial review'. The House of Lords agreed that the same result would have been reached on the basis of Article 8 ECHR. Their Lordships were aware that relying on the common law and the ECHR might not always result in the same outcome. Reference was made to the decision in *R* v. *Ministry of Defence ex p. Smith* [1996] QB 517.

Importantly, the House of Lords held that in the future where there were violations of Convention rights, it was no longer appropriate to ask whether a decision was unreasonable. Rather the correct question was whether the infringement was proportionate. English courts had experience of applying proportionality where there had been an infringement of European Union Law. In *Daly*, Lord Steyn rejected the use of the heightened test for reasonableness which had been used by Sir Thomas Bingham MR in *Ex p. Smith*. His Lordship referred to the judgment of Lord Clyde in *De Freitas* v. *Permanent Secretary of Ministry of Agriculture, Fisheries, Lands and Housing* [1999] 1 AC 69, where it was stated that the court should ask whether:

1. 'the legislative objective is sufficiently important to justify limiting a fundamental right';

2. 'the measures designed to meet the legislative objective are rationally connected to it'; and

3. 'the means used to impair the right or freedom are no more than is necessary to accomplish the objective'.

CORNERSTONE

Proportionality and the Human Rights Act 1998

As a consequence of the Human Rights Act 1998, where there has been a violation of a Convention right, the courts will use proportionality as a ground for review. In order for a decision to be proportionate it needs to be shown that there is a legitimate objective which is sufficiently important to justify limiting a fundamental right, and that the measures used to achieve this objective are rationally connected to it. Consequentially, there needs to be a link between the measure and the objective.

It is important to note that the test for proportionality requires a higher standard of review of executive decision-making. In *Daly* Lord Cooke had observed that whilst the application of the reasonableness test and that of proportionality may reach the same result, cases such as *Ex p. Smith* demonstrated the limitations of the former. Lord Cooke observed:

'The view that the standards are substantially the same appears to have received its quietus in *Smith and Grady* v. *United Kingdom* (1999) 29 EHRR 493 . . . And I think that the day will come when it will be more widely recognised that *Associated Provincial Picture Houses Ltd* v. *Wednesbury Corpn* [1948] 1 KB 223 was an unfortunately retrogressive decision in English administrative law, in so far as it suggested that there are degrees of unreasonableness and that only a very extreme degree can bring an administrative decision within the legitimate scope of judicial invalidation. The depth of judicial review and the deference due to administrative discretion vary with the subject matter. It may well be, however, that the law can never be satisfied in any administrative field merely by a finding that the decision under review is not capricious or absurd' (at [32]).

We can see above that Lord Cooke was critical of the unreasonableness test, namely that there needs to be unreasonableness of 'only a very extreme degree' before the courts will find the decision invalid. His Lordship implicitly questioned the survival of *Wednesbury* unreasonableness. This heightened review of proportionality has constitutional implications. The courts can question not just whether the decision is extreme, irrational or is one that no other reasonable decision would reach; as now the courts can ask whether the decision was more than was necessary to accomplish the executive's objective. Decisions which exceed what was required to meet this legitimate objective can be challenged by the courts.

Lord Steyn observed that the Court of Appeal in *R* v. *Ministry of Defence ex p. Smith* [1996] QB 517 'reluctantly felt compelled to reject a limitation on homosexuals in the army' which violated Articles 8 and 14, because the decision was found not to be unreasonable. However, the ECtHR found that it was not proportionate. His Lordship distinguished the two tests, because firstly 'the doctrine of proportionality may require the reviewing court to assess the balance which the decision-maker has struck, not merely whether it is within the range of rational or reasonable decisions', and secondly 'the proportionality test may go further than the traditional grounds of review inasmuch as it may require attention to be directed to the relative weight accorded to interests and considerations' (at [27]).

Recently, in *Bank Mellat* v. *Her Majesty's Treasury (No.2)* [2013] UKSC 39 Lord Reed reconsidered the requirements of the proportionality test and approved the use of a fourth limb. His Lordship stated that the test adopted at Strasbourg was not the same as the test used domestically. This was because:

> '[T]he Strasbourg court recognises that it may be less well placed than a national court to decide whether an appropriate balance has been struck in the particular national context. For that reason, in the Convention case law the principle of proportionality is indissolubly linked to the concept of the margin of appreciation. That concept does not apply in the same way at the national level, where the degree of restraint practised by courts in applying the principle of proportionality, and the extent to which they will respect the judgment of the primary decision-maker, will depend upon the context, and will in part reflect national traditions and institutional culture. For these reasons, the approach adopted to proportionality at the national level cannot simply mirror that of the Strasbourg court' [72].

Rather than mirroring Strasbourg, the domestic courts have been influenced by other common law jurisdictions. The test in *De Freitas* was based on South African, Zimbabwean and Canadian jurisprudence.

Take note

Domestic courts should not adopt the margin of appreciation because this is an international concept which, whilst useful to the ECtHR, is not suitable for the domestic courts because they are much better placed to review a decision. This is because they understand the local political and social conditions.

Lord Reed accepted the inclusion of a fourth limb, which had been first used in *Huang* v. *Secretary of State for the Home Department* [2007] UKHL 11. This was because the fourth limb had originated along with the original test in *R* v. *Oakes* [1986] 1 SCR 103. The fourth limb was 'whether, balancing the severity of the measure's effects on the rights of the persons to whom it applies against the importance of the objective, to the extent that the measure will contribute to its achievement, the former outweighs the latter'. His Lordship observed that, '[i]n essence, the question at step four is whether the impact of the rights infringement is disproportionate to the likely benefit of the impugned measure.' It is not sufficient that the interference is the least drastic measure available to achieve the legislative aim, as the court must balance the importance of the measure against the impact on the individual whose rights have been breached.

The approach post *Daly*

Lord Bingham stated in *A* v. *Secretary of State for the Home Department observed*:

> 'In *Smith and Grady* v. *United Kingdom* (1999) 29 EHRR 493 the traditional Wednesbury approach to judicial review . . . was held to afford inadequate protection (by the ECtHR) . . . It is now recognised that "domestic courts must themselves form a judgment whether a Convention right has been breached" and that "the intensity of review is somewhat greater under the proportionality approach": *R (Daly)* v. *Secretary of State for the Home Department* [2001] 2 AC 532.'

Thus, in *A* v. *Secretary of State for the Home Department* [2004] the House of Lords held that the Home Secretary's decision to detain suspected foreign terrorists without trial breached the ECHR. Thomas Hickman (2008), reviewing the introduction of proportionality post *Daly*, has commented (making reference to decisions such as *R (Begum)* v. *Governors of Denbigh High School* [2006] UKHL 15) that, '[t]he House of Lords has established that proportionality is concerned only with the outcome of the process of decision-making, not the manner in which it was conducted.'

APPLICATION

The government has announced that any openly homosexual member of the armed forces will be dismissed. The government's legal adviser has informed the Secretary of State for Defence that following the decision of the Court of Appeal in *Ex p. Smith* the department could go ahead with this policy.

Lieutenant Oakes is homosexual and has recently had her sexuality made public by a former partner. She was questioned by her superior officer and in line with governmental policy dismissed. Lieutenant Oakes wishes to bring an application to judicially review the decision to dismiss her.

Lieutenant Oakes will be able bring an application for judicial review and can argue that the decision was not proportionate. Applying the test for proportionality, there needs to be a legitimate aim which the government policy is trying to achieve, that the decision to dismiss Lieutenant Oakes is connected to the legitimate aim, and that the measure does not violate rights beyond what is really necessary to achieve the objective. Finally, it is necessary to consider the fourth limb and balance the importance of the legitimate aim against the impact on the individual whose rights have been violated.

The role of proportionality beyond violations of the Convention rights

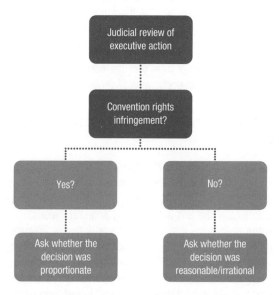

Figure 13.3 When to use proportionality as a ground for judicial review

Having two tests, depending on whether or not Convention rights are involved, has been criticised and many commentators, both judicial and academic, have questioned the confinement of proportionality to cases involving ECHR violations (see Figure 13.3). Nicholas Dobson (2003) has considered the status of *Wednesbury* unreasonableness after the decision in *Daly*. Commenting on the aftermath of *Daly*, Dobson observed that, '*Wednesbury* essentially concerns proper adherence to statutory discretion and to that extent its core principles would seem still to be relevant.' Lord Slynn in *Alconbury Developments* had rejected the need to distin-

> **Take note**
> For decisions where there are no violations on Convention rights, then the traditional *Wednesbury* unreasonableness test must be used.

guish *Wednesbury* unreasonableness and proportionality. Following the key decision in *Daly*, the Court of Appeal in *R (Association of British Civilian Internees: Far East Region)* v. *Secretary of State for Defence* [2003] EWCA Civ 473 questioned the justification for retaining *Wednesbury* unreasonableness as a ground for judicial review.

The Court of Appeal in *R (Association of British Civilian Internees: Far East Region)* v. *Secretary of State for Defence* is an example of judicial willingness to use proportionality as a ground for review beyond breaches of the ECHR. Dyson LJ had stated that:

> 'Support for the recognition of proportionality as part of English domestic law in cases which do not involve Community law or the Convention is to be found (in Daly and Alconbury Developments) . . . It seems to us that the case for this is indeed a strong one . . . The criteria of proportionality are more precise and sophisticated . . . It is true that sometimes proportionality may require the reviewing court to assess for itself the balance that has been struck by the decision-maker, and that may produce a different result from one that would be arrived at on

an application of the Wednesbury test. But the strictness of the Wednesbury test has been relaxed in recent years even in areas which have nothing to do with fundamental rights . . . The Wednesbury test is moving closer to proportionality and in some cases it is not possible to see any daylight between the two tests . . . Although we did not hear argument on the point, we have difficulty in seeing what justification there now is for retaining the Wednesbury test . . . But we consider that it is not for this court to perform its burial rites' [35]–[35].

We can see that the Court of Appeal was clear that the continued use of the *Wednesbury* test had little justification, given the sophisticated application of proportionality as a ground for review.

What is wrong with unreasonableness as a ground for judicial review?

Lord Lester and Professor Jeffrey Jowell (1987) criticised *Wednesbury* unreasonableness and argued that it should be replaced by proportionality. They criticised unreasonableness as permitting the court to hide the reasons for its decisions under the vagueness of the test, which permits the court to find rational decisions as irrational and the test is 'confusing and tautologous'.

However, there are some academics that support the retention of *Wednesbury* unreasonableness. Paul Daly (2011) has argued that despite strong judicial and academic criticism, *Wednesbury* unreasonableness has survived as a ground for judicial review in non-Convention rights cases. Daly argues after reviewing its application and responding to criticisms, that unreasonableness still has a place in the twenty-first century and needs to be better understood rather than be condemned. Commenting on the decision in *R (Association of British Civilian Internees: Far East Region)* v. *Secretary of State for Defence*, Sir Philip Sales (2013) observed that, '[t]here may be an assumption, in light of [this] . . . decision, that the Supreme Court will, when given the opportunity in a suitable case, change the rationality standard of review derived from Wednesbury and GCHQ into a general proportionality standard of review. I suggest, however, that there should be serious pause for reflection before such a step is taken' (p. 223). Sales had criticised the suitably of proportionality as a suitable ground for review in all circumstances, and had stated that that rationality is quite often a better test.

The problem is that proportionality requires the court to engage in a heightened review of the decision and to ask whether it could have been achieved in some other less drastic way. Whilst this is appropriate where Convention rights are infringed, it may be constitutionally inappropriate to do this where the decision involves political decisions and policy matters. Heightened review risks offending the separation of powers and may lead to accusations of judicial activism. Therefore, unreasonableness would permit the courts to permit the executive suitable discretion.

ILLEGALITY AS A GROUND FOR JUDICIAL REVIEW

We shall now look at illegality as a ground for judicial review.

Acting outside of the powers conferred on the decision-maker

CORNERSTONE

Illegality

Lord Diplock in *GCHQ* had observed, '[b]y "illegality" as a ground for judicial review I mean that the decision-maker must understand correctly the law that regulates his decision-making power and must give effect to it.' This essentially means that the decision-maker must act within his powers. This also means that the decision-maker must have regard to how he uses his powers, that he exercises these in a manner that takes into account relevant considerations, and it is used for the proper purpose for which it was intended.

Put simply, the decision-maker must use their decision-making powers lawfully and must not:

- act outside of the powers given to them by statute or the prerogative;
- abuse the discretion given to them by statute or the prerogative by:
  - using the powers given for improper purposes
  - delegating their decision-maker powers
  - fettering their discretion and introducing a rigid policy without exceptions
  - taking into account irrelevant considerations and ignoring relevant considerations
  - reaching a decision by making errors as to the law or facts.

Acting outside of the powers given to a minister by statute or the prerogative

The government is not above the law and the courts will review executive decision-making to see if it is *ultra vires*, which means illegal. A classic example of this is the Home Secretary's decision to order his agents to search Mr Entick's house in *Entick* v. *Carrington* (1765). The court could not find any lawful authority for the Home Secretary to issue a valid search warrant. Therefore, the consequence of this was that the agents had committed trespass. A decision which is *ultra vires* cannot stand and it will be quashed by the courts. In *Entick* the Home Secretary was acting to prevent the distribution of material by people regarded as dangerous to the state, whereas his successor some 200 years later in *Congreve* v. *Home Office* [1976] QB 629 attempted to revoke television licences where these licences had been taken out with the intention of avoiding a planned price increase. The Home Secretary had acted to prevent people surrendering their licences in order to apply for new licences, with the sole intention of avoiding the planned increase in the price of a licence fee. Lord Denning MR stated that there was no statutory power to revoke the licence. His Lordship emphasised the courts' constitutional role, '[to revoke the licences] would be a misuse of the power conferred on him by Parliament: and these courts have the authority – and, I would add, the duty – to correct a misuse of power by a Minister or his department, no matter how much he may resent it or warn us of the consequences if we do'. Clearly, the courts cannot legitimise executive illegality in the interests of expediency.

Often the courts will look at both the literal wording of the statutory provision being relied upon by the decision-maker and the intention that Parliament when enacting the provision. The decision in

Attorney General v. *Fulham Corporation* [1921] 1 Ch 440 concerned a scheme by the local authority to start up a laundry service. The local authority was relying on various Baths and Wash-houses Acts to operate the laundry service. It was argued that the Acts were concerned with washing clothes and the laundry service was not excluded by the Act, but rather it was consequential. Indeed, it was argued by counsel for the local authority that, '[t]here is no practical difference between the case of a woman bringing her clothes to the wash-house and washing them there and the case of her bringing the clothes in a bag and having them washed for her.' However, the court held that the laundry scheme was not directly authorised by the legislation, and it was not something consequential to what Parliament had intended.

> Until the middle of the twentieth century many people did not have their own bathrooms or facilities for washing clothes and had to rely on facilities provided by their local authority. Local bath houses enabled people to wash and washing facilities often provided there meant that people could clean their clothes more quickly than they could do at home.

CONTEXT

We can see that the courts will look beyond the literal meaning of a provision and look at the intention of Parliament, and therefore ask whether the decision-making is acting *ultra vires*. An example of the courts is the decision in *R* v. *Secretary State for Foreign and Commonwealth Affairs ex p. World Development Movement Ltd* [1995] 1 WLR 386. The court ruled that the Foreign Secretary could not use his statutory powers under section 1 of the Overseas Development and Co-operation Act 1980 to fund economically unsound projects. Section 1(1) stated that:

> 'The Secretary of State shall have power, for the purpose of promoting the development or maintaining the economy of a country or territory outside the United Kingdom, or the welfare of its people, to furnish any person or body with assistance, whether financial, technical or of any other nature.'

The court held the Foreign Secretary had no power to invest in the project and therefore was acting illegally. The court was willing to read into the statute the fact that Parliament would not intend for the Foreign Secretary to use the statutory powers to invest in unsound projects.

Abuse of discretion by the decision-maker

An application can be made to judicially review a decision where the decision-maker has abused their discretion. The courts provide a check and balance against the executive abusing the powers conferred by Parliament.

Using the powers given for improper purposes

The courts will ask whether the decision-maker's exercise of the powers given to him have been used for the purposes which were intended by Parliament (see Figure 13.4). Examples of situations where the court held that powers have not been used for the intended purpose include *Wheeler* v. *Leicester City Council* [1985] AC 1054. Here the local authority had used their statutory powers to prevent Leicester Rugby Football Club from using grounds owned by the local authority for one year. This was because some of the players had ignored the local authority's policy on boycotting South Africa and had gone on a tour of South Africa (in the apartheid era when it was ruled by a white minority).

Until 1994, South Africa was ruled by a white minority and non-whites were not permitted to vote. Since the late 1940s a system of apartheid divided white and non-white South Africans. It was an extremely controversial policy and led to many people, including musicians and athletes, boycotting South Africa. However, some high-profile people did go to South Africa to play music or take part in sporting competitions. This racial divide only ended when Nelson Mandela became President, having been elected in the first election where all adult South Africans were entitled to vote.

In *Wheeler* the court ruled that the local authority had misused the statutory power under section 71 of the Race Relations Act 1976 to penalise the club. Lord Templeman stated:

> 'In my opinion, this use by the council of its statutory powers was a misuse of power. The council could not properly seek to use its statutory powers of management or any other statutory powers for the purposes of punishing the club when the club had done no wrong.'

The House of Lords held that this was illegal as the powers conferred had not been intended to be used in such a way to punish a club. However, the powers could have been lawfully used to prevent a racist group from using its facilities. The House quashed the decision.

In *Porter* v. *Magill* [2001] UKHL 67 several members of the conservative controlled Westminster City Council were held to have abused their powers. These councillors had misused their statutory powers to sell council homes by deliberately selling houses in marginal wards in order to gain additional support from voters. The House of Lords was clear that powers conferred by statute must be used only for the purposes for which the power was conferred. Here there had been a politically motivated misuse of power. The House of Lords observed that:

> 'Sometimes misconduct may consist of a single decision made on behalf of a local authority by an individual acting under delegated powers, the decision being formally correct but invalid because made for improper and legally irrelevant reasons.'

In *R* v. *Port Talbot Borough Council ex p. Jones* [1988] 2 All ER 207 a housing officer was found to have misused his power when allocating housing, because he had given priority to a councillor. Therefore, the power conferred had been used for an improper purpose. Another example is *R* v. *Somerset CC ex p. Fewings* [1995] 1 WLR 1037 where a decision was taken to ban hunting on the local authority's land. The Court of Appeal held that the decision had to be based on the local authority's statutory power and banning hunting solely because it was considered morally repugnant amounted to an improper purpose.

An interesting example of a local authority using its powers to pursue a policy is the House of Lords' decision in *Roberts* v. *Hopwood* [1925] AC 578. Here section 62 of the Metropolis Management Act 1855 stated that the local authority, 'shall . . . employ . . . such . . . servants as may be necessary,

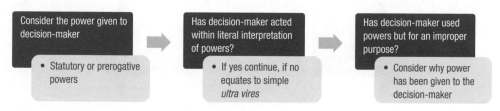

Figure 13.4 Using powers for an improper purpose

and may allow to such . . . servants . . . such . . . wages as (the Council) may think fit'. The local authority used their power under section 62 to introduce a minimum wage for both female and male employees. The House of Lords held that the statutory power had been used for an improper purpose as it was not the intention of Parliament that section 62 would be used to introduce a minimum wage. Rather it was there to ensure that the local authority could perform its services.

> There is a risk that where power is given to do X in order to achieve Y, that the decision-maker will do X, but will do so in order to achieve Z. It might appear that if X is done, then why should the purpose matter? However, it is important that the power is used for the purpose intended by Parliament, as otherwise a decision-maker could be pursuing their own policy, i.e. punishing those who defy its policies on playing sport in a particular country. It matters because the power should only be used for the purpose for which it was given; otherwise the power is open for abuse, whether it is political (*Porter* v. *Magill*), or is being exercised to benefit associates (*Ex p. Jones*).

REFLECTION

Delegation of discretion

If a decision-maker has statutory powers to make a decision regarding a particular subject-matter, are they able to delegate the actual decision-making to another person (see Figure 13.5)? In a government department a minister can delegate powers to civil servants. Where this delegation occurs, the validity of the civil servant's decision cannot be challenged on the grounds that there has been unauthorised delegation. This is because the civil servant is considered the minister's alter-ego. This is known as the *Carltona* principle and was established by the Court of Appeal in *Carltona Ltd* v. *Commissioners of Works* [1943] 2 All ER 560. When we consider the sheer size of modern government departments, it would be completely unrealistic to expect the minister in charge of that department to make every decision. Therefore, a minister may delegate a decision to a civil servant, even where statute expressly delegates discretionary powers to him.

INTERSECTION ....

It should be remembered that where a civil servant makes a decision which has negative consequences (such as resulting in a scandal which affects the minister's department), that the minister depending on the circumstances should take responsibility. In Chapter 7 we explored the convention of individual ministerial responsibility and the role it served in holding the government to account.

Figure 13.5 When can a decision-maker delegate their discretion?

The Home Office (or Home Department) is responsible for security, counter-terrorism, immigration and passports, the police and the criminal records bureau. In 2010, there were over 27,000 civil servants working for the Home Office. See http://www.homeoffice.gov.uk/about-us/our-organisation/

CONTEXT

Is there any limitation on who a minister can delegate to?

In *R* v. *Governor of Brixton Prison ex p. Enahoro* [1963] 2 QB 455 the Home Secretary had the power to deport fugitives under section 7 of the Fugitive Offenders Act 1881. The Home Secretary ordered a fugitive to be deported to Nigeria. However, a deputation from Parliament asked that the Home Secretary reconsider his decision. Consequently, it was argued that the Home Secretary had unlawfully delegated his discretionary powers to Parliament. In his judgment Lord Parker CJ stated that:

- A person making a judicial decision cannot delegate the decision-making.
- In certain types of administrative decisions the decision-maker has no power to delegate the actual decision-making.

Parker CJ categorised the decision as an administrative decision with no power to delegate. However, His Lordship did not find that the Home Secretary had delegated the decision to Parliament. All that the Home Secretary was doing was listening to Parliament's opinion and he was permitted to take this into consideration when he made his decision. His Lordship stated:

> 'I think, to be realistic, he was inviting Parliament to express a view as to whether his decision that it was just was the view also of the majority of the House . . . there is no reason why he should not invite the expression of further opinion, and, if influenced by it, change his mind. Looked at in that way, I cannot see that by inviting Parliament or by allowing Parliament to express an opinion on his decision, he was in any way surrendering or sharing with Parliament what was his statutory responsibility.'

The issue of whether the Home Secretary could delegate his power to deport an individual arose again in *R* v. *Secretary of State for the Home Department ex p. Oladehinde* [1991] 1 AC 254. The decision whether to deport immigrants under section 3 of the Immigration Act 1971 had been delegated to immigration inspectors. The House of Lords ruled that the Home Secretary could delegate this power to suitably senior and qualified immigration inspectors, even if they were not classified as civil servants working within his department, but rather employed under statutory powers. The House of Lords made reference to Parliament's intention and found that there was no implied limitation on the Home Secretary's power to delegate.

An example of a decision-maker exercising a judicial function occurred in *R* v. *Secretary of State for the Home Department ex p. Doody* [1994] 1 AC 531. Here the Home Secretary had the statutory discretion to determine the sentence tariff for a life prisoner. The House of Lords held that despite the sentencing decision being a judicial function, the Home Secretary could delegate the actual decision-making, but only to a junior minister within the Home Department. Therefore the exercise of a judicial function will restrict the *Carltona* principle.

Finally, a minister cannot delegate his statutory discretionary powers to a minister responsible for another government department. Although, it is possible to seek advice from that minister before reaching the decision (see *H Lavender & Son Ltd* v. *Minister of Housing and Local Government* [1970] 1 WLR 1231).

Fettering of discretion

⊕ CORNERSTONE

Fettering of discretion

We have seen that there are limitations on who a decision-maker can delegate his powers to. If a decision-maker has discretionary powers then it is important that he exercises this discretion properly. It is not valid to fetter (i.e. restrict your discretion), as Parliament has given the decision-maker discretion and intends that the discretion will be properly exercised.

In *R* v. *Port of London Authority ex p. Kynoch Ltd* [1919] 1 KB 176 the court held that there would be nothing wrong in an authority adopting a policy for legitimate reasons and refusing to hear someone making an application which fell outside the policy, unless there is something exceptional regarding his application. This would not amount to a **fettering of discretion**, because there is always scope for the decision-maker to take into account exceptional circumstances. However, there will be fettering of discretion if the decision-maker refuses to *ever* listen to and consider any application which falls outside their policy. We can see that a decision-maker when exercising their discretionary powers will adopt a policy to help him apply his discretion in a consistent and fair way. The decision of the Board of Trade in refusing an investment grant was challenged in *British Oxygen Co Ltd* v. *Minister of Technology* [1969] 2 All ER 18. The Board of Trade had a policy that it would not consider applications where the cost of the units was under £25. British Oxygen's application was refused because its units cost £20 each. The Court of Appeal held that there was nothing wrong with the Board of Trade adopting a policy, but that they must be willing to consider exceptions to their general policy.

⊕ CORNERSTONE

Keeping the door ajar

In *British Oxygen Co Ltd* v. *Minister of Technology* [1969] 2 All ER 18 Karminski LJ held that a policy could be lawfully adopted but that the decision-maker must always be willing to keep the door ajar. If the policy permitted no flexibility, then it would amount to an unlawful fettering of discretion:

> 'As a matter of law there is nothing to prevent the Board of Trade adopting or publishing such a policy, providing that it is ready to consider reasons in suitable cases for departing from that policy . . . I do not think that in the present case the Board of Trade, though they may seek to adhere to their policy decision, have closed the door on reconsidering the application on its merits in the exercise of their discretion. In my view declaration is wrong and should be set aside.'

Irrelevant and relevant considerations

When reaching his decision what considerations should the decision-maker take into account? Conversely, what considerations are irrelevant and should not be taken in account? This is a question for the courts and a decision can be challenged where improper considerations have been taken into account. This is because when Parliament gives a minister statutory powers to determine policy, it will often state that in reaching a decision the minister must consider all relevant considerations.

The decision in *Ex p. Fewings* was challenged because the decision-maker had taken into account the consideration of preventing animal cruelty. The Court of Appeal held that animal cruelty could be a relevant consideration, but that the decision was invalid as the local authority had failed to take into account relevant statutory considerations. The Court of Appeal held that the decision-maker's moral views as to the repugnancy of stag hunting were an irrelevant consideration. The decision was quashed by the Court of Appeal. In order to determine what considerations should be taken into account, it will depend on whether the statute expressly states that a consideration must be taken into account, must not be taken into account or that it gives the decision-maker the discretion to take into account 'yet to be identified' (or implied) considerations (see *Ex p. Fewings* at 1050). Cooke J in *CREEDNZ Inc.* v. *Governor-General* [1981] 1 NZLR 172 at 183 considered the correct approach:

> 'What has to be emphasised is that it is only when the statute expressly or impliedly identifies considerations required to be taken into account by the authority as a matter of legal obligation that the court holds a decision invalid on the ground now invoked. It is not enough that a consideration is one that may properly be taken into account, nor even that it is one which many people, including the court itself, would have taken into account if they had to make the decision.'

APPLICATION

The Airport Expansion Act 2014 (fictitious) repeals all existing statutes relating to the power to expand airports and gives the Secretary of State for Transport the power to decide whether to expand airports in England and Wales. Section 13(2) of the Act states, 'In deciding whether to expand an airport the minister must take into account the view of local authorities, other government infrastructure and transport projects and environmental policy and all other relevant considerations.' Lutchester Airport Ltd is seeking to expand and the Secretary of State has refused its application. The Secretary of State has reached his decision after considering the fact that Lutchester Airport is located next to Downville House and the increased flights would disturb visitors, and as a new airport will be built fifty miles away there is no need to expand Lutchester Airport. Lutchester Borough Council is annoyed as it was not consulted about this decision. We can see that the Secretary of State took into account the effect that airport expansion would have on visitors to Downville House. This would be an irrelevant consideration. He had failed to take into account the views of the local authority which was a relevant consideration. However, he did take into account a relevant consideration which was government transport projects, i.e. the construction of a new airport.

Errors of law and fact

The courts can review a decision where the decision-maker has made a mistake as to the facts. Judicial review is permitted where the decision-maker wrongly believes the facts permitted him to make a decision. This is known as error of precedent fact or jurisdictional error. The question here is whether the decision-maker has made an error of law and does not legally have the power to make the decision. In *Anisminic* v. *Foreign Compensation Commission* [1969] 2 AC 147 the decision-maker was held to have made an error of law, as there had been a misinterpretation as to the criteria for compensation. The error could be reviewed.

Errors of fact which are material to the decision reached can also be reviewed by the courts. This is because there was no evidence to support the decision. In *R* v. *Criminal Injuries Compensation Board, ex p. A* [1999] 2 AC 330, A was a victim of rape and buggery (now classified as rape under the Sexual Offences Act 2003) and had applied for compensation from the Criminal Injuries Compensation Board (CICB). The CICB had informed A that she would have to prove that she was a victim of a violent crime. The CICB held that A had not demonstrated this. When the CICB reached its decision it had not been shown a report which suggested that the injuries caused to A's rectum were consistent with buggery. Although the burden was on A to establish that she was a victim of violent crime, the CICB's decision was quashed because it had not requested appropriate evidence from the police and therefore its decision amounted to an error of fact.

More recently in *R (Connolly)* v. *Havering LBC* [2009] EWCA Civ 1059 the Court of Appeal quashed the decision of a planning inspector, who had granted planning permission and was under the mistaken belief that she was in possession of the full history of the site. The Court of Appeal applied the approach from *E* v. *Secretary of State for the Home Department* [2004] EWCA Civ 49, and quashed the decision because it is clear that the fact was not contentious and that it was objectively verifiable, and the applicant challenging the decision was not responsible for the mistake and that the mistake proved material in the decision-maker's reasoning.

LEGITIMATE EXPECTATION AS A GROUND FOR JUDICIAL REVIEW

CORNERSTONE

Legitimate expectation

A decision can also be reviewed where the applicant had a legitimate expectation that the decision-maker would exercise his powers in a certain way. Legitimate expectations can be procedural or substantive. A legitimate expectation is procedural where it is expected that a procedure will be followed in a particular way, and it is substantive where it is expected that a particular decision will be reached.

The term legitimate expectation originated from the judgment of Lord Denning MR in *Schmidt* v. *Secretary of State for Home Affairs* [1969] 2 Ch 149 at 170. Lord Denning had stated that an administrative decision-maker could be bound to allow a person affected by his decision to make representations. However, '[i]t all depends on whether he has some right or interest, or, I would add, some legitimate expectation, of which it would not be fair to deprive him without hearing what he has to say.' We shall see that there is an overlap here with procedural fairness.

Procedural legitimate expectation relates to a policy or practice which gives the claimant an unambiguous and clear representation that the decision-maker will follow a policy in exercising his powers. To put it another way, the claimant should not be in any doubt what the decision-maker meant. In *Council of Civil Service Unions and Others* v. *Minister for the Civil Service* [1985] AC 374 [*GCHQ*] the trade unions representing civil servants working at GCHQ (the government agency responsible for intelligence gathering) challenged the decision of the Prime Minister, in her capacity as Minister for the Civil Service, to prevent civil servants from being members of trade unions. The decision was taken without consulting employees or trade unions. The trade unions argued that the long-term practice of consultation had created a procedural legitimate expectation that consultation would be carried out before a decision such as this would be taken. The House of Lords held that the decision was unfair because of the lack of consultation and that there had been a legitimate expectation that there would be consultation. However, national security considerations could outweigh the need to give effect to the legitimate expectation. Therefore, the decision not to consult was valid.

In *Attorney General of Hong Kong* v. *Ng Yuen Shiu* [1983] 2 AC 629 the Hong Kong government had issued a policy which stated that before deporting illegal immigrants who had entered Hong Kong, each immigrant would be invited to make representations before the decision to deport them would be taken. The government of Hong Kong decided to deport the claimant without inviting him to a hearing. Lord Fraser stated that:

> 'The justification for (making the decision-maker honour its promise) is primarily that, when a public authority has promised to follow a certain procedure, it is in the interest of good administration that it should act fairly and should implement its promise, so long as implementation does not interfere with its statutory duty.'

Here there was nothing to justify not honouring the claimant's legitimate expectation, as the consultation and hearing were not inconsistent with the government's statutory duties.

A clear and unambiguous representation can also create a substantive legitimate expectation, which rather than stating that a policy will be followed, will instead amount to an undertaking that the decision-maker will exercise his powers in a particular way.

CORNERSTONE

R v. *North and East Devon Health Authority ex p. Coughlan* [2001] QB 213

In this case the Court of Appeal held that a decision to close a nursing home and move the residents elsewhere was unfair and would not be permitted by the court. The residents had been promised that they would have a home for life at the premises and this was held to amount to a clear and unambiguous representation, which created a substantive legitimate expectation. Therefore, the decision-maker was prevented from going back on this previous promise because there was no overriding public interest which justified the change of policy. It was held that:

> 'Where the court considers that a lawful promise or practice has induced a legitimate expectation of a *benefit which is substantive*, not simply procedural, authority now establishes that here too the court will in a proper case decide whether to frustrate the expectation is so unfair that to take a new and different course will amount to an abuse of power. Here, once the legitimacy of the expectation is established, the court will have the task of weighing the requirements of fairness against any overriding interest relied upon for the change of policy.'

On balance in *Ex p. Coughlan* there was no overriding public interest to justify the decision-maker changing its policy. The reasons stated by the Court of Appeal were:

- the importance of the promise which had been made to the residents;
- the promise had only been made to a few residents and not to a large amount of people; and
- there would only be financial consequences in forcing the decision-maker to honour its promise.

The unfairness in the decision made by the decision-maker to go back on its promise amounted to an abuse of power and the decision could be quashed by the court. However, it must be noted that substantive legitimate expectation operates on a limited basis.

Could a pre-election promise give rise to a legitimate expectation?

In *R* v. *Secretary of State for Education and Employment ex p. Begbie* [2000] 1 WLR 1115 a child had been offered a place at an independent school under a state-funded scheme. After the 1997 General Election the Labour government decided to end the scheme. The Secretary of State decided to stop funding the education of children beyond the age of eleven. It was argued that the child had a legitimate expectation that their schooling would be funded by the state until they reached the age of eighteen. This was because the Labour party in its pre-election manifesto had stated that whilst it would end the scheme, it would permit children currently on the scheme to continue to be funded. This position had been confirmed by the local MP who had received confirmation of this from the then Shadow Secretary of State. This argument was rejected by the Court of Appeal because a pre-election promise could not be regarded as giving rise to a legitimate expectation.

Five propositions regarding legitimate expectation were accepted by the Court of Appeal:

1. 'the rule that a public authority should not defeat a person's legitimate expectation is an aspect of the rule that it must act fairly and reasonably';
2. 'the rule operates in the field of substantive as well as procedural rights';
3. 'the categories of unfairness are not closed';
4. 'the making of an unambiguous and unqualified representation is a sufficient, but not necessary, trigger of the duty to act fairly'; and
5. 'it is not necessary for a person to have changed his position as a result of such representations for an obligation to fulfil a legitimate expectation to subsist'.

The Court of Appeal accepted that substantive and procedural rights can be protected; therefore the courts can compel a decision-maker to exercise his power in a certain way to give effect to a promise made. The need for an unambiguous and unqualified representation is important to establish legitimate expectation, but its absence may not be fatal to a claim. Finally, detrimental reliance by the claimant is not required. However, the court was clear that reliance must not be understated as, '[i]t is very much the exception, rather than the rule, that detrimental reliance will not be present when the court finds unfairness in the defeating of a legitimate expectation.'

Will a lack of detriment be fatal?

In *R (Bibi)* v. *Newham London Borough Council* [2002] 1 WLR 237 the applicant successfully argued that the decision should be set aside on the ground that their legitimate expectation had not been taken into account. The local authority had wrongly believed that refugees who were homeless were entitled to security of tenure. This had been communicated to the applicant. The Court of Appeal held that detrimental reliance was not a perquisite to establish a legitimate expectation. The reason for this was that:

> 'To disregard the legitimate expectation because no concrete detriment can be shown would be to place the weakest in society at a particular disadvantage. It would mean that those who

have a choice and the means to exercise it in reliance on some official practice or promise would gain a legal toehold inaccessible to those who, lacking any means of escape, are compelled simply to place their trust in what has been represented to them.'

The effect of a qualification?

We can see that legitimate expectation can be created from an unambiguous and unqualified assurance to the applicant. This can be given personally or through a circular, policy or government statement. The claimant in *R (Bancoult)* v. *Secretary of State for Foreign and Commonwealth Affairs (No.2)* [2008] UKHL 61 had argued that the Foreign Secretary had created a legitimate expectation that the Chagos islanders would be allowed to return home to their homeland. The islanders had previously been deported by the British authorities to permit the building of a United States airbase on the largest island, Diego Garcia. After the Divisional Court ruled against the government, the Foreign Secretary had stated in a press notice: '[t]he work we are doing on the feasibility of resettling the (islanders) now takes on a new importance. We started the feasibility work a year ago and are now well underway with phase two of the study. Furthermore, we will put in place a new Immigration Ordinance which will allow the (islanders) to return to the outer islands while observing our Treaty obligations. This Government has not defended what was done or said 30 years ago.' The majority of the House of Lords held that this public statement did not amount to a legitimate expectation and the government would not be prevented from changing its policy. According to Lord Carswell this was because there was an on-going feasibility study about resettling the islanders and therefore, the statement could not be regarded as unequivocal. His Lordship noted that that the Foreign Secretary's press statement was directed to a large number of people and was 'not an assurance directed towards one individual or a small number of people, whereas in Coughlan . . . the Court of Appeal regarded such a limitation as a significant feature in favour of the applicant's claim'. The relevance of this is that the impact of forcing the government to be bound by the press notice would have a significant impact on resources.

Lord Carswell also noted that, 'if the Government were obliged to resettle the Chagossians, the consequences could be more than financial, as it could give rise to friction with the United States.' This is important because the Court of Appeal in *Coughlan* had stated that a legitimate expectation needed to be balanced against the public interest in permitting the decision-maker to depart from its promise. As we have seen in *Coughlan*, the Court of Appeal stated that because the only consequences were financial there was no public interest to prevent the decision-maker honouring its promise of a home for life. Whereas, in *Bancoult*, the enforcement of the press notice would have significant foreign policy considerations. The minority in *Bancoult* argued that the Foreign Secretary's press notice could give rise to a legitimate expectation as it was capable of amounting to a clear and unambiguous representation. Lord Bingham argued that the notice was 'devoid of relevant qualification' and that '[t]he Government could not lawfully resile from its representation without compelling reason, which was not shown.' In any event, His Lordship held that the claimant did not need to demonstrate that there had been detrimental reliance.

The risk that a decision-maker will fetter their discretion

If the courts prevent the decision-maker from changing a policy or from going back on a promise, then this approach would risk fettering the decision-maker's discretion.

PROCEDURAL IMPROPRIETY AS A GROUND FOR JUDICIAL REVIEW

CORNERSTONE

Procedural impropriety

The procedure used to make a decision must be fair. The level of fairness will depend on the type of decision which is being made. We shall see that procedural impropriety will be a ground for judicial review where it is alleged that one of the requirements is missing.

Lord Diplock in *Council of Civil Service Unions and Others* v. *Minister for the Civil Service* [*GCHQ*] had stated that procedural impropriety was a ground for judicial review:

'I have described the third head as "procedural impropriety" rather than failure to observe basic rules of natural justice or failure to act with procedural fairness towards the person who will be affected by the decision. This is because susceptibility to judicial review under this head covers also failure by an administrative tribunal to observe procedural rules that are expressly laid down in the legislative instrument by which its jurisdiction is conferred, even where such failure does not involve any denial of natural justice.'

His Lordship was clear that this ground was wider than just the obligation to observe the common law requirements of natural justice or procedural fairness. The common law has developed the concept of natural justice and the requirements needed to ensure the decision is fair.

Should natural justice apply to administrative decisions?

The controversial decision in *Local Government Board* v. *Arlidge* [1915] AC 120 concerned the exercise of statutory powers under the Housing, Town Planning Act 1909, which permitted the local authority to declare a dwelling-house unfit for human habitation. A person affected by a decision made pursuant to the Act appealed. The Board dismissed the appeal without allowing the appellant to be heard orally before reaching its decision, or without permitting the appellant to see its report. The House of Lords was clear that natural justice did not extend to administrative decisions. The decision-maker must comply with his statutory duties, but other than complying with the statute, the procedure it adopted was a matter for the decision-maker.

Lord Shaw's judgment in *Local Government Board* v. *Arlidge* [1915] stated that the courts should not impose the requirements of natural justice which arose when legal issues were determined to be administrative decision-making. His Lordship stated:

'Judicial methods may, in many points of administration, be entirely unsuitable, and produce delays, expense, and public and private injury. The department must obey the statute. For instance, in the present case it must hold a public local inquiry, and upon a point of law it must have a decision of the Law Courts . . . if administration is to be beneficial and effective, it must be the master of its own procedure.'

We can see that His Lordship had acknowledged that there were some basic requirements for the procedure which the decision-maker had adopted. The decision-maker must permit both sides to speak before reaching its decision:

'For it must always be borne in mind that its procedure if not in defiance of elementary standards – say, by hearing one side and refusing to hear the other – is simply the plan which it adopts to satisfy itself that the decision come to by a local authority was a good or a bad decision.'

Lord Shaw had criticised the Court of Appeal for applying judicial standards to an administrative decision, as this approach was regarded as an usurpation of the decision-maker's role by the courts.

Natural justice applies to both judicial and administrative decisions

CORNERSTONE

Ridge v. *Baldwin* [1964] AC 40

The House of Lords decision in *Ridge* v. *Baldwin* [1964] AC 40 is an important one because their Lordships held that the requirements for natural justice applied to administrative decisions, rather than just judicial or quasi-judicial decisions. A Chief Constable had been charged with conspiracy to obstruct the course of justice and had been acquitted by a jury. Nonetheless, as a result of negative comments made by the trial judge regarding the Chief Constable's character, the watch committee decided to dismiss him. The majority of the House of Lords held that the decision to dismiss him was void because of the failure to observe the rules of natural justice. This was because the watch committee had not informed the Chief Constable of the charges against him and he was not allowed a chance to be heard.

In *Ridge* v. *Baldwin* [1964] the House of Lords heard that natural justice applied to an administrative decision. Lord Hodson had stated:

'The cases seem to me to show that persons acting in a capacity which is not on the face of it judicial but rather executive or administrative have been held by the courts to be subject to the principles of natural justice.'

Lord Devlin had observed that:

'I do not find it necessary to determine whether before 1919 the power to dismiss for neglect of duty could be exercised administratively and without any sort of judicial inquiry. Nor do I need to decide whether or not the power to dismiss for inadequacy is purely administrative. I am satisfied that in all matters to which the regulations apply the power to dismiss must be exercised in accordance with them.'

Right to a fair hearing

CORNERSTONE

Natural justice

Natural justice means that when the decision-maker exercises his decision-making powers the procedure used to reach this decision must be fair.

A decision, or hearing to decide the issue, must be carried out in a fair way. Article 6(1) of the European Convention on Human Rights (ECHR) states that:

'In the determination of his civil rights and obligations or of any criminal charge against him, everyone is entitled to a fair and public hearing within a reasonable time by an independent and impartial tribunal established by law.'

Article 6(3) ECHR outlines the minimum rights of someone charged with a criminal offence. These are:

(a) to be informed promptly, in a language which he understands and in detail, of the nature and cause of the accusation against him;

(b) to have adequate time and the facilities for the preparation of his defence;

(c) to defend himself in person or through legal assistance of his own choosing or, if he has not sufficient means to pay for legal assistance, to be given it free when the interests of justice so require;

(d) to examine or have examined witnesses against him and to obtain the attendance and examination of witnesses on his behalf under the same conditions as witnesses against him;

(e) to have the free assistance of an interpreter if he cannot understand or speak the language used in court.

> ### Take note
>
> The chapter is concerned with common law requirements, rather than the statutory requirements. If statute requires the procedure to be carried out in a certain way then this procedure must be followed.

We can see that in both civil and criminal matters decisions reached using procedures which are not fair will breach Article 6. We are concerned here with administrative decisions and the requirements of natural justice. It should be noted that the decision and the consequences for a person affected by it, will be important factors when the courts determine the extent of the requirements needed to satisfy natural justice.

Extent of fairness required?

Lord Bridge in *Lloyd* v. *McMahon* [1987] AC 625 observed that 'the so-called rules of natural justice are not engraved on tablets of stone'. The level of fairness required will depend on the type of decision and the circumstances behind it. In *McInnes* v. *Onslow Fane* [1978] 1 WLR 1520 Meggary VC observed that there was a distinction between a person who had made an application which was then refused, and on the other hand where someone had been granted a right and this right was now being revoked. In revocation cases the applicant was entitled to notices of the charges against him and the right to be heard at a hearing. We can see that there is a sliding scale of what is required by the requirement of procedural fairness.

CORNERSTONE

R v. *Secretary of State for the Home Department ex p. Doody* [1994] 1 AC 531

The level of fairness required was considered by the House of Lords in *Ex p. Doody*. This case concerned prisoners who were serving a mandatory life sentence. The Home Secretary fixed the period which each prisoner would have to serve until their imprisonment could be reviewed. The Home Secretary had consulted the trial judge and the Lord Chief Justice for their recommendations, but had not revealed these recommendations to the prisoners and had not given the prisoners an opportunity to make representations before he reached his decision.

The House of Lords in *Ex p. Doody* quashed the Home Secretary's decision and held that the prisoners were entitled to:

- make written representations;
- know the judicial recommendations; and
- know the reasons why the Home Secretary had chosen not to follow the judicial recommendations.

Lord Mustill stated, '[t]he only issue is whether the way in which the scheme is administered falls below the minimum standard of fairness.' According to Lord Mustill, the key question for the court will be to determine, '[w]hat does fairness require in the present case?' His Lordship outlined six propositions from established case law:

1. 'Where an Act of Parliament confers an administrative power there is a presumption that it will be exercised in a manner which is fair in all the circumstances.

2. The standards of fairness are not immutable. They may change with the passage of time, both in the general and in their application to decisions of a particular type.

3. The principles of fairness are not to be applied by rote identically in every situation. What fairness demands is dependent on the context of the decision, and this is to be taken into account in all its aspects.

4. An essential feature of the context is the statute which creates the discretion, as regards both its language and the shape of the legal and administrative system within which the decision is taken.

5. Fairness will very often require that a person who may be adversely affected by the decision will have an opportunity to make representations on his own behalf either before the decision is taken with a view to producing a favourable result; or after it is taken, with a view to procuring its modification; or both.

6. Since the person affected usually cannot make worthwhile representations without knowing what factors may weigh against his interests, fairness will very often require that he is informed of the gist of the case which he has to answer.'

It is clear that the common law will require a decision-maker to exercise the power given to him fairly. Fairness will not demand the same procedural requirements for every decision. Each decision, depending on the circumstances, will require differing requirements to meet the minimum level of fairness required. Lord Mustill held that a life prisoner would have the right to make representations to the Home Secretary before the decision was reached. His Lordship acknowledged that there is no general duty to give reasons for an administrative decision. However, the circumstances of the decisions might imply such a right. His Lordship, given the seriousness of the decision, considered that there was an implied right here.

The requirements of common law fairness were considered in *R (on the application of Manchester College of Higher Education and Media Technology Ltd)* v. *Secretary of State for the Home Department* [2010] EWHC 3496 (Admin). The case concerned the suspension of the claimant's licence to sponsor overseas students. The factors identified by Lord Mustill in *Ex p. Doody* were considered, especially the point that the level of fairness would depend on the circumstances. It was held that where a decision was taken to suspend the claimant's licence without prior consultation then there would be a breach of the common law duty of fairness. Mr Justice Pelling QC stated, 'that the common law rule of fairness required in the circumstances of this case that the claimant would be consulted before such a draconian step was taken' (at [25]).

The right to know the case against you and time to prepare your defence

It is important to know the case against you. Unless you are aware of the allegations or alleged breaches, then how can you counter these at the hearing or in written representations?

There must be suitable time for a defence to be prepared and sufficient notice should be given before the hearing takes place. In *R* v. *Thames Magistrates Court ex p. Polemis (The Corinthic)* [1974] 1 WLR 1371 a ship's master was summoned at 10.30am to appear before the Magistrates' Court at 2.00pm, after there was an accusation that oil had leaked from the vessel. The fact that there had been insufficient time to prepare a defence meant that the defendant had lost the right to be heard.

The right to be heard and to make representations

The right to be heard does not as a general rule entitle the applicant to an oral hearing, as the applicant could put across his representations through written representations. In *R* v. *Army Board of the Defence Council ex p. Anderson* [1991] 3 WLR 42 Taylor LJ stated that the right to make oral representations will depend 'upon the subject matter and circumstances of the particular case and upon the nature of the decision to be made. It will also depend upon whether there are substantial issues of fact which cannot be satisfactorily resolved on the available written evidence.' Whether an oral hearing is required will depend on the subject matter (whether a person is having a right deprived or merely making an application) and whether the court considers that the degree of fairness requires it. Where the level of fairness required is low, then unless there is sufficient evidential ambiguity, written representations can satisfy the minimum requirement of fairness.

However, at a hearing there is no general right to legal representation. Lord Denning MR took the view in *Enderby Town Football Club* v. *Football Association* [1971] Ch 591 that:

> 'In many cases it may be a good thing for the proceedings of a domestic tribunal to be conducted informally without legal representation. Justice can often be done in them better by a good layman than by a bad lawyer.'

This is because a good layman might be better than a lawyer at understanding the regulations in dispute.

In *R* v. *Secretary of State for the Home Department ex p. Tarrant* [1984] 2 WLR 613 it was stated that fairness may require legal representation in circumstances which include:

- the seriousness of the charge faced;
- whether points of law were likely to arise; or
- that the prisoner is not competent to present his own case.

The right to know the decision-maker's reasons

In *Ex p. Doody* it was accepted that as a general rule the decision-maker is not required to give reasons for his decision. However, where the decisions concern something as fundamentally important as personal liberty, then reasons must be given. The Court of Appeal in *R* v. *Civil Service Appeal Board ex p. Cunningham* [1991] 4 All ER 310 had to decide whether the decision-maker was right not to give decisions. The majority held that although there was no general duty at common law to give reasons for why an administrative decision was made, however, where the decision appeared irrational because of the low figure which had been awarded, then a reason as to why the Board had

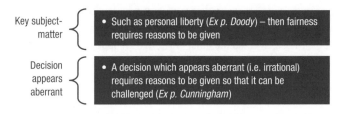

Figure 13.6 When must reasons be given?

reached this decision must be given. The reduction of a research grant was challenged in *R* v. *Higher Education Funding Council ex p. Institute of Dental Surgery* [1994] 1 WLR 242. The Council had given no reasons as to why it had decided to reduce the amount of funding. The court held that academic decisions did not generally require reasons to be given. Sedley J clarified the law as to when a decision must be given. Reiterating that at common law there is no general duty to give reasons, he stated that reasons would need to be given in certain circumstances (see Figure 13.6).

Whether reasons will have to be given is a question to be determined on a case by case basis. Even if reasons have to be given then there is no requirement that they are sufficiently detailed.

Al-Fayed was an Egyptian national who had lived in the United Kingdom for many years and had been refused a British passport. He challenged the decision of the Home Secretary to refuse him a passport. The Court of Appeal in *R* v. *Secretary of State for the Home Department ex p. Al-Fayed (No.1)* [1998] 1 WLR 763 held that although there was no statutory requirement requiring the Home Secretary to give reasons, the Home Secretary must inform the applicant of the areas which weighed against his application. Lord Woolf MR stated that the applicant did not require the full reasons for the refusal, just the areas of concern. This was because the applicant could not argue that the decision was wrong unless he knew the broad areas of concern.

> Mr Al-Fayed is a famous businessman who once owned Harrods, a world famous department store in Kensington, London.

CONTEXT

The rule against bias

APPLICATION

Imagine that you have made an application for planning permission to build an extension on your home and the decision whether to allow or reject your application was to be made by a planning committee. The committee is chaired by your next-door neighbour, who had indicated that he objects to his garden being overshadowed by your proposed extension. You are then informed by the committee that your application has been refused. In these circumstances, you could seek to judicially review the decision on the ground that the decision was potentially biased. It is important that in circumstances such as this that decisions made by public bodies are seen to be fair.

In *R* v. *Sussex Justices ex p. McCarthy* [1924] 1 KB 256 the clerk who was advising the magistrates on a point of law was also a member of the firm of solicitors who were representing one of the parties in the case. The magistrates convicted the other party, and on appeal the court held that his conviction must be quashed. The issue was not whether the clerk has been biased or had advised upon whether to convict, rather it was not proper that he should be acting as a clerk in the circumstances. Lord Hewart CJ stated that:

> '[A] long line of cases shows that it is not merely of some importance but is of fundamental importance that justice should not only be done, but should manifestly and undoubtedly be seen to be done . . . The question therefore is not whether in this case the deputy clerk made any observation or offered any criticism which he might not properly have made or offered; the question is whether he was so related to the case in its civil aspect as to be unfit to act as clerk to the justices in the criminal matter. The answer to that question depends not upon what actually was done but upon what might appear to be done. Nothing is to be done which creates even a suspicion that there has been an improper interference with the course of justice' (at 259).

It is clear that Lord Hewart CJ was concerned that justice should be seen to be done, rather than whether on the facts it had been done. Citizens must have faith in the legal system and judges cannot be seen to be biased, even if they are not.

The rule that a judge or administrative decision-maker must not be biased and should be seen to be impartial is very important. This is covered by Article 6 of the ECHR.

INTERSECTION

The Lord Chancellor's judicial role was regarded as potentially being incompatible with Article 6 because of his position in government. This meant that Lord Irvine only sat in cases where there government did not have an interest, so as to avoid the appearance of bias. His successor, Lord Faulkner declared that he would no longer sit as a judge. In Chapter 8 we discussed the importance of judges not being viewed as biased and that judges should be seen to be independent of the government.

Types of bias and consequences on the decision and the decision-maker

- Where actual bias is proved then the decision-maker must step down and the decision will be quashed.

- Where the decision-maker has a direct interest in the issues involved, then there will be presumed bias and the decision-maker is automatically disqualified and any decision taken will be quashed.

- Where the decision-maker has an indirect interest in the issues involved, then this will not give rise to automatic disqualification.

We will now look at each of the above in turn and look at examples where the court has had to consider whether the decision-maker was biased. It is important to note that these apply not just to judges, but to other types of decisions made by public bodies, such as government ministers and local authorities. A person affected by an allegation of bias can judicially review the decision.

Actual bias

An example of actual bias would be where it is proved that a judge or administrative decision-maker had taken a bribe. In this case the decision would be quashed as there was clear evidence of bias.

Presumed bias: direct interest

There is no need to prove actual bias, just that the decision-maker has a direct interest in the matter. According to Kate Malleson (2002), '[o]nce a judge is shown to have a direct interest no examination of the circumstances of the alleged bias will be required and disqualification will follow automatically' (at p. 55). Traditionally, the direct interest needed to be financial. The most famous example of this was the case of *Dimes* v. *Grand Junction Canal Proprietors* (1854) 10 ER 301.

CORNERSTONE

Dimes v. *Grand Junction Canal Proprietors* **(1854) 10 ER 301**

The Lord Chancellor, Lord Cottenham, had an investment of several thousand pounds in the claimant company. In the 1840s this was a considerable sum. The Lord Chancellor had not declared this interest when he had upheld the decision of the Vice-Chancellor who had ruled in the claimant's favour. The decision was appealed and the House of Lords held that the Lord Chancellor should have been disqualified because of his direct financial interest and held that his decision be quashed.

Could the decision of the Lord Chancellor be challenged on the grounds of bias? Lord Campbell in *Dimes* v. *Grand Junction Canal Proprietors* (1854) 10 ER 301 at 793–794 stated that:

'No one can suppose that Lord Cottenham could be, in the remotest degree, influenced by the interest that he had in this concern; but, my Lords, it is of the last importance that the maxim that no man is to be a judge in his own cause should be held sacred. And that is not to be confined to a cause in which he is a party, but applies to a cause in which he has an interest. Since I have had the honour to be Chief Justice of the Court of Queen's Bench, we have again and again set aside proceedings in inferior tribunals because an individual, who had an interest in a cause, took a part in the decision. And it will have a most salutary influence on these tribunals when it is known that this high Court of last resort, in a case in which the Lord Chancellor of England had an interest, considered that his decree was on that account a decree not according to law, and was set aside. This will be a lesson to all inferior tribunals to take care not only that in their decrees they are not influenced by their personal interest, but to avoid the appearance of labouring under such an influence.'

It is worth considering what Lord Campbell was saying here:

- That no one is questioning the Lord Chancellor's integrity nor is anyone saying that he had actual bias.
- The court must prevent any appearance of bias arising from the decision-maker's direct interest in the case.
- No person can be a judge in their own cause.
- This case sets an example at the highest level that decision-makers must be seen to be impartial.

CORNERSTONE

R v. *Bow Street Metropolitan Stipendiary Magistrate ex p. Pinochet Ugarte (No.2)* [2000] 1 AC 119

In this case the former Chilean dictator, Augusto Pinochet, had come to the United Kingdom seeking medical treatment. Amnesty International and other groups had sought to extradite Pinochet to Spain to face charges for the crimes that were committed by the state during his rule. The House of Lords in *R* v. *Bow Street Metropolitan Stipendiary Magistrate ex p. Pinochet Ugarte (No.1)* [2000] 1 AC 61 ruled that as a former head of state he did not have immunity and could be extradited to face trial in Spain. One of the judges, Lord Hoffmann, was an unpaid director of a company which was owned by Amnesty International. The House of Lords agreed that Lord Hoffmann's position amounted to a direct interest in the case, since the company's role was to 'to procure the abolition of torture, extra judicial execution and disappearance' and this was the issue in the case. It was not possible to distinguish the company from Lord Hoffmann in his capacity as a director. Additionally, Lord Hoffmann's wife, Lady Hoffmann, worked for Amnesty International. Neither Pinochet's lawyers nor the Law Lords believed that Lord Hoffmann was personally biased against Pinochet.

Lord Goff in *R* v. *Bow Street Metropolitan Stipendiary Magistrate ex p. Pinochet Ugarte (No.3)* [2000] 1 AC 147 considered whether Lord Hoffmann's association with one of the parties in the case could have been regarded as giving rise to bias:

> 'The effect for present purposes is that Lord Hoffmann, as chairperson of one member of that organisation, [the company], is so closely associated with another member of that organisation, [Amnesty International], that he can properly be said to have an interest in the outcome of proceedings to which [Amnesty International] has become party. This conclusion is reinforced, so far as the present case is concerned, by the evidence of [the company] commissioning a report by [Amnesty International] relating to breaches of human rights in Chile, and calling for those responsible to be brought to justice. It follows that Lord Hoffmann had an interest in the outcome of the present proceedings and so was disqualified from sitting as a judge in those proceedings.
>
> 'It is important to observe that this conclusion is, in my opinion, in no way dependent on Lord Hoffmann personally holding any view, or having any objective, regarding the question whether Senator Pinochet should be extradited, nor is it dependent on any bias or apparent bias on his part. Any suggestion of bias on his part was, of course, disclaimed by those representing Senator Pinochet. It arises simply from Lord Hoffmann's involvement in [the company]; the close relationship between [Amnesty International] . . . and [the company], which here means that for present purposes they can be regarded as being, in practical terms, one organisation; and the participation of [Amnesty International] in the present proceedings in which as a result it either is, or must be treated as, a party.'

Looking at the decision of the House of Lords it is apparent that:

- Direct interest can apply to non-financial interests, such as being involved with a company that has an interest in the decision. This is very important as the decision extended the nature of interest beyond a pecuniary one. However, in *Locabail (UK) Ltd* v. *Bayfield Properties Ltd* [2000] 2 WLR 870 the Court of Appeal held that a minor interest, if it was too small to have an effect on the decision-maker, would not give rise to automatic disqualification bias.

• There need not be evidence that Lord Hoffmann was personally biased. It was sufficient that his connection with the company and its connection with Amnesty International gave rise to automatic-disqualification bias.

The consequence was that the decision in *R* v. *Bow Street Metropolitan Stipendiary Magistrate ex p. Pinochet Ugarte (No.1)* was quashed and the question of whether Pinochet could be extradited was reconsidered by the House of Lords in *R* v. *Bow Street Metropolitan Stipendiary Magistrate ex p. Pinochet Ugarte (No.3)* [2000] 1 AC 147 (see Figure 13.7).

Lord Hoffmann subsequently defended his decision not to recuse himself from the appeal (i.e. stand down). The BBC reported that Lord Hoffmann had defended his decision by arguing that as a judge he was not biased. It was irrelevant that his wife worked for Amnesty International. You can read the article at http://news.bbc.co.uk/1/hi/uk/235456.stm.

CONTEXT

Apparent bias: indirect interest

Where there is an allegation of apparent bias the decision-maker is not automatically disqualified. Instead the question for the court to decide is whether an indirect interest existed which could lead a

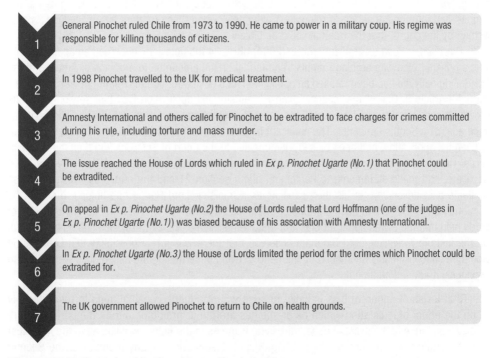

1	General Pinochet ruled Chile from 1973 to 1990. He came to power in a military coup. His regime was responsible for killing thousands of citizens.
2	In 1998 Pinochet travelled to the UK for medical treatment.
3	Amnesty International and others called for Pinochet to be extradited to face charges for crimes committed during his rule, including torture and mass murder.
4	The issue reached the House of Lords which ruled in *Ex p. Pinochet Ugarte (No.1)* that Pinochet could be extradited.
5	On appeal in *Ex p. Pinochet Ugarte (No.2)* the House of Lords ruled that Lord Hoffmann (one of the judges in *Ex p. Pinochet Ugarte (No.1)*) was biased because of his association with Amnesty International.
6	In *Ex p. Pinochet Ugarte (No.3)* the House of Lords limited the period for the crimes which Pinochet could be extradited for.
7	The UK government allowed Pinochet to return to Chile on health grounds.

Figure 13.7 Pinochet and the three House of Lords decisions

reasonable and fair minded observer to believe that there was a real possibility of bias. There is no need to prove that the decision-maker was actually biased. It is important to appreciate that an indirect interest is an interest which exists, but is one which does not affect the decision-maker personally.

CORNERSTONE

Porter v. *Magill* [2001] UKHL 67

The test used for whether there is apparent bias comes from the case of *Porter* v. *Magill* [2001] UKHL 67, where Lord Hope had stated that, '[t]he question is whether the fair-minded and informed observer, having considered the facts, would conclude that there was a real possibility that the tribunal was biased.' Only where this test is satisfied can the decision-maker be disqualified for apparent bias.

The case of *R (Kaur)* v. *Institute of Legal Executives Appeal Tribunal* [2011] EWCA Civ 1168 is an example of apparent bias. In this case the vice-president of ILEX and other council members had sat on a disciplinary panel, where an ILEX member was accused of cheating in an exam. The Court of Appeal held that the panel was biased. Rix LJ giving judgment argued that the court should not have to make a choice between automatic direct interest bias and apparent indirect interest bias, as both doctrines have the same requirement that a judge should recuse themselves or be disqualified from sitting, 'where there is a real possibility on the objective appearances of things, assessed by the fair minded and informed observer (a role which ultimately, when these matters are challenged, is performed by the court), that the tribunal could be biased.'

In *Davidson* v. *Scottish Ministers (No.2)* [2004] UKHL 34 the decision concerned an applicant who was a prisoner who was arguing that his treatment in prison amounted to a breach of Article 3 of the ECHR. Originally, he had been refused an application for a declarator that his treatment was incompatible with Article 3. One of the reasons given for refusing his application was that section 21 of the Crown Proceedings Act 1947 prevented the court from granting an interim order for specific performance against a Scottish minister. The applicant believed that Lord Hardie, one of the judges who had refused his application, had been biased. He appealed to the Court of Sessions and then the House of Lords. He argued that the Extra Division had not been impartial, because Lord Hardie, whilst Lord Advocate, had made statements to Parliament about section 21 and the remedies which would be available post devolution. In his then capacity as a minister, Lord Hardie had helped to shape the Scotland Act 1998 and had been a promoter of the legislation which was at issue here. The House of Lords held that there was apparent bias and that the decision of the Extra Division should be vitiated. On the facts in *Davidson*, Lord Bingham observed that there was a real possibility that Lord Hardie would be subconsciously influenced by the need to avoid undermining the assurances which he had previously made to Parliament:

'[T]hat a risk of apparent bias is liable to arise where a judge is called upon to rule judicially on the effect of legislation which he or she has drafted or promoted during the parliamentary process. Since in the present case there is no issue as to the facts, no issue as to the legal test to be applied and (in my opinion) no significant misdirection by any member of the Second Division, I should for my part be very reluctant to disturb its unanimous decision. I am however of the clear opinion that its conclusion was justified by the nature and extent of Lord Hardie's involvement in the passage of the Scotland Act. The fair-minded and informed observer, having considered the facts, would conclude that there was a real possibility that Lord Hardie, sitting judicially, would subconsciously strive to avoid reaching a conclusion which would undermine the very clear assurances he had given to Parliament' (at [17]).

In *Lawal* v. *Northern Spirit Ltd* [2003] UKHL 35 the House of Lords held that there could be apparent bias where a barrister who was appearing for one of the parties in an employment dispute, had sat as a judge in the Employment Appeal Tribunal and knew one, or more, of the lay members of the tribunal which had heard the present appeal. Lord Steyn held that there was a real possibility of bias on the part of the lay members of the tribunal, because they might have subconsciously been biased towards the barrister who had served with them. Lord Steyn stated that the observer from the test in *Porter* v. *Magill* would be influenced by the fact that the lay members would have previously looked to the barrister for instructions on the law, and there would be likely to exist 'a fairly close relationship of trust and confidence with the judge'.

APPLICATION

A High Court judge has been having an on–off affair with a barrister. The judge is very professional and when this barrister represents a client before her, she always makes sure that her judgment is impartial. In a personal injury claim before the judge, the barrister is representing the defendant and the judge dismisses the personal injury claim and finds in favour of the defendant. The claimant, Mrs De Keyser, hears rumours about the relationship between the judge and the barrister, and consequentially alleges that the judge was biased. It would be difficult to establish that the judge was actually biased, however if the judge had a direct interest it would be possible to presume that he was biased (*Ex p. Pinochet Ugarte*). It would be difficult to establish here that the judge had a direct interest and therefore Mrs De Keyser could argue that the judge had an indirect interest. We would need to see if the test in *Porter* v. *Magill* is satisfied before we can establish that there is apparent bias.

KEY POINTS

- Judicial review has an important constitutional significance.
- There are a number of different grounds for judicial review: illegality, procedural impropriety, legitimate expectation, unreasonableness, irrationality, proportionality and bias.
- There are many sub-elements to illegality, including unauthorised delegation and simple *ultra vires*.
- It is possible to give rise to both a procedural and substantive legitimate expectation.
- If Convention rights have been violated the courts will use proportionality as a ground for review, rather than unreasonableness.
- There are different types of bias, including actual bias and direct interest (automatic disqualification) bias.

CORE CASES

Case	About	Importance
Associated Provincial Picture Houses Ltd v. Wednesbury Corporation [1948]	The case involved a decision to ban children from going to the cinema on a Sunday.	Lord Greene MR considered what was meant by unreasonableness. The case gave rise to what was to become known as *Wednesbury* unreasonableness.
Council for Civil Service Unions v. *Minister of the Civil Service* [1985]	The government decided to prevent civil servants at GCHQ from being members of trade unions.	The House of Lords held that the prerogative could be judicially reviewed. There was no longer a distinction between statutory and prerogative powers. Lord Diplock identified the grounds of judicial review and Lord Roskill provided a list of non-justiciable prerogative powers.
R v. North and East Devon Heath Authority ex p. Coughlan [2001]	The Court of Appeal held that a decision to close a nursing home and move the residents elsewhere was unfair and would not be permitted by the court. This was because there was a legitimate expectation that the residents would have a home for life.	A clear and unambiguous representation can also create a substantive legitimate expectation, which rather than stating that a policy will be followed, will instead amount to an undertaking that the decision-maker will exercise his powers in a particular way.
Ridge v. *Baldwin* [1964]	This case involved the dismissal of a Chief Constable.	The House of Lords held that the rules of natural justice applied to both administrative and judicial decisions. This decision is extremely important in the development of judicial review.
R v. Secretary of State for the Home Department ex p. Doody [2001]	This case concerned prisoners who were serving a mandatory life sentence. The Home Secretary had fixed the period that each prisoner would have to serve until his imprisonment could be reviewed.	The House of Lords considered the level of fairness required for a decision of this type.

Case	About	Importance
Dimes v. *Grand Junction Canal Proprietors* (1854)	This case concerns judicial bias. The Lord Chancellor owned shares in the Grand Junction Canal, which had been a party in a case that he had been involved in.	No one was alleging that the Lord Chancellor had been actually biased, rather that he could be presumed to be biased because of his direct pecuniary (financial) interest in the decision.
R v. *Bow Street Metropolitan Stipendiary Magistrate ex p. Pinochet Ugarte (No.2)* [2000]	This case involved the attempts by human rights campaigners to extradite the former President of Chile to Spain, so that he could face trial for the crimes that he had committed in Chile. The House of Lords had to determine whether a former head of state could be extradited. The House of Lords held that he could be. However, Lord Hoffmann was linked to Amnesty International, which was one of the parties, and they employed his wife. The question was whether Lord Hoffmann had been biased.	The House of Lords held that whilst no one was alleging that Lord Hoffmann had been actually biased, he had a direct non-pecuniary interest and ought to have excused himself. The decision as to whether to extradite Pinochet had to be retaken.
Porter v. *Magill* [2001]	A case concerning Westminster Council.	This case established the two-stage test for apparent bias, which would occur where there was an indirect interest.

FURTHER READING

Daly, P. 'Wednesbury's reason and structure' [2011] *Public Law* 238
This article offers a defence of *Wednesbury* unreasonableness.

Dobson, N. 'The long trek away from Wednesbury irrationality?' [2003] *Journal of Local Government Law* 129
This article reviews the judicial approach to *Wednesbury* unreasonableness.

Hickman, T. 'The substance and structure of proportionality' [2008] *Public Law* 694
This article reviews the development of proportionality.

Lester, Lord and Jowell, J. 'Beyond Wednesbury: substantive principles of administrative law' [1987] *Public Law* 36
This article is a critique of *Wednesbury* unreasonableness.

Malleson, K. 'Safeguarding judicial impartiality' [2002] 22(1) *Legal Studies* 53
Refer to this article for a detailed look at the rule against judicial bias.

Sales, P. 'Rationality, proportionality and the development of the law' [2013] *Law Quarterly Review* 223

This article considers the development of proportionality and looks at whether it should replace rationality as a ground for review.

Wade, H.W.R. and Forsyth, C. *Administrative Law* 10th edn (Oxford University Press: Oxford, 2009)
A very comprehensive and detailed book which covers the key areas of administrative law.

Glossary

Alternative Vote In May 2011, there was a referendum on replacing First Past the Post with the Alternative Vote. The Alternative Vote system operates to allow voters to list their candidates by preference. If a candidate achieves 50 per cent he will win outright. If no candidate receives 50 per cent of the votes, then the weakest candidate is eliminated and their votes are given to the voter's second favoured candidate. The process will continue until one candidate achieves the important 50 per cent required.

Bias A decision can be challenged where the decision-maker is biased. Bias can arise where there is actual bias, a direct or indirect interest.

Cabinet government Under George I, II and III, there was the development of cabinet government with the business of state being run by the government, rather than under the monarch's direction.

Checks and balances Having checks and balances means that one branch of government will review the activities of the other branches to ensure that the power given to them is used properly.

Civil Service The Civil Service forms part of the executive and is politically neutral. The Civil Service is headed by the Permanent Secretary, who is not a politician and will remain in office despite a change in government.

Coalition The current government is a coalition government. The Conservative–Liberal Democrat government is the first peace-time coalition government since the 1930s.

Coalition Agreement The 2010 Coalition Agreement outlined the relationship between the Conservatives and Liberal Democrats. It listed the policies which each party would agree to support.

Codified A codified constitution is one where all the sources are found in a single document.

Collective ministerial responsibility The convention of collective ministerial responsibility operates to ensure that what is said during cabinet meetings is not made public.

Commonwealth An organisation comprised of former members of the British Empire. It is headed by Her Majesty, the Queen.

Constitution A constitution is a collection of rules, practices and laws which relate to the political life of a country and the key rights of any citizen. A constitution is intended to regulate government and it will contain the rules on how the courts, the legislature and the executive operate, the rules about elections, the power of the head of state and protection from police and executive oppression.

Constitutional conventions Constitutional conventions are an important source of the constitution and are crucial for the effective operation of the United Kingdom's constitutional system. Conventions regulate the conduct of the monarch, the government, individual minsters, Parliament and judges.

Constituency A constituency is an area represented by a Member of Parliament. The voters in each constituency will determine who represents them in Parliament.

Constitutional monarchy The monarch is the head of state, but the personal prerogative powers of the monarch are regulated by constitutional conventions, which are non-legal rules.

Crown The Crown is shorthand for the power which is exercised by the government through prerogative and statutory powers. The Crown can be used to describe the monarch's powers or those powers which are exercised by the government.

Declaration of incompatibility Where an Act of Parliament breaches the Convention rights the courts may make a declaration which states that the Act is incompatible. Such power is found under section 4 HRA 1998. The declaration does not affect the validity of the Act.

Devolution Where powers are devolved from central government and from the Westminster Parliament.

Devolution Acts The 'Devolution Acts' 1998 are the Scotland Act 1998, the Government of Wales Act 1998, and the Northern Ireland Act 1998. They devolved powers from Westminster to Scotland, Wales and Northern Ireland.

English Civil Wars Two civil wars were fought between Parliament and the Crown in the 1640s, and another between Parliament and royalists in 1650s. Parliament triumphed and the monarchy was abolished.

Executive In the United Kingdom the executive is comprised of the monarch, the government (the Prime Minister, ministers who attend cabinet and junior ministers), the emergency services, the armed forces, local government, government departments and the Civil Service.

Federal A federal constitution is one where power is shared between central government and the regions or states.

Fettering of discretion If a decision-maker has discretionary powers then it is important that he exercises this discretion properly. It is not valid to fetter (i.e. restrict your discretion), as Parliament has given the decision-maker discretion and intends that the discretion will be properly exercised.

First Past the Post The method of electing an MP is called First Past the Post. This system allows the person with the most votes to become the MP. This system is controversial for many reasons, principally that it permits an MP to be elected without having a majority of the total votes.

Glorious Revolution Parliament invited James II's son-in-law, William of Orange, to invade. In 1689 William and his wife Mary became joint monarchs. This is known as the Glorious Revolution and marks the supremacy of Parliament over the monarchy.

Hansard The record of parliamentary debate. The courts can refer to this in order to interpret Parliament's intention.

Holyrood Holyrood Palace is the Queen's official residence in Scotland, and is also the name used to describe the Scottish Parliament.

Individual ministerial responsibility The convention of individual ministerial responsibility is an important method of executive accountability. Ministers are expected as a matter of convention to act responsibily, and to ultimately resign in the event of either problems in their departments or their own personal life.

Irrationality According to Lord Diplock, a decision can be challenged where it 'is so outrageous in its defiance of logic or of accepted moral standards that no sensible person who had applied his mind to the question to be decided could have arrived at it'.

Judicial A term used to describe the functions/actions of judges.

Judicial review The purpose of judicial review is to hold the executive at both a national and local level to account, which includes governmental agencies and anyone else who is responsible for making decisions of a public law nature.

Judiciary The judiciary refers to judges who carry out the function of the judicial branch of the state. The head of the judiciary in England and Wales is the Lord Chief Justice.

Justiciable This is used to describe areas of executive decision-making which can be reviewed by the courts.

Law Lords The Appellate Jurisdiction Act 1876 created the Lords of Appeal in Ordinary, who are commonly known as the Law Lords.

Legislature The United Kingdom's Parliament is based at Westminster and is bicameral. This means that there are two chambers, the House of Commons and the House of Lords.

Legitimate expectation A decision can also be reviewed where the applicant had a legitimate expectation that the decision-maker would exercise his powers in a certain way. Legitimate expectations can be procedural or substantive. A legitimate expectation is procedural where it is expected that a procedure will be followed in a particular way, and it is substantive where it is expected that a particular decision will be reached.

Lord Chancellor A senior cabinet minister who is also the Secretary of State for Justice. The office of Lord Chancellor was reformed by the Constitutional Reform Act 2005.

Magna Carta King John was forced to sign the Magna Carta at Runnymede in 1215. The rebel barons wanted to prevent the king from abusing his power and stated that the king could not raise taxation without the barons' consent.

Margin of appreciation Because of the large number of political and cultural differences between the member states, the ECtHR has developed a margin of appreciation, which essentially gives each state discretionary scope and avoids setting uniform standards for strict observance of each Article.

Mirror Principle The relationship between Strasbourg and domestic courts has given rise to the Mirror Principle, where domestic courts will develop domestic law in line with Strasbourg. They will only depart from the jurisprudence of Strasbourg in exceptional circumstances.

Natural justice Natural justice requires that decisions are made fairly and that a fair procedure is used.

Ombudsman Complaints can be made to the Ombudsman concerning United Kingdom public bodies, governmental departments and the NHS in England.

Ouster clause This is where an Act of Parliament attempts to restrict a decision from being reviewed by the courts.

Parliamentary Sovereignty Parliament is the highest source of law and can make or change any law that it wishes. The courts must give effect to an Act of Parliament and cannot declare it to be void.

Prerogative powers According to Dicey the prerogative was 'the residue of discretionary power or arbitrary authority which at any one time is legally left in the hands of the crown'.

Prime Minister The Prime Minister is the head of the government and has considerable power. Prime Ministers dominate the cabinet. The Prime Minister determines the choice of his cabinet, and can dismiss cabinet ministers and reshuffle important posts.

Private members' bills Either an MP, or a member of the House of Lords, can introduce private members' bills. The ways that a private members' bill can be introduced include by ballot, the ten minute rule and by presentation.

Proportionality In order for a decision to be proportionate it needs to be shown that there is a legitimate objective which is sufficiently important to justify limiting a fundamental right, that the measures used to achieve this objective are rationally connected to it, i.e. there is a link between the two. Finally, it must be showed that the measure does not violate rights beyond what is really necessary to achieve the objective.

Protectorate A period in history where Oliver Cromwell ruled as Lord Protector.

Public authority A public authority cannot act in a way which is incompatible with the Convention rights. A public authority can either be a core or hybrid public authority, and could include a local council or a private company which manages a prison.

Public bill Public bills are introduced to Parliament by the government.

Public body The decision being reviewed must have been made by a public body. A public body could include a private company which is exercising public law functions.

Public inquiry An important aspect of administrative justice and indeed executive accountability are public inquiries. Inquiries are viewed as an important review of government policy or to investigate a specific event such as a national emergency.

Queen in Parliament Together the House of Commons, the House of Lords and the Queen in Parliament form Parliament. The monarch plays an important role as her approval is required before proposed legislation can become law.

Referendum This is where matters of national importance are put to the people for a direct vote on that issue. Referendums have been held on membership of what is now the European Union and changing the voting system.

Royal assent This is one of the personal prerogative powers of the monarch. A bill must receive royal assent before it becomes law. As a matter of convention the monarch cannot refuse royal assent.

Rule of law The rule of law means that the government and its agencies must act in accordance with the law, that the government is not above the law, and that the law should be sufficiently certain and accessible. There are different versions of the rule of law.

Salisbury Convention The Salisbury Convention exists to ensure that the House of Lords does not veto bills which were contained in the government's election manifesto.

Select committee Select committees oversee the work of specific government departments. The committees have no power to compel ministers to attend. Ministers are not allowed to sit on the committees. This is important as the committees serve to review executive action and to scrutinise policies, etc.

Separation of powers According to this theory, which is associated with the French writer Montesquieu, the three branches of government – the executive (which is responsible for carrying out governmental functions), the legislative (which in the United Kingdom is Parliament and is responsible for making laws) and the judicial (which is carried out by the courts) – functions must be carried by separate bodies and by different people.

Sewel Convention The Sewel Convention was created to restrict the Westminster Parliament from legislating for Scotland, where the subject-matter is one which has been devolved to the Scottish Parliament under the Scotland Act 1998.

Standing In order to bring an applicant for judicial review the claimant must have standing, that is *locus standi*. Section 31(3) of the Senior Courts Act 1981 states that 'the court shall not grant leave to make such an application unless it considers that the applicant has a sufficient interest in the matter to which the application relates'. This means that unless a person (or a group) has sufficient interest then they are unable to bring an application for judicial review.

Strasbourg The European Court of Human Rights (ECtHR) is based in Strasbourg and it hears petitions from individuals and states concerning alleged violations of human rights.

Stuarts The Scottish royal dynasty which inherited the English Crown in 1603. The Stuarts proved to be very controversial and two kings were deposed. James I (1603–25) believed in the divine right of kings and that the king was above the law. This was a view shared by Charles I (1625–49) and eventually Charles and his Parliament fought two civil wars. Charles I was executed in 1649. The monarchy was restored in 1660 and Charles II ruled until 1685. James II succeeded his brother in 1685 and clashed with Parliament. James II was deposed in 1688 and Parliament offered the throne to James' son-in-law William and daughter Mary. After their deaths the last Stuart monarch, Anne, inherited the throne.

Tribunal In the United Kingdom there are many different types of tribunals. The procedures used in tribunals will be different to the procedure used in courts. The tribunal may be comprised of legal and non-legal members.

Ultra vires A decision is *ultra vires* where the decision-maker acts outside of their lawful powers.

***Wednesbury* unreasonableness** A decision can be challenged where the court is of the opinion that the decision-maker has acted unreasonably. This requires the court to assess whether the decision is one which no other reasonable decision-maker would make.

Vertical effect This is used within the human rights context, as section 6 HRA 1998 only permits Convention rights to be enforced vertically, which means against public authorities.

Victim A victim is someone who has been directly affected by a violation of a Convention right.

Westminster This is used to describe Parliament.

Whitehall This is used to describe central government.

Index